CW01262318

DISTORTED IMAGINATION

Also by Ziauddin Sardar

Science, Technology and Development in the Muslim World
Muhammad: Aspects of a Biography
Islam: Outline of a Classification Scheme
The Future of Muslim Civilization
Science and Technology in the Middle East
Islamic Futures: the Shape of Ideas to Come
Information and the Muslim World
Explorations in Islamic Science
Decorum and Discourse: Critical Islamic Perspectives
Unfinished Journeys: Adventures in Familiar Places

Edited Works

Hajj Studies
The Touch of Midas: Science, Values and Environment in Islam and the West
Building Information Systems in the Islamic World
The Revenge of Athena: Science, Exploitation and the Third World
An Early Crescent: the Future of Knowledge and the Environment in Islam
Faces of Islam: Conversations on Contemporary Issues

Also by Merryl Wyn Davies

Knowing One Another: Shaping an Islamic Anthropology

Edited Works

Beyond Frontiers: Islam and Contemporary Needs
Faces of Islam: Conversations on Contemporary Issues

Ziauddin Sardar & Merryl Wyn Davies

DISTORTED IMAGINATION

Lessons from the Rushdie Affair

Grey Seal   *London*
Berita   *Kuala Lumpur*

First Published 1990 by Grey Seal Books
28 Burgoyne Road, London N4 1AD, England

© Ziauddin Sardar and Merryl Wyn Davies 1990

All rights reserved. No part of this publication may be reproduced or transmitted in any form or by any means, electronic or mechanical, including photocopy, recording or any information storage or retrieval system, without permission in writing from the publishers or their appointed agents.

British Library Cataloguing in Publication Data

Sardar, Ziauddin
   Distorted imagination: lessons from the Rushdie affair.
   1. Islam, related to Western culture, history
   I. Title II. Davies, Merryl Wyn
   297.09

ISBN 1-85640-000-X (U.K.)
ISBN 967-969-261-2 (Malaysia)

First published 1990 in ASEAN countries by
Berita Publishing Sdn. Bhd.
22 Jalan Liku, 59100 Kuala Lumpur, Malaysia

For Maha, Zaid and Zain
who are not amused and
who have to live in the aftermath

Contents

Introduction
Post-modern Blues 1

One
The Fire of Secularism 8

Two
The Images of Ignorance 34

Three
Enter, the Brown Sahib 76

Four
The Legacy of Muslim History 88

Five
The Other Side of Midnight 115

Six
Deconstructing Satan 142

Seven
Megalomaniacs, Mullahs and the Media 184

Eight
The Limits of Forbearance 238

Nine
The End of Civilization? 267

Bibliography 280
Index 293

Ziauddin Sardar, an expert on science and technology in the Muslim world and on information science, is an independent futurist and an internationally published scholar and journalist. He has contributed to numerous publications, and has worked for the British science journals *Nature* and *New Scientist*, and was Consulting Editor and a major contributor to *Inquiry*. In the world of broadcasting, he reported for London Weekend Television's *Eastern Eye* and presented the series *Encounters with Islam* for BBC Television. He was born in Pakistan, brought up and educated in London where he lives with his wife and three children between his frequent and extensive travels around the developing world.

Merryl Wyn Davies began her career in local newspapers before moving into broadcasting. She first worked in news and current affairs radio and television at BBC Wales before spending nearly a decade with BBC Television's Religious Programmes department. She worked on BBC TV's award-winning documentary series *Everyman*, *Heart of the Matter* and *Global Report*, and was responsible for such notable programmes as 'Coal and Prayer' and 'Koestler'. She produced the series *Encounters with Islam* before leaving the BBC to write her first book. She is a well-known writer on Islamic issues, has contributed to *Inquiry* magazine, and edited a new book on Islam and contemporary needs. Born in south Wales, and ever Welsh at heart, Ms Davies lives and works in London.

Sardar and Davies are co-founders of ISF Productions, an independent television production company which specializes in making programmes about Islam, the Muslim world and Third World issues. During the past year, they have brought out two series of programmes, *Faces of Islam* and *Alternatives*.

Introduction
Post-modern Blues

When *The Satanic Verses* was published in London on 26 September 1988, deep passions and accumulated resentment throughout the Muslim world were unleashed. World-wide demonstrations, calls for prosecution for blasphemy and withdrawal of the book, the totally uncharacteristic act of book-burning, and at the height of the affair, the announcement by Ayatollah Khomeini of a death sentence against the author were some of the results. In the Western world, these reactions produced horror and bewilderment and brought to the fore the age-old prejudices and phobias against Islam and Muslims. The 'Rushdie affair' became a matter of taking sides, defending positions and erecting barricades.

So frantic has been the activity of defending high ideals from presumed onslaughts that it is questionable whether the opponents can any longer hear, much less understand, each other. More certain is that the hue and cry has drowned out more elusive arguments that do not fall into neat, easily defendable redoubts. In the clamour there is much that has never been heard, despite acres of media coverage.

In this book we will examine some of the soundless background to this confrontation within a multicultural society, where controversy is nurtured but understanding and dialogue discouraged. Our concern is to bring together opposing views so that a dialogue can be initiated to assist everyone in drawing some constructive lessons from an affair that has rocked us all back to some highly revealing first principles. But first, the following true story may provide a backdrop to the Rushdie affair.

In a secondary school in Hackney, East London, a Pakistani boy listened attentively to the story of Richard the Lion Heart, but he had difficulty relating to the adversary, Saladin. The boy tried to inform the teacher that there was no such character as Saladin. If he was actually talking about Salahuddin Ayubbi, the Muslim general who conquered Jerusalem, then Salahuddin was a much braver and more magnanimous character than Richard the Lion Heart, and, at the very least, deserved detailed attention rather than mere dismissal. But the teacher could not tolerate persistent interruptions from this student—he forced the boy to stand outside the classroom while he continued his deliberations on Saladin.

A few weeks later the same history teacher began his lesson on the Indian mutiny, to be met by immediate protests from the Pakistani student: 'that was no mutiny', the boy declared, 'it was a struggle for freedom from the British'. But the teacher ignored the boy and continued to describe the achievements of Clive and the barbarism of Tippu Sultan and Haider Ali, whom the boy knew all about—they were the heroes he had brought with him from his homeland. Finally, unable to get a reasoned response from the teacher, the Pakistani boy followed his ancestors and rebelled. He turned the classroom tables upside down, threw chairs all over the place, and fired chalk pellets at the teacher. The boy was eventually subdued and marched to the headmaster's office for 'six of the best'. That not-so-long-ago boy recently demonstrated against *The Satanic Verses*, and his sons and daughters marched through London beside him.

The boy's classroom rebellion and the demonstrations against *The Satanic Verses* are attempts to recover an appropriated history: the real issues raised by the Rushdie affair are all about reclaiming history and the survival of cultural identity. In an increasingly uniform world, such issues are part of the temper of our times; learning the lessons of this affair are essential for the future, not merely for any one society but for everyone from all nations. In recent times it has become popular to talk about One World shared by a diversity of people, that our future lies in mutual co-operation because all our tomorrows will be increasingly interconnected. What the Rushdie affair demonstrates is just how much work has still to be done to turn easy platitudes into a genuine *modus vivendi*, to strip away the many layers of unintelligibility which divide and make conflict, and to create an atmosphere of comprehension where we can talk together about what really matters.

Communication and comprehension depend upon information. But comprehension, communication and information do not occur in a vacuum. We bring the whole of ourselves into any communication, and what we take from it will in large measure depend upon the quality of the information we have available. What has become important is what each side, behind its own barricade, thinks, perceives or assumes it can detect in the action and response of its opponent. If we are to bring down the partitions that prevent communication being heard, which is still a long way from making it mutually intelligible, then we need to examine the context within which this whole dialogue of the unhearing is taking place. That context begins among a marginalized minority who are subject to a whole variety of harrassments, a group of people acutely aware of their powerlessness and exclusion from the mainstream of society—the Muslim community in Britain, which can represent other minority Muslim and ethnic communities in both developed and developing countries. It begins with the axioms of art in a modern secular society and the vantage point of a typically post-modern author. But it extends far beyond the brief history of Muslim settlement in Britain or the fashionableness of post-modern thought. Rejecting the notion of the end of history and the collapsing of relevant time scales, we have found the only way to address the real issues is to set out the long march of continuing history, to bring together a host of material normally separated that fragments our understanding and distracts our mutual comprehension.

Our main aim in this book is to provide a basis for mutual understanding. The Rushdie affair has a long history, an emotionally charged present, and could, unfortunately, have a devastatingly long future. Any one who is interested in comprehending the true import of the Rushdie affair has to be ready to traverse a territory that will take him or her into totally new domains of history and cultural meaning. Whether *The Satanic Verses* is an original work of fiction or not is secondary to the fact that it fits neatly into, indeed is a logical culmination of, the well-known tradition of Orientalism, the scholarly and literary tradition responsible for the Western image of Islam. On the Western side of the divide, understanding Orientalism is not only a prerequisite for understanding the Rushdie affair, it is a natural step towards Western people understanding themselves and their own perceptions. For Muslims, the context is provided by secularism, its history and its rise as *the* dominant worldview. In a secular world, where religion is relegated to personal preference and minor matters of conscience and where God has been killed, people who take their religion seriously appear not only out of step with modern times but quite abnormal. Their actions are judged against the backdrop of a bloody conflict between organized religion and forces of reason and liberty that has nothing to do with their own history. The secularization of European history and religion is one where gains have been secured after an intense physical, political and intellectual war. Understanding secularism and its history is, therefore, the prerequisite for Muslims to make themselves understood; it is also the prerequisite for their survival as Muslims.

The Rushdie affair cannot easily be pigeonholed or written down in simplistic terms. Every raised Muslim voice is immediately overwhelmed by the demand to state its position on a number of issues. It is not possible, however, to respond to the demands in the way they are posed without taking a journey none of the questioners have yet been prepared to undertake. This book is that journey. It is not an attempt to avoid the questions but the only possible way to define how we relate to the questions. The Rushdie affair is not a reaction to the past but a struggle about the nature of our common future. What is involved are questions about equity and justice that have been distorted by history and cannot be resolved without recourse to rethinking received history. There is a need on both sides of the barricades to attempt to experience history as others know it in order to take the measure of just what is at issue. We present a reading of the history of Europe and the West and of Muslim civilization. It is a rationally argued position with which many people may disagree. Our claim is that even if one disagrees with the argument, it contains more than enough substance to set a constructive agenda for discussion. The making of the future is about a willingness to engage in genuine dialogue around rational and valid disagreements. This is the only alternative to continuing crude power relations in which finer sentiments and noble values on both sides are trampled into the dust.

Central to our book is the concept of distorted imagination: the intellectual and cultural tool the West has fashioned to explain Islam and Muslims. The distorted imagination is a deliberate and calculated exercise that impedes mutual understanding between Islam and the West. For Muslims the distorted imagination confronts them everywhere with images of ignorance. The ignorance fosters attitudes and questions of monumental irrelevance to the believing Muslim, attitudes and questions that prevent any discussion taking place for the lack of a common language for that dialogue. The whole tradition of Orientalism is founded on the supposedly 'objective' proposition that Muslims are partial witnesses to their own religion and history. It gives weight and credence only to non-Muslim 'observers', who, by the way, are equally partial, never objective and long overdue for an examination of their motivations and purposes. To make a quarter of mankind voiceless appendages to their own history and identity is to invite conflict. To consign a fourth of humanity to the dustbin of erroneous history is a lunatic action that invites catastrophe. Muslims inhabit a cherished world of meaning formed by Islam. One is not required to believe as they do, nor to subscribe uncritically to everything they say. But one is required to acknowledge that they do have a consistent, rational position that belongs in every informed assessment of the present and future of the world, as well as the Rushdie affair.

The Muslim is expected to accept the distorted imagination as self-description. Internalizing the images of ignorance is the price for their entry into modernity. It is not only too high a price, it is a price no civilized people should tolerate or be prepared to impose by active or tacit means. We do not present a reading of history to reject the West in toto—there are no people and no individuals in today's world exempt from coming to terms with the West. The re-reading of the history of the West aims to demonstrate how clearly it appears to others that the West now maintains a distorted image of itself, a seemingly infinite ability to sustain unreflective ignorance about itself, to internalize this ignorance in a cynical enterprise of domination that belies and denies everything the West itself claims as its best achievement. Tolerance is not to be judged by the comfort and complacency of those with power. If you want to learn whether tolerance or justice, equity or fair dealing exist, then you must ask those without power and be prepared to learn from their experience. Until that openness exists there can be no plural world, but only the meaninglessness that reduces liberty for all people.

The Satanic Verses reads like a re-run of a cul de sac of history, Orientalism. As Timothy Brenan argued in his *Salman Rushdie and the Third World*, 'it projects itself as a rival Qur'an with Rushdie as its prophet and the devil as its supernatural voice'. Another in the continuous historic succession of Orientalist rewriting of the Qur'an and Muslim history, this one finds its substance in the post-modernist culture of nihilism, meaninglessness, confusion, ambiguity of reality, panic, cynicism and perpetual doubt. 'In this fertile indecision, this apotheosis of self-questioning, the counter-Qur'an of the novel finds its theology'. We examine the novel to see how the distorted imagination projects images of ignorance that embrace the reconstructed theology of Rushdie. So pervasive are these images that the defenders of Rushdie's freedom of expression are ignorant of what he has actually written in the book. We insist that everyone has a duty to defend with understanding and not to defy from ignorance. The willingness to experience the knowledge of those who are profoundly offended by Rushdie is the measure of the potential for developing a genuine plural society.

It is argued that Muslims are intolerant and bent upon destroying the tolerance based on freedom of expression that is part of Weste civilization. The facts of the Rushdie affair do not bear this construction. Absolute freedom of expression does not exist in Western civilization: the concept of freedom of expression within the law is variously determined from country to country. Why limits exist and where they should properly be set is the proper issue that urgently needs to be addressed. Such a discussion, however, can only have meaning when freedom of expression is tested against some rather basic measures. Freedom surely cannot be said to exist nor be defensible where opportunity to exercise this right is unequally held and practised. Freedom of expression is alleged to be the guarantor of informed judgement through the opportunity to encounter a diversity of opinion that, however erroneous or partial they may be, by their very diversity improve our store of knowledge and power of discernment. It is an established principle of Islamic law that the prerequisite of a duty is itself a duty. If freedom of expression is to have any validity for all people, then the prerequisite of provision for equality of opportunity and balance must be seen to exist. Unfortunately, they palpably do not exist, as the coverage of the Rushdie affair has amply demonstrated. It is our argument that the realization of the West's best ideals are now perverted by a group of omnipotent/helpless children with weak egos and socially distorted superegos, who have transformed art into god and themselves into high priests and guardians of morality and the ever expanding outer limits (*hudud*) of secular fundamentalism, and have thereby made themselves the custodians of the soul of society—those generally acknowledged to be the *literati*.

When one's ideology, in this case secular fundamentalism, becomes the yardstick by which reality is measured, one exists in a totally insulated space that permit's no counter-reality. In this insulated space it is not possible to see the other side's objectivity with any objectivity. Every defender of Rushdie's freedom to do what he wishes without social accountability saw the argument only in singular, monolithic terms, or in Rushdie's own words, in 'the light of secularism and the darkness of religion'. It is not possible to understand the position of the other side, let alone comprehend its arguments, when one's own value, secularism, is seen as *the* fundamental value to which all other values must defer. In reality, Rushdie's defenders have offered no argument except the argument of absolute freedom without responsibility, an argument that has no place in a civilized society.

The Rushdie affair has evolved into a power struggle, a genuine post-modern impasse. Secularism has a comprehensible meaning for those who embrace this ideology. But secularism is nothing more than a power structure of considerable intolerance when it demands that it alone must determine what is acceptable for everyone in the modern world. Secularism in its current embodiment of absolute panic and total doubt, post-modernism, is and will continue to be opposed by those who refuse either to choose or be pressurized into marginalization and meaninglessness. There is nothing freedom-loving nor liberal in insisting that the dominant position of secularism remain intact.

The Rushdie affair has shown us that words have power, that they matter. Their power is that they contain meaning, represent real systems of dealing with and organizing reality. No civilized society can disown the power of words; it has a duty to comprehend that is not merely prudential but touches upon everything that qualifies and defines the highest ideals of being civilized. Muslims are tired of being written about as barbarians and demand that the mote of barbarism in the eye of Western civilization, somewhat belatedly, be removed. We do not want to see a world that relentlessly treks to uniform universal barbarism. In such a world it is not just Muslims who will lose their identities, but all people will see their identities reduced, their finest ideals corrupted. We see this as the only destination of the universalizing mission that now seems to dominate the world, a mission that not only excludes but seeks to eradicate finally and irrevocably, while at the same time alienating and eradicating all the richness of Western identity from within itself. We believe that alternative futures exist, but they will have to be based upon plurality and will demand new thinking from all people. It is in the certainty that the Rushdie affair will not subside to a whimper that we see hope.

The vast majority of Muslims wish Salman Rushdie no physical harm; but equally, they are not able to forgive him. They would be fools to do so on two counts. If they do not defend their cultural and historic territory, they cannot hope to survive the future without losing their identities. Because of the intrinsic and deep connection between Muslim identity, the Prophetic paradigm and the Qur'an, no one who has abused or ridiculed the Prophet in recent times has been allowed to go unchallenged. Moreover, they should not forgive because 'their forgiveness [would have] made possible the deepest and sweetest corruption of all, namely the idea that he [has done] nothing wrong' (*The Satanic Verses*, p. 26).

One
The Fire of Secularism

The Satanic Verses is an offensive book. This is the substance of the Muslim protest, as well as a substantive reason for the vociferous defence of Salman Rushdie. The opponents' differing views of the world allow no common ground for dialogue. For one party the offence contained in the book transgresses the acceptable limits of freedom of expression; for the other the offensive nature of the book is a necessary part of the exercise of freedom of expression. Mutual incomprehension obviates the possibility of any debate on what is tolerable in a plural society.

The Rushdie affair is proof that a genuine plural society does not exist. More sadly, it demonstrates that, as yet, there is little desire in Western society to create a plural society. There is diversity in both Western society and the modern world order, but diversity is not necessarily plurality.

The Rushdie affair is a confrontation brought about by a post-modernist author in true post-modernist fashion, trying to write a traditional worldview out of history. The author is vigorously defended by post-modernist secularists, whose position his text vindicates. Opposite is the fully fledged post-modernist defence of a traditional worldview. There is nothing eccentric or idiosyncratic about this impasse; it is a conflict about the nature of the future that has ramifications for all the world's peoples. Hysteria and obfuscation have so far been the hallmark of knee-jerk responses on both sides. But the issues and alignment of opinions involved will not simply fade away—they will have to be faced. They are not so simple or straightforward as the media cacophony suggests.

However we wish to think about modernity, we end up describing a condition abstracted from the experience of the West, from just one civilization and one history. The content of modernity includes a secular nation-state, representative democracy, science and technology, industry and material abundance, individualism, mass communications, freedom of expression, personal liberty and rationality. Modernity is a globalizing force, a universalizing enterprise of great power; no part of the world is now free from its incursion. Today, modernity is the norm that subsumes all diversity and its strategy for dealing with difference is its ruling ideology—secularism. Neither modernity nor secularism can be defined without reference to the Western civilization where they were forged, where they are claimed as discontinuities. But they represent even more radical discontinuities for non-Western civilizations. What it is to be modern depends upon secularism, an ideology that has broken away from the roots of Western civilization through a process that has been shaped in all its essentials by the nature of the institutions and ideas it has renounced in its struggle to become 'free'.

Within Western civilization, secularism has dethroned the ruling orthodoxy, the uniquely powerful institution of the Church, which was made to accommodate people who conscientiously refused to submit to its authority and, hence, to its uniform world of meaning. The freedom of each individual to chose from among multiple worlds of private meaning is the promise of secularism; shared meaning has been transcended for the betterment of all citizens. The price that all parties have been asked to pay for this betterment is that no sectional belief can be left beyond the reach of the freedom to question, to doubt and to disparage. Secularists defend the principle that all tenets must be subjected to the test of rationality, whether or not it is pertinent to those beliefs. This liberty for all sectional beliefs to contend for attention and defend themselves within the conventions of doubt and disparagement has been chosen as the proper protection for the conscientious existence of dissident groups; it is, therefore, seen as a means to tolerance. This is how the modern world works to keep choices and, hence, the future open. It is less easy to see that this tolerance and diversity of sectional belief comes to be underpinned by one ruling orthodoxy—secularism—that alone can be trusted with freedom, liberty and the power of determination and thereby becomes the supreme value. The one thing that cannot be questioned is secularism itself.

The virtues of secularism are so ingrained as the normative ideal of Western civilization that it is hard for its adherents to perceive that the cumulative historic choices of their civilization are now an orthodoxy, a given of the modern world wherein Western societies are the dominant powers. One choice that is not open is a non-secular future for those who maintain their beliefs and seek an integrated, holistic world of meaning. So close is the identification between modernity and secularism that adopting secularism is the natural, progressive and, therefore, superior diagnostic criterion for entering upon modernity. Secularism is believed to be neutral, value free and best able to offer the power to choose rationally and eclectically from a range of lesser values. Secularism is regarded as the guarantor of genuine freedom from coercion, generating the liberty to progress beyond all the social patterns that have retarded the development of non-Western peoples. Its claim is to leave the individual free to choose a private world of meaning. This choice is founded upon the absolute right to doubt and the supreme value of doubt, not just within Western civilization but for any civilization throughout the world.

For all non-Western civilizations that would be modern, however, secularism is not a choice, certainly not a choice that arises from within. The unconscious template by which all modern goods and services are manufactured is the genetic code of Western modernity. Appropriation of those goods and services then replicates the society of its inception, wherever it goes. The modernizing history of non-Western civilizations is acceptance of Western terms that neither are chosen nor have meaning within their own history or culture. Rather, modernity is the abandonment of traditional meaning where secularism may have no coherence or conceptual validity, except in the annihilation of all that has gone before, all that defines the identity and existence of a civilization. Therefore, internalizing modernity means renunciation of a distinct history and the recognition that the organizing ideas of that history and culture have no contribution to make to the present or the future. Modernity is the end of authenticity, the assumption of another self.

For a non-Western civilization, global modernization, in fact, means the acceptance of meaninglessness, because the modernity that is spreading has been efficiently destroying the stability and internal dynamics of traditional cultures without providing the benefits advertised to make the condition bearable. The non-Western world has suffered physical and social degradation of its environment; it remains a net contributor to the ever increasing wealth of the West while the vast majority of its people live in poverty; and for the tools of modernity it remains acutely dependent on the economy and politics of the West. For the last forty years while modernity developed the Third World has been a surrogate for the ideological conflicts of Western civilization in its two modes: capitalism and communism. As the West has been able to envisage no continuity of otherness abroad, it has been determined to make no accommodation to the pockets of otherness within.

The triumph of modernity and secularism has been achieved by pursuing their own internal logic. The triumph of the Enlightenment was the breaking free from old certainties, renouncing old ideas and their notion of truth, deconstructing them with the weapon of reason. The progress of rational truths of modernity has been effected to make the future open, to free the way for newness that is endlessly open to revision. In the process, however, powerful institutions have been created whose existence is seen as essential to facilitating the continuance of more and more progress, the secular nation-state and science and technology being the most obvious. The juggernaut

The Fire of Secularism

must roll on even though Western civilization, the instigator and beneficiary of modernity, has come to recognize a crisis: the loss of any rational truth that can be substantiated, the dissolution of all choices, a condition termed post-modernism.

Throughout Western societies there is urgent debate about post-modernism, embracing all fields from science to politics and religion. In this search for a post-modern resolution of the crisis of modernity, art is a crucial area of expression. The artist is the contemporary high priest setting out the mysteries of the human condition, its contradictions and the meaninglessness of its quest to explicate existence. A post-modernist author such as Salman Rushdie can blend, borrow, mix and match from all languages and imageries to validate the primacy of duplicity, truthlessness, doubt and ambiguity. The artist holds up a mirror to life to reveal a basic tenet of post-modernism, meaninglessness. However, this mirror image, or mirage, is not disinterested. It is a definable position that can be located in a tradition of thought; its manipulations or simulations have a determined ideological programme, a subtext of their own. As Rushdie has himself written '. . . every story one chooses to tell is a kind of censorship, it prevents other tales' (*Shame*, pp. 70–1). In their fabrications the authors/artists have no responsibility to the languages and sources from which their choices are made. But there is a responsibility that is never absent: to confirm the supremacy of secularism by the portrayal of the modern condition according to the dictates of secularism. It is not just meaninglessness and doubt that are vindicated by post-modernist writing, it is the specific kind of meaninglessness and doubt that confirms the necessity of secularism, the inescapability of this route from the past into the future.

The burning of a book is a symbolic act, an emotive gesture. It is an act of powerlessness against a powerful institution of the modern world. The peaceful ritual burning of *The Satanic Verses* evokes a host of potent images that confirm the central place of the icon of the *Book* in modern Western society. The outraged response to the act of defiance by a marginalized minority who have no entree to the levers of power is positive proof that it is through art and the *Book* that the project of modernity has been brought into being, that secularism will brook no interference with its dominance.

Power and territory belong to secularism; the rights of secularism are absolute, irrespective of the impact upon others. It is the duty of secularism to bring all others within its ambit of progress. The *Book*, irrespective of its contents and especially when its text does not respect sacred sensitivities, offers a service to those who believe in sacreds and are thereby incapable of self-examination. Such pre-modern believers and their beliefs are ripe for deconstruction to bring them into the modern world. As Rushdie stated in his essay 'Outside the Whale', 'the modern world lacks not only hiding places, but certainties'. The modern world is to be found outside the whale, where there 'is the unceasing storm, the continual quarrel, the dialectic of history'. In this storm we are all products of history who must directly face the turbulence. With no hiding places and no certainties, those who clothe themselves in the sou'westers of belief are seeking shelter from reality. They are shrouding themselves in certainties that are mere illusions, the worse in which to face the unceasing, continual storm. The storm is a force that must have conflict and cannot be calmed by those buffeted by its superior might. In the conflicting pressure systems of politics and history, we will be changed by the elements. It is not for the storm-tossed jetsam to seek to impose direction upon their course, for the ocean swell will decide where, or if or when, there will be a landing. In this Salman Rushdie is, in fact, arguing for keeping a faith—keeping faith with the rising tide of uncertainty that is the temper of the secular world. He is keeping afloat the ship of doubt triumphant.

Dogmatic secularism is so sure of its doubt that it neglects to notice it has become a certainty, the constant of the inconstancy of existence. In *The Satanic Verses*, Rushdie asked, 'what is the opposite of faith?' He answered, 'not disbelief. Too final, certain, closed, itself a kind of belief. Doubt.' Yet to retain doubt is itself an act of faithful defiance—the defiance of any belief, except doubt. To be a doubter is to regard belief as illicit, or inferior, or suspect, a denial of freedom. To champion doubt is to let all things contend before the sceptical imagination that alone is free to choose. Any exercise of choice, even that of unbelief, would be a selection of a certainty and can only be accepted as a private peccadillo that must remain marginal to the wider world, whatever importance it may have for an individual. The freedom and openness guaranteed by secular doubt is the only bulwark against imperialistic belief and totalitarian certainty which impose conformity. They are the history of belief from which secularism was born and at great cost has liberated all people through the advancement of modernity. But if all systems of belief must be subjugated by secular dominance, then secularism is the imperial power par excellence; it is totalitarian since it determines you can have any belief you choose, so long as it is not useful in negotiating the future of society.

Doubt is a recognizable position that creates around itself an ordered world of contending forces whose only rationale is to preserve conflict so that one may doubt. The conflicting storm demands sacred processes that service and maintain doubt. Just as doubt did not come easily into history, so must it be protected vigilantly from any slide back into the strangulating straightjacket of belief. Therefore, everything must be subjected routinely to questioning, including ridicule and abuse. To be free to doubt, all things must be open. It is hard for the doubter to conceive that this freedom can itself be an act of force, an imposition, in effect, upon others. Doubt, as Rushdie so clearly intimates is not final, not closed; it creates an open world for everyone. So it must appear to the doubter, for surely openness is the guarantee even for those who must believe, who must be certain. Surely they do not have to read the books; they can switch off their television sets; they need not exercise the freedoms others have secured on their behalf. This is the virtue of doubt triumphant.

Within the righteous miasma of doubt there is nothing wrong with being wrong. Being wrong is a freedom from which much good can come. Freedom is upheld by continual testing of its limits. Freedom is the freedom to outrage, or it is no freedom at all. It may in some senses be wrong to outrage, nevertheless it is a healthy freedom. One can even see this freedom to outrage as a positive service to those afflicted by certainty. The sceptical attitude must mock and deride, scorn and traduce, to ensure that freedom exists, that doubt holds sway, that no new pernicious certainties have entered unobserved to overturn the secular hegemony. Thus doubt serves the cause of the diversity of certainty, ensuring we are not curtailed by some aspiring certainty bent upon imposing itself. Only doubt is fit to offer this selfless service; it is not something one can expect from any certainty. The one freedom the believer does not have in the world of doubt triumphant is the freedom from abuse, the right to respect *within one's own terms*, the right to define oneself on par with the holders of the ring of modern power—the secular worldview.

The doubtful freedom to ridicule takes itself seriously, so seriously that it has created a blind spot in failing to observe how potent a power structure it has become: no one has power to contend on any terms except those laid down by the secular world. Hence, book-burning leads to outrage, leads to power politics, for politics and history are all we have and their nature is to breed false certainties, and thereby conflict. This is the storm that has been determined by doubt. As Salman Rushdie presciently noted, there are no hiding places when doubt determines all, according to the rules of the secular world order.

Doubt is not a Western invention: all traditions incorporate some notion of doubt. But perpetual doubt and its host, secularism, are purely Western inventions; they are the product of a particular history unique to Europe—a history with book-burning and suppression of thought at its core. The *Book Irrespective* (irrespective of its contents) and the *Book Respectless* (respecting nothing as beyond abusive criticism) have been the cornerstones of the creation of the secular worldview because of the pervasiveness of book burning and the lack of freedom of expression in European history. It is from the ashes of a book-burning order that secularism wrested its modern dominance. The problem with secularism is that it overwrites everything, all other histories and politics, with its own historical experience. Here our concern is to understand the world that made secularism; later we will have to consider how distorted an imagination secularism becomes when imprinted upon other peoples' history, when the rest of the world is subsumed within the particulars of the Western secularizing experience.

The Making of Secular Hegemony

The term 'secular' derives from the Latin *saeculum*, meaning 'present world'. It denotes a process of transferring territory, property and services from ecclesiatical authority. Initially it meant transference of control from the magisterium of the Roman Catholic Church, a perpetual and mystical community, to the transient and spiritually inferior community of the present world, giving control to the kings who were the state. This transfer involved much more than a realignment of territorial control or ownership of property. What began the process of secularization was a reaction to the operation of religion in society; as it gathered pace and scope over the centuries, secularization has retained this essential feature. A reaction to religion is not the same as a reaction against religion. Many features of Western secularization have indeed been justified, as was the first reformation, as the search for a more correct, a truer relationship with the sacred. If it was a reaction against something, then the opponent was not religion *qua* religion but authority over religion. In all its complexity the growth of the secular worldview is incomprehensible without the notion of a Church which claimed sole, infallible authority over the ideas, interpretation and institutional form of religion. The rupture of this authority was, and is, the most radical and enduring patina of thought underlying secularization. It is the freeing of thought from Church authority that resulted in all Western civil liberties being, at base, religious liberties, and these liberties being secured through reaction to a Church. Reaction also has a specific legacy: it caused both parties to define themselves and their opponents around the disputed issues while ignoring the features common to both.

The authority of the Church in Western Christendom was total. The ideal of the Christian vision was the identification of the Church with the whole of organized society. The ideal held sway, in changing form, from the fourth to the eighteenth century. It was only after a process of change that had introduced a multiplicity of religious forms and organizations within some societies that eighteenth-century thinkers could regard the ideal as untenable. But the thinkers of the Enlightenment were still wrestling with and reacting to the authority of the Church, and their efforts were directed to disproving the foundations of Church authority. The Western experience of Church authority was that it formed a total society, which was a compulsory society in the same way as the modern state is a compulsory society, as R.W. Southern has written.

> Just as the modern state requires those who are its members by the accident of birth to keep its laws, to contribute to its defence and public services, to subordinate private interests to the common good, so the medieval church required those who had become its members by the accident (as one may almost call it) of baptism to do all these things and many others. . . . In baptism the godparents made certain promises on behalf of the child which bound him legally for life. From the social point of view a contractual relationship was established between the infant and the church from which there was no receding . . . the obligations attached to baptism could in no circumstances be renounced. (Southern, *Western Society*, p.19)

One of the obligations of baptism was to accept the teachings of the Church, its doctrine and dogma, and one of the coercive powers of the Church was the punishment of heresy. Thomas Aquinas wrote:

> Heresy is a sin which merits not only excommunication but also death, for it is worse to corrupt the Faith which is the life of the soul than to issue counterfeit coins which minister to the secular life. Since counterfeiters are justly killed by princes as enemies to the common good, so heretics also deserve the same punishment. (Aquinas, 2, 2, qu.xi, art.3)

Both heretics and heretical writings were burnt throughout the domain and history of Western Christendom.

The Church's attitude to the importance of maintaining orthodoxy had been laid by St Augustine, who first emphasized the Biblical text, 'Compel them to come in' (Luke 14:23). Paul Johnson has described this 'idea that a heretic should not be expelled but, on the contrary, be compelled to recant and conform, or be destroyed' as 'constructive persecution'. About St Augustine's views, he wrote:

> His second contribution was in some ways even more sinister because it implied constructive censorship. Augustine believed that it was the duty of the orthodox intellectual to identify incipient heresy, bring it to the surface and expose it, and so

force those responsible either to abandon their line of inquiry altogether or accept heretical status. (Johnson, p. 117)

The theory, which grew out of the abusive theological disputes of the early Church, was that doctrinal error inevitably induced moral decay. This trend of thought can be found in Western literature up to the nineteenth century, and is not entirely absent in our own day. Every new ideological movement was seen as a dangerous opening of the floodgates of social chaos; every new thinker was a heretic, thereby an atheist and perforce a libertine, who abandoned any semblance of moral restraint in personal life. Unorthodox ideas lead to social chaos and eventually bring all order in the state crashing down. Given this conception of heresy, it is not surprising that its corollary was the view that only the orthodox believer could be a loyal subject of the state. It is argued that the constitution produced by the French Revolution was the origin of modern totalitarianism. It is possible to argue it was merely a totally secular expression of a very old idea, the secularization on the proper principles of the ideal of the unitary state. The Reign of Terror, as is well established, was not a revenge against the aristocratic class, but the logical consequence, a rooting out of heresy; the majority of those consigned to Madame La Guillotine were revolutionary heretics. Punishment of heresy had always been the function of the state: in Paul Johnson's neat phrase, 'the Church unearthed and the State castigated'. The coercive authority of the Church needed the coercive power and administration of the State, and both regarded orthodoxy as a supreme value. In justice it must be said that the State was often more zealous than the Church in rooting out heretics and consigning them to premature, this-worldly fires of Hell.

As the dogma of the Church was elaborated over the centuries, what was required of orthodoxy burgeoned. A significant number of recurrent heresies shared the theme of a return to the simplicity of the life of the Apostles and the primitive Church, a life of common property and simple faith. The Cathar and Waldensian traditions are as old as Christianity and their attraction was the signal contrast they offered to the abuses of the Church itself. They were deemed heresies to be rigorously put down, notoriously so in the case of the Crusade against the Cathars. The sacraments of the Church became more elaborate, as did the instruments, such as indulgences, perpetual endowed masses, and dispensations, by which the Church offered spiritual relief to the believer. The Church's view of the world was explicit, the reality was spiritual reality; the true Christian life was the life of the religious following a spiritual vocation. The life of this world was irrelevant, or the realm of sin and evil. The metaphysical beliefs of the

Church were matters of doctrine created by the Church, and an essential part of orthodox belief was the infallibility of the Church in doctrinal matters. The Church was *the* literate institution of society, carefully guarding its monopoly over ideas. Diversity of opinion could be indulged, within limits, among the body of the Church, but licence in thought was for the elite and shielded from the masses. Incidentally, this elitist trend was something shared by later rationalist thinkers; Voltaire and his friends indulged in free thought but, as he cautioned, not in front of the servants. The language of the Church was Latin; possession of a Bible or other religious standard text in the vernacular could open people to the charge of dabbling in heresy. The literate output was scrutinized enthusiastically for signs of heresy, and offending works would be consigned to the pyre. What the Church taught and sanctioned was orthodoxy. That orthodoxy came to include the rationalist, philosophical and metaphysical speculations of the mediaeval scholars.

The Church was also a power in society; it has been estimated that by the end of the Middle Ages a third of all property in Europe belonged to the Church. The theoretical authority and power of the Church was total. It was never efficient, was prone to inertia and often was more lenient and enlightened than the secular authorities. It was a mighty magisterium but often had to accommodate secular authorities. European monarchs could find themselves embroiled in conflicts of interest with a powerful body, subject to an autonomous system of law, operating within the boundaries of their states. The kings could not discipline the unruly and errant clerics, but gradually won influence over the Church within their territories. This shift gradually and subtly aligned the notion of orthodoxy within the boundaries of a territorial state. The ideal of a universal Church continued, a practice of the Church within nations proliferated; neither ideal nor practice affected the identification of orthodoxy with citizenship.

The structure of the Church formed during the Middle Ages is, as R.W. Southern noted, 'the most elaborate and thoroughly integrated system of religious thought and belief the world has ever known'. The creations of the mediaeval church in organizations, and some would argue patterns of thought, have shown an astonishing power of survival. We must agree with Southern that:

> The medieval social environment still haunts the modern world in institutions which were formed by its pressures. One reason for the survival is the success with which they were built into and conformed to the pattern of the society that produced them. Church and society were one, and neither could be changed without the other under-

going a similar transformation. This is the clue to a large part of European history whether secular or ecclesiastical. (Southern, *Western Society*, p. 16)

Change was necessarily and inevitably concerned with religion. To effect change in social life, for whatever reason, entailed a reaction to religion; any stance was formed by engaging with central religious issues and the fact of the existence of the Church. It is often overlooked that Marx began his academic career immersed in religious study and debate, which was the location of the intellectual cutting edge in the post-Hegel Germany of his youth. Secularism today is still engaged in reaction to religion, since so many planks of the triumphalist secularist outlook have been constructed upon historical increments in the reaction to religion. The superiority of secularism can best be made evident in contrast with religion. So the notion of what religion comprises, which is most usually its mediaeval image, continues to be a validation of secularism as well as a proof of its superiority.

There is one other survival we must note. The Church was the *power*; those who reacted against religion were for most of European history dissenting minorities. Liberty of thought and expression, therefore, was won to assure the tolerance of these minorities, as well as to embrace those who contended against the power of the state. Conformist or religious ideas are, therefore, always assumed to be the expression of the mainstream. Secularism acquired this attitude of absolute defence of liberty in a particular history. In the course of the Rushdie affair, secularists have been loathe to notice that the positions of power have changed and new responses may be required.

The rise of the secular state and the notion of secular society came much later, after centuries of clamour for reform of the Church. The movement called the Reformation, however, is more accurately termed a revolution both in the practice of and ideas about religion. Inevitably a movement for purified, simplified religious enthusiasm must also affect the nature of state and society. Intending a reform of obvious abuses in the body of the Church, the Reformation thinkers had no notion of changing the identification of orthodox obedience in religion with citizenship. What they sought to change was the content of orthodoxy to which obedience was required. The odour of burning that accompanied the Reformation, on both sides and in both kinds, of humans and books, testifies to the initial aim of replacing one total society with a new total society differently constituted and incorporated.

The religious ideas of the Reformation have had a major influence on Western thought and the genesis of secularism. The most revolutionary change it produced was in the concept of authority. What was overthrown was the authority of the Roman Church which was replaced by a direct appeal to scripture. A major emphasis was placed by all reformed trends, as well as counter-Reformation Catholicism, on education. Since the reformed trends held that all believers must have access to scripture in their own language, they at a stroke ushered in the concept of a mass society. It took a long time to become a reality, but it was an unstoppable consequence of reformulated ideas about religion. The other revolution was in the importance attached to the *saeculum*, the present world. Without the Reformation there could be no secularism, for secularism depends upon the centrality of human society in this world. Luther was the first to make this major redefinition when he introduced the idea of the priesthood of all the believers, including the laity, in the mission of religion as summoned to an earthly vocation. Calvin, as always, went further; his doctrine of election gave the devout believers an assurance of their role in this world and its righteousness which could be unshakable, even though the essence of the doctrine was that the certainty of election was unknowable.

The humanism of the Renaissance played little part in the Reformation; indeed, it was almost wholly swept away by the tide of religious fervour. Scholarship, however, played a great part in making the Reformation, and led many to accept that the makers of the doctrine of the Church had made errors in their formulations. Protestantism would never again accept the infallibility of the Church. In the present world the Reformation man or woman could supersede the knowledge of the early founders of the Church by direct study of improved scriptural texts. The techniques of inquiry were essential to reformed practice. The whole concept of the nature of authority in society was altered. This world became the focus of religious idealism because it was in this world that mankind uncovered and implemented the Will of Providence by moral and intellectual exertions. It is a modern commonplace that there is an opposition between science and religion, with the foundation dramas of this eternal opposition being the burning of Giordano Bruno and the inquisition of Galileo. It is far too simplistic a commonplace. Protestantism gave a positive value, indeed a duty, to the devout believer to study the other book of God, nature, and thus gave an impetus to science. It is hardly fashionable or comprehensible today to remember that the creators of modern science, such as Newton and Descartes, were impelled in their science by their faith, and took their starting point from scriptural ideas.

Without the shift in the concept of authority made by the Reformation, there would have been no notion of the progress of scientific knowledge. The voyages to the new world showed that the fathers of natural philosophy, the ancients of Greece and Rome, had also erred. They had asserted that antipodean man was an impossibility; Reformation man encountered and enslaved them. New knowledge was open and available. The charter of Britain's Royal Society is quite explicit on the point of the link between scientific knowledge and religion, in the new reformed sense. The duty to inquire was fundamental to avoid error, and included the duty to discover error that had occurred in the past or the present so that the devout could properly enact the earthly calling of religion. Therefore, without the Reformation the scientific spirit would have meant far less than it does in the modern world.

Through the Reformation, Europeans acquired a new view of the importance of their place within the natural world. Just as they had a new relationship to scripture, so they would seek to answer a host of new questions about their relationship to nature. The questioning had a profound influence on both the development of science and social thought. Increasingly, the term 'natural', whether it was the original nature of man and his natural rights or the natural laws of the mechanical universe, entered into debate. The importance of the natural was that it could be substantiated by reason; it provided a means of thinking about problems without appeal to doctrine. The natural rights of man were those God-created rights all possessed by virtue of their existence. They could be appealed to beyond the legislation of Church doctrine or that of the State. They became a source for legitimating challenges to authority. What was natural was the original condition before the overwriting of Church or State and, therefore, both ancient and pure. The post-Reformation world began to have a new relationship to time, a new concept of history.

None of the advancement in thought about man's natural condition was disinterested. It had the ideological point of confirming the error of doctrine of the renounced Church or proving its rightness, and providing ground for either the maintenance or alteration of the social condition of the State. The Reformation put the reformulation of the human condition at the top of the European intellectual agenda, and reaction to religion was a central actor in the radical new knowledge that it provoked. The historic conjunction of the Reformation and the so-called voyages of discovery is of major importance for the redefinition of the natural condition of mankind. This is the moment when the non-European makes an entry into European thought.

From the first the non-European role has been to provide a new means of thinking about the human condition outside and beyond those of received doctrine and oppressive legislation. One of the first examples was also one of the most potent: Thomas More's *Utopia*, published in 1516. More's concern was the state of English society; his dialogue with a traveller recently returned from the new world was a means of launching a radical critique of the governance of his society. The detail of his argument drew on Vespucci's report of the life of the Indians of South America in his letter *Novus Mundus*, which described the Indians as the negative of the norms of European existence, especially in holding all property in common. Although this idea had its roots in the Christian tradition, had More used the conventional models from Christian history he would have been writing heresy; such a case could not arise by reference to a non-European people, who on making their physical entry into European consciousness swiftly became the practical models that informed the growth of a European sense of history as progress. These non-Europeans were the evidence of the original condition, the natural existence and character of mankind. They were evidence of where Europeans had been before they enchained themselves within erroneous doctrines and the legislative states built upon those doctrines. Just as the voyages of discovery meant the European, then Western, appropriation of power over the whole globe, so the idea of the non-European informed their intellectual imperialism over the human condition and the invariance with which thinking about the human condition is also thinking about the social and political problems of the West. The non-European has, therefore, always been a creation of Western wish fulfilment, a research laboratory to confirm or confound European ideas, not to be seen directly in their own terms but only in comparison with a European standard. The pattern has a long history and is still alive and well today.

The Reformation was a search for a new orthodoxy that contained within it the seeds of fragmentation, the impossibility of there being a uniform orthodoxy once a coercive authority had been dethroned. But it left a civil problem of considerable proportions. The Reformation had been effected through the authority of the State; the religious choice of rulers became the religious affiliation of their subjects, the most extreme example being the English Reformation, or the English nationalization of religion under the Crown. But diversity of conscientious belief continued to proliferate. It was now the State, rather than the Church, which was legislating the nature of orthodoxy in religion that defined the loyal citizen. The next stage in working out the consequences of the Reformation was all to do with the relationship between religion and civil rights.

From Reformation thought emerged that potent idea, conscience, the individual conscience devoutly and diligently searching the scriptures for certainty. Owen Chadwick noted:

> That reverence for individual conscience, which Christianity nurtured in mankind, weakened the desire for conformity to public rites. The legendary saying of Luther, 'Here stand I, I can do no other', represented so Christlike a Christian attitude that,

though its consequences were not yet seen, the attitude must in time destroy the ideal conformity to rites or to faith by social pressure or by law. Christian conscience was the force which began to make Europe 'secular'; that is to allow many religions or no religion in a state. (Chadwick, *Reformation*, p. 23)

Chadwick touched upon a central theme in Western religious thought. The hold of the Church and the observed abuses of the Church were in its rites and offices. The Western concept of religion was essentially sacramental. What revolted the reformers was the mechanical, even superstitious, view of the sacraments and offices of the Church that the Church itself was purveying through indulgences and relics. When justification by faith alone became central to religion, formal rites and sacraments were diminished in number and made symbolic acts through which faith was nurtured, rather than real acts through which faith and grace were actually received. For the more extreme dissenting wing of Protestantism, conformity to rites could not be *the* test of faith nor *the* practice of religion. Yet orthodoxy in religious rites had been the equivalent of obedience not just to the Church, but also to the social order which was another expression of Church teaching. When faith became the motive force of religion, disobedience to the imposition of formal rites became a feature of social life. New thinking on the question of obedience and social order was inevitable.

Calvin had many contradictory things to say about social order. He clarified the notion of two kingdoms, the heavenly and political. From the Reformation the notion of spiritual and temporal, sacred and secular, as basic dichotomies attained heightened significance in Western thought. What makes it such a paradox is that Calvin worked out the most rigorous Protestant notion of an integrated social and religious order, which retained the right of the consistory, the religious/secular embodiment of the Church, to excommunicate. If there were two kingdoms, then the Christian conscience and its obligations were still the realm from which social order was to derive its inspiration and guidelines of proper action. Yet he also developed the notion of freedom of conscience, which included the idea of the diversity of religious belief and practice in the name of freedom of religious conviction, since religion that is not voluntarily embraced is no religion at all. Calvin could acknowledge areas where freedom could be exercised, areas of legitimate diversity, but he also insisted there was a limit: anyone who advocated a 'papal mass' ought not to be tolerated. In discussing the freedom of conscience he introduced a phrase that became pregnant in the European imagination: 'consciences observe [God's] law, not as if constrained by the necessity of the law, but that freed from the law's yoke they willingly obey

God's will'. Eventually such an idea must affect the notion of civil society. For Calvin there was still the direct connection that civic fair dealing and order depend upon a uniform and enforced orthodoxy.

Those who lived with the experience of the paradox came to see it differently. The muddle of the English Reformation, perhaps, made England the country where people had to wrestle most earnestly with resolving the paradox. The doctrine of the English Reformation was the least 'reformed', and yet, the clear association of conformity to doctrine as the basis of the State was at its most obvious. The pressures for proper doctrinal reform remained and religious thought was influenced by all European currents. The enforcement of censorship through printing monopolies, accompanied by book-burning and harrassment of those who differed from religious orthodoxy, were the State's means of maintaining an uneasy compromise, the quintessential broad Church. The compromise broke down in the English Revolution which battled over both political and religious liberties. This was the era when the presses were suddenly freed and a massive diversity of opinion was presented to the public. The most strident upholders of the idea of freedom of the individual conscience most strongly championed the freedom of the presses. Milton's fervent and ringing *Areopagitica* is the benchmark for all later generations: 'Who ever knew truth put to the wrose, in free and open encounter?' Cromwell insisted on free conscience being the guiding spirit of the New Model Army, that men should know what they fight for and love what they know. Britain took more than a century formally to catch up with the logic of the ideas its Revolution had unleashed, and has not fully done so yet, since it retains a national, established Church with a guaranteed and superior constitutional place in the civil order.

Political debate in the Revolutionary era put a new emphasis on the natural rights of all who inhabited the temporal realm as the underpinning of all civil society. The natural and ancient were in reality radically new ideas validated by the appeal to a tradition that had never existed and was fabricated for a specific political purpose. Obedience to the civil order could be ensured by giving people the interest of their 'natural rights', which would include the freedom of conscience. It is natural, since so many of the heirs of English revolutionary thought made their way to North America, that the first and most enduring secular state should be the United States of America. The drafters of the U.S. Constitution gave a clear exposition of the argument for a secular state, directly derived from religious thought and the experience of religious history. As James Madison wrote: 'Torrents of blood have been spilt in the old world by vain attempts of the secular arm, to extinguish Religious discord, by proscribing all difference in Religious opinion.' In the same vein,

Thomas Jefferson wrote: 'Is [religious] uniformity attainable? Millions of innocent men, women and children, since the introduction of Christianity, have been burnt, tortured, fined, imprisoned; yet we have not advanced one inch toward uniformity. What has been the effect of coercion? To make one-half of the world fools, and the other half hypocrites.' He set out the logic of the situation that echoes the whole spirit of the U.S. Constitution:

> [Well aware] that our civil rights have no dependence upon our religious opinions, more than our opinions in physics or geometry; that, therefore, the proscribing of any citizen as unworthy [of] the public confidence by laying upon him an incapacity of being called to the offices of trust and emolument, unless he profess or renounce this or that religious opinion, is depriving him injuriously of those privileges and advantages to which in common with his fellow citizens he has a natural right; . . . that it is time enough for the rightful purposes of civil government, for its offices to interfere when principles break out into overt acts against peace and good order. (In Koch and Peden, p. 276)

It could hardly be lost on those framing the U.S. Constitution that back in England religious toleration after the Revolution of 1688 did not include this civil principle. The Test Acts continued to debar Catholics and nonconformists from civil offices until the nineteenth century.

The legacy of Reformation was diversity, albeit diversity with a common root in Christianity, Christian heritage and the history of reaction. The Reformation provoked a proliferation of doctrines with the resulting fragmentation of consensus, or as John Redwood put it, 'men found all the values accepted by their society to be in doubt, owing to the lack of agreed opinion over the crucial issues of the origin and purpose of the world'. The vehemence with which different opinions were argued had changed little from the days of the early Church and had similar characteristics, as Redwood's study of the pamphleteering of 1660–1750 shows. In an age of diversity with some limited recognition of toleration, the word 'heresy' acquired new analogies: blasphemy and atheism. Like heresy before them, they were associated with moral turpitude and civil disorder in the minds of those who opposed them.

The Age of Reason, which Redwood described as that of the English Enlightenment, was not an era of a free press. Printing was still controlled through the office of the licenser. Granting of licences was, however, somewhat haphazard. It depended on a partial view of which opinions were the more objectionable. A book or pamphlet could get into print and still be condemned and burnt because it offended an authority who took a different view to that of the licenser. The effect of banning a book already had its modern consequence as noted by Samuel Pepys: it increased interest and put up the price. Christopher Hill has argued that censorship was such a pervasive climate in the seventeenth century that all texts should be read between the lines, as well as along them, if their meaning is to be gleaned—just like pre-glasnost East European writing. He further argued that more ideas were bubbling under the stiffling of censorship than modern historians credit.

The presses which had known brief periods of liberty during the Interregnum were subject to new restraint with the Restoration. The response of writers was self-censorship, a common phenomenon, or writing guardedly, delaying publication or not publishing at all. Samuel Pepys even began to keep his diary in code; and he was by no means the only one. The villains of censorship were the State through the monarchy and the Church, though it was not unknown under the rule of Parliamentarians whose official licenser was none other than the author of *Areopagitica*, Milton. The fluctuating fate of the presses was part and parcel of the wrestling with authority, the changing of the nature and forms of civil society, the working-out of Protestant ideas. In Catholic Europe, censorship through the Index of prohibited books was the norm until its formal end with Vatican II. Licensing of books was employed in all Catholic countries, though it never succeeded in suppressing the trade in illicit books. The era of the English Revolution, with its incipient notions of democracy, with its appeal to the common people through publication as an extension of the quintessential nonconformist virtue, preaching, established a groundswell that would eventually mark the temper of secular society, the liberty of the presses. What had been denied would be valued because it had for so long been absent. The liberty of the presses would be cherished because its denial had been used to underpin an elitist society of authority over the common people, or in parlance of the times, the tyrannies of king and bishops. John Redwood reminded us:

> Seventeenth century thought was God ridden. Whenever a man took up his pen and attempted to write about the weather, the seasons, the structure of the earth, the constitution of the heavens, the nature of political society, the organisation of the Church, social morality or ethics he was by definition taking up his pen to write about God. (Redwood, p. 9)

The overthrow of Church authority over doctrine and dogma flung out many formulated certainties that had to be questioned to be answered anew. Remaking knowledge of the world was not a disinterested process, for there still remained a Church, and there were still many who defended and maintained the old certainty: there was still an establishment to be challenged. But now the questions of the origin and purposes of the world could be approached in defiance of old certainties. One way of proving the rightness and legitimacy of the new doctrines was disproving the basis of old certainties, proving that scripture did not contain the structure of ideas the scholars and the Church had built upon them. The conscience, the inner mind freed from the imposition of law, would discover the truth of God's purposes by inquiry. The agent of inquiry would be reason. In the future, what men and women would be asked to believe would have to be reasonable, for already revulsion at superstition was making inroads through knowledge into the supernatural teachings of earlier times.

Domination by Ridicule

Reason could have some unexpected consequences. Paul Hirst has argued convincingly that the upsurge of witch hunting under the Parliamentarians was a product of a new confidence in the procedures of reason to uncover the truth of the existence of witches. The old ideas of 'compel them to come in' had been associated with a whole battery of techniques of force and judicial torture, against which the reasonable mind revolted. Trial by reasonable procedures would be able to establish truth, so in conscience witches could be tried. The belief in demonic powers and forces was too embedded in scripture to be a matter of indifference to men of religious zeal. The decline of witch trials, according to Hirst, was also a product of lack of confidence in the reliability of the procedures of reason: men could not have confidence that justice was being done. It was still not the case that they ceased to believe in witches. What people believed about witches and demonic forces was not the agent of change; what changed was the authority they invested in the concept of reason to arbitrate what could and could not be done in acting upon belief in social life. John Redwood has argued that the age characterized as the age of reason was in many ways no more rational than preceding ages, that the difference was in the frequency of appeals to the word 'reason' and that there were widely differing opinions of the nature of that reason and the implications of its use.

A world that had been compelled to orthodoxy by authority, invested new authority in reason. The Protestant ideology was straightforward: reason would produce a new orthodoxy which was as uniform as the old certainties, but which people would freely adopt because it was seen to be reasonable—the real meaning of the origin and purpose of the world as God's creation. The technique of reason was disproving the basis of old certainties and formulas and uncovering new truths about the processes of nature and the world. But just as new doctrines proliferated and established diversity of opinion, so the fruits of reasoned inquiry, which was itself diverse, produced differences of opinion. What the private conscience believed by faith could no longer be compelled. In the public arena faith generated more and more matters over which people could have doubts, more and more divergent opinions which caused them to doubt. The creation of consensus, therefore, came to rely not on the fruits of reasoned inquiry but on the supremacy of the methods of reason agreed to be the way everyone should proceed. Britain's Royal Society, therefore, prohibited religious disputation from its proceedings; it secularized itself by insisting on the use of reason in observation and disputation about the natural world.

The new orthodoxy based upon reason had a marked distinction from the consensus on how faith should be operated in society. Faith produced differences over which there could be no compulsion, only toleration of diversity. Where reason produced diversity of opinion, and therefore questions of doubt, further applications of reason were necessary to accumulate more facts to settle the matter of doubt. Eventually all things would come to be subjected to the methodology of reason, which would be renamed the scientific method. The rise of scientism had begun. But reasoned thought did not begin in a vacuum. Old ideas and old constraints not only remained but were often the substance of what reason sought to disprove. Old habits of thought were part of the construction of new ways of thinking, for reacting to them could mean reacting against or reacting for the old certainty in a new form. It was a long time before religion would become irrelevant to scientism.

It was not until the nineteenth century that ideas of a materialist universe appeared and scientism attained its modern form. Materialist, humanist scientism was a natural product of a community torn apart by differences of opinion, where reason had been used to rescue inquiry from disputation that could only be settled by matters of faith, where it was no longer possible to compel uniformity or orthodoxy. It is because of the rupture of doctrine that the questions of the origin and purposes of the world had to be answered anew. It was to confound certain doctrines inherited by the Church that the methods of reason were applied. The basic intention was to show as absurd the doctrinal formulations held by other people. Science came to be seen as the opponent of religion in the narrow sense, for science was putting forward an alternate way of thinking about the universe. Science had to contend with the authority structures of religion, with clergy who saw new ideas as an assault upon faith and, particularly, upon doctrinal orthodoxy.

A world that had been used to certainty, to orthodoxy as the norm because orthodoxy was insisted upon, imposed and compelled, must have found the proliferation of opinion a traumatic experience. Religious conscience now made doubt legitimate, but could not deliver the compelling orthodoxy Western man had come to expect from religion by the new means of free conscience and reason. Once it became valid to doubt, for the ordinary literate citizen there was a sense of absurdity at the vigour used by opposing parties to denounce each other. The pamphleteers of the Enlightenment specialized in an inflationary language to excoriate opinions with which they disagreed. Their targets were routinely accused of blasphemy and atheism, with the familiar connotation of being libertines bent upon social chaos. Every point of view took itself seriously because the substance of the issues on which they differed was so important, so central to their own concept of certainty and vision of how the world should be. Among the literate public that watched the furore unfold, another reaction set in, a reaction that would have been impossible without the legitimacy acquired by doubt, a sense of the ridiculous:

> The atheist hunters could rightly point to a far more insidious growth in English and continental thought than the growth in the importance or at any rate the growing use of the words 'reason' and 'nature'. That insidious growth was the incursion made by irony, wit and ridicule. . . . Many of the atheist-hunters were aware of this in their correspondence and many of their pamphlets and works were designed to appeal to an audience which could either convert those who jeopardized Christianity in this way, or could appeal directly to those who attempted to pervert life by seeking cheap enjoyment at the expense of truth and belief in God's universe. It was the age of ridicule which did far more harm to Christian defences than did the onslaught of reason and nature. (Redwood, p. 14)

The age of ridicule had large areas of doubt and dispute, whole tranches of abusive argument to feed upon. It also drew upon a tradition, for Erasmus's most potent weapon in marshalling the cry for reform of the Church had been to satirize its abuses. But before things can become targets of ridicule, they must be perceived to be open to question. The techniques of hunting error and sensing the presence of error are what makes the satire bite, the jest strike its mark. Where one man saw mystery in faith and argued that denial of that mystery would lead the whole of society to chaos, another argued in devout conscience that there was no mystery but God-created regularity amenable to reasonable understanding. Where one man said there could be neither faith nor salvation without miracles, another contended that God could not be properly worshipped unless the reliance on miraculous intervention of Providence were replaced with the understanding of a rational universe where God's purpose could be implemented without waiting for miraculous intervention.

Between all the difficulties of these arguments, there grew perhaps not indifference but the attitude of a plague on both your houses. There were those who preferred to enjoy the world and the ever-rising material standards of life and to indulge a sense of fun and ridicule at the expense of such arcane and, to the majority, obscure disputation. Indifference could be seen as a positive part of the new balance needed by civil society. Ridicule, disparaging all faithful fervour, could be seen as a healthier attitude, for there could be no assurance that acrimonious words would not give way to the old pattern of violent deeds of suppression by some contending party. Toleration was a positive value that rescued civil society from real warfare. Wit, irony and ridicule defused the real warfare of words to ensure they did not escalate into physical warfare.

There is one thing about the age of ridicule one cannot overlook. It was an age intimately concerned with the issues of liberty and freedom because individual liberties and freedoms were so constrained and brittle, such a long way from being secured. Toleration had been sought against clear evidence of the meaning of intolerance, whose instruments were fire and the sword, imprisonment and torture, censorship and exile. Ridicule, just like every other diversity of opinion had to be tolerated if the march back to intolerance and its well-remembered consequences of bloody turmoil were to be averted. All liberties and freedoms had to be ardently defended, since so few reasonable and essential ones had been allowed and those that had been acquired, however precarious, had been secured at great cost.

In the era of 'Wilkes and Liberty', the presses used ridicule and abuse through a host of literary devices to contend with or defend authority. The most pointed barbs might be wrapped in the stylistic device of parody, with supplements printed to give the key to the identity of the real characters. The non-European could also serve the cause of satire: numerous attacks on the political order exposed venality at home by transporting the entire cast of characters to the Persian court, where their corruption would more obviously impress the reader. Distancing the author of serious purpose from direct reference to their real and serious subject matter through such literary devices was a necessary protection from harrassment, which is also why fiction developed as such a crucial genre. Writers were regularly subjected to charges of seditious libel, which carried fines and imprisonment, and regularly suffered such penalties. As an insulating technique from the ire of authority, it is a well-worn assumption that those who object to the freedom of expression are always those with superior power, whereas the writer is the agent who inches forward the cause of liberty for the common good.

Wherever one looks in Western scholarship after the Reformation, from physics and geometry to philosophy and anthropology, the context of thought was the same: to understand the origin and purposes of the world, to provide solutions to the political and social conundrums of European civilization and to attain freedom from old orthodoxies and resolve the diversity of new doctrines into proper liberties and freedoms for the individual. Western scholarship is about the existential problem of Western man, because ideas of freedom had arisen that were denied by the systems of government within which Western man lived. The orthodoxy and authority of government and the social order it demanded still called upon religious ideas as validation, as well as continued to use sacramental rites to symbolize that authority and dominance. Opposition to the established order also called upon religious ideas to validate radical reforms or revolutions. More and more of the contending arguments concerned understanding the processes and history of the present world in secular terms, so that the ambit of orthodox religion could be curtailed and the authority of doctrinal pronouncement and its derived system of law could cease to impose limitations on the kinds of reforms people thought necessary.

A mass society had been growing in Europe from the time of the Reformation, emerging by increments from mob society through ideas about the importance of the individual conscience and, therefore, individual liberties. The Industrial Revolution made this mass society a reality. Owen Chadwick has argued that one of the features of mass society is that it is a slogan society. Surveying the secularization of the European mind in the nineteenth century, Chadwick averred that secularism, the materialist, humanist, atheist view of mankind, touched the mass of the people far less than the secularists believed. What did come to dominate were slogans that informed the mass of people that certain essential propositions about the materialist universe had been established by scientific inquiry. Surely Chadwick was right in arguing that Darwin or Marx did not by force of their ideas secularize the West, for very few people would have read their works and even fewer understood them. But in the nineteenth century, newspapers could widely circulate slogans portraying in a nutshell what Darwin or Marx were supposed to argue and thus a climate of ideas became established. The ideas of both Darwin and Marx were popularized by propagandists, who had to disseminate slogans to be effective in their cause. In other words, secularism relies upon ignorance and not substance.

The context in which secularism arose *is* the history of Europe and the West. Modern secularism is an inheritor of many traits that are a function of its ancestry. Its passionate fervour on the subject of liberty and freedom are most certainly inculcated by its own historical existential problems of struggling against the lack of liberty and freedom. And these are not long-lost hard-learned lessons. We can today listen to the witness of survivors of the modern relapses into the mass psychosis of Naziism and Stalinism, with their attendant employment of those age-old techniques of book-burning, thought police and destruction of their own defined groups of 'heretics'. Losing the liberty to doubt, being compelled to right thought, is a horror from the past often projected as the possibility of the future, even if we have safely passed the baleful 1984.

Few would deny that secularism is a product of history. But there is one feature of that history, which secularism is decidedly reluctant to acknowledge. The scientific notions of historical progression it has inherited from nineteenth-century evolutionary thought are a universalizing of its own very particular existential experience; they are presumed to be not just universal but the only universals. This notion of historical progression subsumes within itself all other histories, cultures and civilizations; it, therefore, assumes it has the monopoly of knowledge that explains all other histories, cultures and civilizations to their bemused inhabitants. Today, secularism is evolutionary in the sense that it has colonized the future of non-Western cultures by its notions of development and progress. Secularism remains the product of Europe; its concepts of liberty and freedom will have to become the basis of the future of other cultures and civilizations, because they are the universal standard by which liberty and freedom are to be assessed and comprehended. Triumphalist secularism inherits the arrogance of its lineal ancestor as being the only defining society, bearing the only possible definitions of modernity and the future that awaits all other people.

Gathering together the strands that have made the modern secular West is not discontinuity but a marked continuity of historical memory, the continuing relevance and pervasiveness of the techniques that fashioned that history. Today secularism is as proselytizing a creed as any of the orthodoxies it has replaced. Secularism, too, is operating to establish a compulsory orthodoxy, to compel all others to come in. So successful has it become that it has even internalized itself within the religious vision of some Christian thinkers. As Don Cupitt, Dean of Emmanuel College, Cambridge, has recently noted 'today, left-wing postmodernists like me are turning religion into something like art: believers must continuously reinvent their own faith . . . the vulnerability of rational belief to refutation by argument is its strength' (*Weekend Guardian*, 16 December 1989).

The dominance of secularism must be seen in the disparity of attention given to religiously held views and the disparagement that is the obligatory filtering device through which they can claim any attention in the mainstream—a complete reversal of the positions of power that generated secularism, and a position that does not accurately or intelligently reflect the argument over *The Satanic Verses*. The creed of secularism is its methodology, the supreme value of perpetual doubt as the only proper underpinning for critical reason. The unique feature of secularism as a certainty in procedure is that it claims the right to define what is appropriate, tenable and sustainable in beliefs it chooses not to hold. It alleges that its methodology can better serve believers than can their own beliefs. The other trait of secularism that confirms historical continuity is its resistance to plurality. Diversity is not plurality since plurality suggests the participation of equally valid and respected systems of thought and belief in the mutual activity of constructing a society.

Standing up to secularism has thus become a matter of cultural identity and survival for non-Western cultures. In the contemporary world, secularism directs its venom, its ridicule and its abuse not towards Christianity which has already succumbed, but towards those cultures that stubbornly refuse to become an appendage to Western civilization. The arch enemy for secularism is the traditional society in general and Islam in particular. Secularism regards Islam and traditional worldviews just as it regarded Christianity: as mediaeval, against science, rationality, progress, and liberty, according to its own definition of science, rationality, progress and liberty. Just as ridiculing and disproving the sacred has been the essential technique by which secularism has realized itself in history, so it has turned with messianic zeal to applying these techniques to those cultures and civilizations that have yet to make the great transformation in emulation of the West. Relativism notwithstanding, there is nowhere for other people to go except where the West is now: that is the sacred creed upheld by the sacramental rites of modern secularism, and that is the message of and the context in which *The Satanic Verses* was written.

It is, however, not always easy to ridicule a worldview grounded in reason and criticism. To make it amenable to ridicule and abuse one must first produce a caricature, a straw man which is then set on fire. In the case of Islam this caricature, based as it is on ignorance, fear and loathing, has been in the making for almost one thousand years. *The Satanic Verses* imbibes and sustains this tradition. Those who burned a copy of the book may have been foolhardy, benign and even 'fundamentalists', but they made their stand on secularism clear: this far and no further, this is where we draw the line, for

Islam is not Christianity, this is where abuse and violence of the history, tradition and the sacred territory of Islam come to an end. What some see as a mediaeval act within a particular historic context, others see as a symbolic act for the will to survive.

Two
The Images of Ignorance

Sex and violence not only sell books, they can also shape the images of other people, other societies and other civilizations. For the past millennium, caricatures of sex and violence have been used to subjugate and humiliate the people of Islam. This image, the image of the Orient where 'unfathomable mysteries dwell and cruel and barbaric scenes are staged', is thriving today as much as it did in the Middle Ages. It represents all that Europe considers to be evil and depraved, licentious and barbaric, ignorant and stupid, unclean and inferior, monstrous and ugly, fanatic and violent. The Western image of Islam, is, in fact, the darker side of Europe.

Racism. Unbelief. Sex. Hate. Domination. Ignorance. Espionage. These are the basic ingredients which have shaped Europe's relationship with Islam and produced the historic image which is the legacy and chief opinion maker of our time. Europe has always felt disturbed and threatened by Islam; the image-mongering has emerged out of this fear and morbid fascination with the Orient. It was born in ignorance, forged by military and political domination and nourished by racial superiority, religious bigotry and blind faith in the dogmatic assumption that the Occidental civilization is the norm for all human cultures.

From its inception, Islam presented the Christian world with a 'problem'. What was the purpose of the new revelation to an Arabian Prophet over six hundred years after the crucifixion and resurrection of God's own son? Islam contained within itself a recognition of Christianity and its legitimacy: it described itself as the summation of the messages brought by Abraham, Moses, Jesus and all the other prophets; it accepted the virgin birth of Jesus and gave him a prestigious position among all the prophets; it accepted the Bible as one of the books of God (although contaminated by human tamperings). Islam had no 'problem' with Christianity and from its inception kept churches open and provided all the necessary guarantees for the survival of Christianity and its institutions in Muslim lands. But Christianity could not return this ecumenical courtesy; it could only denounce Islam, its Prophet and its followers. When, within one hundred years of Islam's inception,

Europe found it at its borders, Islam became a political problem. In addition, the scholarly achievements of the Muslim civilization made Islam an intellectual problem as well.

The foundation of this image was laid almost one hundred years after the birth of Islam. John of Damascus (d.748), a Christian scholar who was a great friend of the Ummayyad Caliph Yazid, declared Islam to be a pagan cult, the Ka'aba in Makkah an idol, and the Prophet Muhammad an irreligious and licentious man. He claimed that Muhammad cobbled his doctrine from the Old and New Testaments through the instruction of an Arian monk. The writings and accusations of John of Damascus became the classical source of all Christian writings on Islam during the mediaeval period.

The pronouncement of John of Damascus found an echo in Christendom not only because it saw Islam as a distinctively different religion, but also because Muslim society reflected a totally different life style to the one dominant in Europe. As R. W. Southern explained:

> For the greater part of the Middle Ages and most of its area, the West formed a society primarily agrarian, feudal, and monastic, at a time when the strength of Islam lay in its great cities, wealthy courts, and long lines of communication. To Western ideals essentially celibate, sacerdotal, and hierarchical, Islam opposed the outlook of a laity frankly indulgent and sensual, in principle egalitarian, enjoying a remarkable freedom of speculation, with no priests and no monasteries built into the basic structure of society as they were in the West. (Southern, *Western Views*, p. 7)

Faced with a rapidly expanding new religion, which had produced a totally different form of society and appeared to challenge God's promise to the Christian faithful, what could the leaders of Christendom do? They did what they had always done: they turned to the Bible. Paul Alvarus (d.859) found all the answers he needed in the Book of Daniel (Southern's comments are in parentheses):

> The fourth beast shall be the fourth kingdom upon earth, which shall be different from all kingdoms, and shall devour the whole earth, and shall tread it down, and break it in pieces. (In traditional Christian thought this was the Roman Empire, the fourth world power following the Empires of the Assyrians, Persians, and Greeks.)
>
> And the ten horns of the Kingdom are the ten kings that shall arise. (Here were the barbarian invaders who had destroyed the Roman Empire.)
>
> And another shall arise after them and he shall be different from the first; and he shall

subdue the three kings. (Here were the followers of Mahomet with their vast empire triumphing over Greeks, Franks, and Goths.)

And he shall speak great words against the Most High, and shall wear out the saints of the Most High, and think to change times and laws. (Did not Mahomet, the Moslem calendar, and the Koran do these very things?)

And they shall be given into his hand for three and half periods to time. (Here was the crux of the matter. . . . Paul Alvarus interpreted this obscure phrase to mean that Islam would flourish for three and a half periods of seventy years each; that is, 245 years in all. Now since he was writing in 854, and the beginning of the Moslem era was in 622 . . . it is evident that the end of the world was very close. By a curious coincidence . . . the Emir of Cordova Abd ar-Rahman III died in 852 and he was succeeded by Mahomet I, 'the man of damnation of our time'.) (Southern, *Western Views*, pp. 23-4)

Alvarus and his colleagues possessed a brief biography of 'Mahomet', a parody of the life of Jesus, written by Spanish monks, which gave Mahomet's death as the year 666 of the Spanish era. The year 666 is, of course, the number of the Beast of Revelation, the Antichrist. The picture was now complete. Thus was born the image of Muhammad as an Antichrist and of Islam as a sinister conspiracy against Christianity.

As Southern pointed out, this was 'the first and rigidly coherent and comprehensive view of Islam . . . to be developed in the West'. It was a product of total ignorance, but an ignorance of a particular kind:

The men who had developed this view were men writing of what they had deeply experienced, and they related their experience to the one firm foundation available to them—the Bible. They were ignorant of Islam, not because they were far removed from it like the Carolingian scholars, but for the contrary reason that they were in the middle of it. If they saw and understood little of what went around them, and they knew nothing of Islam as a religion, it was they who wished to know nothing. (Southern, *Western Views*, p. 25)

This picture of Islam based on hatred, unbelief and self-imposed ignorance was an insulating device, a way of avoiding unthinkable thoughts that could not be allowed to gain credence. Once created, the image grew more and more entrenched as Islam continued to expand. With the arrival of the Crusades, new imaginative flights of fancy were added to expand the propagandists' image of Islam as a tool to maintain the crusading spirit. The Crusaders brought with them not knowledge but fairy tales designed to focus their hostility towards those who held sway on the ground where Christ had walked. Now Mohamet was a magician who destroyed the Church in Africa and the East. He attracted new converts to his depraved religion by promising them promiscuity. He finally met his end, during one of his fits, with a herd of pigs. At his death a white bull appeared to put the fear of Christ in his followers and carry away Mohamet's laws in his horn. Mohamet's tomb was suspended in mid-air by magnets.

By the middle of the twelfth century this was the distorted image that most people, including the scholars, had of Islam and Prophet Muhammad. The biography of Mohamet by Guibert of Nogen is the earliest in this genre; although Guibert admitted that it was based on imagination, he said 'it is safe to speak evil of one whose malignity exceeds whatever ill can be spoken'. This genre was not limited to biography but extended to other literature and epic poems. It is there in the cycle of popular performance literature known as *chansons de geste* that the Prophet was given the Devil's synonym, Mahound. One of the oldest of the *chansons de geste* is *The Song of Roland*, an epic poem popular throughout the Middle Ages, which described Muslims as pagans who worship a trinity of gods. Underlying the poem is the unspoken assumption that the world of 'Saracens' is a mirror-image of Christendom, structured in exactly the same way but inverted in every moral sense. Thus, a valorous Saracen would have been an ideal chevalier had he been a Christian. When the hero Roland dies he offers his soul freely to the archangels, but when the Saracen Marsilla dies his soul has to be wrestled out of him by 'lively devils'.

The main purpose of such literature was propaganda for the Crusades. The concept of reclaiming the holy places was conceived in determined disinformation by Peter of Cluny. So pervasive was the ignorance of the Crusaders of the Holy Land they set out to reclaim for Christendom that they could not conceive of the existence of Christian communities under Muslim rule. The first slaughters perpetrated by Crusaders in the Holy Land were of their co-religionists, to the total amazement and revulsion of contemporary Muslim writers.

By the twelfth century, the long period of interaction with Muslim civilization in Spain and the Crusader kingdoms had made Europe a substantial borrowing society from its enemy. The concept of the university was appropriated wholesale in form, terminology and course matter from the *madrassas*, which had been in operation for over a century throughout Muslim lands. So avid was the desire for Arabic learning that underpinned the twelfth-century Renaissance, the age of Aquinas, Peter Abelard and Bacon, that the authorities became seriously worried about the impact the imitation of these unacceptable, heretical ideas was having on the fabric of learned Christendom. To counteract the popularity of Arabic poetry, the propagandists produced learned works and popular poetics of a very different nature, works such as Dante's *Divine Comedy*.

Dante (1265–1321), of course, is a pillar of Western literature. 'Maometto' turns up in canto 28 of his *Inferno*:

> No cask ever gapes by loss of end-board or stave like him I saw who was ripped from the chin to the part that breaks wind; between the legs hung the entrails; the vitals appeared, with the foul sack that makes excrement of what is swallowed. While I was all absorbed in the sight of him he looked at me with his hands laid open his breast, saying: 'See now how I split myself; see how Mahomet is mangled! Before me goes Ali in tears, his face cleft from chin to forelock; and all the others thou seest here were in life sowers of scandal and schism and therefore are thus cloven . . .'

John D. Sinclair, writing in 1939, explained in a footnote: 'Mahomet was believed to have been a Christian convert, a priest, a cardinal, an aspirant to the Papacy, then a renegade and schismatic. Ali, his son-in-law and fourth successor, was head of the one party in the great Mahometan schism'.

Travel writing further strengthened the conscious and conscientiously sustained image of ignorance and distorted imagination. The Florentine Ricoldo da Montecroce, who went to Baghdad in 1291, was totally blind to Muslim learning and intellectual achievements, which at the time represented the zenith of civilization. His major concern was to attack Islam which he called lax and Muslims whom he described as confused, mendacious, irrational, violent, and obscure. The Irish Franciscan, Simon Semeonis, travelled to Palestine in 1323 with a copy of the Qur'an which he often quoted; but he could not mention the name of Mahomet once without such opprobrious epithets as pig, beast, son of Beliel, sodomite, and so on. Sir John Mandeville, who travelled around Muslim lands in the middle of the fourteenth century, however, was a little more restrained.

> You ought to know that Muhammad was born in Arabia, and at first was a poor fellow, looking after horses and camels and travelling with merchants of Egypt, which at that time was inhabited by Christians. In the desert of Arabia, on the highroad to Egypt, there was a chapel, and a hermit living in it. And Muhammad went into the chapel to speak to the hermit. And when he entered the chapel, the doorway, which was very low, suddenly grew as tall as the gate of a great palace. This as they say, was the first miracle he did, when he was young. After that Muhammad began to be wise, and rich, and a great astronomer. The prince of the land of Corodan (Khorasan) made him ruler and governor of his land; and he governed it wisely and graciously, so that,

when the prince was dead, he married the princess, who was called Cadrige (Khadija). This Muhammad had epilepsy, and often fell through the violence of that illness; and the lady sorrowed much that she had married him. But he made her believe that each time he fell the angel Gabriel appeared and spoke to him, and that he fell down because of the dazzling brightness of the angel. And therefore the Saracens say that the angel Gabriel often spoke to him. (Mandeville, pp. 108–9)

Unfortunately, the use of imagination and abuse in literary and academic form was not solving the 'problem' of Islam; resisting both conversion and conquest, Islam simply refused to go away. Something else was needed, and it arrived in the shape of philosophy.

However it tried to cope with Islam, Christendom could not help being influenced by Islam's intellectual achievements. The influence of such Muslim philosophers as Avicenna (ibn Sina) and Averroes (ibn Rushd), was beginning to be felt. The view common in Islamic philosophy, and articulated strongly by Avicenna, that man can never have a direct audience with God, began to gain a small foothold in the academic quarters of Christendom. This new view, which undermined the Christian ideas that the souls of the blessed enjoy a direct vision of God, called for a retort. One of the major responses came from St Thomas Aquinas in a lengthy discussion written about 1250. But to defend his theological position, Aquinas had to depend on another Muslim philosopher, Averroes. If the error was inspired by Avicenna, the language and methodology of the retort was supplied by Averroes. While Aquinas's followers rejoiced that their hero could subdue (once again, more imagination than reality), they were not willing to concede that a civilization which could produce philosophers of the rank of Averroes and Avicenna, who taught Aquinas all the philosophy he knew, could have a few positive aspects. Once again xenophobia had the better of them and Averroes's name became synonymous with infidelity. But they saw philosophy as a tool that could be used against Islam and Muslims.

Roger Bacon (d.1294) saw it as his task to use Islamic philosophy to launch a mission of preaching against Islam. 'Philosophy is a special province of the unbeliever: we have it all from them,' he declared. But his efforts fell on the ears of a deaf Pope. Later, the cause was taken up by John Wycliffe who, writing in 1378–84, saw Islam not just as theological heresy but as a heresy of morals and practice. This was an enduring undercurrent of Christian reaction to Islam. Mediaeval Christianity was especially world denying, for the fulfilment of Christian vocation was the life of the religious, a celibate life of poverty and renunciation. In contrast, Islam affirmed the world, its emphasis being placed upon God-guided moral regulation of God-given human appetites within the world. The epitome of the Christian vision of the world was the personality of Jesus, the ideal sinless man. By abstracting all the salient attributes of Jesus, Prophet Muhammad, exemplar of the Muslim worldview, could be shown to be the negative of all the cherished Christian conceptions of ideal values. The European Christian idea was the standard against which Islam was evaluated. It was found not merely to be different but lacking the necessary sophistication and values, the negative image of Europe according to the standard technique of mediaeval comparative thought.

Wycliffe's colleague John of Segovia (d.1458) thought that Islam should be tackled at the fundamental level of the Qur'an. The basic question was, is the Qur'an the word of God or not? If by examination of its text it could be shown to contain contradictions, confusions, errors and traces of composite authorship, these should convince anyone that it was not what it claimed to be. The efforts of Bacon, Wycliffe, John of Segovia and others bore fruit at the Council of Vienna in 1312 which, echoing the words that Luther (1483–1546) was to utter some two hundred years later—that Muslims cannot be converted by persuasion or by sword since their hearts were hardened, they despised the Scriptures, they rejected argument, they clung to the tissue of lies of the Qur'an—proposed that an academic onslaught should be launched on the Saracens and that Arabic professorships should be established in Paris, Oxford, Bologna and Salamanca. The decree was repeated in Basel in 1343, but the chairs of Arabic did not come into existence until the middle of the seventeenth and early eighteenth centuries.

In modern times it is conventional to see the mediaeval era as far removed from the world of secular scientific thought. In cultural matters, however, this separation is more apparent than real. Ways of thinking as well as pervasive images that were formulated in the Middle Ages have remained in the Western pysche and have been continuously drawn upon, reformulated and reworked into 'modern' scholarship. In nothing is this so true as in Western approaches to the study of cultural and social diversity, a point made by Margaret Hodgen in her study of the origins of anthropology:

> The Mind's Fidelity to the old has left its mark on anthropology as well as on other fields of thought. Modern cultural investigation has taken up its abode in a mansion of organizing ideas already designed, built and richly furnished with traditional assumptions more closely related to the early levels of Western theology and philosophy than to the data of human history. Nearly all the principles of inquiry employed by recent generations of scholars in Europe and elsewhere are of great age and antiquity. Were their genealogies consulted, it would become quickly apparent that their antecedents are to be found in the Judaeo-Christian scriptures, in the classics or in the derivative Christian literature of the Middle Ages. (Hodgen, p. 478)

The Scholarship of Hate

Towards the end of the sixteenth century as the notion of 'Europe' slowly began to displace 'Christendom', Islam ceased to present a political threat. At the very moment that the Reconquista expelled the last representatives of Muslim civilization from Spain, Columbus sailed for the new world. A new dimension was opened in the European perception of themselves and the world. From then on the Christian message of dominion over the earth came increasingly to be witnessed through the progressive domination over other peoples of the earth. So a new feature was added to the mediaeval Christian image of Islam: domination as a function of power relationships. At the same time, certain features of the ignorant image of the triumphant imagination were brought into much sharper focus. Racism now became overt, deeply rooted as it was in the belief of the superiority of the European race and civilization. Sex became one of the dominant themes and sexual perversity was seen to be intrinsic in the teachings of the Qur'an, the life of the Prophet Muhammad, and Muslim social and cultural institutions. Violence and aggression were seen universally as major constitutive characteristics of Islam. Ignorance was now institutionalized by the use of reason and academic discourse.

The classical European image of Islam was sharpened by a group of scholars who came to be known as 'Orientalists' and their discipline, not unnaturally, was referred to as 'Orientalism'. At the core of Orientalism were a number of articles of faith and certain strong features. Unlike any other discipline—when, for example, one studies botany one shows certain respect for plants; when one studies entomology, one comes to appreciate insects; a zoologist has certain affinity for wild life; an ecologist cannot be expected to detest the environment—Orientalism came to be based on hate. The Orientalists loathed and feared, and to some extent still do, the subject of their study: Islam and Muslims. Apart from the obvious belief that Western civilization was the norm for all cultures, they also believed that Biblical tradition was the norm for all monotheism. Thus, Orientalism sought not to understand Islam but to dominate it, not to seek empathy with it but to ridicule it, abuse it and demonstrate its inferiority, and, once raped, to envelop it within Western civilization and to turn Muslims into nice, docile, subject people, an extension of the West.

The noted Orientalists of the seventeenth century took special delight in abusing Islam and its followers and in maligning its Prophet. From Edward Pocock (1604–91), the first occupant of the Chair of Arabic at Oxford, to Simon Oakley (1678–1720), author of *History of Saracens*, to George Sale who translated the Qur'an, the dominant theme was hatred and abuse. In his *History*, Oakley repeatedly referred to the Prophet Muhammad as 'the great imposter' and to the Muslim expansion as 'that grievous calamity'. Sale followed Maracci's notes and Latin translation of the Qur'an when he declared in his *Preliminary Discourse* 'that Mohammad was really the author and chief contriver of the Qur'an is beyond doubt, though it is highly probable that he had no small assistance in his design from others' and proceeded to distort the translation of the Qur'an in accordance with received ideas.

In Cambridge, the first chair of Arabic was established in 1632. Its occupant, who was also instrumental in establishing it, was William Bedwell. The Head of Houses in Cambridge established the following as the duties of the new professor of Arabic: (1) 'the advancement of good literature by bringing to light much knowledge which is lockt up in that learned tonge'; (2) 'good service of King and State in our commerce'; and (3) 'in God's good time to enlarging the borders of the Church, and propagation of the Christian religion to them who now sitt in darkness' (Quoted by J.D. Latham). Bedwell, who is regarded as the father of Arabic studies in Britain, had a good command of Arabic and a reasonable reservoir of sources on Islam and Muslims. But what are authentic documents worth in the face of intense hatred? As Alastair Hamilton, Bedwell's biographer, noted:

> The gratuitous venom which Bedwell expends on Islam at every opportunity, even in his dictionary, is striking in its intensity. A manifest exhibition of his attitude can be seen in the title *Mohammedis Imposturae* in the first edition, and *Mahomet Unmasked* in the second, with the recurrent subtitle, 'A Discovery of the manifold forgeries, falsehood and horrible impieties of the blasphemous seducer Mohammad: with a demonstration of the insufficiencies of his law, contained in the cursed Alkoran'. (Hamilton, p. 67)

There is always some noble soul who stands against the tide and offers a sane alternative. In 1670, Henry Stubbe (1632–76), published a more objective study of Islam under the revealing title, *An Account of the Rise and Progress of Mahometanism With the Life of Mahomet and Vindication of Him and His Religion from the Calumnies of the Christians*. Stubbs was ridiculed and suppressed. The Dean of Norwich, Humphrey Prideaux (1648–1724), immediately wrote a refutation, *The True Nature of the Imposter Fully Displayed in the Life of Mahomet*, and life returned to normalcy in Christendom.

In the late eighteenth and nineteenth centuries as colonies began to be established and science and learning advanced, a new awareness of the Orient appeared. Orientalism received a boost from imperialism, anthropology, Darwinism, positivism, utopianism, historicism, Freudianism, Marxism and Spenglerism. It became a paradigm, defended by disciplinary boundaries, professional societies, research programmes, university departments. Born out of ignorance and institutionalized in hate and racism, Orientalism became, in the words of Edward Said, 'a political vision of reality whose structure promoted the difference between the familiar (Europe, West, "us") and the strange (the Orient, the East, "them"). All that had gone before was distilled into this discourse which, while purporting to be a neutral comparison of the Occident and Orient, was an expression of power relationships.' Islam is made comprehensible and intelligible by a network of categories, tables and concepts that simultaneously defined and controlled it. To know was to subordinate. As Said argued, the crucial 'fact' about Orientalist discourse was that it was the Occident that knows and talks about the Orient and Islam, while Muslims can neither comprehend themselves nor talk about 'others'.

Armed with the tools of the new disciplines, Orientalist attacks on Islam became more intense, more confidant, more pervasive. They ascribed ridiculously large and important roles to minorities: Christians, Jews, Ismailis, assassins, Hellenists, certain features of Sufi thought (Hallajism is a 'religion of the cross'), anyone or anything which to their mind represented the antithesis of Islam and could undermine its basis. Thus we have the spectacle of Reinhardt Dozy becoming outraged at the incident of Kerbala where the Prophet's grandson, Hussain, and his handful of followers were martyred by the huge and powerful army of Yazid. But it was not in compassion for the slain that Dozy fulminated, it was in passionate support of Yazid's actions (universally denounced by the Muslims). In Dozy's view, Yazid crushed the arrogant, ideological Islam of the Prophet's city: 'the pagan principle reacting against the Muslim principle'.

Equally ridiculous are the antics of H. Lemmens (1862–1939), who set out to remove Islam altogether from the face of the earth. He endlessly lamented the Arab victory in the seventh century which led to the contraction of Eastern Christianity. He abused the Prophet, whom he described as a voluptuous imposter, and his family, particularly Ali whom he singled out as the incarnation of the new Islamic ideal. He picked out for glorification those elements in Islamic history which present an antithesis of true Islam: he praised the Umayyad dynasty for re-establishing the anti-Islamic Quraysh aristocracy and stopping the egalitarian revolution in its tracks. He described the life of the Prophet as a historical novel concocted later on the basis of the Qur'an, for which he also had nothing but contempt. Lemmens took his abuse so far that a fellow Orientalist, Ignac Goldziher, was forced to say, 'what would be left of the Gospels if he applied his own Qur'anic methods to them?'

Driven by their hate, the Orientalists insisted on seeing Islam as the reverse image of the West—the exact technique of the mediaeval scholars. In the case of the Prophet Muhammad, for example, the attributes of Jesus were present in their negative form. As Jesus was sincere, Muhammad must be insincere. Because Jesus was chaste, Muhammad was sensual and polygamist. Because Jesus loved peace and was defeated and crucified, Muhammad was violent and a politician. William Muir's *Mahomet and Islam* illustrates the point:

> When, again, we come to compare Islam with Christianity, and first in its secular aspects, one is immediately struck with the difference between the two in the virtue of adaptation to the wants and aspirations of humanity. Islam imposes a code, hard, fast, and imperative in every detail, which, however well it may have suited Arabia thirteen centuries ago, is quite unfitted for the varying requirements of other times and places. Yet it binds society hand and foot; there can be no onward upward movement, nor even the attempt to rise.
>
> The Christian code is altogether different. It lays down principles, and not details. If there be one exception, that, namely, in respect of marriage and divorce, it is expressly based on the laws of nature. 'He', said Jesus, 'which made them at the beginning, made them male and female; . . . what, therefore, God hath joined together, let not man put asunder.' The foundations of Christian morality are not less immutable than those of the Coran, but they are infinitely broader, and can be suitably built upon for all generations. Its laws are capable of being applied to the habits, thought, and institutions of all ages, and its doctrines harmonise with every upward step towards freedom, knowledge and philanthropy; indeed, we may say, themselves contain the plastic force which brings these results about.
>
> Again, while the Coran represents God as Creator, Ruler, and Preserver, the Rewarder of good and evil, and the Hearer of prayer, it nowhere recognises Him as a Father, much less the Father of our Lord Jesus Christ. The sentiment of the Moslem partakes, therefore, of the fear of a servant more than the love of a son. The Office of the Holy Spirit as Regenerator is unknown, and the death and resurrection of Christ are denied. There is thus in Islam nothing answering to the grace of redemption, and, consequently, the grand power of the gospel, namely the love of Christ as a constraining influence, is wanting; nor is there the approach to anything that might supply its place.
>
> To put the matter shortly, each religion is an embodiment of its Founder. Mahomet sought power; he fought against those who denied his claims; he put a whole tribe to the sword; he filled his harem with women, bond and free; he cast aside, when they had served his purpose, the Jewish and Christian Scriptures, and he engrafted his faith

on the local superstition of his birthplace. He did all these things under cover of an alleged divine authority, but he did no miracle.

The life of Jesus is all in contrast. He spoke and taught as one having the inherent authority in Himself; but He could also say, 'The works that I do in My Father's name, they bear witness of Me'. He was holy, harmless, undefiled. He pleased not Himself. Though rich, he became poor, that we through His poverty might become rich. He made Himself of no reputation, and took upon Him the form of a servant. He was despised and rejected. He humbled Himself, and became obedient to death, even the death of the cross. (Muir, p. 246–50)

The insistence of Orientalism on seeing Islam as the mirror image of the West has now become its hallmark. Jacques Waardenburg demonstrated this feature of Orientalism in *L'Islam dans le miroir de l'Occident*. He examined five important Orientalists of the late-nineteenth and early-twentieth centuries—Ignaz Goldziher, Duncan Black MacDonald, Carl Becker, C. Snouck Hurgronje and Louis Massignon—each of whom nourished a hostile image of Islam and saw it as a reflection of his own chosen weakness. While Goldziher appreciated Islam's tolerance towards other religions, he hated Muhammad's (alleged) anthropomorphisms and the theology and jurisprudence of Islam. MacDonald considered Islam to be an heretical form of Christianity. Becker thought Islamic civilization was a poor and underdeveloped reflection of its Western counterpart. Snouck Hurgronje's focus on Islamic mysticism led him to denounce its crippling limitations. Massignon's strange love affair with Ismaili mysticism and concern for 'cyclic time' led him to denounce Islam for rejecting the idea of incarnation. While these scholars worked in different areas and used different methods, their goals and the concensus at which they arrived was common: they spent their entire lives trying to prove and expose, to use an Edward Said term, the 'latent inferiority' of Islam.

Reasoned Racism

Orientalism is rooted in the work of Christian churchmen who overtly represented the Church and the Western Judaeo-Christian heritage with its claim to possess the only truth backed by a sense of cultural supremacy and real political might. It received support from all quarters of the intellectual arena. The Enlightenment thinkers rebelled against Christian dogma and challenged the domination of the Church. The work of the French *philosophes* replaced Christianity with reason as the sole criterion and claimant of truth. But did reason lead the Enlightenment intellectuals to a more knowledgeable understanding of Islam?

By the time of the Enlightenment, it had already been decided that Europe's destiny lay with colonizing Islam. Despite their stand for freedom and liberty, reason and liberal thought, Enlightenment thinkers worked with the Orientalists to provide a rational justification for this adventure. For many of them—Voltaire (1694–1778), Montesquieu (1689–1755), Volney (1757–1820), Pascal (1623–62)—Europe occupied a special place: it was to be the destiny of humanity (construed as Western man). Their Eurocentrism thus further locked Islam into an exclusive confrontation with the West. All the basic ingredients of the mediaeval image of Islam were now rationalized as is so evident from the section devoted to the Prophet Muhammad in Pascal's *Pensees*. But unlike their predecessors, the Enlightenment philosophers saw Islam as a civilization.

Voltaire, Montesquieu and Volney, according to Hichem Djait, thought that the 'backwardness of Islamic society could be explained by the failure of its government, that is, of its political institutions, as well as by the structure of its religion'. In *Mohammad and Fanaticism*, Voltaire denounced Islam in hostile terms. Later, in the *Essai sur les moeurs*, he was a little more restrained, but the judgement did not change. He still saw Islam as an embodiment of fanaticism, antihumanism, irrationalism and the violent will to power. But despite this, Muslims did have a few positive aspects.

> Islam was seen, by Voltaire, as moving towards greater tolerance and as approximating, thanks to its loose sexual standards, something like a system of natural religion. Jesus was good, but Christians became intolerant, whereas Muslims were tolerant despite their evil Prophet. Positive development in one case, negative in another: this was Voltaire's way of harmonizing his many contradictory ideas on the subject, of reconciling his prejudices with reason. (Djait, p. 22)

Just as Europe was the norm for all civilizations, Christianity was the norm for all religion. Enlightenment thinkers almost always saw Islam as the antithesis of Christianity. Thus, in *Les Ruines*, Volney announced that 'Mohammad succeeded in building a political and theological empire at the expense of those of Moses's and Jesus's vicars'. Or, in the scene where he has an imam speaking about 'the law of Mohammad', 'God has established Mohammad as his minister on earth; he has handed over the world to him to subdue with the sabre those who refuse to believe in his law'. Volney denounced the 'apostle of a merciful God who preaches nothing but murder and carnage', the spirit of intolerance and exclusiveness that 'shocks every notion of justice'. The mediaeval phrases made a comeback in the garb of the Enlightenment: the Prophet as an ambitious man who put religion to work for 'his worldly aims and his plans of dominion', and the Qur'an as 'a tissue of vague, contradictory declamations, of ridiculous, dangerous precepts'. While Christianity might be irrational, it was gentle and compassionate, Volney declared. Islam, he said, had a contempt for science, which of all things this was indeed bizarre since Western science and philosophy owed an immense debt to Muslim civilization. From whom did the enlightenment philosophers learn their science? Who taught them the use of reason? But even this awkward notion could be sanitized by the conveyor belt of history. The Muslims merely preserved translations of ancient Greek works, to which they added nothing themselves. Thus these literary sources were readily available, as Vico argued, to pass the torch of civilization direct from Greece to Western Europe, while Muslim civilization remained unwarmed even by the embers. To amplify the point, Islam is also based on an utterly crude morality which has all the hallmarks of the barbarity of its origins. In *Travels in Egypt and Syria*, Volney summed up his thoughts on Islam:

> So far from helping to remedy the abuses of government, the spirit of Islamism, one might say, is their original source. To be convinced of this, simply examine the book which is the repository of that spirit. . . . Anyone who reads the Koran will be forced to admit that it has no idea either of man's duties in society or of the formation of the body politic or the principles of the art of governance; in brief, it says nothing about what constitute legislative code. The only law it contains can be reduced to four or five ordnances concerning polygamy, divorce, slavery, and the inheritance rights of the close relatives . . . if amidst the babel of this perpetual delirium any grand design or coherent meaning ever breaks through, it speaks with the voice of an obstinate, impassioned fanaticism. The ear rings with words like *the impious ones, infidels, enemies of God and the Prophet, zeal for God and the Prophet.* . . . There you have the spirit of the Koran! . . . [Muhammad] wanted, not to enlighten but to reign. He sought, not disciples but subjects. Of all the men who have dared to give laws to nations none, assuredly, was ever more ignorant than Mohammad. Of all the absurd creations of the human mind none is more wretched than this book. (Quoted by Djait, p. 25)

The Muhammad described by Volney is diametrically opposite to the Prophet of Islam; while the Enlightenment may have been concerned with reason, its champions were not too worried about truth when it came to Islam.

Once again someone tried to break the mould. Alphonse de Lamartine (1790–1869) was not an orthodox Christian but an independent thinker with religious sympathies. He saw what the others could not see: a religion where reason played all too dominant a part. He thought Islam was simpler, more streamlined and more rational. 'It is practical and contemplative theism. The sort of men who believe in it cannot be converted: one moves from a dogmatic system full of miracles towards a simpler kind of dogma, not the other way round' (Djait, p.31). And Lamartine saw the Prophet of Islam as an altogether different figure than hitherto envisaged. His description of Muhammad, being unique in the history of Western thought on Islam, is worth quoting in full:

> Never has a man set for himself, voluntarily or involuntarily, a more sublime aim, since this aim was superhuman: to subvert superstitions which had been interposed between man and his creator, to render God unto man and man unto God; to restore the rational and sacred idea of divinity amidst the chaos of the material and disfigured gods of idolatry, then existing. Never has a man undertaken a work so far beyond human powers with so feeble means, for he (Muhammad) had in the conception as well as in the execution of such a great design no other instrument than himself, and no other aid, except a handful of men living in a corner of the desert. Finally, never has a man accomplished such a huge and lasting revolution in the world, because in less than two centuries after its appearance, Islam, in faith and in arms, reigned over the whole of Arabia, and conquered, in God's name, Persia, Khorasan, Transoxania, Western India, Syria, Egypt, Abyssinia, all the known continent of North Africa, numerous islands of the Mediterranean, Spain and a part of Gaul.
>
> If greatness of purpose, smallness of means, and astounding results are the true criteria of human genius, who could dare to compare any great man in modern history to Muhammad? The most famous men created arms, laws and empires only. They founded, if anything at all, no more than material powers which often crumbled away before their eyes. This man moved not only armies, legislations, empires, people and dynasties, but millions of men in one-third of the inhabited world; and more than that, he moved the altars, the gods, the religions, the ideas, the beliefs and the souls. On the basis of a Book, every letter of which has become law, he created a spiritual nationality which blended together peoples of every tongue and of every race. He left us the indelible characteristics of this Muslim nationality the hatred of false gods and the passion for the One and Immaterial God. This avenging patriotism against the profanation of Heaven formed the virtue of the followers of Muhammad; the conquest of one-third of the earth to his dogma was his miracle; or rather it was not the miracle of a man but that of reason. The idea of Unity of God, proclaimed amidst the exhaustion of fabulous theogonies, was in itself such a miracle that upon its utterance from his lips it destroyed all the ancient temples of idols and set on fire one-third of the world. His life, his meditations, his heroic revilings against the superstitions of his country, and his boldness in defying the furies of idolatry, his firmness in enduring them for fifteen years at Mecca, his acceptance of the role of public scorn and almost of being a victim of his fellow countrymen: all these and, finally, his flight, his incessant preaching, his wars against odds, his faith in his success and his superhuman security in misfortune, his forbearance in victory, his ambition, which was entirely devoted to

one idea and in no manner striving for an empire; his endless prayers, his mystic conversations with God, his death and his triumph after death: all these attest not to an imposture but to a firm conviction which gave him the power to restore a dogma. This dogma was twofold, the unity of God and the immateriality of God: the former telling what God is, the latter telling what God is not; the one overthrowing false gods with the sword, the other starting an idea with the words.

Philosopher, orator, apostle, legislator, warrior, conqueror of ideas, restorer of rational dogmas, of a cult without images; the founder of twenty terrestrial empires and of one spiritual empire, that is Muhammad. As regards all standards by which human greatness may be measured, we may well ask, is there any man greater than he? (Lamartine, volume II, pp. 276-7)

Even though Lamartine saw through the veil of ignorance, he was still a child of the West, and could not totally break away from the current of the time. He still saw Islam as a fanatical and fatalistic creed, Muslims as somewhat inferior beings, and in the end, his racism got the better of him. He advocated the colonization of the Muslim world, to save it from its impending doom, and suggested how it could be done!

Scheherazade's Alter Egos

Universally, Muslims—in their manifestations as Saracens, Orientals, Arabs, Moors, Ottomans, Indians, Bedouins—were described as primitive, gullible, habitual liars, lazy, lacking initiative, fanatic, violent, suspicious, stupid, unclean, notoriously cowardly, insolent, treacherous, sexually perverted and prone to conscious and unconscious indecent exposure in public. Whether the literary work was a product of 'the giants of those days', or their less accomplished contemporaries, a narrative of the journey 'beyond forbidden frontiers' or or account of a period of stay in 'the Orient', the descriptions of Muslims were always the same. In this respect they were all works of fiction:

In the depth of this oriental stage stands a prodigious cultural repertoire whose individual items evoke a fabulously rich world: the Sphinx, Cleopatra, Eden, Troy, Sodom and Gomorrah, Astarte, Isis and Osiris, Sheba, Babylon, and Genii, the Magi, Nineveh, Prester John, Mohamet, and dozens more; settings, in some cases names only, half-imagined, half-known; monsters, devils, heroes; terrors, pleasures, desires. The European imagination was nourished extensively from this repertoire: between the Middle Ages and the Eighteenth century such major authors as Ariosto, Milton, Marlowe, Tesso, Shakespeare, Cervantes, and the authors of *Chanson of Roland* and the *Poema del Cid* drew on the Orient's riches for their productions, in ways that sharpened the outlines of the imagery, ideas, and figures populating it. (Said, *Orientalism*, p. 63)

At the end of the seventeenth century, Henry Maundrell, in his *Journey from Aleppo to Jerusalem* could only describe the Turks as 'rogues and robbers' who would always cheat at the slightest opportunity. Their basic character traits were 'lust, arrogance, covetousness and the most exquisite hypocrisy'. W.M. Thackeray considered Orientals to be fools and comic figures in his *Notes on a Journey from Cornhill to Grand Cairo*; and Palgrave declared that 'lying to the Oriental is meat, drink and the roof that shelters him' (Burton, *Personal Narrative*, volume 2, p. 211). But by this time these products of the 'distorted imagination' were looking a little stale.

The old image needed a new dimension, some new colours, a few fresh elements of exotica. The arrival of an Arabian princess in the early eighteenth century did just that. Scheherazade took Europe by storm. *The Thousand and One Nights* (*Alf Laila wa Laila*), or 'Arabian Nights' as it was most commonly called, was first translated by Antoine Galland (1646–1715) and appeared in the West in 1704. In their native land, these stories had been circulating, both in their collected and oral forms, for centuries. They were part of a folklore, kept alive by storytellers who improvised as they went along, and used them to entertain large crowds, ordinary folk bored by the tedium of daily chores. Not surprisingly, the stories were diverse, varied from version to version, and evolved to pander to the baser instincts of a largely male audience. They had virtually no literary value. The celebrated bibliophile, al-Nadim, who flourished in the tenth century, described the early editions of *The Thousand and One Nights* in his *al-Fahrist* with these words, 'I have seen it in the complete form a number of times and it is truly a coarse book, with no worth in the telling' (al-Nadim, p. 714). In Europe, however, it acquired not only the status of literature, but also an image of reality.

> These stories met the eighteenth century's hankering after the primitive. The allure of *Les Mille et une nuits* led many Europeans to confuse the real East with the East of the stories. Lady Mary Montagu, for instance, believed the tales to be accurate descriptions of the Oriental society of which she found herself on the periphery in her capacity as British ambassador's wife. She wrote with endearing naivete that these 'very tales were writ by an author of this country and (excepting the enchantments) are a real representation of the manners here'. (Kabbani, *Europe's Myths*, p. 29)

Because the stories describe real physical objects, it produced in the 'European reader's already susceptible imagination a strange "sense of reality in the midst of unreality" '.

The Arabian Nights phenomenon had a tremendous impact on European fiction, poetry and travel narratives. The Orient of the stories was adopted as a framework for romanticism and a metaphor for stating the moral beliefs of Muslim societies and people. Often European writers projected their own repressed sexuality onto their image of the Orient. For example, William Beckford's Oriental tale, *Vathek*, 'a precursor of the kind of Oriental narrative that the nineteenth-century Decadents would produce', had a sinister, over-indulgent, wealthy young Caliph as its hero who allowed nothing to stand between him and his sexual appetites. But the story of the young Caliph is the story of Beckford himself, complete with Beckford's adulterous relationship with Louisa, wife of his cousin, portrayed in the novel by the relationship between Vathek and Nouronihar.

The received ideas about Islam and its Prophet now acquired the Oriental setting of the Arabian nights. All the traditional hostility to Islam, including the description of Prophet Muhammad as an imposter and magician, can be seen, for example, in Thomas Moore's novel, *Lalla Rookh*, published in 1813. Moore made no attempt to differentiate between legend and history, having a Persian fire-worshipper denounce Mohammad as

> A wretch who shrines his lust in heav'n
> And makes a pander of his God.
> (Kabbani, *Europe's Myths*, p. 34)

No one has done more to harden the image of Arabian Nights as the reality of the Orient than Richard Burton (1821–90). Like so many European travellers and adventurers, he sought gratification for his repressed sexuality in the Muslim world while maintaining close links with the British government for espionage purposes. He projected every imaginable kind of sexual perversion onto the Orient. Burton presented Eastern women as sexual objects who were capable of infinite varieties of copulation and deserved equally infinite contempt.

> A peculiarity highly prized by Egyptians; the use of the constrictor vagina muscles, the sphincter for which Abyssinian women are famous. The 'Kabbazah' (holder), as she is called, can sit astraddle upon a man and can provoke the venereal orgasm, not by wriggling and moving but by tightening and loosing the male member with the muscles of her privities, milking it as it were.
> (Kabbani, *Europe's Myths*, p. 59)

Thus, what you could not get in the Victorian home, Burton announced to his contemporaries, you can find in the illicit space that is the Orient. What is not permissible in England is permissible in Egypt where women are used to being treated as chattel. Given such flights of sexual fantasy, it is not surprising that the Victorian traveler and expert on Oriental sex, often described Oriental women as beasts. And like beasts they behaved irrationally, instinctively and freely sought gratification of their sexual desires with anyone, anywhere. Burton had a great reputation but he earned his richest financial rewards late in life with his translation, and especially the footnotes to the *Kama Sutra* and *The Perfumed Garden*. Once he had identified what his public wanted, he gave them the full battery of a scholarship little related to the texts he presented.

Many of Burton's fellow Europeans took his advice to their bosoms, donned their racist safari suits, firmly tied the laces of their imperial shoes, copies of the latest editions of Burton's translations in hand opened to appropriate pages, and went looking for sexual excitement in the East. After all, out there, it was all happening openly in the streets and markets! Here is Flaubert's description of what they got up to in Cairo:

> To amuse the crowd, Mohammad Ali's jester took a woman in a Cairo bazaar one day, set her on the counter of a shop, and coupled with her publicly while the shopkeeper calmly smoked his pipe.
>
> On the road from Cairo to Shubra some time ago a young fellow had himself publicly buggered by a large monkey—as in the story above, to create a good opinion of himself and make people laugh.
>
> A marabout died a while ago—an idiot—who had long passed as a saint marked by God; all the Moslem women came to see him and masturbated him—in the end he died of exhaustion—from morning to night it was a perpetual jacking-off. . . .
>
> *Quid dicis* of the following fact: some time ago a *santon* (ascetic priest) used to walk through the streets of Cairo completely naked except for a cap on his head and another on his prick. To piss he would doff the prick-cap, and sterile women who wanted children would run up, put themselves under the parabola of his urine and rub themselves with it. (Said, *Orientalism*, p. 103)

But the men did not have this arena all to themselves. Women, too, were out there looking for action. In *The Wilder Shores of Love*, Lesley Blanch described four of them: Lady Burton, wife of Sir Richard, Aimee Dubucq, Jane Digby, and the most notorious, Isabelle Eberhardt. Eberhardt (1877–1904), whose diary has been recently published, comes closest to the spirit of Burton with whom she shared a number of character traits: repressed sexuality, insatiable appetite, a keen interest in the permutations and the perception of the Orient as the only place where true sexual liberation can take place. She was an illegitimate daughter of an illegitimate mother, a victim of advances from her mother's Greek Orthodox priest lover, a product of an incestuous relationship with her brother, and a child of a family where suicide was a regular occurrence. She moved with her mother to Bone in Algeria where she is said to have joined a mystical order and converted to Islam. After the death of her mother, she joined the French Intelligence Service in Algeria and, dressed as a man and calling herself Si Mahmound, embarked on her famous career as a desert wanderer and writer. According to Blanch, Eberhardt 'found peace in Islam's faith—and flesh'. But the Algerians saw her as a spy and tried to assassinate her. In reality her sexual appetite could not be satisfied. Unattractive, thin, hairy, and with rotting teeth, she would shout in her nasal voice, 'I want a *tirailleur*, I must have a *tirailleur*', and would grab the first Arab (and only Arabs, no Frenchmen) she could lay her hands on. Savaged by venereal disease, malnutrition, *kif* and alcohol, Eberhardt had spiritual illusions in which she saw herself as a Muslim holy woman. Blanch presented Eberhardt's squalid life as true-blue romanticism, writing that she had 'become completely accepted by the Arabs' and that apart from her weakness for alcohol she had 'profound acceptance of the Moslem faith'. Rana Kabbani, however, put her antics into their true perspective:

> The voyage East for Isabelle was primarily a gateway to sex, as it had been and would be for countless other Europeans. It provided a way of attaining experiences more varied than she could have expected in suburban Geneva. It satisfied her craving for adventure, her delight in disguise, as well as her sexual curiosity. Like the majority of Europeans who made this voyage of self-discovery, she carried with her a great deal of mental baggage, especially the stereotypical notion of the East as a coffer of erotic delights and unlimited freedoms. (Eberhardt, p. vi)

While Burton, Flaubert, Eberhardt and such other writers as Andre Gide, Edward Lane, Charles Doughty and T.E. Lawrence sought the release of their heterosexuality or suppressed homosexuality in the erotic delights of the Orient, they never missed an opportunity to express their sense of religious superiority. It was their old morality, based as it was on the Judaeo-Christian heritage, which brought in the dazzling achievements of civilization and the consequent colonization of the Orient.

In these sordid proceedings, one literary critic, Thomas Carlyle (1795–1881), tried to inject a voice of moderation. He argued that the Orient, as with European society itself, could be better understood in terms of efforts of men of vision and genius. At a lecture on Friday, 8 May 1840, he described a 'Mahomet' totally different from the common European image. He argued that Muhammad was no legend, no shameful sensualist, no magician, but a sincere, heroic prophet, a man of vision and self-conviction, 'a great Man especially, of him I will venture to assert that it is incredible he should have been other than true'. But Carlyle felt that a proviso should be added before he could proceed to describe 'the hero as Prophet':

> We have chosen Mahomet not as the most eminent Prophet; but as the one we are freest to speak of. He is by no means the truest of Prophets; but I do deem him a true one. Further, as there is no danger of our becoming, any of us, Mahometans, I mean to say all the good of him I justly can. It is the way to get to his secrets: let us try to understand what *he* meant with the world; what the world meant and means with him will then be a more answerable question. Our current hypothesis about Mahomet, that he was a scheming imposter, a Falsehood incarnate, that his religion is a mere mass of quackery and fatuity, begins to be now untenable to anyone. (Carlyle, p. 40.)

But, Carlyle warned his audience, 'Mahomet' is one thing; the 'Koran' quite another. 'Nothing but a sense of duty could carry any European through the Koran', for it is 'a wearisome confused jumble, crude, incondite; endless iterations, long-windedness, entanglement; most crude, incondite;—insupportable stupidity, in short!'. Bernard Dold attributed Carlyle's attitude towards the Qur'an to the fact that he studied it through defective translation, which is also why he found Islam's notion of heaven sensual. Carlyle's other heroes in *Heroes and Hero Worship* are Dante and Shakespeare (in 'the hero as poet') and Luther and Knox (in 'the hero as priest'). Dold pointed out that 'when speaking of Muhammad', Carlyle 'spoke well of Islam. When speaking of Dante and Shakespeare, he spoke well of Catholicism. When he spoke of Shakespeare, he spoke ill of Mohammad. Now when he speaks of Luther and Knox, he speaks ill of Catholicism and rather well, once again, of Islam'. Not surprisingly, Carlyle's lecture caused an uproar among the clergy and in other intellectual circles. In the end, Carlyle's intervention, like the efforts of Henry Stubbe some two hundred years before him, turned out to be a minor diversion.

Meanwhile, travel writing continued to reinforce the image of Islam originally conceived by Paul Alvarus, added to by *Chansons de Geste* and Humphrey Prideaux, sharpened by centuries of Orientalism, and served in the mould of Scheherazade. Thus, for Francois de Chateaubriand (1768-1848), fanaticism, barbarism, cruelty, despotism, servility, violence, and unbelief came together in Muslim nations which 'belong essentially to the sword', and have a history that negates civilization itself. 'It would be hard to imagine', wrote Hichem Djait, 'a more Manichaean attitude than Chateaubriand's in the *Itinerary from Paris to Jerusalem* he evoked all the passions of the mediaeval period, reaffirming it as he gloried in the splendours of a brutal and exclusive "we", echoing, continuing, and reappropriating the Middle Ages as the core of a great tradition and a moment of truth in history.'

When they were not decrying the barbarism and fanaticism of the Muslim world or finding avenues for their sexual gratification, European travellers were describing the more stupendous inhabitants of the Orient in a scientific tone. E.W. Lane (1801–76) thus described 1834 *Modern Egypt* as a treasure house of magic and occult, astrology and alchemy, hemp and opium, snake-charmers, jugglers, public dancers, superstitions, supernatural beliefs and bizarre incidents that defied imagination. As befitted these everyday features of Muslim culture, according to Kabbani, he described them in a tone 'deceptively dry in sharp contrast to the kind of material he was describing. This gave his writing a semblance of scholarship and encouraged in his readers a total suspension of disbelief. Beyond fanaticism, sex and the bizarre, there was always the old favourite: straight-to-the-point contempt wrapped in a sense of moral and religious bigotry.' Doughty had total contempt for Islam and the people he mingled with in *Travels in Arabia Deserta*. After declaring that the 'Moslem religion ever makes numbness and death in some part of the human understanding', he ranted about the Prophet of Islam:

> The most venerable image in their minds is the personage of Mohammad . . . (nothing can) amend our opinion of the Arabian man's barbaric ignorance, his sleight and murderous cruelty in the institution of his religious faction; or sweeten our contempt of an hysterical prophetism and polygamous living—Mohammad who persuaded others, lived confident in himself; and died persuaded by the good success of his own doctrine. (Doughty, p. 405.)

In his introduction to the meanderings of Doughty, T.E. Lawrence (1888–1935) wrote that Doughty 'went among these people dispassionately', 'the realism of the book is complete' as 'Doughty tried to tell the full and exact truth of all that he saw'. Lawrence highlighted Doughty's attitude to the Arabs by putting them in more precise terms:

> Semites are black and white and not only in vision, with their inner furnishing; black and white not merely in clarity, but in apposition. Their thoughts live easiest among extremes. They inhabit superlatives by choice. . . . They are limited narrow-minded people whose inert intellects lie incuriously fallow. . . . They show no longing for great industry, no organisation of mind or body anywhere. They invent no system of philosophy or mythologies. . . . (Doughty, volume 2, p. 22)

Lawrence, of course, knew all about truth. He went to the East not to find release for his repressed homosexuality, but to seek the truth. And what truth did he discover? He discovered a legend in his mind and manufactured a mythical hero. He believed about himself what he wrote about Doughty: 'he was very really the hero of his journey, and the Arabs knew how great he was'. What Arabs knew about Lawrence was that all his writings were economical with the truth and written to stir up emotion, that during the war he claimed to champion their cause and following the war he refused to support their demands for the independent Arab kingdom that their British and French allies had promised them in return for their support against the Germans and the Turks, and that he believed in his own sentimental myth. As Rana Kabbani has pointed out:

> The 'Lawrence of Arabia' fabrication kept the man from real scrutiny; it hid his weaknesses, his unreliability, and exaggerated what positive traits he possessed way beyond recognition. Sometimes, the real Lawrence dared to look beyond the real myth he himself had manufactured. (Kabbani, *Europe's Myths*, p. 110)

Prejudices, racism and bigotry found in literature and travel writing received empirical support from the colonial administrators. Evelyn Baring (Lord) Cromer (1841–1917), for example, repeatedly insisted that 'the Egyptian Oriental is one of the most stupid . . . in the World. . . . Stupidity, not cunning is his chief characteristic', that the Egyptian mind 'like that of all oriental races, is naturally inaccurate and incapable of precision of thought and expression', that the Oriental could only show a servile submission to authority, and, most of all, he was quite incapable of ruling himself. He devoted five chapters to delineating such features of Oriental character in *Modern Egypt*. He combined his hatred for the subject people with a sense of racial superiority to produce an image of Muslims which justified all the prejudice and stereotypes one could find in literature:

> Sir Alfred Lyall once said to me: 'Accuracy is abhorrent to the Oriental mind. Every Anglo-Indian should always remember that maxim.' Want of accuracy, which easily degenerates into untruthfulness, is in fact the main characteristic of the Oriental mind.
> The European is a close reasoner; his statement of facts are devoid of any ambiguity; he is a natural logician, albeit he not have studied logic; he is by nature sceptical and requires proof before he can accept the truth of propositions; his trained intelligence works like a piece of mechanism. The mind of the Oriental, on the other hand, like his picturesque streets, is eminently wanting in symmetry. His reasoning is of the most slipshod description. Although the ancient Arabs acquired in a somewhat higher degree the science of dialectics, their descendants are singularly deficient in the logical

faculty. They are often incapable of drawing the most obvious conclusions from any simple premises of which they may admit the truth. (Said, *Orientalism*, p. 38)

The idea that the Orientals were so stupid that they could not govern themselves acquired deep roots during the colonial period. Albert Camus, for example, who identified with the Algerians and, like T.E. Lawrence, had declared himself to be their friend, could not accept the fact that Algerians could govern themselves. Camus expressed his ideas of fair justice for Algeria in these words:

An Algeria constituted of federated settlements and tied to France seems to me preferable, without any possible comparison to simple justice, to an Algeria tied to an empire of Islam which would only bring about an increase of misery and suffering and uproot the French people of Algeria from their native land. (Alloula, p. xii)

An Algeria without France is so far from the imagination of Camus because, for him, despite his declared friendship for them, they are a non-people, a people without a history, and hence without a future. He declared that Algerian cities have no history; and in his fiction treated Algerians themselves as non-people. In *The Stranger* (1939), a young Arab trespassed the world of *colons* to save his sister's honour. He attacked Meursault and Raymond and was killed by Meursault. The Algerian remained unnamed, anonymous. Camus described 'the violent intervention of Meursault and his compatriot Raymond into Algerian society but never recognized, acknowledged, or even named it as a society with its own internal structure, mores, and contradictions'.

Camus's arrogance and deep-seated ignorance was highlighted in 1959 by Ahmad Taleb Ibrahimi, a minister in the Algerian government. Before independence Ibrahimi had admired Camus's writings; but now he wrote in an open letter to Camus:

It is strange to note that you who proclaimed your love for your Arab 'brother' should display such an arrogant contempt for everything Arab, Muslim and Oriental. You, who pretend that Algeria is your 'true country', are totally ignorant of its heritage even to the point of speaking of Algerian cities 'without a past' (from *L'ete*). Even the most superficial knowledge of the history of the Maghrib would have shown you that the Algerian nation is not an epiphenomenon and that its destiny, even if it is Mediterranean, is also African and Arab. (Alloula, p. xiii)

But neither Camus's fiction, nor his hatred is unique. In Andre Gide's *L'Immoraliste*, the hero, Michel, showed the same contempt for Algeria's history and people. He visited Biskra and became friendly with a group of Algerian children. When he returned to the city two years later he discovered that the children did not have time for him, being busy with earning a living. One of them had become a butcher, another was washing dishes in a cafe, another selling bread, still another employed breaking stones on the highway, and one of their brothers had married. 'And was this all that remained?' asked Michel, 'All that life had made of them?'. As Barbara Harlow has written, 'the children's very claim to a historicity of their own is anathema to Gide's aestheticism'.

The description of Muslims in fiction, poetry, travel writing, legends, myths, Orientalism, despatches from colonial administrators, Christian polemics and Enlightenment philosophers all have a predictable similarity; they fuse together to produce a concrete image of inferiority, sexuality and despotism. They are the stuff of Western perceptions of Islam which are then projected onto Muslim society to become the expectations of the Orient that never failed to be fulfilled; they were copied and reproduced again and again, thus giving the image so rooted in ignorance its own internal momentum.

Philosophers of Impotence

By the time the grand historian appeared on the European scene (in Islam he had already existed for eight hundred years), the image of Islam as a fanatical, militant and uncivilized creed had already crystallized. Edward Gibbon (1737-94), for example, simply took his view of Islam from Simon Oakley (1678-1720), the occupant of the fifth chair of Arabic at Oxford. Oakley had shocked European intellectuals by writing in his *History of Saracens* that it was to the Muslims that Europe owed what she knew about philosophy, while also arguing that Islam was a dangerous and militant heresy. But it was Hegel (1770-1831) who first looked at Islam as a civilization.

The central idea in Hegelian thought is development. In history it appears as an evolutionary process moving history through periods and civilizations towards a progressive self-realization of reason. In the Hegelian scheme, history developed through four stages: the Oriental world, the Greek world, the Roman world and, finally, the goal of the evolutionary march of humanity, the German world in which Hegel himself lived. Hegel considered the German world to be the epitome of civilization because it gave full reign to reason by making freedom a cornerstone of the state. In his scheme, Islam was of the Oriental world and its sole purpose was to be a stepping stone to humanity's ultimate realization, the creation of the German world. For him

Islam signified 'the worship of one, the absolute object of attraction and devotion'. But Islam's devotion to One was much too abstract, too excessive; indeed, it excluded an interest in the human world. This is why the Muslim mood swung like a pendulum from fanatic zeal to desperation, from one extreme to another. Because of these extremes, Islamic civilization was self-destructive and on the verge of writing itself off from history. Islam now had nothing to offer except fanaticism, sexual enjoyment and despotism. Europe's destiny lay in swallowing the antithesis of Islam into a new thesis of its own. What is one to make of such attempts to banish Islam from history? Muslim critic, Parvez Manzoor, offered this assessment:

> One wonders how the most subtle European mind of his time could display such provincial arrogance, such spiritual banality and such intellectual shallowness when it came to Islam. He was a moribund child of his age and his image of Islam was forged in the crucible of Western military and political superiority. The Ottoman state was moribund and the rest of the Islamic world lay prostrate at the Europeans' feet. It had no effective voice, no philosophy of history, no awareness of its destiny. It did look as if it was destined to perish forever. Hegel was not perceptive or prophetic enough to scan beyond his cultural horizons. The most cogent argument against his indictment of Islam has been provided by the passing of time. As for his strictures against the abstractness of Islam, anyone who has the slightest acquaintance with Hegelian thought must spontaneously exclaim: 'the kettle calling the pot black!' To a Muslim who has personally experienced the fullness of his devotion and submission to the One, Hegel also appears ridiculously sham and bogus! (Manzoor, 'Eunuchs')

Hegel, thus, clearly spelled out Western anxieties and fears about Islam: 'in the dreamland of European destiny, Islam looms as a nightmare'. Where Hegel led, other philosophers followed. In his monumental work, *Weltgeschichte* (1881–88), L. von Ranke declared Islam to be an antithesis of Christian Europe. Jacob Burckhardt concurred. Ernest Renan declared that 'Muslims were the first victims of Islam'. They must break the hold that Islam has over them, just like Europe had broken the chains of religious tyranny. But Renan was not sure that Muslims, whatever their history, had the capability of measuring up to the norms established by European civilization. The reasons for this lie behind race—the moving spirit behind history. Islam and Christianity were not only two different religions, they were products of two different races: the genius of Christianity was the genius of the Aryan race, and the fanaticism and decadence of Islam rested squarely on the Semitic race. The Oriental mind, Renan declared in a lecture on 'Islam and science', borrowing the idea from Voltaire, is incapable of rational thought and philosophy and was responsible for blocking the development of science and learning in the Muslim world. The little science and philosophy that Muslims had produced was the result of a rebellion against Islam. The view that Muslims had produced no original science, but were only a conveyor belt for transferring Greek learning to Europe, became the orthodoxy until the middle of the twentieth century.

Marx accepted Hegel's idea that history is a process, a man-made process, which could be controlled and modified. For him, history is the arena of human struggle and liberation as well as of promise and salvation. History acquires meaning in the future when salvation comes, not through divine grace, but through collective human action. Thus, Marxism, a Judaeo-Christian heresy, replaced religious eschatology with history. But the liberation and salvation of the Orient required first its destruction. Drawing from Adam Smith and Mills, Marx and Engels made a typological distinction between Western and Oriental history. Their argument was based on the climate and agricultural practices of the Orient. The mode of production in the Orient, they argued, rested on agriculture which in arid zones had to be carried out with huge state-financed and controlled irrigation schemes. It is not surprising, then, that governments in the Orient tended to be too powerful and despotic. Islam provided a typical example. Thus, the liberation of the Orient required destruction of its mode of production:

> Now, sickening as it must be to human feeling to witness those myriads of industrious patriarchal and inoffensive social organizations disorganized and dissolved into their units, thrown into a sea of woes, and their individual members losing at the same time their ancient form of civilization and their hereditary means of subsistence, we must not forget that these idyllic village communities, inoffensive though they may appear, had always been the solid foundation of oriental despotism and that they restrained the human mind in the smallest possible compass, enslaving it beneath the traditional rules, depriving it of all grandeur and historical energies.... (Said, *Orientalism*, p. 153)

Thus England was right to colonize India, where it had a double mission:

> One destructive, the other regenerating—the annihilation of the Asiatic society and the laying of the material foundation of Western society in Asia. (Said, *Orientalism*, p. 154)

As it turned out, both processes were totally destructive. And for Marx the Orient was nothing more than so much human fodder standing between him and the realization of his messianic vision.

Marx's theory of the Oriental mode of production was elaborated by Karl

Wittfogel in his infamous *Oriental Despotism*. The Orient now became a 'hydraulic society' and Islam once again served no other purpose than of 'supplying the Marxist contender with an epithet of abuse!'

As elsewhere, once again we have a voice of sanity, this time supplied by the Konigsberg historian Hans Prutz. In his history of the Crusades, *Kulturgeschichte der Kreuzzuge* (1883), Prutz argued that not only had the West acquired the use of its rational faculties from Islam but also it was through contacts with the Muslim world that Europe learned to liberate itself from the suffocating embrace of the Church. As before, a furore followed and Prutz's voice was drowned in all the noise. A year later, Gustav le Bon in *La Civilization des Arabes* (1884), showed that the European universities had been living off the intellectual efforts of Muslims for over five hundred years.

But both Le Bon and Prutz were overshadowed by Oswald Spengler. In his classic study, *The Decline of the West*, Spengler classified human cultures into three basic types: the classical, the Magian and the Faustian. Here Islam fits into the middle as the best expression of the the Magian type sharing its 'Magian life-feeling' with such other 'religious' cultures of the Orient as Judaism, early Christianity, ancient Chaldean society and Zoroastrianism. Magian cultures, Spengler argued, are intensely dualistic, split between soul and spirit and were fervently messianic. The individuals of the Magian cultures experienced the world as a cavern and projected this experience in their sacred architecture and buildings, such as Christian and pagan basilicas, Hellenic and Jewish temples, structures of Baal worship, Mazdian fire temples and mosques. The best expression of this sacred architecture, derived from the cavernous experience of the world, is the dome; and the first mosque was the Pantheon, as built by the Roman emperor Hadrian! So the only thing that the Muslims could claim to be authentically Islamic dissolved into the dim and distant past of ancient history!

Spengler is totally wrong on almost every count. His data has been shown to be spurious and he has been demolished by a host of scholars. The Muslim scholar, Mohammad Iqbal, known as 'the philosopher of the East', declared in his *Reconstruction of Religious Thought in Islam* that 'his ignorance of Muslim thought on the question of time, as well as the way in which the "I", as a free autonomous centre of experience, has found a place in the religious experience of Islam, is simply appalling'. Despite that, just as most philosophers of history are, one way or another, children of Hegel, the influence of Spengler simply refuses to go away. But it is not just philosophers of history, such as Toynbee, Mumford, Sorokin and Suzuki, who are Spenglerian through and through, but even such politicians as Richard Nixon and policy-makers as

Henry Kissinger have found Spengler rewarding for understanding contemporary realities.

However, it is Arnold Toynbee who imbibed Spengler more than most. In *A Study of History*, Toynbee identified twenty-one civilizations as constituting the totality of human cultures. Borrowing freely from Ibn Khaldun, Toynbee argued that each civilization passes through three phases. The genesis always appears in religion which is soon institutionalized into a 'universal church' and leads to the creation of a 'universal state'. The state collapses when it's centre of culture is attacked by outside barbarians. In the case of Islam, the universal church is the ummah, the global Muslim community, and the universal state is the Abbasid caliphate. The role of the barbarians here is played by Turkish and Mongol hordes of Central Asia, the Berbers of North Africa and the Arab nomads of Arabia. Toynbee also argued that the Muslim civilization consists of two distinctively separate societies: 'the Arabic' and 'the Iranic'. As to the 'fundamental question' of the 'parent society' of which the Abbasid caliphate is the 'final stage', Toynbee identified it as the ancient society of Syria. Once again, the verdict of Parvez Manzoor:

> Islam, seen in this light, is nothing but a response to Hellenism. On the religious plane, the response had to be, the Christian historian laments, a rejection of Christianity because to the Near Eastern mind it represented nothing else but a perversion of the indigenous monotheism by the alien polytheism of Hellenism. Politically, the Abbasid caliphate must, so he reckons, also be construed as the restoration of the last indigenous empire which was devastated by the foreign armies of Alexander, i.e., the Achaemenian. This ridiculous exercise in futility, thus, continues backwards in time until Toynbee is able to locate in the dim and distant horizons of the 'Syriac' society—almost fifteen centuries earlier—'the ultimate source of Muslim empire'. How dogmatic can history get? Here is an historian's counterpart to the 'Jewish origins of Islam': historic scholarship purely as a function of religious faith. Spurious and dogmatic. (Manzoor, 'Eunuchs')

Given Hegel's exercise to banish Islam from the stage of world history, Marx's inane comments on 'Oriental despotism', Spengler's efforts to subsume Islam in Magian cultures, and Toynbee's final assault in an attempt to bury its fifteen hundred years in ancient history, it is not surprising that Parvez Manzoor compared 'these progenitors of modern historical consciousness' to the 'coarse Nietszchian image, to "the eunuchs in the harem of history" whose observations and reflections lack the authentic conviction of penetration!'

But the philosophers of history did succeed in further strengthening the stereotype of Islam as despotic, fanatical, heretical and incapable of self-sustenance. Despite the persistence of this image, indeed its absorption by certain segments of Muslim societies, Islam obstinately refused to go away. It survived the Mongol invasions, internal decadence, collapse of the Caliphate, European imperialism and subsequent colonization, even 'development'. A new strategy was now needed to combat the problem of Islam.

The New Orientalism

When it became clear that Islam could not be ontologically obliterated, the Orientalist efforts shifted to capturing it by describing it, improving it, making it 'modern' by radical surgery. This new Orientalism was the exercise undertaken by such scholars as H.A.R. Gibb in his *Modern Trends in Islam*, W. Cantwell Smith in *Islam in the Modern World*, Kenneth Cragg in *The Call of the Minaret* and *Counsels in Contemporary Islam*, Philip K. Hitti in *Islam and the West* and W. Montgomery Watt in his numerous works. At the same time a new breed of Western scholar appeared who was willing to study Islam on its own terms. It is to scholars such as Reynold Nicholson, Arthur Arberry and Marshall G.S. Hodgson, who devoted their lives to Islamic study, that we owe much contemporary knowledge of ancient Muslim manuscripts and modern holistic interpretations of Islam.

But old habits die hard, if at all. What the Orientalists thought of Islam was equally true of their approach to their subject. In the kinds of questions they asked, Orientalists kept alive the old spirit of Eurocentrism, Christian moral superiority and hostility; the basis remained the same but the manner became mild and polite. The new thesis, in reality merely a reformulation of the old, was that Islam was incompatible with the modern world; and the assertion was justified by attempts to prove what Said has called the 'latent inferiority' of Islam. To give their arguments some validity, the Orientalists often had to present a total inversion of reality. Or perhaps because of the assumptions buried in their methods of identifying and describing, which were laden with all the old Orientalist values, they could only see reality upside down. Thus, talking of the Ikhwan al Muslimun (the Muslim Brotherhood) in Egypt, Smith set out to demonstrate their inherent inferiority and presented not only a totally false picture but also invented a great deal of fiction to buttress his position:

> Unfortunately for some of the members of the *Ikhwan* and even more for many of their sympathizers and fellow-travellers, the reaffirmation of Islam is not a constructive programme based on cogent plans and known objectives or even felt ideals but rather

an outlet of emotion. It is the expression of the hatred, the frustration, vanity and destructive fury of a people who for long have been prey to poverty, impotence and fear. All the discontent of men who find the modern world too much for them can in movements such as *Ikhwan* find action and satisfaction. . . . In this aspect, the new Islamic upsurge is a force not to solve problems but to intoxicate those who can no longer abide the failure to solve them. (Smith, pp. 158–9)

The element of truth in what was presented as an academic analysis is negligible, a distillation of supposed fact that is more akin to slander. *Ikhwan* included among its membership some of the most noted Muslim scholars of our time: Qutb, Abdul Qadir Oudah, Mustafa al-Sabai and Abdul Aziz al-Badri, whose intellectual output makes Smith's own pale by comparison. The rank and file members of Ikhwan were not uneducated fools and troublemakers who had no understanding of the modern world, but scientists, engineers, medical doctors, academics and professionals, who by virtue of their policies and programmes could attract mass support. They did not attack Christians but asked them to join hands in fighting secularism. And, of course, Smith did not have a word to say against the atrocities of Nasser; indeed, he thought them to be essential for the cause of secularism.

To sustain the new Orientalist thesis about Islam in the modern world, Muslim history had to be rewritten. This was a negative variant of Whig history; it was the failure to modernize that was the internal march of historical forces. Philip Hitti's works on these lines have become standard texts. In *Islam and the West*, he presented the Prophet Muhammad as an imposter and the Qur'an as a rather jumbled document based on Christian, Jewish and heathen sources. In the age-old tradition, he stated that Islam made no contribution to mankind with the exception, of course, of the celebrated 'Arabian Nights'. Exotic splendour was not the outcome of creative industry but opulent indulgence, conspicuous consumption by court society spent on concubines, singing girls, a few minor discoveries in science; but on the whole, Islam promoted only ignorance and stifled intellectual activity.

While secularists such as Smith and Hitti were more directly trying to prove that Islam was irrelevant to the modern world and that only secularism could save Muslims from certain oblivion, members of the clergy were aiming at the same goal using that old but now somewhat worn-out stick—Christianity. Kenneth Cragg has devoted his career to arguing that Islam is inferior Christianity, that the only way forward for Muslims is to Christianize Islam, which actually involves secularizing it. Islam is inferior to Christianity, the old priest has argued, because:

1. It lacks the notion of redemption of evil and seeks instead its forcible containment or elimination.
2. By marring the distinction between the sacred and the profane, Islam becomes a political faith. In Christianity, God intervenes positively in the world of human sinfulness. . . . Islam addresses itself to the community and does not address the individual as a proper 'person'.
3. It is the evolving flexibility of commitment that has opened the door to doubt and sin in the West. This is the strength of Christianity. Islam, in contrast, leaves no room for doubters; here God cannot be interrogated and, as such, Islam is totally inappropriate to modernity. If, however, Islam can be Christianized in this respect, the mystery of doubt and sin would bring man much closer to God.
4. The Old Testament prophets by 'confronting to the end the tragedy of human evil' offer a true representation of what prophethood is all about. The Prophet of Islam was not of this temper. The teachings of the Qur'an must therefore be supplemented by the Christian message. (From Jamil Qureshi, in Hussain, pp. 211–13)

Despite what the learned clergyman may declare, and he has repeated these pleas in a number of books, there is absolutely no need to Christianize Islam simply to allow a place for doubt. 'Think', 'ponder', 'reflect' is a message that is repeated again and again in the Qur'an. Thought often leads to doubt; this is why one of the greatest scholars of Islam, al-Ghazzali, had declared that 'he who has not doubted has not believed'. Al-Ghazzali himself had doubted, as his autobiography makes clear. Indeed, most of the great scholars, thinkers and writers of Islam went through a period of doubt; and some never resolved their doubts.

The question of redemption of evil is at the heart of the matter, as it has always been. It is this lack of a central drama of suffering and the expurgation of sin by divine redemptive intervention that has always made Islam appear austere, unforgiving, harsh, lacking in compassion for the human condition, a religion based on fear and not mercy.

The profoundly obvious point is that Islam is not Christianity and to investigate it according to the topography of Christian theology and Christology is bound merely to 'discover' absences. That Islam might be different and yet incorporate many similar notions to cherished Christian values in a different structure of ideas and concepts is a notion that has seldom been entertained and, therefore, never investigated. That the different form and statement of ideas and concepts is no barrier to loving God and believing and relying entirely upon His mercy seems to be beyond the imagination of

Western writers, yet is the truth lived by Muslims for all that. In Christianity, God's mercy and redemptive grace are mediated through the incarnation of Christ; faith and grace are the moving axes of Christian thought. Central to Islam is the pervasiveness of God's mercy and forgiveness, but the access to God and location for the exercise of this mercy is in the person of each and every human individual. Every human being has a direct, immediate relationship to God.

On the surface, Cragg sought to save Islam from the Muslims; but the real goal was to redeem the sins of Christianity and persuade Muslims to accept the Christian idea of God. The believing Christian, having colonized and exploited the Muslim world for over two centuries, having depleted it of all its natural and economic resources, having given a 'deathblow' to its intellectual and educational institutions, having reduced its people to 'poverty, impotence and fear', is now made anew; he, along with his sisters, seeks redemption and invites Muslims to adopt his newly found 'spiritual' secularism! By seeking to explain Islam in Christian terms, the evangelical scholarship of Cragg is not attempting conversion but, as Jamil Qureshi has argued so convincingly, 'subversion'.

The orientalist scholarship of the 1950s and 1960s, as exemplified by W.C. Smith, Philip K. Hitti and Kenneth Cragg, who has continued to write to the present time, has certain redeeming features. One could, as indeed Muslims did, argue with these scholars, point out their underlying assumptions, draw them into dialogue. At the beginning of the 1970s, all this changed as the old strain of Orientalism reappeared, rather like herpes, in a new virulent form.

Return of the Scholarship of Hate

The early 1970s saw a cultural awakening in Muslim societies, at the same time as a drastic rise in the price of oil and the revolution in Iran, which were seen as direct challenges to the West and its domination. Suddenly, Islam had 'returned' in a 'militant' form; it had became 'radical' and 'resurgent', and there was a 'revival' of 'fundamentalism'. The fact that Islam was always there through the entire colonial period and so many 'development decades' was quite irrelevant. The old spectre of the dangerous and unimaginable monolithic energy of Islam acquired a new lease of life as the image of Muslim 'fanaticism' and 'irrationality' awakened in the Western mind. The idea that Muslims were seriously disturbed, and that the roots of this disturbance were buried in their barbarian religion, as the Orientalists of yore had always maintained, returned with a vengeance. The old Orientalism was now crossed with political science and sociology; politeness took a back seat as unashamed frontal attacks were launched on anything remotely conceived as 'Islamic'. Racism, unbelief, sex, hate, domination, ignorance and espionage were once again in the driving seat.

The Orientalist literature of the last two decades is in quantitative terms truly phenomenal. It is not possible or, indeed, all that desirable to take a comprehensive look at this literature. We will, however, examine some typical examples of its more obnoxious representatives in an attempt to give the flavour of its content from the perspective of the right as well as from the left, from scholarship and professional writings, from popular tracts, fiction and travel literature.

One of the best examples of contemporary Islamophobic Orientalism is in *Hagarism: the Making of the Islamic World* by Patricia Crone and Michael Cook. The thesis of *Hagarism*, based on a document called *Doctrina Iacobi* which in 'all probability was written' in the seventh century by Jewish rabbis, is that there is nothing Islamic about Islam; Islam, in fact, is a barbarian conspiracy with Judaic roots. Using *Doctrina Iacobi* as their starting point, Crone and Cook adopted Eurocentrism of the most extreme, purblind kind, which assumes that not a single word written by Muslims can be accepted as evidence. The only way to know anything about Muslims is from those who were not Muslims. This is the purest form of Orientalism: because Prophet Muhammad and his followers migrated from Makkah to Medina, it must be based on the Jewish idea of exodus; because Muslims practise circumcision and sacrifice, the rituals must be borrowed from the Jews; and so forth. The triumphant conclusion of Crone and Cook was that Islam is an amalgam of Jewish texts, theology and ritual tradition. Apart from *Doctrina Iacobi*, what other historical evidence is there for this thesis? The answer: none. Everything is 'probable', there are reasons (always unstated) 'to assume', and 'clues' to any 'reassertions' are almost totally insignificant. The arguments in *Hagarism* might be summarized as follows: as the Jews of the early period shivered in the cold, sneezed and caught flu, and as the early Muslims also shivered in the cold, occasionally sneezed and caught some kind of influenza, Muslims must originally be Jews.

When struck with the depth of the ignorance of Crone and Cook, Leonard Binder found himself totally dumbfounded. There is 'no more outrageously antagonistic critique of Islam than that which calls itself Hagarism':

> The consistent theme of the work is that Islam is deeply flawed both as a religion and a civilization. Virtually no conceivable aspect of Islam is left without direct or indirect critique. Hagarism is described as primitive (p. 12), pagan (p. 13), inconsistent (p. 15),

Distorted Imagination

> parvenu (p. 16) and barbarian (p. 73). The Qur'an is described as 'frequently obscure and inconsequential in both language and content' (p. 18). The significance of Mecca is described as 'secondary' (p. 24). The traditional date of the Prophet's death, as well as the orthodox conception of the role of 'Umar and the historicity of Hasan and Husain are all doubted (pp. 28 *et passim*). Both Judaism and Islam are dominated by rabbinic legalism and the pharisaic spirit, but 'in Judaism the other side of the coin is messianic hope, in Islam it is Sufi resignation' (p. 34). The synthesis of Judaic values and Arab barbarism is described as 'conspiracy' (p. 77), which permitted the 'long term survival' of Hagarene doctrine and the 'consolidation of the conquest society'. (Binder, p. 106)

There is thus nothing in Islam but total barrenness, 'ethical vacuum', intellectual austerity, uniformity, fanaticism and barbarism in all its religious, political and physical dimensions. Why on earth, asked Binder in total astonishment,

> Does anyone believe in Islam? The appeal of Islam seems 'puzzling', write Crone and Cook, in what must be the most astonishing passage in this astonishing book. The answer they give is that, despite its numerous inadequacies, Islam has great appeal in 'the world of men in their families' (p. 147). 'The public order of Islamic society collapsed long ago . . . but the Muslim house contains its *qibla* within itself' (p. 148). Thus do Crone and Cook deny what most others see as the essential and persistent aspect of Islam, and declare its public and political aspects to be mere illusion. Islamic civilization is, then, absolute *differe nce*, a jumble of unrelated atomic particles with no ordered, structured form. (Binder, p. 107)

In *Muhammad*, Michael Cook, co-author of *Hagarism*, set out to recreate the seventeenth-century picture painted by Humphrey Prideaux in *The True Nature of the Imposter Fully Displayed in the Life of Mahmomet*. Despite its title, only thirteen pages were devoted to the life of Prophet Muhammad, the mass made up of the usual mixture of half-truths, distortions, straight fabrication and racism. Most of his material, Cook said, is not to be found in authentic sources: 'the elaborate narrative traditions drawn on here are not to found in the Koran'. So why are they there? Where do they come from? Hagarism? In the end we have a strange genealogical 'sacred history' which, not surprisingly, is 'by Biblical standards rather stereotyped'. After all this Cook concluded:

> Both Judaism and Christianity are religions of profound pathos—Judaism with its dream of ethnic redemption from present wretchedness, Christianity with its individual salvation through the sufferings of a God of love. In each case it is a pathos

which too easily appeals to the emotions of self-pity. Islam, in contrast, is strikingly free of this temptation. The bleakness which we saw in its conception of the relationship between God and man is the authentic, unadulterated bleakness of the universe itself. (Cook, pp. 88–9)

This kind of hatred and Eurocentrism crops up more noticeably in groups with a strong ideological commitment, among Christians of both right and left, Zionists and Marxists. In some cases these groups may express sympathy for the Muslim world, but this sympathy is limited to seeing Islam in the perspective of its own ideological cause. The Marxist, for example, is totally blind to everything in Islam except its purely modern dimensions, and thus ignores its inner cultural life, which is bound up with the past. He or she is committed to revolutionary causes and universality, but in their only valid form—Marxism. We thus have the spectacle of Fred Halliday's *Iran, Dictatorship and Development*, published on the eve of the Iranian revolution, totally oblivious to the revolutionary forces in the country. If only he had a little knowledge of Iranian history and was not blinkered by everything except Marxism, perhaps he would not have overlooked the role of the ulamas (the religious leaders) or marginalized them to total oblivion.

For a treatment of Islam totally blind to everything but its own ideology, we turn to Malise Ruthven's *Islam in the World*, where we find 'believing Muslims' to be inferior beings whose objectivity cannot be trusted. 'Many western scholars accept the Muslim version, though with several modifications'. Ruthven presented something called the 'Mohammadan paradigm'. The Arabs in the time of Muhammad, he said, were very good at poetry. Muhammad himself was a poet who must 'consciously or otherwise, have absorbed some of their techniques and facility of expression'. But he was not only a poet he was also a soothsayer, a *kahin*.

> The *kahins* . . . made repetitious invocations to natural and physical phenomena . . . and were often consulted as oracles in both public and private matters, . . . When prophesying in this manner the *kahins* would . . . give utterance to their visions in breathless, rhythmic cadences known as *saj*, or rhyming prose. . . . It is significant that the first revelation which he (Mohammad) uttered resembled the *saj* of the *kahins* in both form and content. The earliest suras (chapters) of the Qur'an consist, in the main, of shamanistic invocations of natural phenomena . . . lacking in the higher style and more finely wrought language of the poets. (Ruthven, p. 59)

He substantiated his thesis by invoking a Marxist colleague, Maxine Rodinson, to prove that the visions of Muhammad emerged from his unconsciously reflecting the Biblical, Christian and Judaic teachings he must have heard from people in Makkah.

Ruthven then stated that Islam emerged among the Bedouins: 'in pastoral societies prestige and virility are often closely linked, not least because the human community shares many of the features of the animal society by which it lives'. So the Prophet was both 'voluptuous' and war-like. In Medina, his adopted solution was 'a traditional Bedouin one: to prey on the merchant caravans proceeding from Mecca'. To take the animal analogy further, Ruthven said, 'a tribe's women, like its mares, ewes and she-camels, were an essential part of its capital'. By now the unsuspecting reader has the image complete in his or her mind: animals, Bedouins, war, sex, soothsayers, ignorance—it is all there, the mysterious but perverted East of the Arabian Nights.

Islam in the World covered 1,400 years of Islamic history while trying to explain contemporary political events. Ideology always took the upper hand over historical objectivity and facts, and current paranoia about Islam appeared throughout the book disguised as current affairs. The overall goal was to tell the reader that Islam is institutionally and politically stagnant; glorious it may have been in its time, but it is a sure handicap for ours. As such Islam has no future.

The persistence of certain images, words and invective is, of course, not limited to the Marxist left. The ideologues of the right, too, have a claim to this territory. Perhaps the best example is provided by Daniel Pipes, an ex-Harvard advisor to the U.S. State Department (the link between academia and the world of skullduggery, between the School of Oriental and African Studies and MI5/MI6, was always there!). Pipes's political colours and rabid racial superiority were presented in *In the Path of God: Islam and Political Power*. Here we were informed that the mere fact of being a Muslim has profound political consequences: 'Were Iranians Buddhist, a religious leader would not have vanquished the Shah; were Lebanon entirely Christian, the civil war would not have occurred; were Israel Muslim, its neighbours would have accepted its establishment'. It is this kind of banality that has forced one reviewer of Pipes to take his argument to its logical conclusion: 'were Daniel Pipes an ass, he would have grown long ears and would not have written this book; were he a goat, he would have chewed its leaves; and were his father sterile, we wouldn't have heard of him at all!'

The main thesis of *In the Path of God* is that Islamic resurgence is a product of the oil boom, its chief architects being Saudi Arabia and Libya, its main ally the Russians, and its ultimate goal nothing less then the total destruction of the West.

To the extent the Islamic revival is based on the oil boom, it is mirage. . . . The confidence that played so large a role in leading Muslims to experiment with fundamentalism and autonomist solutions will be destroyed. The power of Saudi Arabia and Libya will fade as their disposable funds diminish and the two countries return to their former inconsequential isolation. . . . Iran's moral influence is fated to end as surely as the sheikhdoms' financial power. . . . The Islamic alternative, once so full of promise, will lose its appeal and many Muslims will again regard their religion as an obstacle to progress. . . . In all likelihood, Nasserism will again appeal to Egyptian and Arab youth, Ataturks' legacy will be reinvigorated in Turkey, Pakistan will rediscover its British heritage. . . . The Arabs will find themselves face-to-face with Israel, without external help, and Israel can be expected to emerge from the crucible of the oil boom much strengthened. (Pipes, p. 331–3)

To the extent that it was a conspiracy of Saudi Arabia, Libya, the Russians and the Marxists, Islamic resurgence has already disappeared; the reality of the cultural awakening of Muslims, however, is still there, a constant source of nightmares for political advisers, crusaders for the ideology of Western dominance, Orientalists and professors of political science.

Most of the contemporary grievances of Muslim people are against the nation-states as they were created by the colonial powers and as they are ruled by their surrogates, the brown sahibs. Not surprisingly, one aspect of the cultural revival in Muslim societies is focused on finding an Islamic alternative to the colonial heritage, the 'Islamic state'. And not surprisingly, either, both the notion of the 'Islamic state' and the political process towards its realization became a target of the invective of the new strain of Orientalism.

A good example of professional studies focusing on the notion of the 'Islamic state' and the Muslim political process is provided by research initiated by the Royal Institute of International Affairs (Chatham House, London) on the influence of Islam in 'states with predominantly Muslim populations'. The idea was to examine the role Islam plays as a 'motivator', 'legitimator' or simply a 'justifier' of a particular political policy. The results have been published as *Islam in the Political Process*, edited by James P. Piscatori, and *Islam in Foreign Policy*, edited by Adeed Dawisha. Both studies contain articles by a number of Western experts on major Muslim states: Pakistan, Malaysia, Saudi Arabia, Algeria, Egypt, Turkey, Iran, Senegal, Libya, Nigeria, Morocco and Indonesia. While the individual findings varied from author to author, depending on the particularities of chosen countries, the underlying assumption of all the contributors was the same: Islam is seen in terms of the rulers, the first and second generation of brown sahibs, and not in terms of the ruled; in terms of the confused concessions that the governments of Muslim states have been forced to make to appease the masses, not in terms of what is actually being demanded. Not a single contributor was willing to accept the reality that Muslim people have an authentic vision of their own future which is in sharp contrast to the outlook of the Westernized elite who rule them. The overall recommendation of the two books was thus that Muslim masses should be beaten into shape and 'modernized', and governments must move away from a fundamentalist approach if the Muslim world is to survive the challenge confronting it.

In the xenophobic discourse of Orientalism, the distinction between scholarship and invective is not always easy to make. In the Chatham House studies, the contributors were restrained while they ground their own axes. In P.J. Vatikiotis's *Islam and the State*, scholarship took a back seat while invective had a field day. In a style reminiscent of the Islamophobic Orientalism of the Middle Ages and combining the pathology of the secularist dogma, Vatikiotis attacked the notion of Islam as a political faith which he saw as the greatest threat to modern civilization. He located the fanaticism of Muslim barbarians at the heart of their faith: the Prophet was 'a militant preacher who combined possession of the Word of God with a particularistic ethos' to produce a mechanism for the conquest of the world; 'the Koranic conception of politics ... is confrontationist, or rather Manichean, emphasizing rectitude versus error, and an armed confrontation between them'; and Islam postulates 'that the unbelievers are enemies of God (see Khomeini), who are pitted against the believers, who are friends of God (and the Ayatollah).' However, Vatikiotis undermined his entire argument and revealed his own misrepresentations when a few lines after the above invective he admitted that 'the basic structure of political ideas in the Koran though activist and militant, is somewhat neutral ...'

But the realization that the political ideas in the Qur'an are neutral did not stop Vatikiotis from building his case on the mountain of fabrications he had created. Having projected Islam as a militant and violent worldview, he showed that such an ideology must appropriate the state for its own ends. The reason behind Vatikiotis's paranoia is a simple realization: contemporary Muslims may acquire power without abandoning their faith. As he himself stated, 'in order to work for the power and glory of this earthly city, man in Islam does not have to kill God'. If Muslims were to acquire earthly power and even ruled their nation-states competently and compassionately, justly and humanely, what would happen to the Enlightenment dream of a universal polity of secularism, of the vision of Europe as the centre of the universe?

If invective and fabrication are the basis of much of Western scholarship about Islam (although one must acknowledge there are exceptions), what could one expect of polemics produced for mass consumption? In this arena, anything goes:

> Thus you can readily equate Islam with almost any Muslim: Ayatollah Khomeini is the readiest candidate for this. Then you can go and compare Islam to everything you dislike, regardless of what you say is factually accurate. As an example there is the Manor Books paperback publication of Khomeini's *Islamic Government* under the title *Ayatollah Khomeini's Mein Kampf*. Accompanying this text is an analysis of it by one George Carpozi, Jr. (a senior *New York Post* reporter) who for the reasons of his own claims that Khomeini is an Arab and that Islam began in the fifth century B.C. Carpozi's analysis begins euphoniously as follows: Like Adolph Hitler in another time, Ayatollah Ruhollah Khomeini is a tyrant, a hater, a baiter, a threat to world order and peace. The principal difference between the author of *Mein Kampf* and the compiler of the vapid *Islamic Government* is that one was an atheist while the other pretends to be a man of God. (Said, *Covering Islam*, pp. 39–40)

To prove the point further, we can look at John Laffin's *The Dagger of Islam*. Laffin, who once worked for the Israeli secret service, set out to warn the West of the inherently violent nature of Islam and the Muslim world. The 'demonic' character of Islam, according to Laffin, stems from the stultifying doctrines of the Qur'an itself. There is no such thing as a Muslim intellect, no ability on the part of Muslims to think in abstract terms, no practice of 'contemplation' as in the Christian tradition. Any discernible refinement in Muslim civilization comes not as a result of Islam but from people whom the Muslims have subjugated. The 'brutal' and 'coercive' nature of Islam, Laffin said, also comes from the 'vengeful' and 'violent' behaviour of the Prophet Muhammad himself. Muhammad was an unscrupulous opportunist for whom ends justified the means and whose cardinal crime was that he was political.

The same sentiments are also prevalent in fiction. From John Updike's *The Coup* to Leon Uris's *Hajj* to Phillip Caputo's *Horn of Africa*, the message is loud and clear. Caputo's novel contains all the relevant ingredients in liberal measure.

Horn of Africa is about violence and treachery. Racism is not even skin deep as Caputo's sense of racial superiority and 'civilization' jumps out of every page. We find Cairo to be 'a fly plagued decaying mess' with taxi drivers 'cursing as only Arabs can'. The language of the local has 'that demeaning invective for which Arabic seems to have been invented'. The Palestinians are 'prepared to trample on every law and convention in pursuit of their aim', their creed is 'the romantic worship of violence, violence for its own sake'. The inhabitants of Jubaya have the same light in their eyes as the hero had seen in the eyes of Palestinian guerrillas, 'the gleam of something darker than madness—belief, an absolute belief in the rightness of one's religion or political dogma or personal destiny'. Indeed, the eyes tell everything: 'I knew it from his shining eyes: he was a fanatic'. The whole narrative is divided into two clear-cut divisions: the white characters, on the one hand, are civilized, polite, humane and, even when they are committing acts of mass murder, rational; the Muslims, on the other, are blood thirsty, alien, barbaric and savage. But the characterization and narrative are secondary to the point-of-view of the author: Caputo's 'personal vision' of violence and of 'a certain kind of man' prone to such violence. The passion simmering throughout *Horn of Africa* is hatred.

Ideological tracts do not only come disguised as fiction; often they arrive in the form of travel narrative. Consider, for example, *The Voices of Marrakech* by Elias Canetti, where we see a Morocco reminiscent of Burton's Orient and Flaubert's Egypt: barbaric, backward, violent and incomprehensible. Indeed, it is attractive only because it is totally mysterious and escapes civilized definition. Much of Canetti's narrative—he was really writing fiction, using 'travel' as a label of convenience—concerned the copulation and beating of donkeys, disfigured beggars, maltreatment of camels, the bizarre and horrific; no one in today's Morocco seemed to be normal. Canetti discovered all the miserable animals, destitute natives, and decrepit 'creatures' of Marrakech and piled them one on the other. Inhumanity and barbarism were always on the surface, even when the locals were dealing with their beasts of burden: 'we often see needless thrusts and blows, which disgust the least humane; and the use of the whip, especially when the driver appears in the semi-bestial negro shape, is universally excessive'.

With the 'semi-bestial negro shape' the notions of sex, racism and hatred that shaped the image of Islam in the West, came full circle. The distorted imagination so consciously created by John of Damascus, Dante and *Songs of Roland*, and nurtured by countless writers, travellers and philosophers, still shapes the West's understanding of Islam. These images have been perpetuated for over one thousand years, and are still alive and thriving in modern scholarship and literature. The centuries of hatred and Islamophobia have now become a permanent feature of the Western psyche. It seems that Western writers are quite incapable of seeing Muslims as human beings, as real people with real histories, real grievances, real aspirations. Somehow Western writers cannot describe the Muslim in other than savage or barbaric terms, cannot see her or his world other than as the dark side of Europe. Even when on best behaviour, Western writers cannot talk to Muslims, but can only talk at them or down to them; the 'Islam' they purport to understand is always some empirical reality in some remote village or the fantasy of some deranged individual, but never the normal conscience that shapes the outlook of a billion people. Western writers are so convinced of the superiority of their civilization, so sure of the superiority of their moral and political positions that any non-Western conception of a single humanity has become anathema to them. Can the hatred and xenophobia, Eurocentrism and bigotry, ignorance and paranoia of the old and new writings on Islam and the Muslim world be surpassed? Unfortunately, it can. Only one kind of individual is programmed to achieve this unsurpassable distinction.

Three
Enter, the Brown Sahib

Throughout the Middle Ages and the period of colonization, Europe used Christianity as a stick to beat Islam. Orientalism, literature and philosophy had fossilized the view of Muslims as backward people, whose lack of progress was a function of their adherence to Islam. Colonial policy had confined religious law to the realm of customary personal law: Islam was traditional and therefore anti-modern and anti-progress. After the Second World War when Muslim societies began to gain their independence, a new weapon of mass destruction appeared: modernity and its bed-fellow, secularism. Muslim societies could not move forward without rejecting Islam. Indeed, the very survival of Muslims as human beings was at stake. To survive in a modern world one had to be modern, and anti-modern societies were doomed. The deep anger against Islam for blocking humanity's evolution towards universal Christianity, by the 'false prophecy' of Muhammad, now turned to an active contempt combined with pity. A rationalized Eurocentrism abetted the development strategies designed to Westernize Islam and undermine its cultural and social roots.

The West was confident that in modernity it had a weapon which would conquer Islam by relegating it to the position that Christianity was increasingly occupying in Europe and North America: that of a set of beliefs and rituals limited to personal piety and totally divorced from social, cultural, intellectual and political aspects of the modern world. There were two main reasons for this confidence. The colonial powers had left the Muslim world with a network of economic and intellectual resources designed only to serve the interests of the metropolitan colonial power. Independence did nothing to dent the continuing physical dependence of new nations upon the old colonial powers for basic survival. The economy of new nations could only work within the terms of trade set down by the industrial countries; they lacked the resources to build themselves into sustainable nations without reference to the demands and inbuilt advantages of the industrialized nations the colonies had been created to serve. Even worse, they inherited a network of modern services, such as education and health, that had been designed to serve the needs of the colonial expatriot and the indigenous elite corps of functionaries who serviced their administration. The very boundaries of these new nations were artificial creations, whose rationale was to be found in the history of foreign powers. The scramble between European nations to dominate territory determined where the boundaries were drawn, not the self-sustaining viability of the unit created. And if the boundaries contained dissimilar populations, then that was to the advantage of the colonial power; inherent tensions could be manipulated to facilitate domination, the game of divide and rule could be played out to the advantage of the colonial ruler. Independence meant having to wrestle with resolving all the legitimate grievances that had been suppressed only by the imposition of foreign domination. Human, ethnic, religious, language and economic distortions that would vex the wisdom of Solomon were the inheritance of these new nations. Every group expected independence to bring them the answers to their own special problems. New nations would be advised to leave the past behind them, to become thoroughly Westernized. To achieve this mission of newness, the departing colonial powers had left an important not-so-departing legacy: the brown sahibs.

The Making of an Alienated Elite

The brown sahib is a descendant of the pre-colonial monarchies and feudal landlords and a product of colonial administrations, which set out to produce a 'go-between' between the rulers and the ruled, as Varindra Tarzie Vittachi has pointed out, with 'calculated deliberation':

> When the imperial age began crumbling, the inheritors of the power found themselves at a fork in the road to the future. One road was signposted: 'Their way'. The other: 'Our way'. . . . They did not think that it was a difficult choice to make. Jawaharlal Nehru, Aung Sang, Soloman Bandaraniaka, Lee Kuan Yew, Abdul Rahman and their counterparts in the Dutch and French colonies and, later, in Africa—like Nkrumah, and Kenyatta—were all deeply and broadly colonised in their minds. (Vittachi, p. 17)

This colonization of the mind was achieved by over a century of conscious policy. Macaulay had alluded to it in 1835 in his Minute of [Indian] Education: 'we must at present do our best to form a class who may be intepreters between us and the millions whom we govern; a class of persons, Indian in blood and colour, but English in taste, in opinion, in morals, and in intellect'. The first step towards this goal involved a systematic effort to give, in the words of William Hunter, Director-General of the Statistical Department of India, writing in 1871, 'the educational system of the Musalman' a 'deathblow'. Thus Muslim institutions of learning were systematically uprooted and their products, who were among the leaders of those who challenged British domination, were abused, ridiculed and identified as the prime cause of Muslim backwardness. What the British did in India, Malaysia and parts of the West Indies, the French did in the Maghrib, Francophone Africa and other parts of the West Indies and the Dutch in Indonesia. In all cases the goal was the same: to rearrange, in the words of Vittachi, the 'neural intellectual circuitry' of the co-opted individuals 'in a colonial pattern' and to 'replace a clear white colonialism with a murky brown colonialism'.

The brown sahibs were selected from among those groups who offered the least resistance to the colonial administration. They came from two main classes: the physically and psychologically battered pre-colonial monarchies and ruling elites who had been transformed into feudal landlords during the colonial period, and the middle-class traitors who had been rewarded for their efforts with junior positions in the colonial administration. (After all, would the East India Company have succeeded in taking over the Mughal Empire with such ease had it not had at its disposal a network of informers ever ready to sell their people short for this or that favour?) Apart from an acute sense of inferiority, vis-a-vis indigenous culture, the groups and individuals selected for brown sahibdom shared three other main features: they had the wealth with which to buy education in the mother country, they possessed skills with which to manipulate the masses, and they had a sense of hereditary right in taking over the colonial administration.

The elite co-opted as brown sahibs were subjected to an educational system that differed from that provided in their traditional cultures. Special colonial high schools were set up, often by Christian missionaries, where junior brown sahibs were indoctrinated into the ways of Europe and taught that European civilization was the yardstick by which all cultures are measured. Thus, the journey for child and young man from home to school often became a journey between two worlds. This feeling of being in two worlds was accentuated by sending the young men to the metropolitan universities of Oxford, Cambridge, London, Paris and other European cities as part of the socialization process to fill higher positions in the colonial society. The more wealthy aspirants to brown sahibdom could afford to skip the first stage of indoctrination at colonial schools—they went straight to Eton, Rugby and Harrow where they learned the true art of colonial administration and contempt for other cultures.

Not surprisingly, the brown sahibs identified strongly with the colonial culture. But this belonging to two cultures and to none produced serious psychological problems. The brown sahibs faced perpetual identity crises and were compelled to change identities as often as they changed jackets from their wardrobes, at one time trying to identify with the indigenous culture, at another behaving as Europeans—Indian one minute, white the next. In all cases it was a put-up job: on the one hand, they knew, from their experiences on the playing fields of Eton, Rugby and Oxbridge, that they could never be accepted as *pukkah* sahibs; and on the other, they hated the indigenous culture and their Indian selves. Sometimes this crisis produced strange sexual neuroses. Frantz Fanon, for example, told of a West Indian who on his arrival in France hurried to a brothel to emphasize his supremacy, so that 'when my restless hands rest on this white breast I grasp white civilization and dignity and make them mine' (p. 12).

The perpetual goal of the brown sahibs—to grasp European civilization—meant downgrading local history, literature and culture and identifying strongly with European history and cultural artefacts. They considered every element of indigenous culture to be backward and worthy only of being dumped onto the scrap-heap of history. They took particular pride in their ignorance of their own history and often paraded their ignorance in public. When M.R. Singer studied the brown sahib in the early 1960s, he was surprised to note that for them 'the British parliament is the mother of democracy, and Hobbes, Burke, Locke and Hume were absolutely correct'; it was forgivable for a brown sahib not to know the basic facts about the Mughals, or anything about the great literary works of Urdu and Hindi, or even the basic tenets of Islam, but it was 'downright unthinkable for him not to know who signed the Magna Carta' (Singer, p. 47).

Once a cadre of brown sahibs had emerged, the colonial powers departed in the confident knowledge that the mental inheritance of those who had taken over from them would ensure total loyalty and obedience. And that is exactly what happened: surrogate brown sahibs kept newly emerging Muslim states on their pre-planned courses, right down to the patterns of exploitation. Their preoccupation was with strengthening their hold on the countries they now ruled and their attention was turned inwards, devoted to making brown sahibdom the domestic pattern of nationhood. In Malaya, for example, the British colonialists handed power over to Tunku Abdul Rahman, a prince educated at Cambridge where he spent his time much as did the characters in *Brideshead Revisted*. He was as far removed from the vast majority of Malayans as Kuala Lumpur is from London, where the Tunku was called to the bar. Once in power, the Tunku, as Shaharuddin Maaruf has pointed out, 'merely continued the development philosophy of the former colonial powers and shared its biases and prejudices'. The allegiance to Western prejudices of Tunku and such other brown sahib rulers as Nehru, Sukarno and Bandaraniaka was not always explicit, but was implicit in everything they did—'the model left behind by colonialism was taken for granted as historically given' to be implemented in all its aspects. The brown sahibs even accepted the view of the natives propagated by European colonialists. Thus Tunku believed, contrary to his own experience and local scholarship, the myth of the lazy native, the Malay as good-for-nothing layabout. 'He overlooked the suffering of the masses under the centuries of feudalism and colonial capitalism: ". . . my people are said to be lazy because they don't have to work, and less still struggle in order to live." Whenever confronted by development problems demanding serious attention and reform, Tunku would brush them aside. Poverty, he said, was not an issue because though poor, the masses were happy and contented. Development and wealth, he argued, would change this' (Maaruf, p. 122). Tunku's thought and action echoed what brown sahib rulers all over the newly independent Muslim world believed and practised.

At this stage the brown sahibs themselves did not have literary ambitions. They were content to move into the gymkhanas and other social and sporting clubs—which in the colonial days were the exclusive domain of white men—and appropriate them as the exclusive reserve of the brown sahib. Here they drank whisky and brandy, ate ham and bacon, wore suits and ties, spoke English, denigrated the indecent and decadent habits of the natives, and generally abused and ridiculed non-Western cultures, history and worldviews.

The Brown Sahib Comes of Age

In the first decades of the post-independence world, the brown sahibs were preoccupied with establishing a strong foothold in the countries they had inherited from the colonial powers. Today, the second generation of brown sahibs have become writers and commentators, novelists and international celebrities. Their basic characteristics remain the same, but now they have acquired global pretensions. In the Western perspective hatred is focused on non-Europeans, but in the perspective of the brown sahibs that focus of Eurocentric fear and loathing is incorporated in themselves. Vittachi has written, 'within their own countries and in their own sets and clubby cliques the brown sahibs will indulge themselves in tearing their own kind apart, limb from limb, skin from bone, with finger-licking tooth-sucking glee'. In a world that is shrinking, when Oriental minorities are establishing themselves in Western states, this activity is not limited to the brown sahibs' own countries any more. Brown sahibdom has now attained an international dimension. In the early phases of the post-colonial history,

> The characteristic mode of communication in the world of brown sahib is the anonymous letter . . . and the writer as always has no personal axe to grind, oh no, and is acting entirely pro bono. . . . But most subcontinental anonymous letters seem to have a distinctive characteristic: there is not even a suggestion of a fact or truth in them, unlike in poison-pen correspondence elsewhere in which the poison consists precisely of a small germ of truth. The brown sahib's world is the only place where there is smoke without any fire. The lie is laid on someone not as a distorted or flawed fact but as a spiteful wish, a curse. (Vittachi, p. 139)

Today, the old 'mode of communication' has given way to poisonous novels and travel writing—after all, what need is there in a world rampant with a new strain of Orientalism claiming its victims indiscriminately for the brown sahib to remain anonymous?

The father of all brown sahibs with literary ambitions was Rudyard Kipling. Of English parents, Kipling was born, brought up and spent his early life in India. He was therefore a cultural hybrid, of a superior crop but doomed to live and identify with the inferior Indians. Throughout his life, he struggled with his two halves, between the hero who identified with the values and superiority of Western civilization which had rejected him, and the under-socialized Indian who could not comprehend the diversity of subcontinental life. This is why some authors have spoken of the two voices of Kipling, the saxophone and the oboe:

> The saxophone was, one suspects, Kipling's martial, violent, self-righteous self which rejected pacifism and glorified soldiery, went through spells of depression, was fascinated by the grotesque and the macabre, and lived with an abiding fear of madness and death. The oboe was Kipling's Indianness and his awe for the culture and the mind of India, his bewilderment at India's heterogeneity and complexity, her incoherence and ancient mastery, her resistance to the mechanization of work as well as man, and ultimately her androgyny. The antonyms were masculine hardness and imperial responsibility on the one hand, and feminine softness and cross-cultural empathy, on the other. The saxophone won out, but the oboe continued to play outside Kipling's earshot, trying to keep alive a subjugated strain of his civilization in the perceived weakness of another. (Nandy, *Intimate Enemy*, p. 70)

What was the link between the two Kiplings? 'It was', in the uncompromising words of Nandy, 'blind violence and hunger for revenge'. Like

Kipling, his brown sahib progeny have sensed that the glorification of the values of Western civilization is the ultimate basis of the doctrine of social evolution. In Kipling's days it justified colonialism; in our time it justifies secularism and the ascendancy of Europe into a global and universal civilization. The brown sahib, therefore, is a rabid defender of everything Western; and since he cannot banish his Oriental self within him, like Kipling he turns on himself and his own kind.

V.S. Naipaul is, of course, one of two internationally-known literary brown sahibs roaming the globe, the other being Salman Rushdie. One of the main characteristics of brown sahibs, which Vittachi overlooked, is that each one considers himself to be the only true representative of the ideology of the colonial masters. The violent hatred surging within their captured minds is often directed towards other brown sahibs. Thus, when asked what he thinks about Rushdie, Naipaul replied, 'I don't know his books, but I have been aware of his statements. I found them usually left-wing and trivial and antiquated. I found them about fifty years out of date.' Asked what he thought of the Ayatollah Khomeini's death threat to the author of *The Satanic Verses*, Naipaul answered: 'It's an extreme form of literary criticism', and broke into a laugh (*The Independent*, 17 March 1989; *The Sunday Oberver*, Bombay, 17 March 1989).

But it is not only Rushdie's work that Naipaul (or *Nai* Paul, *nai* meaning new in Urdu, the new Paul bringing white man's contempt and secular message to the East) does not know. A casual glance at *Among the Believers: an Islamic Journey* reveals the abject depths of his ignorance. He began his journey in Iran by admitting that he is totally ignorant both of Iran and Islam. He had always known Muslims, so he said, but he knew nothing of their religion:

> The doctrine, or what I thought was its doctrine, didn't attract me. It didn't seem worth inquiring into; and over the years, in spite of travel, I had added little to the knowledge gathered in my Trinidad childhood. The glories of this religion were in the remote past; it has generated nothing like a Renaissance. Muslim countries, where not colonies, were despotisms; and nearly all, before oil, were poor. (Naipaul, p. 16)

His knowledge of Iran is not much better either:

> I hadn't followed Iranian affairs closely; but it seems to me, going only by the graffiti of Iranians abroad, that religion had come late to Iranian protest. It was only when the revolution had started that I understood that it had a religious leader. (Naipaul p. 14)

This ignorance is all-pervasive, intrinsic and deeply rooted; it cannot be cured by a dose of knowledge. When his Communist guide suggested 'to understand I should go to the holy city of Qom and talk to people on the streets', he declined, not just because of his obvious difficulty with the local language but more because he did not want his prejudices shattered. His ignorance is multi-layered and revealed on almost every occasion. For example, when he heard the name of Avicenna, he exclaimed: 'Avicenna! To me only a name, someone from the Middle ages: it had never occurred to me that he was a Persian'. But had he read Chaucer, he would have known who Avicenna was.

Naipaul was surprised to learn that the Iranians were talking about a constitution: 'They might not have ideas about a constitution—a constitution was, after all, a concept from outside the Muslim world'. But any contemporary text on constitutional history would have told him that the first written constitution in the world is connected with the Medina state of the Prophet Muhammad. A life based on the Qur'an, he wrote, is simple: 'it has rules for everything; and everyone had to learn the rules'. Even the distorted edition of the Qur'an by his own publisher would have shown him that the Qur'an has few rules; indeed, one-third of the Qur'an is devoted to exhorting the believers to think, ponder, reflect. Over dinner at the Holiday Inn, Kuala Lumpur, he was surprised to see a fashion show on a Friday. It is meant, he told his readers, for non-Muslims, or 'Muslims not observing the Sabbath'. Obviously his childhood friends in Trinidad did not tell him that Friday and Sabbath have no connection whatsoever. When he was told that students at the seminaries in Qom study for six years, he was amazed: 'What did they study all that time?'

Naipaul's ignorance, however, is not limited to religion, history or current affairs, but it extends even to methodology. In a market in Karachi he picked up a copy of *Chachanama*, a story book rather like the Arabian Nights, which relates stories of conquest. It is totally composed of fairy tales and is treated as such even by school children in Pakistan. No journalist, no historian, no one with even a modicum of critical training, would use *Chachanama* as an historical source, which would be akin to trying to write the history of the Renaissance by talking to a taxi-driver. But this intrepid brown sahib first told us that

> The *Chachanama* is Arab or Muslim genre writing, a 'pleasant story of conquest', and it was written five hundred years after the conquest of Sind. The author was Persian; his source was an Arabic manuscript preserved by the family of the conqueror, Bin Qasim. (Naipaul. p. 126)

He then related its content as objective history. So we learn the whole history of the subcontinent, arrival of Islam, conquest of Sind by Mohammad bin Qasim, *etc.*, from a book of fairy tales.

When not relying on the *Chachanama*, Naipaul's source of information is his own ignorance and prejudices. Islam is thus a 'religion of fear and reward, oddly compounded with war and worldly grief . . . ' Islam expanded by a simple rule: 'conquest first, Islam later: it was the pattern of Arab expansion'. 'What was required from the conquered people was not conversion to Islam, but tribute and taxes, treasure, slaves, and women'.

Naipaul began his chapters on Pakistan by recalling an article in the *Tehran Times* which talked about 'the history of Pakistan.' The writer, he commented, 'hadn't gone into that history, and he had ignored its nature'. He then revealed his total ignorance of Pakistan's history. He wrote that Mohammad Ali Jinnah, founder of Pakistan, died three months after the creation of Pakistan: in fact, he could have asked any child in any street in any city of Pakistan to be told that Jinnah died in September 1948, thirteen months after independence. He stated that the majority of those who migrated from India to Pakistan settled in Sind: in fact, they settled in the Punjab, where over one-third of Pakistan's population live. He then stated that Zulfiqar Ali Bhutto, who came from Sind, was 'the country's first native leader'. Where did previous presidents and prime ministers of Pakistan—Khwajah Nazimuddin, Mohammad Ayub Khan, Iskander Mirza, Agha Muhammad Yahya Khan, Liadquat Ali Khan, Husain Shahid Suhrawardy, Ghulam Mohammad, Malik Feroz Khan Noon, Chaudry Mohammad Ali, Mohammad Ali Bogra, Ismail Chundrigar—come from? Mars? Indeed, it seems that most of the people Naipaul encountered were of extraterrestrial origin. A certain Mr Mirza, 'described as one of the most distinguished men of Pakistan', is typical. This 'distinguished' man was almost as ignorant as Naipaul himself, tried to monopolize his time and announced, 'I am God-intoxicated' at the slightest opportunity. If Naipaul had met Mr Mirza in a lunatic asylum, one would have believed in his character a little more. Despite the fact that Pakistan was created for Islam, we are told, everyone is running out of the country, 'leaving the land of faith for the land of money'. Are we to believe that migrant labour is unique to Pakistan? How came Naipaul's forefathers to end up in Trinidad? What about the European and American job hunters in the Middle East? What about the United States, a country composed almost entirely of migrant populations? And how were Australia, New Zealand and Canada created? Just as the people he encountered are false, so are his statistics. For example, he stated that the literacy rate of Pakistan is 1 per cent, whereas it is actually over 32 per cent; and it was almost 100 per cent before the British arrived.

When arrogance is combined with ignorance, a lethal amalgam is produced. Naipaul seems to be proud of his ignorance; he reaffirmed it again and again, taking a certain delight in stating his ignorant views. It is worth contrasting his position with that of Nick Danziger, a modern, young explorer of the Orient, who prepared himself for his journey by extensive reading and research. Even though, on one occasion, he was forced to admit:

> I was increasingly aware that I was poorly read, and the sheer weight of my ignorance outweighed whatever chance discoveries of knowledge I might make. My aim was to look at everything with a completely fresh eye, or to try to see it from a different point of view from my own, but I remained in danger of being the victim of my own preconceptions and prejudices. I badly needed academic knowledge to back up or shoot down the conclusions I was reaching by myself. (*Danziger's Travels*. London: Paladin, 1988, p. 34)

No such realization for Naipaul, however. In this world, things exist in two clear-cut categories: secularism is good, but Islam and anything to do with it is bad. He is full of praise for the 'despotism' of Bhutto but bitter about Zia's 'despotism' simply because Zia tried to justify his action in Islamic terms; military dictatorship in Pakistan is bad because Pakistan is an Islamic republic, but the military dictatorship in Indonesia is good because it is a secular republic. Acceptance of Islam as one's faith is giving in to the imperialism of Islam; acceptance of Western values and culture is the triumph of liberalism. Given the division of the world into black and white, it is no wonder Naipaul cannot understand why people educated in the West are 'converted' to Islam. Why are most Muslim activists to be found in the science and engineering faculties of the universities? These are complex questions for Naipaul and he cannot understand them. His first reaction is the well-chosen path of the ignorant: ridicule.

Naipaul's ignorance is not limited to Islam or the history and culture of the countries he chooses to write about: his knowledge of the civilization whose values and cultures he takes as the norm is also limited. He may think that Salman Rushdie's opinions are fifty years out of date, but his own understanding of the West is straight from the nineteenth century. His confidence in science is reminiscent of 1930s and 1940s; he is totally unaware of the debates in sociology and anthropology about cultural relativism, and he seems to read nothing except the trash he picks up here or there (it would have helped if had actually read 'the standard textbook', Philip K. Hitti's *History of the Arabs*, he boasts about). He started his journey with fixed, ignorant notions of Islam and at the end of his travels his preconceptions remained unchanged; the state of his knowledge at the end is the same as in the beginning. His basic sources of information, according to his own admission, were graffiti and travel agents; direct contact with people and cultures added nothing. He walked through Iran, Pakistan, Malaysia and Indonesia blindfolded. He could easily have written the whole book without leaving his house.

Naipaul's hatred of Islam and India (as expressed in his *India: a Wounded Civilization* and other books) is a product of the programming he and others like him endured during their transformation into brown sahibs. The perpetual identity crises and self-hate that brown sahibs go through produce and epidemic of self-blame. And just like herpes, which no matter how hard is scratched irritates more and more, this self-blame takes the brown sahib to his logical conclusion: in a final suicidal attempt to become what he can never become he eradicates the one thing that can save him from the brink of insanity, his original identity. He thus fulfills the ultimate desire of his programmers, the white sahib, by going the distance that even the white sahib would not go. This is why the noted Indian thinker Ashis Nandy in his *Traditions, Tyranny and Utopias* described Naipaul's work as 'inhuman and ethnocidal'.

In his desperate attempt to obliterate his indigenous identity and submerge it into the European self, the brown sahib seeks to present his original culture and civilization as a pre-modern extension of the culture and civilization of the 'mother country'. As the sahib and memsahib have always had problems with the non-European, Western persons do not define themselves in terms of meaning but in terms of the power they exert over other people in particular and the world and nature in general. Western society has always seen the non-Western world as a mirror of itself. The outside world exists to fulfill the Western self. All civilization is Western civilization, all history is Western history. Cultures are packed in an hierarchical order: every culture is walking the incline of history, slightly out of breath, trying to reach up to become like the culture of modernity, the zenith of Western civilization. All societies are marching towards a single utopia, the ultimate Western organizing principle for society: secularism. The brown sahibs make their positions legitimate within the Western culture by the desire and ambition to prove that non-Western cultures are nothing more than an appendage of Western civilization; non-Western history is nothing more than an extension of the history of secularism. They thus internalize the distorted imagination and its images of ignorance as the only possible description of the non-European and, therefore, of themselves.

The literary endeavours of the brown sahib are a product of this grand Western project. His brown colour ensures the eagerness of many Europeans to listen to his authentic voice and thus have their own prejudices confirmed. But by appropriating the history and sacred territory of non-Western cultures and secularizing them, reducing them to an appendage of Western civilization and a mere segment in the history of secularism, the brown sahib makes totally superfluous all non-Western worldviews that give meaning to the life of three-quarters of mankind. Non-Western cultures and histories, indeed the non-Western people themselves, are effectively written out of existence. The triumph of the West and secularism is thus complete.

Four
The Legacy of Muslim History

Whether the standard treatment is meted out in academic and professional works, literature and fiction, or newspapers and television, there can be little doubt that the total picture that emerges from the perpetual onslaught suggests Islam to be a mediaeval monolith—a monolith with fanatical, inarticulate and incoherent followers; prone to degenerate into violence at the slightest excuse; zealously against reason, thought and literature; for book burning; intolerant of free thought and free expression; and ready to suppress critical material even to the extent of assassination.

It will come as a surprise to many that the reality is somewhat different. Islam does not sanction suppression of thought or banish freedom of expression. It is not against reason or criticism. It has not banned poetry, fiction or any other form of literature. It does not approve of violence or promote fanaticism. It does not accept that people should be sentenced without due and appropriate legal procedure. It has not exiled doubt. It does not even believe that its own worldview should be imposed on others. And though it may be difficult to comprehend in the current climate, many of its followers are coherent and articulate, capable of original thought and innovative expression. But more than that. Islam is rooted in argument and reason, thought and discourse, criticism and counter-criticism, diversity and plurality. An objective look at the Qur'an, the life of the Prophet Muhammad and Islamic history will amply demonstrate this point.

The link between the divine and the human in Islam is the Qur'an. Simultaneously, the Qur'an informs and guides, teaches and inspires, persuades and convinces. It is not only revelation: it is also truth, knowledge, wisdom, law, destiny and remembrance. The Qur'an performs these functions on the basis of a discourse, the fundamental unit of which is the question. The Qur'an asks a series of questions, again and again; and the answers to these questions are to be found by the use of reason and thought, physical exertion as well as inner reflection, and, of course, in the Qur'an itself. This is why, above all, the Qur'an is the Noble Reading. It is not surprising, then, that the Qur'an has been appropriated in Muslim history as a sacred text of devotion, prayer and piety; as a guide to thought and reason; as a moral document of universal and eternal import; as a reverential source of mystical speculation; as a dynamic source for a just social order; as an infallible guide to spiritual illumination. By virtue of the Qur'an, Muslims are incorporated as a book-centred community. Islam is the most striking expression of what might be called documentary faith. As Muslims can only have an interpretive relationship with the Qur'an, every generation of Muslims endeavours to derive significance and meaning for their epoch from the Book of Guidance. The response to the Book's meaning creates the *ummah*, the global Muslim community; in their mutuality, the one is definitive and the other derivative.

The definitive is definitive in terms of values and principles, not in their actualization in history. Being divine in origin, form and meaning, the Qur'an is altogether autonomous of the human and is a norm unto itself. It creates and follows its own logic, rationality, rhetoric and exegesis; it engenders and sustains its own worldview, methodology, sciences, disciplines and hermeneutics; it is unique in its language, expression and semantics, being both literal and symbolic. As such, it provides objective criteria by which Muslims try to conduct their lives and shape their communities and by which their conduct and behaviour is measured. The Qur'an gives us certain basic principles, attitudes, values, norms and sign posts—the *hudud*, the outer limits of behaviour. All of these are not subject to any change; but how they are implemented in society can vary from time to time and place to place. For example, the uncompromising stand of the Qur'an on the equality of all human beings, without exception, before God is immutable. How this principle of equality is actualized in society is shown partly in terms of other immutable principles and left partly as a challenge to Muslim societies. A Muslim society is thus judged by how it implements this absolute principle socially, economically and politically. The actualization of this principle, obviously, requires constant physical and intellectual exertion, continuous identification of forces that undermine this principle, and constant reflection, debate and involvement to ensure that the principle of equality is upheld in society. Consider another example: the declaration of the Qur'an that usury is a basic source of exploitation and must be avoided. Once again this principle is immutable. How an economic system without interest is realized is a challenge that Muslims can meet by reflecting logically on the question, by examining how historic Muslim societies actualized the principle, by developing new theories and ideas, by being aware of changes in modes of production and by guarding against new mechanisms of exploitation entering the economic system. Here again, a Muslim society is judged by how close it comes to putting this principle into practice. The Qur'anic principles, therefore, envisage a dynamic society, constantly adjusting and readjusting, adapting to change and changing things.

Islam is neither monolithic nor averse to change. On the contrary, it both expects and invites change, and by its very nature, encourages diversity in intellectual and societal expression. But unlike secularism and modernity, which are forever tearing down and building up with no solid base on which to work, Islam provides the fundamental building blocks for readjusting or reconstructing society to ensure continuity in the midst of change.

The message of the Qur'an, therefore, is not static; it is gradually and continuously unfolding. Muslims do not believe that they have a total understanding of the Qur'an, once and for all. The Qur'an itself declares: 'It is He who has sent down upon thee the Book wherein are the verses clear that are the Essence of the Book, and the others that are metaphorical' (3:7). The point here is not the ambiguity of the divine message, but the limitation and insufficiency of human language and experience. New human experiences and developments in science and thought bring new insights into the message of the Qur'an. And each Muslim generation by its efforts to understand the Qur'an sheds new light on its message.

The Qur'an is not only a book, it is *the* Book, the fulcrum of Muslim society. However, by the very nature of its revelation, the Qur'an is not a 'book' in the ordinary sense of the term. This is not only because its message is eternal, internally consistent and constantly unfolding, but also because it was revealed piecemeal over a period of twenty-three years to the Prophet Muhammad. The Qur'an also represents a commentary on the struggle of the Prophet against the pagan Quraysh, the powerful tribe of Makkah. Thus, an understanding of the Qur'an involves the understanding of the Sira, the life of the Prophet Muhammad. This message of the Qur'an is not limited to a particular time and place, but the Sira provides the best example of the values and principles of the Qur'an in action and guidance on how these can be adopted by individuals and implemented in society.

Furthermore, to understand the Qur'an one should have access to it in its original language; it is not easy to appreciate the message of the Qur'an in translation. Muslims have always held that due to the richness, beauty and subtlety of its Arabic, the Qur'an cannot be translated. This is not to say that translations do not exist; indeed, it has been translated into almost every language. But translations do not convey the original meaning and beauty of the Qur'an. In some cases they can lead to distortions and introduce nuances and emphases which are not in the original Arabic. In other cases, the Qur'an has been deliberately mistranslated and distorted: English translations provide the best example. A translation widely available in the West is that by N.J. Dawood, published by Penguin. By comparing it to that of the noted Muslim scholar Mohammad Asad, it is easy to see the distortions. For instance, consider verses 5:33-4 (Surah Al-Maidah, 'The Repast') which have been used by many gullible Muslims to justify the death sentence on Salman Rushdie. Dawood translated the verses:

> Those who make war against Allah and his Apostle and spread disorders in the land shall be put to death or crucified or have their hands and feet cut off on alternate sides, or be banished from the country. They shall be held to shame in this world and sternly punished in the next; except those that repent before you reduce them. For you must know that Allah is forgiving and merciful.

That 'shall be' make these verses read like a command; and a non-Muslim reading them would conclude that the Qur'an orders believers to crucify and cut hands and feet off those who attack them. But read the translation of Mohammad Asad:

> It is but a just recompense for those who make war on God and His Apostle, and endeavour to spread corruption on earth, that they are being slain in great numbers, or crucified in great numbers, or have, in the result of their perverseness, their hands and feet cut off in great numbers, or are being (entirely) banished from (the face of) the earth: such is their ignominy in this world. But in the life to come (yet more) awesome suffering awaits them—save for such (of them) as repent ere you (O believers) become more powerful than they: for you must know that God is much-forgiving, a dispenser of grace.

The distinction between the two translations lies not only in the 'shall' and 'are' but also in the absence from Dawood of 'in great numbers'. The word used for slain, *yuqattalu*, denotes, according to a fundamental rule of Arabic grammar, 'they are being slain in great numbers'; the notion of great numbers is essential to the form of the term used. Asad told us, because he knew what certain Orientalists had suggested, that these verses are not and cannot be legal injunctions.

> [The verses] must be read in the *present tense* when they reveal themselves to be *a statement of fact*: a declaration of the inescapability of the retribution which 'those who make a war on God' bring upon themselves. Their hostility to ethical imperatives causes them to lose sight of all moral values; and their consequent mutual discord and 'perverseness' gives rise to unending strife among themselves for the sake of worldly gain and power: they kill one another in great numbers, and torture and mutilate one

other in great numbers, with the result that the whole communities are wiped out, as the Qur'an puts it, 'banished from (the face of) the earth'. It is this interpretation alone that takes full account of all the expressions occurring in this verse—the reference to 'great numbers' in connection with deeds of extreme violence, the 'banishment from the earth', and lastly, the fact that these horrors are expressed in the terms used by the Pharoah, the 'enemy of God'. (Asad, *Message*, p. 148)

Moreover, as the verses also serve as a commentary on what was happening in the milieu in which the Prophet Muhammad moved, they describe what the non-Muslims were doing to themselves. It is a far cry from what Muslims 'shall' do, which is what Dawood tries to convey, to what unbelievers 'are' doing to each other! It is hardly surprising then that Muslims regard Dawood's translation, which seeks to recast the entire order of the original, as thoroughly obnoxious, misleading and distorted: in fact, the distorted imagination in translation. The only adequate way to gain access to the meaning of the Qur'an in translation is to scan a number of different translations.

Criticism and Abuse

A civilization which is centred around the Book, which devotes one-third of its contents to asking its readers to think, exercise reason, read, ponder and reflect, is not likely to look down upon books and book persons. The idea of the book, or *kitab*, is fundamental to Islam; it is fundamental not only in the sense that as a religious and metaphysical worldview Islam is based on the Book of God, the Qur'an, but also in the sense that the book is a basic tool of discourse, a vehicle for the dissemination of thought and ideas, a prime instrument of criticism and counter-criticism, and a basic means of intellectual and literary expression. Given this central role of the book in Islam, it is hardly likely that Islam would be against freedom of expression.

Indeed, freedom of expression has a divine sanction in Islam. No one, no man-made law, can take this birthright away from anyone. Moreover, freedom of expression is not only a right in Islam but an obligation. One who tries to deny criticism and counter-criticism is openly at war with Islam. This is why criticism has been institutionalized in the Islamic concept of *muhaasabah*, which embraces both criticism and self-criticism, including intellectual, political and social criticism, correction of errors, being prepared to accept corrections, trial, giving account, and taking disciplinary measures or actions. The Prophet explained the obligation to criticize by asking his followers to imagine a ship at sea which was carrying passengers. Some of them were seated on the deck while others were seated below. One of those below started drilling a hole where he was sitting. So, if the other passengers were to stop him (and this would be a duty on the passengers below and on deck), his life will be saved along with the lives of the other passengers and crew: if they let him carry on, *laissez-faire*, and connive at his individuality, they will all drown.

Like all freedoms, however, Islam couples freedom of expression with social responsibility. In the West, the book has become an icon, its contents are irrelevant: freedom of expression is equated with the book itself. In Islam, the book is symbolic, but its contents are important too. It can be used to offer any criticism, question anything including even the notion of the divine itself, focus discussion on any aspect of the entire spectrum of human experience and ideas. But, because it is held in such high esteem, it cannot be allowed to be used as a vehicle for abuse or the dishonour of individuals in society in the name of criticism. Criticize as much as you wish, tear arguments or ideas limb from limb, but do not attack the honour or the person by abuse, ridicule or mockery. This is the responsibility that Islam places on the freedom of expression of writers. Islamic law protects the individual from such abuse of freedom of expression: if it is proved that someone attacked the honour of another person, then irrespective of whether the victim can prove that he or she is a man or woman of honour, the culprit stands to be punished. This is in sharp contrast to the Western law of defamation, where the person filing suit has first to prove that he is a person of honour; such a law cannot protect those who are weak and have a low social standing. In Islam, the words do not have to harm the victim, nor does the victim have to prove his or her 'honourable' position in society; it is the writer who has to defend the work and prove that defamation has not taken place.

If Islam believes in argument and discourse, it is clear that it does not stifle the freedom to believe. The Qur'an categorically declares that 'there is no compulsion in religion'. One is free to believe what one likes, and Muslims are asked to argue with unbelievers kindly and with wisdom. Furthermore, the Qur'an, contrary to the general impression, sanctions no worldly punishment for the apostate. The punishment for such individuals is in the hereafter. Nor do we see in the life of the Prophet Muhammad death sanctioned as a punishment for apostasy. Indeed, we do not find a single incident where an apostate was killed simply for apostasy, although there are one or two incidents reported in the authentic traditions of apostates being killed who had either murdered Muslims or declared war on the Muslim community. There are two authentic traditions of the Prophet's own treatment of apostates. One reports that 'an Arab of the desert came to the Holy Prophet and accepted Islam at his hand; then fever overtook him while he was still in Medina. So he came to the Holy Prophet and said, Give back my pledge; and the Holy Prophet refused. Then he came again and said, Give me back my pledge; and the Holy Prophet refused. Then he came again and said, Give me back my pledge, and the Holy Prophet refused, then he went away.' The Prophet allowed the man to work out that his fever was not connected with his conversion; and when he insisted on taking his pledge away he allowed him to return unharmed. Another tradition reports that 'there was a Christian who became a Muslim, read the Baqara and al-Imran and used to write the Holy Qur'an for the Prophet. He then went over to Christianity again, and he used to say, Muhammad does not know anything except what I wrote for him'. This was in Medina after the revelations of the second (al-Baqara) and third chapters (al-Imran) of the Qur'an, when a Muslim state was well established. But, yet again, the apostate was allowed to look after his own fate in the hereafter.

A few instances of apostasy in the time of the Prophet Muhammad were connected with hostile intensions or declarations of war on the Muslims. For example, Imam Bukhari, the famous compiler of the authentic collection of hadith, described apostates as fighters or associated their names with the enemies of Islam; often he described an apostate as the one who 'forsakes his religion and separates himself from the community' or alternatively 'who forsakes his community'. This condition of 'forsaking the community' and joining a hostile camp, particularly, at the time war, is considered by Muslim jurists as a capital offence.

Thus, unless an apostate has declared open (physical) war on the Muslim community, there is no basis in Islam that can be used to justify a capital punishment. Moreover, a state cannot unilaterally sentence a man, whatever his crime, to death without benefit of trial. Even worse, to put a bounty on a person's head is a total mockery of the Islamic notion of justice and cannot, by any stretch of imagination, be sanctioned on the basis of the Qur'an or the example of the Prophet Muhammad.

However, despite the injunctions of the Qur'an and the example of the Prophet, certain Muslim jurists have sanctioned capital punishment for apostasy. S.A. Rahman, a former chief justice of Pakistan, has made a detailed study of the basis for the opinions of jurists in his *Punishment of Apostasy in Islam*. Justice Rahman concluded:

> The *fuqaha* (jurists) acknowledge generally that no punishment for apostasy is prescribed in the Qur'an. Their principal reliance for the view that apostasy must be punished with death is on certain *qauli* (verbal) ahadith, but . . . the relevant occasion

or the circumstances to which they might have reference are not fully explained. Some of these sayings have been subjected to qualifications and exceptions by some very acute minds among the jurisconsults, and it is only a justifiable further step that a presumption about their factual basis being *hirab* or *muharibah* (active hostility to the community) should be raised. . . . Historically speaking, the defectors from the faith, in olden times, almost invariably joined the enemy ranks and became violent antagonists of Muslims. That seems to be the genesis of prescription of the capital sentence for apostasy and no necessity was apparently felt of analysing the circumstances of each individual case to discover whether the elements of *hirab* (hostility) coexisted with apostasy or not. In course of time, decisions justifiable on their own facts hardened into a general rule prescribing the extreme penalty for apostasy. (S.A. Rahman, pp. 133–4)

Justice Rahman's conclusion is that it should be the Qur'an and the example of the Prophet Muhammad which provide guidance on this matter rather than the rulings of the jurists of yore, who themselves held differing opinions on the matter. Rahman stated that there is 'no necessity to punish a peaceful defection from the faith', a conclusion with which most thinking Muslims will immediately agree.

Given Islam's attitude to sanctity of human life, capital punishment is not something with which Muslims can play at will. Indeed, even imprisonment without a guilty verdict in an open court of law cannot be allowed under Islam. To arrest someone only on suspicion and throw him into prison without proper court proceedings and without providing him a reasonable opportunity to present his defence is contrary to all the teachings of Islam. Any government guilty of such actions, as the late A.A. Mawdudi categorically declared, should itself be brought in front of a court of law:

The crimes of the state cannot be justified on the authority of the Qur'an or the traditions of the Prophet Muhammad when the state murders its citizens openly and secretly without any hesitation or the slightest of pretext, because they are opposed to its unjust policies and actions or criticize it for its misdeeds, and also provides protection to its hired assassins who have been guilty of the heinous crime of murder of an innocent person resulting in the fact, that neither the police take any action against such criminals nor can any proof or witnesses against these criminals be produced in the courts of law. The very existence of such a government is a crime. (Mawdudi, pp. 25–6)

Mawdudi insisted that according to Islam no one can be imprisoned, let alone suffer a capital punishment, to use the words of Caliph Umar, 'except in pursuance of justice', by which is meant the due process of law.

Even in such cases where treason is proved beyond doubt, no action can be taken without a hearing in an open court of law. In a famous decision before the conquest of Makkah, the Prophet illustrated the correct procedure in such cases. On this occasion, the Prophet was making preparations for the attack on Makkah when one of his companions, Hatib bin Abi Baltaa sent a letter through a woman to the authorities in Makkah informing him about the impending attack. When the Prophet came to know of this, he ordered Ali and Zubair to 'go quickly on the route to Makkah, at such and such place, you will find a woman carrying a letter. Recover the letter from her and bring it to me.' So they went and found the woman exactly where the Prophet had said. This was indeed a clear case of treachery. The Prophet summoned Hatib to the open court of the Mosque in Medina and in the presence of hundreds of people asked him to explain his position. The accused said: 'O God's Messenger (may God's blessings be upon you) I have not revolted against Islam, nor have I done this with the intention of betraying a military secret. The truth of the matter is that my wife and children are living in Makkah and I do not have my tribe to protect them there. I had written this letter so that the leaders of the Quraysh may be indebted to me and may protect my wife and children out of gratitude.' Umar rose and respectfully submitted: 'O Prophet, please permit me to put this traitor to the sword'. The prophet replied: 'He is one of those people who had participated in the Battle of Badr, and the explanation he has advanced in his defence would seem to be correct'. Mawdudi explained:

> The Prophet acquitted Hatib on two accounts. Firstly, that his past records were very clean and showed that he could not have betrayed the cause of Islam, since on the occasion of the Battle of Badr when there were heavy odds against the Muslims, he had risked his life for them. Secondly, his family was in fact in danger at Makkah. Therefore, if he had some human weakness for his children and written this letter, then this punishment was quite sufficient for him that his secret offence was divulged in public for he had been disgraced and humiliated in the eyes of the Believers. (Mawdudi, p. 29)

A Paradise of Books

The vast book publishing industry in the Western world is truly awesome and certainly cannot be praised enough. But this recent Western achievement cannot eclipse an equally awesome, sophisticated and wide-ranging publication industry that first grew in the Muslim civilization around the middle of the eighth century, almost one thousand years before books appeared in the same quantity and quality in the West. The vast industry was still in existence when Europe began to occupy Muslim lands, and was systematically killed off by the colonial powers, along with the Muslim systems of education and medicine and other cultural institutions.

Given Islam's love for knowledge and its elevation of scholars and writers to exalted positions, the evolution of a publishing industry was a foregone conclusion at the advent of Islam. The Qur'an advised the believer to pray, 'O my Sustainer, cause me to grow in knowledge' (20:114), and asked directly, 'Can they who know and they who do not know be deemed equal?' (39:9). To these Qur'anic injunctions can be added numerous authentic traditions of the Prophet:

> If any one travels on the road in search for knowledge God will cause him to travel on one of the roads to paradise, the angels will lower their wings from good pleasure with one who seeks knowledge, and the inhabitants of the heavens and the earth and the fish in the depth of the water will ask forgiveness for him.
>
> Studying together for an hour during the night is better than spending the whole night in devotions. (*Mishkat Al-Masabih*, volume 1, book II)

Within one hundred years after the advent of Islam, a sophisticated and highly integrated book industry was flourishing in the Muslim world. Techniques were evolved for each stage of book production: composition, copying, illustrating, binding, publishing, storing and selling. Reading books, as well as hearing them being dictated, became one of the major occupations and pastimes. In certain major cities, such as Baghdad and Damascus, almost half the population was involved in some aspect of book production and publication. However, book production was both an industry and an institution, an institution with its own customs and practices, its own checks against fraud and misrepresentation and, above all, an institution that ensured that learning and books were not the prerogative of a select few but were available to all those who desired them. It also ensured that the scholars and authors themselves also benefited, both economically and in terms of recognition from their work.

There were two key institutions in the publishing industry: the mosque where the publication of a work originated, and the *warraq* from whom the final product could be bought. The *warraqs* were the copiers of manuscripts, representatives of the scholarly world as well as entrepreneurs. The mosque was the central focus of intellectual activity, where writers and scholars recounted the results of their studies to audiences of young people, other scholars and interested laymen. As the cultural basis of the intellectual activity was common to all, anyone and everyone could take part in discussion.

When a writer wished to publish a book, he first made notes and then wrote out an original manuscript (*asl*) which was initially called the 'draft' (*muswadda*). While such a draft naturally had a value, it did not constitute publication. The word used for publication, *kharraja*, means 'let (it) go out' or even 'come out' or 'be published'. The author was thus required to present his book to the public. This he did in the mosque by oral reading or dictation. Scholars would dictate numerous volumes of their work in the mosques where the general public gathered to hear them and professional *warraqs* copied and turned them into books. Even when the books were especially commissioned, they would still be published in this way. For example, a prominent ninth-century philologist, al-Farra (d.822), was asked by a friend to write a book to guide him in the understanding of the Qur'an so that he would not be ashamed when the Emir, to whom he was attached, asked him questions about any passage from it. Al-Farra, who lived in Baghdad, agreed. He also announced that he would dictate a book of this nature in the mosque—and it is in this way that the work was published.

Writers of that period were not class based, but came from all walks of life. For example, Al-Ahmar (d.810), who taught the children of Harun al-Rashid, gave his lectures drenched in musk and incense and supplied his audience with all necessary writing materials. His contemporary, al-Farra, however, was modestly dressed, sat on the floor while his audience squatted in the dust in front of him. Normally the author would sit crosslegged with his listeners seated in a circle. Next to him would be his most trusted student who would faithfully transcribe all that his teacher said. Authors would dictate thousands of pages in this way. The philologist al-Bawardi dictated from memory 30,000 pages on linguistic topics; al-Tabari, the noted historian and commentator on the Qur'an, also dictated the same number; the Egyptian scholar Jalal al-Din al-Suyuti (d.1550) dictated some 600 books. These were incredible feats of memory by our standards, but coming from a tradition that valued oral communication, where good memory was considered an indispensable tool for writers, it is not all that surprising nor uncommon. How were these scholars able to devote so much time to the performance of such intellectual feats? According to Johannes Pederson, author of the highly acclaimed study, *The Arabic Book*, it was largely because most of them lived a life of 'great contentment'. Learning, the life of the intellect, was 'intimately bound up with religion, and to devote oneself to both afforded an inner satisfaction and was service to God. . . . it not only made men of letters willing to accept deprivation; even more, it prompted others to lend them aid'. The mosques received a wide variety of aid and grants for scholars from a variety of institutions. No matter what their social origins, the subsistence of the scholars was assured, often in 'liberal measures'.

But writers also made a living from their output. The manuscripts that the *warraqs* transcribed during public dictations had little value unless they carried the ijaza—that is, they were copies authorized by their authors. The process of obtaining an *ijaza* was long and complicated, but it ensured that the rights of the author were preserved and plagiarism was kept at bay. Once the *warraq* made a copy of the author's work, it was read back to him three or more times in public. On each reading, the author would make amendments or additions which required further readings. Only when the author was finally satisfied, did he place the *ijaza* (licence) on the copies that he approved. The *ijaza* signified that he granted permission 'to transmit the work from him' in the form as approved. If the author of a particular work was dead, then the copy was read out by a distinguished scholar, who charged an honorarium for his service and gave his *ijaza* to the manuscript.

The function of getting the *ijaza* and distributing the approved manuscripts was performed by the *warraqs*. The *ijaza* did not give the *warraq* copyright over the work; it was simply an assurance that he passed the book in the form determined by the author and was empowered to transmit the book in the same form to others. The more established *warraqs* went to incredible lengths to acquire new manuscripts. And, of course, there were some who were not entirely honest. For example, al-Farra's commentary on the Qur'an took some years to write and was dictated publicly. There were so many listeners that their numbers could not be determined, including some eighty *quadis* (judges). Two *warraqs*, Salam ibn Asim and Abu Nasr ibn al-Jahm, also attended the dictation. However, when the dictation was completed, the *warraqs* withheld the book from publication; they would only release it on being paid one dirham for every five pages. Al-Farra received many complaints from eager readers, but his attempts to change the minds of the *warraqs* produced no results. He then announced that he would hold a new discourse on the same subject in a considerably expanded form—a new edition of the book, in fact, making the first edition obsolete. At that point the *warraqs* gave in and agreed to supply the original edition at the price demanded by the readers—one dirham for ten pages.

Within two hundred years after the death of the Prophet Muhammad, the book industry was to be found in almost every corner of the Muslim world. Indeed, the whole of Muslim civilization revolved around the book. Libraries (royal, public, specialized, private) had become common; bookshops were to found almost everywhere (small, large, those adjacent to mosques, in the centres of cities, in collectives, in special sections of the bazaars); and bookmen (authors, translators, copiers, illuminators, librarians, booksellers, collectors) from all classes and sections of society, of all nationalities and ethnic backgrounds, vied with each other in the production and distribution of books.

Just how common and important the book was to Muslim civilization can be seen in ibn Jammah's advice to his students in his *Books as the Tools of the Scholars*, written in 1273:

> Books are needed in all useful scholarly pursuits. A student, therefore, must in every possible manner try to get hold of them. He must try to buy, or hire, or borrow them, since these are the ways to get hold of them. However, the acquisition, collection, and possession of books in great numbers should not become the student's only claim to scholarship. . . . Do not bother with copying books that you can buy. It is more important to spend your time studying books than copying them. And do not be content with borrowing books that you can buy or hire. . . . The lending of books to others is recommendable, if no harm to either borrower or lender is involved. Some people disapprove of borrowing books, but the other attitude is the more correct and preferable one, since lending something to someone else is in itself a meritorious action and, in the case of books, in addition serves to promote knowledge. (Quoted by Rosenthal, *Technique*, pp. 8–9)

There was no shortage of libraries from which to borrow books in the Muslim civilization. Around the middle of the thirteenth century, historians list thirty-six libraries in Baghdad alone; and that does not include the House of Wisdom, the royal library, which had one of the largest collections anywhere. The historian al-Maqrizi described the opening of the House of Wisdom in 1004:

> On the 8th day of Jumada II AH 395 (1004) was opened the building called 'The House of Wisdom'. The students took up their residence. The books were brought from the libraries of the Inhabited Castles (residences of the Fatimid Caliphs) and the public was admitted. Whosoever wanted was at liberty to copy any book he wished to copy, or whoever required to read a certain book found in the library could do so. Scholars studied the Qur'an, astronomy, grammar, lexicography and medicine. The building was, moreover, adorned by carpets, and all doors and corridors had curtains, and managers, servants, porters and other menials were appointed to maintain the establishment. Out of the library of Caliph al-Hakim those books were brought which he had gathered—books in all sciences and literatures and of exquisite calligraphy such as no king had ever been able to bring together. Al-Hakim permitted admittance to everyone, without distinction of rank, who wished to read or consult any of the books. (Cited by Stone)

There were similar libraries in Cairo, Aleppo and the major cities of Iran, Central Asia and Mesopotamia. In addition to the central government libraries, there was a huge network of public libraries in most big cities, and prestigious private collections which attracted scholars from all parts of the Muslim world.

Of course, one could always buy books. A manuscript of that period was about the size of the modern book, containing good quality paper with writing on both sides, and bound in leather covers. An average bookshop contained several hundred titles, but larger bookshops had many more on offer. The celebrated bookshop of ibn al-Nadim, the tenth-century bibliophile and bookseller, was said to be on an upper story of a large building where buyers came to examine manuscripts, enjoy refreshment and exchange ideas. *Al-Fahrist*, the catalogue of books that ibn Nadim sold (contained in the shop or to which he had access), listed more than sixty thousand titles in an unlimited range of subjects: language and calligraphy, Christian and Jewish scriptures, the Qur'an and commentaries on the Qur'an, linguistic works, histories and genealogies, official government works, court accounts, pre-Islamic and Islamic poetry, works by various schools of Muslim thought (including the rationalists, the Shia and the ascetics), biographies of numerous men of learning, Greek and Islamic philosophy, mathematics, astronomy, Greek and Islamic medicine, literature, popular fiction, travel (India, China, Indochina), magic, miscellaneous subjects and fables! The first section of the first Chapter of *al-Fahrist* was devoted to various styles of writing (including Chinese), qualities of paper and 'excellencies of penmanship' and 'excellencies of the book'.

Are these the products of a civilization that burns books?

Fruits of Freedom

Muslim writers and scholars of the classical age, which spans over 800 years from the seventh to fifteenth centuries, made full use of the freedom of expression and thought ushered in by Islam. The Qur'an exalted the use of reason, and reasoned discourse became the basic tool of intellectual conflict:

> Behold, God enjoins justice, and the doing of good, and generosity towards (one's) fellow-men; and He forbids all that is shameful and all that runs counter to reason, as well as envy; and He exhorts you (repeatedly) so that you might bear (all this) in mind. (The Qur'an 19:90)

The term translated here as 'counter to reason' is *al-munkar*. The Muslim scholar and commentator of the Qur'an, Mohammad Asad explained the term:

> *Al-munkar* has here its original meaning of 'that which the mind (or the moral sense) rejects', respectively, 'ought to reject'. Zamakshari is more specific, and explains this term as signifying in the above context 'that which (men's) intellect disown' or 'declare to be untrue' . . . : in other words, all that runs counter to reason and good sense (which, obviously, must not be confused with that which is *beyond* man's comprehension). This eminently convincing explanation relates not merely to intellectually unacceptable propositions (in the abstract sense of the term) but also to grossly unreasonable and, therefore, reprehensible actions or attitudes and is, thus, fully in tune with the rational approach of the Qur'an to questions of ethics as well as with its insistence on reasonableness and moderation in man's behaviour. Hence my reading of *al-munkar*, in this and in similar instances, as 'all that runs counter to reason'. (Asad, *Message*, pp. 409–10)

Thus, a great deal of the energies of Muslim writers and thinkers was focused on the question of what should 'the intellect disown', what ran 'counter to reason' not just in worldly matters but also, indeed particularly so, in religious matters. Almost all philosophy that emerged in Muslim civilization was an outcome of reasoned discourse and discussion.

Mutazilism, the rationalist school of thought whose followers also came to be known as freethinkers, appeared less than one hundred years after the advent of Islam. It owes its origins to two young scholars, Wasil bin Ata and Amr ibn Ubayad, both of whom were born in 699. They attended the lectures of the Muslim ascetic Hasan al Basri (d.728), who is attributed by some scholars as being one of the first Sufis. During one his lectures, Hasan al Basri was approached by two men with conflicting views on the state of a believer who had committed a great sin. The first man argued that the perpetrator of a grave sin should be considered as a Muslim and not labelled as an unbeliever, and that his case should be left with God. The second man put forward the argument that the committer of a mortal sin had *ipso facto* deviated from the path of Islam and could not possibly be considered a believer. Before Hasan al Basri could reply, his young students Wasil and Ubayad intervened to present a third option: such a person, they suggested, was neither a believer nor an unbeliever. Hasan al Basri was not amused and said, you have seceded from us. So Wasil and Ubayad broke away from the circle of the master, went to another corner of the mosque and began teaching their views which came to be known as *manzilah bayn al-manzilatayn*: the state intermediate between belief and unbelief. Mutazilism developed as a philosophical movement to interpret the dogmas of religion in terms of reason; most mutazilites were independent thinkers with individualistic views on religious and philosophical questions. Apart from the third option of the state between belief and unbelief, which most Mutazilite philosophers found themselves to be in, the Mutazilite doctrine had four other fundamental principles: divine unity, divine justice, the promise of reward and threat of punishment, and the doing of right and prohibiting the doing of wrong.

The opposition to Mutazilite thought—and it was angry, outraged and forceful opposition—came from Asharism. Asharites held that human reason alone could not account for religious beliefs and the nature of revelation. The Asharite doctrines focused on the attributes of God and their relation with His essence, createdness or uncreatedness of the Qur'an, the possibility of the vision of God and the notion of freedom of will. The founder of the Asharite school was Abu Hasan al-Ashari who was born in 874 in Basra. The young al-Ashari was a devout freethinker and the favourite pupil and intimate friend of al-Jubbai (d.915), the head of the Mutazilite party at the time. One day, according to the biographer, ibn Khallikan (d.1282):

> Ashari proposed to Jubbai the case of three brothers, one of whom was a true believer, virtuous and pious; the second an infidel, a debauchee and a reprobate; and the third an infant: they all died, and Ashari wished to know what had become of them. To this Jubbai answered: 'The virtuous brother holds a high station in paradise; the infidel is in the depths of hell; and the child amongst those who have obtained salvation'. 'Suppose now', Ashari said, 'that the child should wish to ascend to the place occupied by his virtuous brother, would he be allowed to do so?'. 'No', replied Jubbai, 'it would be said to him: 'Thy brother arrived at this place through his numerous works of obedience towards God, and thou hast no such works to set forward'. 'Suppose then', said Ashari, 'that the child say: 'That is not my fault; you did not let me live long enough, neither did you give me the means of proving my obedience'. 'In that case', answered Jubbai, 'the Almighty would say: "I knew that if I had allowed thee to live, thou wouldst have been disobedient and incurred the severe punishment (of Hell); I therefore acted for thy advantage"'. 'Well', said Ashari, 'and suppose the infidel brother were to say: 'O God of the universe! since you knew what awaited him, you must have known what awaited me; why then did you act for his advantage and not for mine?'. Jubbai had not a word to offer in reply. (Quoted by Nicholson, p.377)

A few days later Ashari made a public announcement. On a Friday, while sitting in the chair from which he taught in the great mosque in Basra, he cried out at the top of his voice:

> They who know me know who I am: as for those who do not know me I will tell them. I am Ali b. Ismail al-Ashari, and I used to hold that the Qur'an was created, that

the eyes of men shall not see God, and that we ourselves are the authors of evil deeds. Now I have returned to the truth; I renounce these opinions, and I undertake to refute the Mutazilites and expose their infamy and turpitude. (Quoted by Nicholson, p. 378)

Both Asharites and Mutazilites were shunned by Sufis, the mystics who argued for a life of simplicity and inner reflection, based on the doctrine of love as developed by, among others, the female mystic Rabiah al-Basri. A Sufi, in the words of Ali ibn Uthman al-Hujwiri, the author of *Kashf al-Mahjub*, is 'one who has lost consciousness of the subjective self or ego, and subsists in God; who is liberated from the nature of things (as apprehended by the ego) and is in continuous rapport with the Reality of Realities'. However, when arguing for this spiritual journey towards God, the Sufis' only weapon was reasoned discourse. Here is the explanation of one of the key doctrines of Sufiism from the seventeenth-century Malayan Sufi, Nural al-Din al-Raniri:

> The Sufis too based their view upon reason and Tradition. . . . They contemplated and perceived with their intellectual vision, and they experienced directly (rasa) with their spiritual testing that being (or existence) is but one, and that is the Being of God, Who cannot be seen with the physical eye (*mata kepala*) in this abode of the world. That which the physical eye sees in the world, which has no Being like the Being of God. So the Being of God is the Real Being and Absolute (*mutlaq*), and the being of the world is metaphorical being and limited (*muqayyad*), a shadow (*zill*) and a possession (*milk*) of God's Being. (Quoted by Al-Attas, *Commentary*, pp. 87-8)

Between the positions of the Sufis, the Asharites and the Mutazilites were numerous other strands of philosophy, all of which recognized the right of reason to arbitrate between theological positions and disputes. For example, Tahawism was founded by al-Tahawi (d. 933); Maturidism was founded by al-Maturidi (b. 853), who based his system on freedom from similitude and divine wisdom; and the Zahirite tradition was initiated by Dawud bin Khalaf al-Isfahani (d. 909), author of *Kitab al-Zuhra*, whose celebrated champion was the Spanish philosopher ibn Hazm. Ibn Hazm believed in the literal interpretation of the Qur'an and thus rejected all forms of analogy and deduction from whatever quarter it came, whether Mutazilite, Asharite, liberal or Sufi, and declared all of them to be heretical. Indeed, there were so many schools of thought, interpretation, philosophy and ideas that the term *Zindiqs* was used to describe all forms of freethinkers and associated heretics. All these positions were vigorously defended and writers, confident of their thought and positions in society, jealously guarded their independence.

The fruits of all this independence and free thought kept the copiers, booksellers and the reading public busy and enthralled as expositions led to refutations which in turn led to counter-refutations. The most noted refutation was the devastating attack by al-Ghazzali on philosophy, *The Incoherence of the Philosophers*, and ibn Rushd's equally celebrated retort, *The Incoherence of the Incoherence*. But almost every major Muslim thinker wrote some kind of refutation of some kind of intellectual position. This galaxy of thinkers and polymaths in sheer numbers and quality of thought are witness to a thinking faith, a faith that believes in questioning and constant probing. Rationalist philosophers (al-Kindi, Zakaria al-Razi, al-Farabi, Miskawaih, ibn Sina, ibn Bajjah, ibn Tufail, ibn Rushd, Nasir al-Din Tusi), middle-of-the-roaders (al-Ghazzali, Fakhr al-Din Razi, Sadr al-Din Shirazi, ibn Khaldun), Sufis (al-Hajjaj, Rabia Basri, Junaid of Baghdad, Abd al-Qadir Jilani, Shahab al-Din Suhrawardi, ibn al-Arabi, Jalal al-Din Rumi, Sadi Sharazi, Hamza Fansuri, Nur al-Din al-Raniri), literalists (ibn Hazm, ibn Tammiyah), scholars and political thinkers (Abu Hanifah, al-Shafi, al-Mawardi, Nizam al-Mulk Tusi) demonstrate the diversity and depth of thought that remains unparalleled to modern times. Surely, these are not the fruits of a civilization that suppresses free thought and muffles free and open expression.

Writers Without Cramp

The freedom of expression that Islamic civilization enjoyed was not limited in the classical period to works of philosophy, theology, mysticism and scholarship. It found its expression in literature, too. However, in the current climate it is not sufficient for us simply to make that statement, having no validity in post-modern Western culture. Thus, to demonstrate that Islam places great emphasis on literature and has promoted it throughout the ages, we shall summarize the types of literature that have their origins in Muslim civilization.

The development of a monumental publishing industry and the evolution of a diverse range of thought, as R.A. Nicholson has pointed out, 'was accompanied by an outburst of intellectual activity such as the East had never witnessed before.' Every citizen became a student, and men travelled all over the known world, returning home 'like bees laden with honey, to impart the precious stores which they had accumulated to crowds of eager disciples, and to compile with incredible industry those works of encyclopaedic range and erudition from which modern science, in the widest sense of the word, has derived far more than is generally supposed.'

The philosophical novel first appeared in Muslim Spain; the biographical dictionary was invented by Muslims; bibliography was unknown before its emergence in Muslim intellectual circles; *adab* or the literature of manners and the literature of aphorisms are uniquely Islamic; the encyclopaedic works were first produced not by the philosophes of the Enlightenment as is generally thought but by such Muslim scholars as the Brethren of Purity; and in mystical poetry no other civilization can match the contribution of Muslims.

The apex of Muslim literature, not surprisingly, is the Qur'an which has, in the words of H.A.R. Gibb, 'neither forerunners nor successors in its own idiom'. The Qur'an cannot be surpassed in its style and quality of expression.

> [This] very quality which gives it its literary distinction renders it impossible to translate with any success into another language, and Islamic orthodoxy wisely discountenances any attempt to do so. The vigour and intensity of its language becomes vapid, the grammatical forms lose their subtle implications, the arresting rhetorical constructions become shapeless, and little is left but a seemingly confused and repetitious compilation, loosely strung together without life or artistry, and redeemed only by occasional flashes of mystical beauty or profound insight. (Gibb, *Arabic Literature*, p. 36)

It was due to the position of the Qur'an in Muslim society that literature and literary criticism flourished. But it was not only the Qur'an which encouraged literary expression; the Prophet Muhammad himself had a great love for poetry and literary narrative. He became particularly close to three poets who used poetry to defend Islam against attack from enemies: Hassan b. Thabit, Kab b. Malik and Abdullah b. Rawahah. There are a number of traditions about the Prophet's encounters with poets, and many companions of the Prophet also wrote poetry. The first four caliphs not only patronized poetry but wrote poetry themselves, and many of their poems are recorded by ibn Hisham in his *Sirat*.

Not surprisingly, new themes and new types of poetry emerged in Arabia after the advent of Islam. The most noted of Muslim poetry is, of course, the remarkable independent love-poem, the ghazal. Other forms include the muswashshah (strophic poem), qasida (formal ode), nasib (elegiac prelude to the qasida), zajal (popular strophic poem) and saj (rhyming prose). There is also the great tradition of mystical poetry.

One of the first mystical poets of Islam was Hasan al Basri (d.728), in whose circle the founders of the Mutazilite philosophy studied. He was followed by the famous woman saint Rabiah al Basri (d.801). A host of mystical poets came after the pioneers: Ibn al-Rumi (d.896) created a new introspective and analytical poetry, in which each poem developed a single theme in an organic unity; Ibn al-Arabi (d.1165) wrote three hundred books and countless poems; Abdul Qadir Jilani (d.1166) of India; Farid al Din Attar (d.1229), author of the *Memoirs of the Saints* and *Conference of the Birds*; Firdawsi (d.1020), whose *Shanama* contained 60,000 verses, also produced a biographical anthology of poets and writers of the preceding century or so, presenting their most successful verses, literary 'paragraphs' and metaphorical descriptions and imagery, under the title *The Solitaire of the Age*; Jalal-al-Din Rumi (d.1207) of Konya, whose *The Mathanawi* contained epic mystical poems, often relating a moral narrative; Sadi Shahzis (b.1194), whose *Gulistan* (The Rose Garden) and *Bustan* (The Fruit Garden) taught the plainest truth in the plainest way, had an epigram for every time and every occasion; Hafiz (d.1389) dominated the fourteenth century with his lyrical poetry; Hamzah Fansuri (d.1607), the Malay mystic poet; and Mohammad Iqbal (d.1938), the poet-philosopher of the Indian subcontinent, revived the tradition of mystical poetry with *The Mysteries of Selflessness* and numerous other works. These are just the tip of the iceberg.

While the mystical poets are reasonably well known today, poets of other types have not fared so well—perhaps with the exception of Omar Khayyam who is not held in particularly high esteem in his native land. From the peak of the classical age, Abu Nawas (d.810) and Mutanabbi (d.965) are the best known. Abu Nawas is known to Europeans through *Thousand and One Nights* as the boon companion and court jester of 'the good Haroun Alraschid' and the hero of countless droll adventures and facetious anecdotes. Born Hasan bin Hani of humble parents, he gained the title of Abu Nawas (father of the lock of hair) from two locks which hung down onto his shoulders. As depicted in *Thousand and One Nights* he was genuinely a scoundrel who boasted of his immorality, drunkenness and blasphemy. His *Diwan* contained poems in many different styles: panegyric, satire, songs, elegies and religious poems. However, love and wine were his chief motives for writing poetry.

Abu Nawas's antics were checked by his contemporary, Abu l-Atahiya (d.828), who also shared the court of Harun al-Rashid. Abu l-Atahiya is said to have fallen in love with a slave girl who was not responsive. It was not just that she sternly refused to return his passion, she also took no notice of his poems in which he celebrated her charms and agonized over the suffering she made him endure. In despair he turned to Sufism and wrote some of greatest mystical poems in Islamic literature.

Abu l-Tayyib Ahmad b. Husayn al-Mutanabbi, who came from Kufa, was a few steps ahead of Abu Nawas. He declared himself to be a prophet and developed a large following. Eventually, his antics led to a brief imprisonment. When released he wandered all over the Muslim lands and eventually came to Aleppo, where he joined the entourage of poets to the court of Sayuf al-Dawla. He soon gained favour with the ruler and became his favourite poet. That poetry gave him power was a fact which did not go unnoticed by Mutanabbi; apart from bragging about it, he used it to good effect to gain favours and wealth. Ibn Khallikan described his poetry as 'perfection', while Thaalibi (d.1038) was highly critical of both his poetry and his behaviour.

While there were court poets, there were also poets who were against courts. Abu l-Ala al-Marri (d.1057), declared in his *Saqtu l-Zand* (*The Park of the Fire-Stick*) that he never eulogized anyone in the hope of gaining a reward but only to practise his art. The main focus of his poems is death, the ultimate goal of mankind; the freethinking sage, al-Marri declared, should pray to be delivered as speedily as possible from the miseries of life and should refuse to inflict upon others what, by no fault of his own, he is doomed to suffer. Towards the end of his life, he became a vegetarian and adopted an ascetic lifestyle. Al-Marri's main concern is expressed in this quatrain:

Methinks, I am thrice imprisoned—ask not me
Of news that need no telling—
By loss of sight, confinement to my house,
And this vile body for my spirit's dwelling.
(Nicholson, p.315)

In addition to love poetry, odes and mystical verse, many other types of poetry were pioneered in the Muslim civilization. The *muwashshah* genre combined elaboration with standardization and required the *envoi* to be sharp, pungent and in colloquial speech. The poetry of nature was pioneered by ibn Hamdis (d.1132), who has been called the 'Arabic Wordsworth'. A whole genre (*saj*) of rhymed prose was developed in *The Golden Necklaces* by Fakhr ad-Din ar-Razi (d.1209), a philosopher and the greatest humanist of his time. Ibn Majid of Najd, who is said to have piloted Vasco da Gama from Africa to the Indian coast, took rhymed prose into a new domain when he published in 1489 a manual in prose and verse on the art of navigation for pilots and mariners. The genre of satirical poetry in local dialect was initiated by the Egyptian ash-Shirbani (d.1687).

Where poetry led, prose soon followed. The narrative tradition in Islam received a boost from the Qur'an which contains a chapter entitled 'The Story' ('Al Qasas', 28). Various chapters in the Qur'an relate the stories of the prophets Hud, Yunus, Maryam, Luqman, Yusuf and Ibrahim, as well as stories of people of ancient times. The Prophet was reported to be fond of listening to such storytellers as Tamim al Dari, who was the first storyteller to use the mosque. The preaching of Islam in the early period was also accompanied by storytelling. Among the earliest story writers were Abd Allah bin Sallam, Kab al Ahbar and the Persian Wahab bin Munabbih. According to al-Jahiz, there were twenty-eight well known storytellers in the early times of Islam, for the Caliphs always like to be accompanied by them. Among the companions of the Prophet, al Aswad bin Sari became a well-known storyteller.

Almost every town had its own storyteller for both the populace and high level officials. Within a century of the establishment of the Medina state, narrative literature had evolved into a number of sophisticated institutions, among which were:

1. Narratives of the Prophets
2. Instructional narratives: e.g., religious stories, glorious tales, moral stories, anecdotes
3. Romance of heroes: e.g., 'Romance of Antarah', 'Romance of Bani Hilal', 'Story of Bakr and Taghlib', 'Story of Kisra Anushirwan', 'Romance of Sayf bin Dhi Yazan'
4. Linguistic narratives: e.g., 'Maqamat al Hamzani', written in 939; 'Maqaman al Hariri', written in 1122
5. Philosophical narratives: e.g., 'al Tawabi', written by ibn Shahid in 1075; 'Risalah al Ghufran', written by al Maari in 1057; 'Hai Ebn Yokdhan', written by ibn Tufail in 1185.

The romance made an appearance in Islamic literature during the Abbasid period. Related to the populace by Qussas al Am ('the Storytellers of the Folks'), their authorship remains unknown. Probably each storyteller added and substracted from the romances as the stories developed. Among the most famous is the Romance of Antarah bin Shadad, which described the exploits of Antarah in the battlefield and his dual efforts to win the love of Ablah and become a recognized poet. One romance originated against the background of confrontation between Egypt and Abyssinia in the fourteenth century, another was based on the exploits of Alexander the Great, and another related the story of the paternal uncle of Prophet Muhammad. The Romance of the Beni Hilal illustrates the nature of these narratives. The Beni Hilal, said to come from the south of Arabia and Yemen, moved north with their camels and herds looking for good pastures. This romance is a long and complex epic, made up of a large number of stories and incidents that vary from country to country. For example, the figure of authority may be, depending on the version, the Sharif of Makkah, the Caliph of Baghdad, the Sultan of Egypt, the Turkish Pasha of Algiers or the King of Fez, but the main line of the story remained more or less the same. It had a large number of characters, a host of heroes and heroines, with heroines having particularly strong and assertive personalities. The stories were tales of love and war, with an emphasis on courage and generosity, the overall mood tragic, as hero after hero was killed fighting for the water and grazing lands his people needed to survive.

The linguistic narrative, or *maqamat* literature, was a unique creation of the Muslim civilization, exploiting the stylistic effects of rhymed prose and a vocabulary so fine that it was quite incomprehensible to the ordinary, untutored speaker of Arabic. The stories themselves dealt with ordinary problems of daily life, dramatically constructed and described, often in interaction with some protagonist who the hero or the narrator encountered. The master of the genre was Abu Muhammad al-Qasim al-Hariri (d.1122). Born in Basra, al-Hariri's *Maqamat* is considered a masterpiece of Arabic literature. The adventures of its hero, Abu Zayd, were related by Harith b. Hammam, the alter ego of the author himself. Hariri is reported to have modelled his hero on a stranger he met while sitting in the mosque—Abu Zayd of Saruj, whose native town had been plundered by the Greeks who took his daughter and drove him into a life of exile and poverty. Hariri was so impressed by the stranger's powers of improvisation that he began work the same evening on his *Maqamat* of the Banyu Haram. Written in rhymed prose, Abu Zayd emerged from the *Maqamat* as a fascinating knave. The narrative contained several superb discourses and a number of edifying sermons and lamentations peppered with wit and jest.

The best example of the philosophical narrative is ibn Tufail's *Hai Ebn Yokdhan*, an allegorical novel that explored the theme of solitude and the use of reason in ascertaining the Truth. Hai was generated spontaneously onto an island and brought up by a deer. He developed a keen sense of observation, made a number of empirical discoveries, including the use of implements and the correspondence between animals and plants, and began to realize that the world had a designer:

> And when he perceived that all things which did exist were His Workmanship, he looked them over again, considering attentively the Power of the Efficient, and admiring the wonderfulness of the workmanship, and such accurate wisdom, and subtle knowledge. And there appeared to him in the most minute creatures (much more in greater) such footsteps of wisdom, and wonders of the work of creation, and he was swallowed up with admiration, and fully assured that these things could not proceed from any other than a Voluntary Agent of Infinite Perfection, nay, that was above all Perfection; such a one, to whom the weight of the least atom was not unknown, whether in heaven or earth; no, nor any other thing, whether lesser or greater than it. (Ibn Tufail, p. 90)

With the use of unaided wisdom, Hai came to recognize the existence of God and finally reached 'illuminative wisdom'.

In addition to these categories of narrative, there were other important types of Muslim literature, perhaps the most important being *adab* literature initiated by Ibn al-Muqaffa (d.757). His moralizing animal fables of Bidpai, *Kalila wa-Dimma*, are read to this day and enjoyed by countless numbers. *Adab* literature offered the cream of what had been said in verse, prose, aphorism and pithy anecdote on every conceivable subject. It laid down the rules of conduct for princes, court officers, secretaries and administrators of all kinds and supplied the professional knowledge required for the performance of their duties in the form of manuals, anecdotes and romances. The genre was founded on the belief that 'manners maketh man' and paid much implicit and explicit attention to exemplary linguistic usage. These works were at the very heart of prose belles-letters of the Muslim civilization, drawing on political literature, philosophy, ethical theory and typology, inspirational thought and scholarship in many other fields. The emphasis was always on the literary aspects of the material presented.

The archetypal representative of adab literature was al-Jahiz, 'the goggle eyed' (d.868 or 869). He was a sceptic who looked at everything with a searching and critical spirit. His range was truly enormous, covering such as lore, Arabic rhetoric and poetry, national and ethnic characteristics, ethics, human sexual behaviour, various professions and ways of earning a living. His favourite method of argument was the dialectical device which involved taking both sides of a question, seeing the good and bad of a subject or attacking two seemingly opposite points of view. Some forty books of al-Jahiz are still extant, including his masterpiece, *The Book of Animals*.

After al-Jahiz, Abu Hayyan al-Tawhidi (d.1009) took *adab* literature even further, concentrating on philosophy and religion. The systematic theory of Arabic philology was already worked out by al-Khalil (d.791), whose student Sibawaih (d.793) produced a systematic exposition of grammar simply called *The Book*. Professional philologists then complemented *adab* literature by adding collections called *Majalis* (sessions) and *Amali* (dictations). The most famous of the dictations are those of Al-Qali (d.967), who was born in Armenia, studied in Baghdad, but established himself in Cordova where he delivered his famous *Dictations*, which are still widely read today.

A basic component of *adab* literature was the proverb used for literary embellishment. The proverb along with the aphorism and literary anecdote evolved a genre around themselves, the vitality of which can be seen in the continuous development of new proverbs; indeed, the large reservoir of proverbs known in mediaeval literature have no counterpart in the equally large collection of proverbs developed in modern times. Both the proverb and aphorism are basic components of such anecdotal works as Al-Ghazzali's *Book of Council for Kings*, Qadi al-Tanukhi's (d.944) *Deliverance after Distress* and *Collection of Histories* and Al-Abshihi's (d.1446) *The Literary Delectus*.

Other genre such as biography and travel writing have been extremely well served by Muslim writers. Biography, of course, was handmaiden to religious sciences, with the biography of the Prophet Muhammad, the *sira*, being developed as a precise science and fine art. The first full-scale biography of the Prophet was produced by ibn Ishaq (d.786), followed by a host of other writers. Among other biographies worth noting are Al-Baladhuri's (d.892) historical survey, *The Genealogies of the Nobles*; Yaqut's (d.1229) *Dictionary of Men of Letters* and *Geographical Dictionary or Gazetteer*, the latter including historical notices of the provinces and biographical data of important personages connected with them; and the celebrated biographical dictionary of ibn Khallikan (d.1282), *The Obituaries of Eminent Men*, where he endeavoured to attain the utmost accuracy to the extent of omitting all persons whose dates of death he could not reliably establish. Among the more celebrated autobiographies are *Deliverance From Error*, in which al-Ghazzali explained how he reconciled his doubts; the adventurous *Autobiography* of the Arab knight Usama ibn Munqidh (d.1188); and the long *Autobiography* of ibn Khaldun's, which focused on his scholarly pursuits and contained numerous quotations from poetry, artistic correspondence and eloquent lectures.

A few Muslim travel writers are well known in the West, perhaps ibn Battuta's (d.1377) *Travels* being the most widely read. But ibn Fadlan's *Eaters of the Dead*, an account of his adventures in Scandinavia written in 921, is also widely known (and is more fun to read, given his interest in sex and violence). Also of particular interest are the accounts of the Spanish Jew ibn Yaqub, who went to the Court of Otto the Great as an emissary of Islam in the same year that ibn Fadlan was sent to Scandinavia; the fascinating adventures of a Persian ship captain from Ramhurmuz, *The Wonders of India*, written about 950; the unique travels of mystical quest of Naser-e Khosraw, undertaken in the eleventh century and related in his *Book of Travels*; and the work of the Syrian Abd al-Ghani of Nablus (d.1731), who originated a new kind of mystical travel writing. A traveller who was quite at home on Christian ships and enjoyed a good discussion with Europeans was the Spanish scribe ibn Jubayr (d.1217). He left Granada in 1183 on a pilgrimage to Makkah, catching a Genoese ship from Ceuta to Alexandria and later a Christian merchant ship from Acre, which also carried some two thousand Christians to the Holy Land. Ibn Jubayr's pilgrimage to Makkah served as a model for many who followed, and the genre of pilgrimage narratives is still alive and prospering.

Historiography is not considered in the West as a branch of literature, but in the Muslim civilization it was widely cultivated and highly esteemed as a literary genre, with literary style being the prerequisite for the writing of history. This can be clearly seen in the work of ibn Khaldun (d.1406) where the writing of effective history is shown to depend on literary skill. The lasting fame of his *Muqaddama*, the first volume of a large world history, rests not only on the fundamental contribution it makes to knowledge, its discovery of the pivotal role of certain important factors in the formation and development of human society, but also on its literary style which is praised by all his contemporaries and is reminiscent of the classical style of al-Jahiz.

Literary tools such as thesauri, dictionaries and encyclopaedias were also widely available in the Muslim world. One of the first literary thesauri came from Ibn Qutaiba of Merv (d.889), whose *The Fountains of Story* appeared in ten books, each of which dealt with a given subject, such as sovereignty, war, friendship, asceticism, etc. Ibn Qutaiba also wrote the *Book of Subjects of Knowledge* and *The Book of Poetry and Poets*. Apart from ordinary dictionaries, there emerged centennial dictionaries, produced in particular by Ibn Hajar (d.1449); historical dictionaries of which the most noted is a twelve-volume version from As-Sakhawi (d.1497), the twelfth volume of which deals with women. Among the encyclopaedias, an abridged version of Al-Masudi's (d.959) monumental work, covering history, geography, philosophy and religion, *The Golden Meadows*, has survived to our times. And the serial tracts which accumulate into an encylopaediac work, the genre of *Rasail* or epistles, were pioneered by the Brethren of Purity around 983, which may come as a shock to Marshall Cavendish devotees.

A genre unique to Muslim civilization was that of the biographical dictionary. The majority were meant to be histories of specific subjects, written by focusing on the biography and achievements of writers and scholars who had made major contributions to these subjects. The emphasis was always on figures of cultural significance, rulers and government officials usually being ignored:

> ... the conception that underlies the oldest biographical dictionaries is that the history of the Islamic community is essentially the contribution of individual men and women to the building up and transmission of its specific culture; that it is these persons (rather than the political governors) who represent or reflect the active forces in Muslim society in their respective spheres; and that their individual contributions are worthy of being recorded for future generations. (Gibb, 'Islamic Biographical Literature', p. 54)

Thus biographical dictionaries present the most accurate picture of cultural life in the classical civilization of Islam. Entries recorded educational, religious, cultural, scientific and literary activities, giving the fullest and most complete picture of intellectual life of the Muslim community throughout its history.

Literary criticism, as it has a currency nowadays, was an original creation of Muslim civilization. Its canon, though developed for Arabic, could be transformed easily to other languages. Its prime concern was with the analysis of the figures of speech in both poetry and prose and to heighten the understanding of the wonder of language. Among the masters of systematic literary criticism were Al-Asmai (d.831) whose area was poetic criticism; Abu Obaida (d.825) who examined historical style and expression; the Abbasid prince ibn al-Mutazz (d.908); the rhetorician Qudama b. Jafar (d.922); and ibn al-Jauzi (d.1200) who satirized Sufi literature in *The Deceits of the Devil*. But perhaps the best known today is the eleventh-century literary critic al-Jurjani, the author of *The Secrets of Eloquence*. He is considered to be the first to conceive a monistic theory concerning form and content in literature. In his *Asrar al-Balagaha*, he declared that 'it is not the words (of an author) which illumine the heart, but the inner thought or implications of the words'. The best course for an author aiming to achieve excellence in style, he stated, 'is to leave thoughts on their own devices, and let them decide the words in which they would be expressed. If thoughts were left to their own spontaneous course they would choose for themselves only the most becoming of words and forms of expression'. Any deliberate attempt at literary embellishment would lead only 'to error and to censure'.

This brief survey of Muslim literature is neither meant to be exhaustive, comprehensive nor all that representative, since it concentrates more on freethinkers than on what one might call 'orthodox' writers. But it is meant to show that Muslim civilization is not short of freethinking literati and eminent heretics. Indeed, there seems to be a positive glut of this variety. They provide a good indication of the diversity of thought and varieties of literary genre which is unmatched even in the contemporary world. These are not the products of a civilization that looks with disfavour at its whistleblowers, outlaws free thought or stifles free expression.

Five
The Other Side of Midnight

The mock trial of Islam as a religion, culture and civilization has reached a new crescendo nearly two years after the publication of Salman Rushdie's *The Satanic Verses*. The novel, however, does not emerge unbidden from the mind of the author, but derives from the Western literary tradition to which it contributes. For the past decade, Rushdie has been a feted literary lion, albeit of a new breed. His reputation was established with the publication of the 1981 Booker Prize novel, *Midnight's Children*, and heightened in 1983 by *Shame*, which, alas, did not win British prizes. But by that time Rushdie was regularly being described, after a reviewer's felicitous phrase, as an Indian Gunter Grass, and was well ensconced among the literati. His name is regularly bracketed with those of Marquez and Kundera, and he is a fixture within the particular world of international literature. The cause celebre of *The Satanic Verses* has been seen as an incendiary clash between the mores of that literary world and the world Rushdie writes about in each of these novels: the subcontinent and especially the Muslims of and from the subcontinent.

These three novels that have carved a niche for Rushdie in international literature have also defined a new type of author. What was so excitedly hailed with his arrival on the literary scene was a one-world syncretism of art. Here was an author authentically articulating another world culture with the style, metaphor, preoccupations and language (allowing for Indian idioms as idiosyncrasy) of Western literature. The slogans of one-worldism had an obvious and able literary embodiment—this heady new mixture of interconnection and interdependence was the hallmark of a new era. What is so applauded in Rushdie's work is the merging of elements into a decidedly post-modern text. The novel is regarded as a particularly European art form. Art, especially the novel, holds a crucial position in the history of Western civilization as the bastion of embattled freedom that has urged the Western conscience to 'progress', to free itself from the shackles of dogma, to think, feel and express itself more humanely. In the novel the human predicament and the predicament of being human have been explored to the betterment and enrichment of all humanity. The claim is sincere, and there is no hint of irony in restating such an engrained commonplace. The irony is that the entire Rushdie affair has, as yet, generated so little reflection on the validity and accuracy of this commonplace.

The shock and indignation the Muslim response to *The Satanic Verses* has produced in literary circles arises from the assumed place and function of art in modern society and the particular place of Rushdie within modern literature. Rushdie, the man from two worlds, was seen as the integrated culmination of a global process. It is the nature, including the limitations, of this globalizing process that are the real, unexplored text of this affair. If the Western literary world, the repository of the conscience of Western civilization, is taken by surprise, then its reaction is indicative of something authentic and profound in the perspective of Western civilization. The warning signs of the coming storm were there in the text of Rushdie's earlier works for those who knew how to read them: so dense and determined a text as *The Satanic Verses* could hardly be a sudden rush of insight forcing itself off the page as the author is at work. But there is another reason for seeing the entire thrust of *The Satanic Verses* as deliberate: few modern authors are so consistent in the style and themes they select, and so dedicated in prefiguring the next novel in its predecessor. The attitudes and ideas that made the offence contained in *The Satanic Verses* possible and necessary, deliberate and purposeful, are to be found throughout the body of Rushdie's mature work. It is not only legitimate, it is essential to set the context for *The Satanic Verses* by examining the earlier works.

In *Midnight's Children*, the ever-prescient Rushdie noted that to tell one life he had to swallow the whole world. To comprehend the significance of the Rushdie affair we, too, have had to swallow the whole world. Our argument is that the taste and palatability of this meal of pickles will depend upon one's identity, just as the nature of the tales presented by Rushdie depends upon identity. Identity is determined not by one's place of origin but is a conscious choice of worldview that seasons the repast. Identity is shaped by place of origin, allegiance to traditions, the resonance of culture, the inheritance of history, the fortunes of one's place within society and its economic and political structures. But identity is not just a ragbag of odd elements; it has a determining principle provided by one's worldview. However people may protest that modern secularism is a suspension of choice, it like any other cardinal principle comes with a framework of values that indelibly marks the persona and melds the complex elements of identity into a whole. We chose our identity not because we can randomly make ourselves, but because we can and must select a worldview, a value framework, that will modulate our relationship to all the facets of human existence. That worldview affects everything we do, especially how novels are written and how they are read. It is the worldview that distorts the imagination. The trail of the distorted imagination is distinctive and coherent. The resonance of the Rushdie affair embraces more than *The Satanic Verses*; it is there in *Midnight's Children* and *Shame*.

Rushdie's genre is magical realism; his style is monotonal, as well as derivative, since he constantly provides hints and allusions to literary and historical sources. It is in the allusions that the dissonance arises among his readers. According to his reviewers, Rushdie is the man who integrates two worlds. The real issue that needs to be made clear is the disparity his texts can occasion, depending upon the perspective of the reader. The argument of writers of this genre is that reality is too subtle and complex to be approached directly in fiction. In fantasy we can grasp aspects of truth too easily obscured or too overlaid by conventions of prejudice, sacredness, ideology and indoctrination to be apprehended in straight fiction, let alone in factual, reasoned argument. It is also, perhaps, the secularists' only means of handling the spiritual dimension that is no longer valid, yet inspires the artist as the sense of something beyond everyday common sense. It provides the reverberations behind motivations, actions and events that prove the validity, yet have no mentionable name or genre, except in dreams. So in Rushdie's novels all the characters are possessed, slip into and out of dreams, are transformed and transmuted between different dimensions of consciousness while the backgrounds and foregrounds they inhabit are constantly shimmering, enlarging and shrinking like mirages.

His work shows a marked internal consistency and mutual cross-reference in magical realism and in the themes. On both the profound and overt levels the themes of *The Satanic Verses*, as well as some early drafts of incidents in that novel, are evident in his earlier work. The content of *The Satanic Verses*, therefore, reveals no surprises. The transgression that so offends Muslims is but the logical resolution of ideas contained in earlier novels, the culmination and clarification of a theme Rushdie has been working towards for some time.

Rushdie has spoken of his work as though *Midnight's Children*, *Shame* and *The Satanic Verses* are a kind of trilogy of themes he knows: India, Pakistan and migrants from the subcontinent in England. Certainly these works cohere on many levels and need to be looked at together, especially if one wants to uncover what Salman Rushdie knows. *Midnight's Children* and *Shame* speak of the state of mind and perspective with which Rushdie set about writing of revelation and the formation of Islam in *The Satanic Verses*.

Darkness at Noon

Midnight's Children is the story of Saleem Sinai and his adversary/antithesis, the lurking menace Shiva, who hardly appears in the book. Both are born on the stroke of midnight introducing 15 August 1947, the day of India's independence. The novel, Tristram Shandy-like, sets the scene for the birth of its narrator and central character with the family history of Saleem Sinai.

The opening incident relates how Saleem's grandfather, Aadam Aziz, loses his faith while prostrating himself in prayer. He draws blood when his nose strikes against a frosty tussock of Kashmiri earth under his prayer mat and vows 'never again to kiss earth for any god or man'. As an exposition of the loss of faith this is a vicarious and trivial happening, but it is surrounded by many potential indicators. There is an effortlessness about the process of losing one's faith; it just slips from the person. The loss, simply accomplished and irrevocable, raises a question that seemingly does not concern Rushdie, nor trouble him: how does one lose one's faith? Throughout his work we are confronted by a kind of inevitability about the loss of one's faith that is self-evident. Its consequences matter tremendously and are a genuine preoccupation of Rushdie. The process—how and why it happens, the experience of faith that precedes its loss and precipitates the realization—is absent as a question. It is consequences that are wrestled with and become the perspective from which the practice and nature of religious faith are examined by Rushdie.

Encapsulated in the opening of *Midnight's Children* are all the themes Rushdie juggles in his work: loss of faith and its attendant vacancy; vulnerability to women and the problematique of male/female relationships; and history that impinges, imposes upon and distorts people and places in many ways to set the scenes for Rushdie's mirages.

The Heidelberg-trained Dr Aziz is called to treat a young girl whom, for the preservation of the conventions of modesty, he examines through a hole in a sheet. The recurrent but varying illnesses of Naseen are a potent image of how relationships are formed: partition, things seen through a hole, imagination gluing together salient ideas, another collection of primal notions that reverberate through all the novels with the lurking menace of woman attached. Much the same notion is used to express Rushdie's' acquaintance with Pakistan in *Shame*. He sees the country summed up in how he has come to know his younger sister on irregular visits at different stages of her growth. At another level he is viewing everything through a hole, the hole of vacancy caused by the loss of faith. What Rushdie glimpses standing behind that hole in a sheet is the world of people and history. It is a perplexing world full of the 'storm tossed' confusion of conflicting ideas, as Rushdie has expressed it elsewhere. Of course the point of perspective is in the mind, and what the mind permits, given the circumstances, is merely a badly fitting collage, a prescient reminder at the very outset.

Dr Aziz is at Amritsar to witness the massacre instigated by Major Dyer. He acquires a permanent bruise on his chest from being crushed under the bodies of the dead and dying. Dr Aziz's bruise is a recurrent refrain in *Midnight's Children*, whereas in *Shame* the recurrent bruise is the *gatta*, the mark on the forehead of the devout caused by long hours of prostration in prayer: the bruise of history and the bruise of religion; the bruise of vulnerability and the bruise invulnerable. History and religion leave their imprint upon the subcontinent and its people; these impressions are the texture of context in which Rushdie's themes are pursued.

The modest, silent girl behind the hole in the sheet emerges to marry Dr Aziz and develop into the indefatigable Reverend Mother. All of Rushdie's women are problematic; none admit of easy, stable or appealing relationships. In fact, there are few appealing women in Rushdie's novels, and even those who appeal do so only in phases before being transformed. In *Shame*, Rushdie talks of the oppression of women, which is, of course, the oppression of women in Islam; in *The Satanic Verses* the theme becomes the question of women goddesses and the war with patriarchy. While Rushdie is looking for the grand explanations of what makes women a problem, which he locates in their subjugation by men, the subtext of his writing is the awfulness of women who make men impotent and incapable.

At the moment of India's independence, when Saleem Sinai and Shiva are born, the babies' name tags are switched. The real child of the Sinai's, Shiva, is given to a street entertainer to raise as best he can. And the street entertainer's child, who is in reality the illegitimate son of William Methwold, becomes Saleem Sinai, the narrator of the novel. So the backdrop of colonial history has been introduced, and the theme of brown sahibdom would appear to have its representation, too, for William Methwold does not leave the lives of those who buy his houses untouched. The locus that embodies all the conflicting strands of the novel is Saleem Sinai, the author's alter ego. The tales are vulnerability, history, loss of faith, women, religion, hauntings and life through the confusion and conflict of the author. But then the teller of the tale, Saleem Sinai, and his later evocations in the subsequent novels are not weaklings but especially privileged viewers for all their inner angst, voyeurs who look from a godlike height at the panoply below their reified eyesight. The point of perspective is distinctive, uniting Saleem in *Midnight's Children* with the multiple voices of *Shame* and Saladin Chamcha in *The Satanic Verses*, with Salman Rushdie giving us intimations of his intensely modern preoccupation with the self-consciousness of artistic creativity.

The childhood of Saleem Sinai and his friends is lovingly told in engaging detail in the amiable ambiance of Bombay, itself a fond character in the novel. Saleem Sinai falls in love with the game of snakes and ladders because 'implicit in the game is the unchanging twoness of things' and 'metaphorically, all conceivable oppositions'. Duality marches through all the novels as a central theme which touches every point in the resonant meaning of the words good and evil, from the trite and banal to the cosmogonic. The trouble with the game of snakes and ladders, Rushdie tells us, is that it lacks the crucial dimension of this eternal truth, duality, which is ambiguity. In the opposed duality of Saleem/Shiva, Omar Khayyam Shakil/Sufiya Zenobia and Gibreel Farishta/Saladin Chamcha in *Midnight's Children, Shame* and *The Satanic Verses*, there is only ambiguity in duality and its march through the events and themes, making duality a heady, complex, ambiguous brew that—outside and inside, different and indistinguishable, negative and positive, repellent and attractive, interchangeable at each point on the scale it touches—culminates in the very nature of the divine itself when we eventually get there.

Saleem has all the ambiguity a proto-narrator should have. Endowed by the magic of the time of his birth, he is heir to strange powers, and hears voices in his head. The child's first awareness of the voices is immediately related to the experience of the Prophets. He outrages his family by announcing that archangels are speaking to him. The blasphemy brings immediate physical retribution from Saleems' father, a blow that marks him for life. It is the All India Radio in his head that makes Saleem the story teller who manufacturers the subcontinent for us in *Midnight's Children*; the link this establishes between Prophets and artistic creativity (Rushdie's, of course) is clearly signalled as a grand theme of the author. Saleem renounces his notion of archangels as he more deeply explores the nature of the voices in his head in secret, but Rushdie does not renounce his theme.

When concussion at the age of ten makes Saleem aware of the other children of midnight, 420 of them had died from malnutrition, disease and everyday misfortunes. In Urdu, the number 420 (*Char saw Bees*) has the connotation of wickedness, 'the number associated with fraud, deception and trickery'. But Saleem rejects this significance as 'an excursion into fantasy depending upon a view of life which is both excessively theological and barbarically cruel'. What were the powers of these magic children? There was his closest supporter, Parvati-the-witch, the 'natural', 'real' magician who grew up among the magicians' colony in the shadow of the Jama Masjid in Delhi. There were twins who, despite excessive plainness, had the ability to make any man who saw them fall desperately, hopelessly and often fatally in love. There was the beggar girl whose beauty was so intense it blinded her mother—she had to live with a sack over her face until she was mutilated, making her a very successful beggar since the mark of her former beauty was clear. A boy with the ability of stepping into mirrors and re-emerging through any reflective surface in the land. A girl who could multiply fish, a werewolf, a boy who could increase or reduce his size at will, a girl whose words could inflict physical wounds, a boy who could eat metal, a girl whose green fingers could grow prize vegetables in the desert, and one boy who was a time traveller. Perhaps it is not unlike, as Rushdie notes, the stories of freaks that abound in the newspapers of India or, for that matter, the characters that live in all those Orientalist novels and travel literature.

Saleem sets himself the task of organizing the Midnight's Children Conference (MCC) and infusing them with purpose. They were born at the beginning of a new era, yet that date is but a fleeting instant in the Age of Darkness, Kali-Yuga, which began on Friday, 18 February 3102 BC and will last 432,000 years! The narrator/author notes, 'born and raised in the Muslim tradition, I find myself overwhelmed all of a sudden by an older learning'.

Midnight's Children, for all the horror of its later stages, can very well stand as an act of love. Its exuberance is located firmly in the land of India and peopled with richly drawn characters who palpably engage the affections of the author enroute to endearing themselves to the reader. Indeed, the power of the later sections, what makes them so appalling and keeps the bitterness and venom of the author in balance, is the fact they grow out of a loved and lovingly peopled landscape. If the style is magical realism, then there is just enough of both magic and realism to act as a passport into the world of the novel, to fix the reader within the novel as a solid domain where our emotions and our caring can be engaged. But those are the sections in India; Pakistan is quite another matter. In Pakistan everything is more arid, characters retreat into not quite cardboard, more papier-mache figures. The only ones we can genuinely care about are Ayooba, Shaheed and Farooq, the three teenaged soldiers overwhelmed and doomed by war—the victims. Everyone else, including the once-adorable Brass Monkey, becomes one-dimensional, unapproachable and pretty distasteful; in short, as all the literary devices signal, they stink.

The novel concerns coming to terms with 'independent India', and tangentially the newly reconstituted subcontinent. Rushdie's perspective on place is nurtured by the particularities of his beloved Bombay. Bombay gives the author a delight in eclecticism that freely ranges over the possibilities offered by his native heath. Yet what he offers as possibilities for India is confined by his device of duality, the dichotomy of two contending principles vying for the upper hand. Into this dichotomy he tries to suggest a third principle, a notion of newness.

In his portrayal of India, Rushdie keeps to the well worn path marked out by Orientalism. 'What grows best in the heat: fantasy; unreason; lust'; and his chosen style amplifies this notion while searching, as he clearly indicates, for the form that lies within reality and the meaning which reveals itself only in flashes. From one perspective, what he writes about India or the subcontinent as a whole can easily sit within the whole range of modern writing generated by the latest upsurge of Western fascination with things Eastern. Fantasy, myth, possession by dreams, a feeling of ancient wisdom along with marvels and grotesqueries, surely this has always been the stuff of literature about India? The Orientalist construction of the East was a projection of Western wish fulfillment, as well as a subtle justification for domination; a two-pronged imposition upon India that has made it endlessly fascinating to Western writers. This is not to say there is not a germ of truth in parody. If Rushdie is walking this narrow line, exploring myth and fantasy as it exists within and of the East on its own terms, then he is bound to be faced with difficulties, beset by ambiguities and is begging to be misunderstood on all sides. More importantly, the reader is justified in questioning how successfully Rushdie uses his material to illumine something beyond the reach of Western writers: we can question the autochthonous meaning. It is at this level that Rushdie's vision, his version of truth is bleakest, most barren and ultimately rejectionist of the very world he writes about.

The dilemma of a new nation is indeed singular in the modern world. Precisely as Rushdie indicates, the problem is that they are not new at all but a construction imposed upon a people with millennia of history. But there is a great deal of shallowness in the way he deals with this theme. His continual references to communalism never lead him to consider, for example, that communalism is taken as such a blight because it so directly contradicts the ethos of the unitary nation-state, which could be the limitation and failing of the nation-state, not communalism. The brown sahibs make their appearance in *Midnight's Children*, in that pithy passage about the nation's businessmen turning white. But there are no deeper insights than what is in the end merely a sophisticated, well-turned barb. There is no penetration into the genesis of the brown sahib, only the quip about William Methwold leaving a human legacy behind before departing Bombay. The brown sahib as colonial bastard. The timescale of the brown sahib's genesis is collapsed; he emerges at the end of colonialism, his unexplored sphere of influence the neo-imperialist world of the modern nation-state. It is a slight nod, with a distortedly condensed history, to the reality behind the emergence of the brown sahib who is the conscious creation, not inadvertent offspring, of a long-held colonial policy to foster the workings of a neo-imperialist world order. Rushdie lays down markers but considers no further how both aspects of the nature of the brown sahib has affected the aspirations of independent newness.

We do see that poverty, violence and corruption are part of the inheritance of the new nations, but we receive little insight into their nature. They are abstract actors on the fringes, and as abstractions not penetrated for insight. There is a world of have-and-lack, one of the axes of opposition of Saleem and Shiva, but little pondering that this dichotomy is accentuated within the newly independent nation by a strong legacy of history and by the existence of a world outside the confines of the subcontinent. India's poor are not a problem of India's making alone. Rushdie's thesis, presented through the device of the *Midnight's Children*, is a metaphor that can be taken in two ways, but the two ways he poses are themselves reductionist interpretations. We see less of the subcontinent than we think, perhaps because the author thinks less widely or deeply about the subcontinent per se than we imagine. He gives us either the last throw of reactionary backwardness or an undefined and failed hope of freedom. This is a doubly reductionist vision because, caught in a vacuum of an unreal setting, there is no chance to examine the pressures each idea would have to confront; and anyhow both are presented as doomed.

There is nothing here of a society ravaged and destabilized during the colonial era that must wrestle with that legacy. India was a nation impoverished deliberately by the building of an economic infrastructure under colonialism; that infrastructure was there merely to serve the needs of the metropolitan power, not needs as perceived or defined from within the subcontinent. That is a legacy every new nation has had to cope with. The other notion is of a new nation, as symbolized by the *Midnight's Children*, that rushed too fast into the world of modernizing. But there is nothing of the constraints of this modernization drive, the derivative and dependent nature of the exercise and how this worked to flaw what happened within the confines of the subcontinent. Real India is buried somewhere in the background, and the metaphor and particular experience of the narrator, on reflection, give us fewer flashes of insight than the pace of the novel portends. In so far as Rushdie does define his third option, newness, it is a humane newness that looks remarkably like Western secular liberalism, creator of the very failed modernization he bemoans as doomed, a principle not derived from within but selected to be imposed to shape the raw material available from the subcontinent.

What one does not find in Rushdie is any genuine radicalism, or even the perception that a fourth, very different kind of radicalism exists in the subcontinent. This is the radicalism of a writer such as Ashis Nandy, whose argument is that many an Indian radical is no more than a caricature of the Western/Westernized observer, a person easily written off as a fanatic precisely because he or she speaks with an autochthonous voice that is inaudible to the Western/Westernized observer. The fourth option is that of reformulating a tradition according to distinctive notions supplied by the tradition itself. There are moral principles within the ancient traditions that are not immovable through time, that can be drawn upon in new ways to respond to contemporary challenges to shape a newness that cannot simply be judged by Western-derived standards. It is the West that has declared that all ancient traditions are static, while the West alone has the 'progressive' tradition. From within the ancient traditions, this is a fallacy of the most imperialist kind because autonomous change is a genuine aspiration. It is a real hope, however, that is incomprehensible to the distorted imagination imposed upon the East by the describing and defining civilization of the West, for this newness from within tradition would be an alternative to the West.

There is a vague glimmer of this idea in the reference to Aadam Aziz who at one point dedicates himself 'to an attempt to fuse the skills of Western and hakimi medicine'. The essence is that tradition provides a vantage point of ideas that are capable of criticizing the far-from-infallible Western wisdom, and thus enables a new construction of contemporary knowledge that combines elements of the West with traditional wisdom. This is far more subtle than Rushdie's dismissal acknowledges, for significant work has been done on studying hakimi medicine, and its holistic approach is nowadays of considerable interest to Western medical experts. The hakimi system continues to be most effective in delivering medical care to the bulk of the rural poor, which is part of its attraction to those trained in Western medicine.

A consideration of the fourth option that grants it validity is nowhere to be found in Rushdie's writing, not in the characters of *Midnight's Children*, nor in any of his later works. In the end Rushdie judges that the aspirations and possibilities of independence have all failed. The standards he uses to substantiate this are all derivative Western standards, while the culprits are all localized villains found within the traditionalism of the subcontinent or demonstrating a rapacity seen only from the localized angle of the subcontinent.

Rushdie elegantly weaves a discussion of the nature of his chosen literary style into the fabric of *Midnight's Children*. He is eager to make clear the connection between the style and the reality he is discussing. So in *Midnight's*

Children we are told that 'matter of fact descriptions of the outre and bizarre and their reverse, namely heightened, stylized versions of the everyday', are techniques as well as attitudes of mind.

In the beautifully written closing passage of the book, Rushdie, using the metaphor of pickling, tells us he reconciles himself to the inevitable distortions of this stylistic process; the intensification of taste is a small matter since the art is to change the flavour in degree and not in kind. The objective then has been to root his style in reality and present the form or meaning that stands behind this heightened flavouring of storytelling. That which is most bizarre in reality, the war scenes and the events of the Emergency, provoke the most nightmarish telling, both as matters of fact and through needful escape into dreams and stylization, but their substance is a real history that happened to real people. The author has his justification, but there is another way of seeing it. The stylistic device, the substance of post-modern writing, is making an ideological point. It may hint that form stands behind and under reality, but that form can only be seen in confusion, its reality is conflict. The meaning of the stylistic metier is doubt about contending forces in the form that may be lurking behind the storytelling or life. In this ideological sense the style is not the storytelling, it is the story.

The other stylistic element is pointing to the importance of 'recurrence' and 'correspondences' and the importance of the naming of things. This is a real Rushdieism: he uses the techniques constantly in his trilogy of novels and cannot refrain from telling his readers how and what he is about. 'As a people we are obsessed with correspondences. Similarities between this and that, between apparently unconnected things make us clap our hands delightedly when we find them out'.

One reason for this emphasis is that his Western readers are unlikely to be informed of the sources from which the game derives. The elegant word games are deliberate devices for pointing to significant matters; they apply not only where the author signals them but when the studious reader finds them littered throughout the novel. Therefore, familiarity with the culture gives another subtext that can be quite different from the one available to the unschooled reader. Saleem *Sinai* is fated by his name to wander in barrenness, while being saddled with all the other connections of the letter 'S' that are pointed out to us:

> Our names contain our fates; living as we do in a place where names have not acquired the meaninglessness of the West, . . . *Sinai* contains Ibn Sina, master magician, Sufi adept; and also Sin the moon, the ancient god of Hadhramaut, . . . But Sin is also the letter S, as sinuous as a snake; serpents lie coiled within the name. . . . but when all

that is said and done; when Ibn Sina is forgotten and the moon has set; when snakes lie hidden and revelations end, it is the name of the desert—of barrenness, infertility, dust; the name of the end. (*Midnight's Children*, pp. 304–5)

Midnight's Children opens with the primal event, the loss of faith by Aadam Aziz. The whole question of religious faith is tangential to the main theme of *Midnight's Children*, but it is a constant running sore that niggles at the author. With hindsight the dispersed references in *Midnight's Children* read like early warnings and first drafts of things to come, a prefiguring of ideas more fully realized in *The Satanic Verses*. In the response to Saleem Sinai's claim that archangels are talking to him, the author clearly shows he does not doubt the kind of response such claims would elicit. Saleem Sinai outrages all around him. Yet he continues to reflect on the matter and seems hooked by the thought that when Prophet Muhammad first experienced revelation he thought he was going mad. This very notion reads like the draft version that later became *The Satanic Verses*, where the same idea is again mentioned, to be echoed in the later novel in the paranoid schizophrenia of Gibreel Farishta. With Rushdie, recurrences are not only internal to each novel; one should keep an eye open for the recurrences between his novels.

There is one other reverberating reference one cannot fail to note in *Midnight's Children*, a world of receptivity somehow missing at the root of Rushdie's writing about Islam. One can think of no writer who is attuned to Muslim consciousness, who claims affinity to this cultural background who would find it necessary to refer to the *Fatiha* as 'the exordium', the Latin term for beginning or introductory portion, as Rushdie does in the opening scene of *Midnight's Children*. Why, one wonders, when he claims to be writing of the Third World from within the Third World must he so clearly distance himself from it? Are the most famous seven verses of the Qur'an not capable of being named in their own terms? Or are they only capable of being apprehended by an alien, imposed convention of comprehension? That is a long walk away from writing of the heritage, and daily experience of Rushdie's sector of the Third World from within. The *Fatiha* is the opening surah or chapter of the Qur'an. It is the most frequently recited chapter, since it is the basis of every cycle in the five daily prayers. The *Fatiha* means the opening; it is also known as the *Umm ul Kitab*, the mother or essence of the Book, the Qur'an, encapsulating the religious worldview of Islam. It is the most basic reverberation of Islam within the Muslim; traditionally along with the Azan, the call to prayer, it is the first words a child hears at birth. Rushdie has elsewhere insisted that connection to locale and its cultural heritage must be judged by the felicity and authenticity of a writer's use of the idiomatic speech patterns and terminology of their subject matter and characters. To a subcontinental Muslim, or a Muslim from any background, the term 'exordium' would be unknown, impossible.

The reference is small, but significant. Rushdie has stated that he stands at a particular angle to Islam. His perspective as it unfolds through the entire course of his writing is best described as an angle of attack formed by the Orientalist view of Islam. His portrayal of the religion, his worrying at ideas, his speculative thinking about Islam are shaped not by the world of Muslim ideas but those imposed upon it by Orientalists. Significantly, considering the place he has been given in the literary pantheon, his writing about Islam is not influenced by or attuned to the nuances of Muslim sensitivities, thought or speech. So divorced is Rushdie from the texture of Muslim feeling that every reference to the substance of Islam, as distinct from Muslims, throughout *Midnight's Children* can be read as a deliberate denigration, an intended insult. Thus, God has 'been named after a carved idol in a pagan shrine built around a giant meteorite: Al-Lah, in the Qa'aba, the shrine of the great Black Stone'. But the Arabic term 'Al-Lah' is linguistically the one God.

Repeatedly in all three novels, Rushdie reiterates his fixation with the Black Stone, as if it were or must be seen to be the most significant fact about the Haramain, the holy precincts of Makkah at the centre of which stands the Ka'aba, the direction to which all Muslims around the world turn for prayer. When Rushdie selects a detail, he invariably selects from among the most emotive. It is the world of meaning that resonates behind emotion and simple faith and so totally escapes him, which makes the Muslim reader gasp. In Muslim consciousness the Ka'aba is a house of prayer originally built by Prophet Abraham for the worship of One God, who has no representation. The Arabic word for man, *insan*, has the Qur'anic connotation of a being prone to forgetfulness. That the Ka'aba, a house of worship dedicated to the unity of God, became a shrine of polytheistic worship and was reclaimed for its original purpose through the prophetic career of Muhammad *is* the meaning of the emotive bond. It is fundamental to the Islamic worldview in which the Ka'aba links the Qur'anic revelation to the whole succession of revelation in history back to the first, the primal revelation of Islam given to Prophet Adam (phonetic transliteration of the Arabic: Aadam). The Ka'aba stands for the Muslim concept of successive revelation uniting them to the entire Judaeo–Christian prophetic tradition and other prophets named and unnamed in the Qur'an. Its meaning is that while human perversity in history has repeatedly lost the significance of revelation, it is always available to be refound, recovered. Therefore, it validates in Muslim thought both history as change and continuity in history, and contributes to the distinctive Muslim concept of cyclical history, rather than the modern Western linear history.

Rushdie's recurrent reference to the Black Stone has its ambiguity. The stone-built cube, the Ka'aba, is the most common image known to Muslims; millions of homes throughout the Muslim world will have some representation of the Ka'aba showing it draped in black cloth, the *kiswa*. There is also a Black Stone (which in actuality is a shiny grey) embedded in the wall of the Ka'aba. Every Muslim learns the story of the black stone, which is associated not with the original building of the Ka'aba but the early career of Prophet Muhammad. Before Muhammad became a prophet, he was known to his fellow citizens as Al Amin, the trustworthy, and asked by the rival factions of the community to determine who should have the honour of replacing the Black Stone in the wall of the Ka'aba after its rebuilding. The significance of the incident is as a demonstration of the probity of character of the man who became their Prophet. It is the association with the life of the Beloved Prophet that leads Muslim pilgrims to strive to touch the black stone when they circumambulate the Ka'aba.

Rushdie gives us the diminution of religion to the secular vision of the history of comparative religion, not a form of exposition growing from a particular community, but one imposed upon them by describers and definers. It is a writing lacking in empathy for the faith, and what comprises the experience of faith. Since the consequences of loss of faith is his theme, then its product is apparent everywhere; it results in a deadening of sensitivity to the rich texture and layering of meaning experienced and known by those with faith and leads to propounding effective inaccuracies. It renders inaudible, invisible and irrelevant 1,400 years of thought, intellectual endeavour, literary creativity and cultural achievement; it writes out of history a quarter of mankind that already are a closed book to a Western audience. Rushdie comes to confirm this closure, not to inform. There is no requirement of believing to be able to intimate something of the meaning cherished by those whose beliefs one does not share. It is the crucial litmus test of artistic imagination, however. It is also the basis for a valid claim of justified comment as opposed to bias or opinionated perversity. The trouble is, a modicum of basic information, unadulterated by the distorted imagination, is necessary before readers can assess the quality of artistic imagination they are offered. And that is precisely where Rushdie is supposed to enter and service the international literary scene.

Then there is the case of Ahmed Sinai, whose dream had been to make a rearrangement of the Qur'an in chronological order. The interest of the reference is that in all his books, Rushdie himself invariably cites the translation of the Qur'an by N.J. Dawood based on such a system. This is, incidentally, one of the most erroneous and mischievous translations and by virtue of its form, one incomprehensibly unfamiliar to Muslims.

From reading *Midnight's Children* it is clear that the author's affection and fondness for Bombay has something to do with its non-conformist eclecticism, not merely in lifestyle but also in matters spiritual. In *Midnight's Children* the more flexible world of Hindu pantheism is ever present as a motif; the author notes himself overwhelmed by a sense of more ancient knowledge, offering a range of different ideas about reality and spiritual endeavour to ponder. This includes the author's fascination with and attraction to the notion of goddesses. The name Bombay itself, he speculates, possibly derives from the original reigning female deity of the region, Mumbadevi. Characters bred in this distinct locale no doubt find it easy to think about a whole diversity of religious ideas, finding such a range of alternatives on their doorstep.

A dissonant reading of Rushdie shows a confusion in his rejectionist attitude towards Islam. On the one hand this strict monotheistic religion has bred a puritan orthodoxy, which is contradicted by the practices of many of its adherents who are, indeed, prone to superstition and many forms of obscurantism. Therefore, Islam as religion is false. On the other hand Islam, despite all the superstition rampant among Muslims, is inferior because it does not acknowledge a multiplicity of gods and goddesses, even as intermediaries to the One God. The multiplicity of gods and goddesses offers complex intricacies of experience and expression of spiritual creativity, a highly secularist notion of religion and theism. The two views are mutually contradictory, but strategically useful to bolster rejection and indicative of Rushdie's perverse indifference to what a believing Muslim really believes, experiences or holds to be important.

Fame Is The Spur

Given the clearly signalled partition in the author's affections between India and Pakistan and the effect it has on his literary style, we should be prepared for *Shame*, this second novel entirely about Pakistan. Its style is again magical realism, but more phantasmic than its predecessor. The construction is more problematic than *Midnight's Children*. Rather than using a personalized narrator, the story is told by a disembodied third person, whom the author interrupts with asides about the real world: he discusses his writing style, he pinpoints allusions and correspondences, lest his signals in the narrative escape us, and he introduces ideas he obviously lacks the confidence or means to accommodate within the narrative.

Purportedly *Shame* is about Omar Khayyam Shakil, a character conceived in shamelessness, and Sufiya Zenobia, his antithesis who attracts and stalks him and embodies all the shame no one else in the novel or its country is prepared to acknowledge. These central characters, however, are peripheral to the story for most of its duration; they are picked up and put down in short order in the midst of another narrative. Unlike the experience of *Midnight's Children*, where to explain one life we have to swallow the world and can see the point of digesting it all, these central characters are over-consciously produced stereotypes with all the devices of their creation showing, wheeled on and off stage mechanically. It is difficult to have much affection for stage props, particularly unlovely ones; what the author cannot achieve is well beyond the scope of a mere reader. Nevertheless, these characters are necessary to extract the moral of the other tale that occupies most of the novel—a thinly veiled excursion through the history of Pakistan, the rivalry between Iskander Harrapa (Zulfikar Ali Bhutto) and Reza Hyder (General Zia-ul-Haq), and their menages. Such plot as there is is designed to move us through the essential incidents of that history and provide a denouement in which the stereotype of shame, after ingesting too much, turns into a beast of wrath and consumes all the characters not so far accounted for by history. The detail is in the history, merely made appropriately phantasmic, and the author's asides; not in the novel at all. In this Pakistan, the papier mache is rendered down to cardboard hoardings, covering what the author insists on telling us he is not really talking about, Pakistan, but which is the only thing in the novel one can identify and get much of a feeling for.

The narrative of the fate of Omar Khayyam Shakil and Sufiya Zenobia, of Bilquis and Reza Hyder, and of Iskie and Rani Harrappa and their little father-worshipping daughter the 'virgin Ironpants' Arjumand (Benazir Bhutto) is one part of *Shame*. The course of the narrative mirrors the history of Pakistan, with Hyder and Harrappa being transparent parodies of the two recent leaders of the country. In Rushdie's view there is little to choose between the failed hope of those who preside over the second generation since Independence, Bhutto and General Zia ul Haq. The starkness that is the conclusion of *Midnight's Children* is the whole of *Shame*. The narrative gets into its stride approximately where its predecessor left off. The ambiguous territory of the narrative is discussed in one of the author's asides:

> The country in this story is not Pakistan, or not quite. There are two countries, real and fictional, occupying the same space, or almost the same space. My story, my fictional country exist, like myself, at a slight angle to reality. (*Shame*, p. 29)

This point is taken up again to discuss the inhibitions the ambiguity gives the narrative:

> But suppose this were a realistic novel! Just think what else I might have to put in. . . . And now I must stop saying what I am not writing about. . . . every story one chooses to tell is a kind of censorship, it prevents the telling of other tales. (*Shame*, pp. 69, 71)

So this is a universal modern fairy tale about Pakistan which is not about Pakistan. How universal the tale is is questionable, since while we get an off-centred portrait, it is so near the outlines of what is conventionally known about Pakistan that the style points only to the country the author is allegedly not writing about. So thinly veiled is the portrait that most of the time we wonder just how near is this risque fairy story to reality. On balance, the whole battery of stylistic devices worked out in *Midnight's Children* and recurring in *The Satanic Verses* are made transparent by Rushdie's own rationale. They are an insubstantial claim to fiction, which claims the justification of 'truth' through imagination; they are deliberately based on factual reality, a device to prevent the books being banned, while leaving the reader still wondering just what is real and what is jumbled reality. The winner in the end is doubt, Rushdie's favourite and essential ideological point.

As a fairy tale the characters are grosser and more extreme than those drawn in *Midnight's Children*. Yet they are lineal descendants if for no other reason than that they answer the question posed in the earlier novel of what grows best in the heat: 'fantasy; unreason; lust'. The hoary old Orientalist fabulations of the East are writ large in *Shame*. A goodly number of the characters seem to have roots and would not be out of place in Kipling alongside the phantoms that haunt Mowberrie Jakes and the demon in *The Mark of the Beast*. Haunting and dreams, a minor theme introduced in *Midnight's Children* in the experience of Mary Pereira, recurs with the two central characters of *Shame*, neither of whom can sleep properly; the idea will crop up yet again in *The Satanic Verses*. Deprived of the ability to sleep and, therefore, perhaps the healing power of dreams, they become phantasms in their waking lives unable to deal with reality, especially prone to religious (fantasies) experience. This was less true of Mary Pereira but will be much more telling in the case of Gibreel Farishta.

However universal this fairy tale is intended to be, it so closely resembles the experience of Pakistan that the author must from time to time burst in to establish the credentials of his relationship to Pakistan:

> Although I have known Pakistan for a long time, I have never lived there for longer than six months at a stretch. Once I went for just two weeks. Between these sixmonthses and fortnights there have been gaps of varying duration. I have learned Pakistan in slices, . . . I think what I'm confessing is that, however I choose to write about over-there, I am forced to reflect that world in fragments of broken mirrors. . . . I must reconcile myself to the inevitability of the missing bits. (*Shame*, p. 69)

This passage is strikingly reminiscent of the incident in *Midnight's Children* when Aadam Aziz falls in love with his future bride by examining her in small sections through a hole in a white sheet. This notion of a vacancy through which reality is perceived runs throughout *Midnight's Children*. When the technique moves to Pakistan in *Shame* it loses a great deal of its artistic force, since it merely heightens the ever-present question of what is imagined and what comes from actual events that occurred in Pakistan. It also begs the not inconsiderable question of the weight and significance that must be allowed for the admitted missing bits.

History quite rightly does not belong only to participants. But any writer will be judged by the appositeness and pertinence of his presentation of what did not happen to him, the quality and character with which he gets inside the temper of recreated people, places and events, the kind of 'truth' he brings forth by trespassing. The judgement on an author's poaching of his story will not only be made by those involved in the history he writes about, but by every reader. The explanation and argument is linked to another digression about Omar Khayyam that interweaves with another theme of Rushdie's asides, migration:

> Omar Khayyam's position as a poet is curious. He was never very popular in his native Persia; and he exists in the West in a translation that is really a complete reworking of his verses, in many cases very different from the spirit (to say nothing of the content) of the original. I, too, am a translated man. I have been *borne across*. It is generally believed that something is always lost in translation; I cling to the notion—and use, in evidence, the success of Fitzgerald-Khayyam—that something can also be gained. (*Shame*, p. 29)

This idea of the translated man recurs as the essence of Saladin Chamcha in *The Satanic Verses*.

Sufiya Zenobia is a more complex creation who begins, we are told, with the author reading a British newspaper report of an Asian father who murdered his obviously loved daughter for allegedly making love to a white boy. The father's Asian friends and relatives all refused to condemn him. From the newspaper story the author fantasizes about this young girl, who becomes for him Anahita Muhammad, known as Anna; who would speak with an East End accent; who would understand the language her parents spoke at home, but would obstinately refuse to speak a word of it herself; to whom Mecca would mean ballrooms.

Both the central characters of *Shame* then contain allusions to real people and real incidents. But they are also used as embodiments of the ideas that the author wishes to manipulate: shamelessness for Omar Khayyam Shakil and shame for Sufiya Zenobia. These themes are not merely the experience of other people, they are part of the author's own experience of Pakistan. Even the imaginary characters, those who are not obviously modelled on recognizable historic people off-centred by the author, also have their parallels in real life. Part of the creative process is making them stand for ideas the author wishes to discuss. In Anahita Muhammad, the anonymous murdered daughter named in imagination by the author, we have the germ of the daughters of the Shaandaar Cafe in *The Satanic Verses*, one of whom when discovered to be having a sexual liaison is attacked with a carving knife by her mother and survives only because of her skill in martial arts.

It is surely an odd conception that notions of shame are unique, or especially pertinent only to the East. A theme can only be universal when it has its recurrent echoes in all human situations, even if its form is culturally reconstituted. If we have to go running back to the East to see real 'shame, poppy shame' that is lost on the Western world, then we are dealing with a particular cultural notion that fits in well with the received Orientalist vision of the East as violent and barbaric. However, one can not only imagine but can know of many societies where shame is found on every street. One can also draw to mind quite a few instances where young people are shamelessly slaughtered on the altar of pride by family and nation; the means of inflicting cruel punishment are many and varied, but the consequences are painful, fatal and very real. On balance Rushdie particularizes his great theme in such a way as to prevent its having any wider ramifications. His localizing of the story robs it of anything other than a very limited currency. He leaves the reader thinking only of Pakistan and, by extension, of the Muslim world and no further.

Repatriation can only be a consequence of migration. The author tells us that migration is about a loss of history, translation and dreaming:

> When individuals come unstuck from their native land, they are called migrants. When nations do the same thing (Bangladesh) the act is called secession. What is the best thing about migrant peoples and seceded nations? I think it is their hopefulness. (*Shame*, p. 86)

Rushdie deals with migration as a distinct form of historical discontinuity, a very fashionable idea. But his discussion of migration and its effects are more pertinent to *The Satanic Verses* where they are a central notion, than to *Shame* where they are a subliminal feature of the narrative. In both instances he is oblivious to the fact that migration is a central tenet of Islam, indeed the instance from which the Muslim calendar takes its start. For the Muslims who migrated to Pakistan at Partition, the connotation of *hegira*, the migration of Muhammad from Makkah to Medina, was movement to reconnect with identity and history, potentially to heal a discontinuity, not create one. It is a resonance entirely absent in Rushdie's writing.

As a view of migration as a general or universal phenomenon, Rushdie's ideas seem rather one dimensional. True, migration can entail some kind of discontinuity, uprooting and translation, but the range of responses he envisages seem to narrow and reduce the complexity of examples available from the real world. The notion of being cut free from history, memory and time is, after all, completely at odds with the migrant responses of Scots, Irish and Welsh whose diaspora have all contributed wholeheartedly to the recreation of tradition in their native heath, indeed have been influential in creating the world's image of the lands they left behind. It is a distinctively European notion that nationality should be a unitary, homogenized, and totally coterminus cultural identity. Many would claim this to be an historical and distinctive flaw in the European imagination, and one not far removed from the European obsession with and practice of racism. It is quite probable, to use the Celtic example again, that there is at least as much, if not more, Gaelic, Erse and Welsh spoken overseas as in Scotland, Ireland and Wales. And language is the receptacle of conceptual thought, the reservoir of memory and the resonance of the history of a civilization, the vehicle of its continued existence and viability. Perhaps this is why Rushdie always portrays young Asians in Britain as refusing to speak the native tongue of their parents.

There is another response to migration that Rushdie should see, yet misses: migrants clinging more fiercely to traditions of the homeland as a means of defining their identities in new lands that are hostile to them. The point is pertinent to Rushdie's creation Sufiya Zenobia. Surely it is a valid question to ask whether the vengeful father's act of murder is not more attributable to the special circumstances of England rather than being explicable only by removing it to Pakistan? The response of building exclusive walls of distinctiveness to preserve a cherished tradition is not a new one. It has been practised for cultural and religious reasons by Jewish communities of the diaspora, the idea of assimilation being a recent innovation as well as one that has not dented the sense of distinct identity. There are acres of literary and scholarly works suggesting that in migration 'old' ways are recast in a concrete they never had in the homeland, that tradition is subtly remade to make imperishable and inflexible something that was always a growing, changing, adapting force before it shifted locale. Far from coming adrift from history, many migrants cling more tenaciously to history in order to insulate themselves from the present and to cope with newness. This kind of translation of the migrant is not represented in Rushdie's writing, which tends to support the notion that it is the author's singular experience of migration that is universalized and imposed upon every migrant character he creates.

Rushdie wants the reader to unravel a few more layers of his fairy tale about the country that is not Pakistan. 'My story's palimpset-country has, I repeat, no name of its own.' But tiring of this prevarication he determines to give it a name and chooses that supposedly real *bon mot* used by General Napier, which is, in Rushdie's context, triple-edged. Historically, Napier apocryphally despatched the one word telegram 'Peccavi', to convey the meaning 'I have gained possession of Sind', now a province of Pakistan. So the fairy-story country is called 'Peccavistan'. The translation of the Latin is 'I have sinned', which could convey the meaning of the fairy-tale name as 'the land of sinners'. And in the narrative and asides the grievous faults of this land are many and interrelated:

> Repression is a seamless garment; a society which is authoritarian in its social and sexual codes, which crushes its women beneath the intolerable burdens of honour and propriety, breeds repressions of other kinds as well. Contrariwise: dictators are always—or at least in public, on other people's behalf—puritanical. (*Shame*, p. 173)

One cannot argue with the analysis that one repression begets another. The insight comes from properly understanding how repression is generated and validated, and what kind of alternatives there are to repression. But that is to rush ahead to the substance of *The Satanic Verses*. The female tales are those of Bilquis Hyder, who becomes demented and is secluded; Rani Harappa, who is married and neglected in seclusion; Good News Hyder, who hangs herself, unable to bear any longer the burden of perpetual childbirth and motherhood; and, of course, Sufiya Zenobia, who absorbs everyone's unfelt shame and explodes in the final denouement. The male tales are those of the shameless, which includes the dictators, one elected, one not, Iskander Harappa and Reza Hyder.

The dictators provide reason for another aside that considers the nature of the fairy-tale duel between Harappa and Hyder by way of an analysis of Buchner's play *Danton's Death*, as discussed by the author and two Pakistani friends. The political context of this aside is just another expression of the author's perennial fascination with duality that runs throughout these three novels. The complications are not what matters, the important point is that Rushdie's vision of everything is fundamentally dualistic and his artistic genre is playing out the permutations and sorting out the nature of the interconnections and operative levels of duality. If one does not subscribe to the Manichaean ideology, then the thrust of the novels must appear reductive and dismissive of much that is important but cast aside to maintain the author's view of what makes characters and events significant.

In *Shame*, everything that pertains to the idea of duality reads like a lofty imposition from the far remove of the author upon characters who in their narrative portrayal are themselves too cardboard thin to sustain the weight. And since Iskander Harappa and Reza Hyder are both downright awful, it is hard too see what useful insight this dualistic analysis, whether extrinsic or intrinsic to their natures, can possibly offer. We are on more useful but still trite ground with his comment on the recurrence and persistence of dictatorship. We are not allowed to forget that this discussion of dictators, courtesy of *Danton's Death*, has topical relevance: 'My friends and I had liked Danton's Death; in the age of Khomeini, etc., it seemed most apposite'. This must be linked with the recurrent references in the asides and the fairy story, emphasizing the point that Pakistan/Peccavistan was founded upon a religious rationale, conceived as God's country. As for the topical reference, we are of course told that Pakistan was an Islamic Republic before Khomeini came on the scene, and its relationship to 'Islamic fundamentalism' is different. As a direct consideration of the phenomenon we are told:

> Few mythologies survive close examination, however. And they can become very unpopular indeed if they're rammed down people's throats. . . . In the end you get sick of it, lose faith in the faith, if not qua faith then certainly as the basis of a state. And then the dictator falls, and it is discovered that he has brought God down with him, that the justifying myth of the nation has been unmade. This leaves only two options: disintegration, or a new dictatorship . . . no, there is a third, and I shall not be so pessimistic as to deny its possibility. The third option is the substitution of a new myth for the old one. Here are three such myths, all available from stock at short notice: liberty, equality, fraternity. I recommend them highly. (*Shame*, p. 251)

As in *Midnight's Children*, the new nation has two alternatives and a third option. The recipe is consistent.

There is a great deal of pertinent, warranted and needed pointing-the-finger at the shortcomings, hypocrisy, corruption, backsliding, pettifogging petty and downright self-righteous pomposity of Muslims in Rushdie's portrayal, which derives from the Pakistani model, but has relevance to the rest of the Muslim world. One finds nothing in Rushdie that has not been said by many another, Muslim and non-Muslim, in similar terms. Pointing-the-finger is one thing. What one fails to find in Rushdie is any insight, any intuitive artistic truth through fiction to illuminate the accuracy of his name-calling and make it a genuine or significant analysis of the problems. His barbs are accurate enough, but they are descriptive; as analysis, whether political, social or religious, they are shallow in the extreme. Overall they lead one to the conclusion that here one has a genuine Orientalist-indoctrinated, secular-minded brown sahib whose response to the problem of his own Muslim identity, which he is saddled with wherever he goes, is to produce *bona fide* poison-pen letters.

Rushdie's analysis of Islamic 'fundamentalism' fails to distinguish the thing itself. He seems to think its meaning self-evident, yet for anyone with a knowledge of the Muslim world and modern Islamic thought the term itself has no definitional power; it obscures the things that are interesting and relevant in understanding people, and more importantly, how those people conceive of realizing their aspirations. It is only a definition for Western pundits who use it as a blanket phrase of bogyism. It is certainly true that Islamic fundamentalism, as popularly understood in the West, can be manipulated for political opportunism and has been in more countries than Pakistan. He is quite right to argue that politicians, from the top down, make use of words and symbols of power that people are reluctant to oppose. In this sense 'fundamentalism' is not much different from a number of versions of Islamic 'isms' that have been put on offer by political leaders. Beyond that, to say that Rushdie's analysis is idiotic and simplistic is to give him the benefit of a doubt he clearly does not deserve.

On the broad frame of history, Islam is not the only system of belief that has outlived the collective shortcomings of its practitioners. On the direct point for 1,400 years, Muslim aspiration for an Islamic state has retained its potency, because it is a vision of a just social order that is the inseparable and necessary expression of personal commitment to faith. The aspiration exists irrespective of and despite political opportunism and arcane argument on how such a state should be organized. The 'fundamentalism' of the quest for an Islamic state quite simply has a legitimacy within the Islamic worldview that far exceeds any historic attempt to realize the ideal. Christianity has not lost its validity through history because it has been manipulated by institutions or individuals in ways that can be dubbed unChristian. Liberation theology is today a vibrant attempt to write the moral and ethical vision of Christianity upon the institutions and practice of whole societies, whose power brokers also lay claim to running Christian societies and dub the rising force of idealism heretical, Marxist-inspired subversion. Marxism itself is a system of belief that is still maintained by people while nations trek determinedly from every article of practice that is central to their creed. It even survives the dismantling of communist states and the mass rejection of the Communist Party throughout Eastern Europe. Quite simply, this ramming down the throats, leading inevitably to the bringing down not just of dictators but of God as well, is too naive to illuminate anything. It reads like the author's expression of wish fulfilment rather than insight into the complexities of what is happening inside the Muslim world today.

To describe Islam as a mythology that cannot survive close examination is a point-of-view certainly. It is a far from extraordinary, partial, opinionated point-of-view. It is the exported wisdom of generations of Western writers on Islam. What it leaves out of the picture is Islam as a civilization derived from religious inspiration that has been the stuff of scholarship, thought and analysis, a whole civilizational world of ideas and their history as held and experienced by the believing Muslim. A believer who stands within his or her own tradition is a character that never receives close, let alone sympathetic or empathetic, attention in the artistic vision of Rushdie. Any cursory examination of the works currently being produced by Muslim writers, under the only appropriate heading of Islamic thought, would show the vitality and variety of ideas that are being debated, often spurred on by the desire to recover the high ground from political opportunism. Clearly this is not a world familiar to Rushdie any more than to the rest of Western society. The point is not whether one is arguing for or against Islam, or even whether one thinks Islam is a good or a bad thing. The point is that by the transparency of his analysis, Rushdie is showing his own notion of Islam, giving us another instance of his angle of attack, while demonstrating how little concerned he is to come to terms with what Muslims themselves are thinking and saying. Rushdie is writing about Islam while censoring the majority of believing Muslims out of all his tales.

In *Shame* his preoccupation is with Islam as lived by Muslims. His idea of Islam is as a series of religious rules pertaining to personal piety. Nowhere in his analysis does he acknowledge the moral and ethical ideas, the conceptual principles about the nature of society and the relationship of the individual to the collective which are at the core of Islam. Rushdie abolishes Islam as civilization. Beyond this deconstruction, what passes for analysis takes very little account of Pakistan as part of the world, just as his view of India paid little heed to the influence of the real world on the failed hopes and ruined dreams of independence. For Muslims around the world 'fundamentalism'—what it is or should mean—has to tackle a whole series of impediments foisted on it by discontinuities created in history: decline from within and imposition from without, which includes colonialism and the modernizing experiments.

Pakistan, or rather the Indian subcontinent, is a prime example of a deliberate colonial policy of confining Islam to the minimalist redoubt of personal piety and personal customary law that has distorted the emphasis of Islamic thought and practice that so-called 'fundamentalism' is designed to counteract. The consequence is that the bulk of Islamic law has had no practice for centuries and only limited currency as a field of abstract thought in which Muslim scholars whose education does not embrace knowledge of this world have specialized. At the same time, those Muslims who have worldly knowledge are deficient in specialized expertise in the vast field of Islamic jurisprudence and classical heritage. Thinking about resolving that problem is certainly not the stock-in-trade of dictators from the top down, but it is widespread in Pakistan, as elsewhere in the Muslim world, among a whole range of people holding a wide range of opinions.

The other strand of empathy with a Muslim consciousness that one can never find in Rushdie, yet has a serious impact upon 'fundamentalism' of all kinds, is the sense of the Muslim as someone facing a hostile world. That would be a worthy topic for an artist as well as fuel for a reasoned analysis of political events in the Muslim world. But that could obviously not come from Rushdie, whose consistent angle of attack is clearly formed by Orientalist notions of Islam. Therefore, Rushdie falls back upon a dualistic set of options—disintegration or a new dictatorship—to which he adds his own third option, the substitution of a new myth 'available from stock at short notice: liberty, equality, fraternity. I recommend them highly.' And so he may.

The point is that there are about one billion Muslims around the world who not merely believe but know in the roots of their being that the best source of these ideals is Islam—the quest for liberty, equality and fraternity, along with justice, mercy, tolerance and a host of other values they have been taught and *know* as the essence of the Islamic moral and ethical vision of human purpose in the world. That is precisely what 'fundamentalism' means to them. It is from this source, Islam, that they are struggling to bring these ideals into reality in the life of their societies, which is not what Salman Rushdie means at all, nor an option he would appear capable of comprehending or articulating through his 'art' in even one of his characters.

From the horror of certainty, which is Rushdie personified, to the shamefully inadequate way the religiously inclined characters in his novels are personified is an easy step. Loss of faith is his theme; the nature of faith, the faithful experience is not. Loss of faith humanizes, faith is a grotesque. The consequence is to be found in all his novels in mocking, demeaning, scourging and scandalizing the cardboard cut-out representatives of the 'faithful' to exorcise them from his mental background, to distance them from the self Rushdie has intentionally built for himself. The 'faithful' are not perfect—they are not what they ought to be—are they what they can only be?—they have let down what cannot be believed in—are they not exactly as the thing that cannot be believed in intends? The mutually contradictory confusion is a Rushdieism. The loss of faith kills God; it makes religion merely a human endeavour, so there can never be the space to comprehend the distinction that motivates the faithful: that God exists, therefore, there is always hope and potential to acknowledge error and reform. The only conclusion is that the faithful are the culprits: villify them, humiliate them, take everything they cherish and hold sacred and trample on it, leave nothing they hold to for hope, comfort and security undesecrated. Get all the angst off one's own shoulders and place it at a distance from one's own purified and uplifted, secularly enlightened self. Leave what cannot be incorporated, contemplated or endured as the realm fit only for ridicule and abuse.

In *Shame* the interruptive voice of the author speaking nakedly to the reader gives a clear demonstration of how Salman Rushdie goes about making his stories and the meaning he intends them to have. We are also given much essential information about the ideas of the author unmasked from behind his storytelling and his connections with his subject matter which includes this comment:

> I tell myself this will be a novel of leavetaking, my last words on the East from which, many years ago, I began to come loose. I do not always believe myself when I say this. It is part of the world to which, whether I like it or not, I am still joined, if only by elastic bands. (*Shame*, p. 28)

Rushdie has made the claim that he is a Third World writer, that he writes as an insider about the guts and sinews of India and Pakistan and not as a Western European with a brief acquaintance with the subcontinent would. This is not a claim that we are sweeping away or necessarily denying. The brown sahib can easily contain Salman Rushdie within the diverse repertoire of the subcontinent. Brown sahibdom, migration and consequent translation, indoctrination in or mere personal affinity for the Orientalist vision of the Orient all play their part in his writing. Identifying these strands is to locate an author and his genre, the better to understand what he has to say. The claim of writing as an insider does not of itself make Rushdie any more authentic or authoritative, neither does it insulate him from ignorance or inaccuracy, nor make him freer to take liberties than anyone else. It is perfectly possible to admire much in Rushdie's ability as a writer while feeling that he illumines only a narrow trove of the human condition, that we learn more about the human dilemma of Salman Rushdie than he has to tell us about the broad canvases on which he sets his own anguish about why the subcontinent is not better than it is.

At the end of the day one locates Salman Rushdie's writings to understand the artistic truth he provides, the manner in which, if at all, he illumines his themes. Because Rushdie is a brown sahib his Western readers assume he gives them an artistic truth superior to the Western preoccupation with the Orient. It takes knowledge of the context, the diversity of the Orient, the wealth and meaning of its tradition and history, to assess its real worth. When examined thus Rushdie emerges as little more than the distorted imagination writ large.

Six
Deconstructing Satan

'What kind of idea are you?' is the intellectual question asked in *The Satanic Verses*, its importance emphasized by Rushdie, both in publicizing the book and in reacting to protesters. It is recurrent and in two parts: 'any new idea is asked two questions. When it's weak: will it compromise? . . . How do you behave when you win?' Although valid and important, the way the question is posed does not require anyone to concede it is *the* central question of most enduring significance to the existence or the practice of faith. If this is the question, then the thrust of the narrative must be seen as its discussion. And the discussion partakes of the nature of the narrative, convoluted, difficult to follow, episodic, entangled with a whole range of subsidiary possibilities, ultimately leaving no clear conclusion except the triumph of the other question posed by Rushdie that alone admits of answer: 'What is the opposite of faith? Not disbelief. Too final, certain, closed. Itself a kind of belief. Doubt.'

We do not demur from Timothy Brennan's observation that *The Satanic Verses* is essentially a religious book, in the sense that it is about the nature of religion. It is not a book about migration or translation, the level on which most reviewers have been content to treat the text. To understand the controversy surrounding this book requires taking it seriously as a religious book—then the blasphemous passages can be perceived as expressions of a broader project. As a religious book, *The Satanic Verses* is not disinterested; it has its own theology and projects itself, as Brennan wrote, 'as a rival Qur'an'. 'To ask, "Is my sense of right divine, or only a form of arrogance?" is to subscribe to the religion of doubt that Rushdie would like to see expand and flourish.' As a religious book, *The Satanic Verses* is an ideological text deliberately constructed on the basis of an overt ideology: secularism. Muslims, of course, have no special right to declare secularism illicit as a choice for other people, but they do have an entirely legitimate right to demur when other people's secularism unwarrantably impinges on their choice of belief. Such is the case of *The Satanic Verses*, which manufactures its secular credo through erroneous manipulation of a clearly indicated religion —Islam—through blasphemy, scurrility, ridicule and abuse. Its transgressions are advanced for an audience well prepared for its argument, a Western readership. However, the subtle codification employed within the book depends upon a knowledge of Islam that is neither current nor general among that audience. The level of comprehension of the book shown by the media coverage of the Rushdie affair is proof of the impossibility of engaging in a rational debate on the substantive issues it raises. So constructed is the status quo that whatever Muslims say or do, they can only appear ridiculous to Westerners.

Many Western critics have said that they cannot understand why Muslims are raising such a fuss. They have read the passages complained of and fail to see what is so offensive. This response is as multi-layered and worthy of analysis as Rushdie's book, for they are mutually revealing. The Western reader arrives at the novel, however well intentioned, with a landscape of history and ideas already in mind, shaped by scholarly Orientalist outpourings; therefore, there is nothing in this novel they might not have expected. Then there is another layer of response, shaped by secularism. Religious text is given in history and its reality lost in the accidents of history; however, the fundamentalist takes it literally. The recovery of text must be through the study of motivation and humanness. More humane than religious tradition, secularism is the only true illuminator of the intersection of the sacred with time, since it is the only open-minded element. The leap of imagination is what links people to the era of text; therefore, the artist is well fitted to helping people approach the characters who speak of the sacred, the prophets. For the Western reader all this is self-evident and arises from both the nature of the sacred text they are used to, and the history of ideas and events that links them to their sacred textual sources. The artist saying the unsayable, thinking the unthinkable, has been part not merely of the quest but a prime agent in securing what are called human freedoms; that is how history has been made. In the way he handles his source material, the themes he selects and the attitude with which he treats them, Rushdie is part of that process.

The trouble among Muslims is incomprehensible, since to be understood it must be seen as the product of not just a different sacred text but a different history of ideas and events linked to that text. What Western readers do not see, are ignorant of, is the entirely different constellation of thought and feeling occasioned by Islam for Muslims. In part, the consternation of the Western audience must come from having assumed that Rushdie would be a bridge between these two civilizations, rather than a manifestation of their own with the idiomatic turn of phrase of the subcontinent.

An underlying 'idea' of the novel is that good and evil exist side by side, inhabiting the same space, are so much a part of each human being and even

God, so Rushdie alleges, as to be at times indistinguishable or at least confusing. The whole episode of the so-called satanic verses, which were supposed to have been revealed to the Prophet Muhammad by the Devil and later abrogated, is used to illustrate this notion. Its echoes are seen in the development of the central characters, Gibreel Farishta and Saladin Chamcha, and in their transformation once they are born anew after the midair explosion that lands them on the shores of England. Other echoes are in Salman Farsi, the migrant's adulteraton of a revelation when acting as a scribe to Mahound, which also mirrors the prophet's temptation. However, before we discuss the origins of the historic story, it is necessary to say a few words about the nature and character of the Qur'an.

Power of the Word

For Muslims the Qur'an *is* the word of God. It was revealed through the agency of the angel Gibreel (Gabriel) to the Prophet Muhammad over the course of twenty-three years, from 609 to 632 CE. An essential article of belief for a Muslim is to accept the Qur'an as a direct, literal narration of God's word. The literal truth of the Qur'an is the divine origin of its specific Arabic text, rather than the divine inspiration accorded by Christian fundamentalists to the Bible. Since the Qur'an itself cautions the believer that it uses metaphor and allegory to express that which is beyond ordinary human experience, it is clear that Muslims do not take every word as the exact counterpart of common phenomena or the literal expression of the nature of metaphysical reality. The language of the Qur'an is of particular significance; it is totally different from the ordinary language used by the Prophet Muhammad himself in the course of his life as the Messenger, which are amply recorded in the *hadith*, or his sayings and traditions. The hadith are today the source book for the Sunnah, the practical example given by the Prophet of how to live an Islamic life and an essential second source of Islam. The literary style and language of the Qur'an is clearly distinguished from historic or contemporary Arabic, whether it be poetry or prose, spoken or written. There is not the slightest resemblance in any surviving text of any form of Arabic to the language of the Qur'an, the power and eloquence of which makes an immediate impact, even on those who do not understand Arabic.

The literary style of the Qur'an makes it impossible to add or substract anything without doing violence to the whole—any alteration would be like changing a note or two in Beethoven's *Ninth Symphony*, and would resound like the obvious false notes in the symphony's performance. The Qur'an itself challenges its readers to produce even a single verse of its quality: 'And if you are in doubt as to that which We have revealed to our servant, then produce a surah like unto it and call on your helpers besides Allah, if you are truthful' (2:23). This challenge has indisputably stood the test of time as is acknowledged by all commentators of East or West, Muslim or non-Muslim.

It was the practice of the Prophet Muhammad to memorize the revelations himself, as did many of his companions, and he appointed scribes to write down the revelations almost immediately. It was his custom during each Ramadan, the fasting month, to recite and review the whole of the Qur'an that had been revealed to that point, and he regularly recited verses in the prayers. As the Qur'an refers to itself as a Book, the revelations had to be written in the form of a book, with chapters and between covers. The Book was complete in every detail just before the death of the Prophet. Not just the whole book was known, from cover to cover, but the existence of every word in that Book was known without any doubt since the time of the first revelation. Moveover, the details of when and where each verse was revealed are also accurately known.

The authorship of the Qur'an as the literal word of God is the source of the authority of its text, the completed guidance of God to mankind, valid for all time. The content of the text points to and reinforces the process by which it was applied to the organization of the daily life of the Prophet and the formation of a community of believers. Knowing the times and places in which it was revealed became an essential element in interpreting the meaning of the Qur'an. Information on historical context was necessary to distinguish between the eternally valid principles and the time-bound specifics to which revelation refers. For these reasons Islam is a civilization fully rooted in history. The worldview of Islam has been created by the consistent exertions of Muslims to clarify the origins of their identity in the most meticulous and punctilious detail. The Prophet Muhammad cautioned his followers to make the distinction between the words of divine revelation, his words as a Prophet under divine guidance which provided the example for Muslims to follow, and his words as an ordinary human being who expressed opinions which could be subject to correction. The body of *hadith* records numerous instances of his making these distinctions clear. By the insistence of the Prophet and the exertions of the community, the Qur'an is completely distinct from the body of *hadith*, the record of the words, deeds and tacit agreements of the Prophet which began to be collected and codified at a much later date and which have always been the subject of critical method before being accepted as authentic.

The focus on history and the processes of history has a special significance in the Qur'an, which acknowledges previous revelations from God that have been granted to numerous prophets. It is an article of belief equally incumbent upon Muslims to believe in other books of God and other prophets of God, for each of them brought the same religion—the message of Islam, submission to God. The distinction which is extensively discussed in the Qur'an is the process by which this pure message was lost, distorted or corrupted by the processes of history and the influence of human nature. Preserving the purity of the text of the Qur'an is central to the identity, ethic and ethos of Muslims. It is for this reason that meticulous scholarship was brought to bear by generation after generation of Muslim scholars to know the Qur'an and the Prophet as historical realities. The historic accumulation of this process is the rational and emotional response of all Muslims to anything which might in any circumstance dilute, distort or cast doubt on these established relationships: authorship, authority, community and the specifics of the Qur'an's identity.

The notion of the leap of faith and cloud of unknowing are totally foreign to the Muslim consciousness where the basics of religion are concerned. The functional position of revealed text and Prophetic example amply demonstrate the rationalist temper and the sound rationalist methodology with which early Muslims set about collecting, preserving, codifying and critically examining their historical record. This process of historiography is human, a work of the intellect in the context of time and has itself been the subject of perennial critical analysis by Muslims through history to the present day. What consistently leads Muslims to charge Orientalist writers on Islam with distortion, misrepresentation and misunderstanding is their eclectic selection from within this vast body of evidence, their taking odd references out of context without acknowledging the other contending body of records. In the formation of the Orientalist view of Islam, the Muslim has no voice. Western writers assume that because central matters of faith are concerned, Muslims cannot possibly be 'objective' and, therefore, must have distorted the record themselves. For the Muslim, however, knowledge and reason are two of the inescapable constituents of *iman*, faith, and necessary precursors and accompaniments to faith. Unless this major distinction at the very core of their worldview is understood, it is not possible to comprehend the Muslim reaction to Rushdie or properly to lay a foundation for analysis of his book and its elevation to a cause celebre.

The Sting

The story of the so-called satanic verses should be viewed in this background. In Rushdie, Mahound is offered a compromise by the Grandee of Jahilia; he returns to Mount Cone where he wrestles with Gibreel Farishta, who at this point is the dual identity of the Archangel Gibreel and the Prophet. After revelation, Mahound returns to attend the poetry competition underway in Jahilia. Rushdie actually quotes Surah An-Najam (the Star), chapter 53, verses 1–18, then adds the so-called satanic verses. These verses reverberate through Gibreel Farishta's head in a number of places in the novel.

Rushdie did not invent the satanic verses, for they form part of the historical record and occur in the writings of exegetes and biographers. The way he inserts them into the story of Mahound closely parallels the way they are reported in the historical record. What Rushdie signally fails to do, however, is to notice the discussion of this episode within the historical record, to give any play to the reasons why this incident has been rejected. Of the major classical historians of Islam, Al-Tabari and ibn Saad have mentioned the incident, although they vary considerably in the detail. They were explicitly recording all events and stories concerning the Prophet that were known to exist.

As reported by Tabari, 'Satan cast on his [Muhammad's] tongue, because of his inner debates and what he desired to bring to his people, the words: "These are the high flying cranes; verily their intercession is accepted with approval".' The incident occurred while Prophet Muhammad was reciting Surah An-Najam at prayers in the mosque. At the end of the surah the Prophet and all the Muslims prostrated themselves. 'Those polytheists of the Quraysh and others who were in the mosque likewise prostrated themselves because of the reference to their gods which they had heard.' Tabari said that when Muslims who had fled persecution in Makkah by taking refuge in Abyssinia under the protection of the Negus heard of this event, they returned to their home city. Gabriel came to the Prophet and told him that he had recited words that had not been brought to him from God, which upset the Prophet. Then God cancelled what Satan had cast by the revelation of Surah 22:52. Thus having removed the sorrow Muhammad felt, God revealed Surah 53:21–23, 26. When Muhammad brought this revelation before the people, the Quraysh declared he had altered what he had previously stated and brought something else. The words of the satanic verses were on the lips of all the polytheists and their abrogation led them to become ill-disposed and more violent to the Muslims. At this point the Muslims returning from Abyssinia arrived, but could only enter the city under protection or in secrecy.

Tabari gave a second version of this same incident in which the wording of the satanic verses themselves was different, ending with the word *la-turja*, meaning to be desired or hoped for, instead of *turtada*, meaning accepted with approval. Also different in the two versions are the subsequent events. In the second version when Gabriel is reviewing the surah with the Prophet and they come to the two phrases Satan had cast upon his tongue, Gabriel tells the Prophet he did not bring them. Then God reveals the following verses:

> They are constantly trying to tempt you away from that which we have revealed to you, so that you may substitute in its place something of your own, in which case they would have actively taken you as a friend. And if We had not made you firm, you might have indeed inclined to them a little. Then We would have made you taste a double punishment in this life and double punishment after death and then you would not have found any helper against us. (Qur'an 17:73-5)

This made the Prophet feel guilty and afraid until such time as the following verses were revealed:

> Whenever We sent a Messenger or a Prophet before you and he framed a desire, Satan put obstacles in it. Then Allah removes the obstacles placed by Satan and He firmly establishes His signs. (Qur'an 22:52)

This version then notes that when those who had emigrated to Abyssinia heard that all the people of Makkah had accepted Islam, they returned but found that the people had reversed their decision when the satanic verses were abrogated.

This then is the story of the satanic verses as reported by the classical Muslim historian al-Tabari. It is not unknown to classical writers, nor has it been suppressed by them; rather, it has been subjected to the critical process and rejected as a spurious invention that does not form part of the authentic tradition. The incident has, however, been written about extensively by modern Orientalists, provoking again a reasoned response from modern Muslim scholars. The contention between Muslim scholars and Orientalists is the partiality and lack of rigour with which this incident is accepted by Western writers, in contrast to the more exhaustive methodology used by classical Muslim scholars. The story is totally rejected by Muslim historians for the following reasons:

1. Traditionally, any event in the early history of Islam is only accepted as authentic if it is reported by most, if not all, classical historians. The satanic verses story is either ignored or rejected as preposterous folklore by all the major classical historians, including ibn Ishaq, ibn Hisham, al-Suhayli, ibn Kathir, al-Bayhaqi, Qadi Iyad, ibn Khuzayma, al-Razi, al-Qurtabi, al-Ayni and al-Shawkani.

2. Al-Tabari is considered the most uncritical of classical historians, because

he was a chronicler who reported every event and story that was circulating during the time of the Prophet in Makkah, often without critical evaluation. He was a compendium-maker—the separation of historical fact from fable he left to others.

3. A chronological examination of the story reveals irrational elements. The satanic-verses incident happened after the first batch of Muslims had migrated to Abyssinia. We know that this migration took place in the month of Rajab during the fifth year of the Prophetic mission, or eight years before the migration of the Prophet Muhammad to Medina—*the hijra*, which marks the beginning of the Muslim calendar. The verses (17:73-5) which were revealed to 'admonish' the Prophet, according to the story, were not in fact revealed until after the event of the *miraj*, or the ascension of the Prophet, which occurred two to three years before the hijra. The verses which were revealed to abrogate the so-called satanic verses (22:52) were revealed in the first year of the hijra, that is eight to nine years after the satanic verses incident. It is straining credulity to believe that the Prophet was 'admonished' six years after the event; that the offending verses, which undermined the very basis of the Qur'anic message and bear no relation whatsoever to any other passage or reference in it, were tolerated for nine years before they were abrogated. Further, if the sequence of events in the second version is taken, the subsequent verses of Surah al-Najam which led the Quraysh to institute renewed and harsher repression of the Muslims, which is historically well attested, was without any reason, since this section of the surah was revealed only after the abrogation of the satanic verses by Surah 22:53—which would mean after the hijra or when the Muslims had already left Makkah!

4. When the satanic verses are placed in the body of verses in Surah al-Najam where they were supposed to be, which would be the meaning of Tabari's first version of the incident, then the whole sense of the verses becomes meaningless and a clear contradiction emerges: on the one hand, the dieties are being praised, and in the next verses they are totally discredited. It is also difficult to believe that the idolators would have been fooled by the passage to believe that the Prophet was making a conciliatory gesture towards them.

5. Again on purely rational grounds, the satanic verses were the antithesis of everything the Qur'an had said up to that particular event and continued to say after the incident. If there was even an iota of truth in the story, it would have caused a major scandal in the early history of Islam and the incident would have been reported in the extensive hadith literature.

6. Nothing in early Islamic history or the hadith literature is accepted without thorough criticism based on certain rules and principles. As Manazir Ahsan explained:

> The Muslim traditionalists quite often evaluate hadith on the basis of *riwaya* (the statement or the news based on the chain of narrators and the text of the hadith) as well as *diraya* (credibility of the statement). It means that if something has been attributed to the Prophet of Islam through apparently sound hadith, it will not automatically be accepted if it goes against the Qur'an and other established traditions and cannot be justified by reasoning. It is here that even if one regards the story of the 'satanic verses' as sound on the ground that it has been narrated by a number of Muslim scholars or because it conforms to the requirements of a true narration (which it lacks), no Muslim traditionalist will accept this story because it stands in clear contradiction to the established beliefs of Muslims. (Ahsan, 'Satanic Verses')

Internal and external evidence then leads Muslims to reject this whole incident as preposterous. Further, it leads them to note that Western writers who have speculated on the incident have not studied the evidence relating to the time sequence of verses cited in Tabari, which would demolish their speculative reasons for accepting the incident. Then again one can see that the authoritative collections of hadith, those of al-Bukhari, Muslim, Abu Dawud, Nasai and Ahmad bin Hanbal, record an incident where the Prophet recited the verses of Surah Najam in a prayer at the Ka'aba when the idolators of Makkah who were present were so overawed by the eloquence of the Qur'an that they joined him in the prostration. Given that these listeners described the Qur'an as magic and the Prophet himself as a magician, one has an instance that invites speculation. It is as a work of speculation invented by either pagan Quraysh or later zindiqs, non-Muslims concealing their unbelief by pretending to be members of the ummah (Muslim community), that the divergent forms of the satanic verses incident have been interpreted by Muslim commentators. If one is to speculate, then the historical circumstances make it more plausible to attribute motives to the non-Muslims for needing to justify their joining the Muslims in their prostration than to the Prophet for trying to mollify the pagans.

Is Muslim anger at Rushdie simply a matter that he has reiterated the incident of the satanic verses? Since we have shown that the incident occurs in the Muslims' own historical record, this would unquestionably be unjust. To join the ranks of the Orientalists and again retail a rejected incident without acknowledgement of the long history of analysis which has demolished its credibility would clearly pigeon-hole Rushdie's position vis-a-vis his Muslim background and the contemporary Muslim community, but could hardly constitute grounds for the furore that now embroils a world-wide literary community and their governments. It would be a matter for annoyance and no more. The reasons for Muslim anger, profound offence and dubbing of Rushdie's words as blasphemy reach much deeper and are far more central to the entire thrust of his book than this one incident. It is the precision and careful selection of the satanic verses as a vehicle for advancing his proposition about the nature of religion and revelation, the encrusted and encoded thesis of Rushdie's book, that so offends.

The argument worked out through the character of Gibreel Farishta is that revelation arises from within the desires, personality and psychology of human prophets; hence, revelation is not divine. All the strands of handling the satanic verses, and the echoes in other strands of the book reiterate this point. The character of Gibreel Farishta takes the reader within Rushdie's view of revelation, to establish through one incident, carefully chosen, that we should not look to God but to men, and especially to men doing violence to women, to understand the nature of the founding of 'one of the world's great religions', and by implication and clear inference, all religion.

Beyond Rushdie's opinion of the derivation of revelation, which is for the Muslim and every other religious person a clear blasphemy, there is the calculated nature of the construction of argument which constitutes a second blasphemy. The second strand is the mixing of fact and fiction to create confusion and to promote doubt, making the recovery of truth more difficult for readers. For the Muslim, truth is attainable through knowledge; knowledge is both a constituent of faith and a means to attaining faith. Knowledge succeeds by distinguishing fact from fiction and making their separation clear. This is the invariable practice of traditional Muslim thought; its insistent emphasis is the separation and clear demarcation of fact from fable, so that the irreducible substance of faith can be known. Commentators on Rushdie's book constantly stress that he is, after all, setting the whole thing in fiction, and what is more, as a dream. The point for the Muslim is that by working in fiction with that which is fact, and debatable fact at that, the only conceivable result is to publish a confusion. By virtue of Rushdie's reputation and the support of his publishing agents, this confusion will become widespread among those without the means to judge or to evaluate the facts contained within the fiction. Knowingly to spread confusion, especially to such an audience, is a blasphemy and a *fitna* (strife), since it defies one of the most central tenets of Islamic consciousness. This is not the notion that God needs to be defended from impudent artistic licence, as many a critic has seemed to suggest. God's Word, divine guidance, is a mercy granted to strengthen that God-created faculty within each human being to distinguish truth from error, to exercise moral and intellectual discernment. The failure to exercise this faculty of discernment is, according to the Qur'an, one of the reasons for the corruptions and sufferings human beings have brought upon themselves in history. It is people who need defending from the ease with which confusion, forgetfulness and erroneous ideas can lead them away from God and His eternal messages which are a means for human perfectability. So it is not the defence of God which so preoccupies Muslim protesters but the defence of those historical, factual and knowable distinctions between the divine and human imagination which make God knowable in the complexity of this world and its history. The charge of blasphemy defines a challenge to the essentials of faith such that it prejudices the maintenance or existence of faith by people. To so mingle fact and fiction that there is no hope of disentangling them is to achieve such a blasphemy.

We should note here that Muslims are not the only people who are concerned about the encroachment of fiction upon fact. In quite another context there is widespread concern about the rise of 'faction', the drama documentary, the historically based reconstruction—a powerful new genre of communication. The cause for concern is exactly the same as that argued by Muslims. Without imputing any devious or destructive motive and even with the highest of motives, faction must lead to the blurring of distinctions between events that are knowable and matters of interpretation and opinion. The test when applied to Rushdie must be whether he is writing fantasy or fiction, and to what extent he bases his fiction on fact and the relationship between his fiction and the facts he draws them from.

If we identify the nature of revelation and the role of prophethood as central to Rushdie's concern, then we cannot avoid the way in which he treats the characters of those who experience these events in a variety of ways in the novel. Each of these characters is part of Rushdie's musings on the institution, a reflection or refraction of the ideas he is seeking to convey. Not least of the sources of offence to Muslims is the parody Rushdie presents of the beloved Prophet Muhammad in the shape of Mahound. The offence operates on a number of different levels. First, there is the selection of the name Mahound—a term, as Rushdie acknowledges, of conscious abuse. Then there is the reviling of the person of Mahound by character notes and details that are clearly extracted from the historical record of the person of Prophet Muhammad. All this is a calculated disrespect, a transgression on the reverence in which Muslims view the Prophet. The blasphemy occurs at a much more profound level. It is the subtle mingling of fact to present a distorted picture of the relationship of the Prophet to revelation. In Rushdie's version the substance of revelation, the Qur'an, includes the detail of the Sunnah, the historical record of the Prophet's actions. For Rushdie, revelation is the outward name for the inward desires of a prophet; the history and personality of the prophet determines the nature of the message he conveys to his followers, so this is a logical conflation, the only possible relationship between prophet and text that can be put forward. For the Muslim it is a direct contradiction of the nature of the relationship between the Qur'an and the example of the prophetic Sunnah, which are distinct from each other as the two prime sources for the creation of Islamic civilization and the nature of the faith of Islam.

The Circumference of Guidance

The prophets play a central role in the worldview of Islam. The Qur'an mentions that all peoples have received prophets from God to guide them to the realization of a divine creator. As such, Muslims believe in all the prophets of God and accord them due respect and reverence. Among the prophets named in the Qur'an are Noah, Moses, Jesus and Abraham as Nuh, Musa, Isa and Ibrahim. For Muslims, prophets are not divine, but mortal human beings. However, they are not ordinary men, for they have special characteristics which are known and which elevate them to the status of prophethood. The Muslim conception of prophethood, *risallah*, has been written about by the Indian scholar, Abu Hasan Ali Nadwi, who clearly referred to all prophets and accorded all prophets with the same inherent characteristics. It is unthinkable from a Muslim perspective to see one prophet as a negative reflection of another, since all those 'named and unnamed' by the Qur'an have been chosen by God to fulfil His purpose, His mercy to mankind. The moral conduct of prophets is above reproach: in every affair they are noble, truthful, straightforward and generous. Their intellects are sound and well balanced, their decisions are dictated by wisdom, caution and prudence. It is only in the matter of their prophetic missions that they claim any distinction or mastery in worldly affairs. What they preach about the extra-physical world is not derived from knowledge currently available to the people of their times; in fact, they are often not conversant with the sciences of their age. They surpass others in moral excellence and are models of virtue and righteousness. The prophets have knowledge of reality with an oracular guarantee of truth and certitude unparalleled by the discoveries of the senses and intellect. Such realities are to them personal perceptions beyond doubt or contention. The prophets never claim to wield power over the forces of nature, nor do they claim to have answers to all questions. They await revelation from God for enlightenment, but it is not within their power to obtain revelation to their liking at their own will. Sometimes the revelation is against what they had desired, and it may even admonish them or counsel against their wishes. The prophets are in close communion with the Almighty whose assistance would always appear to be available to them. Sometimes supernatural phenomena would appear to be against the natural law of causation, or to be miracles which cannot be explained away by reason except as the will of God. The prophets, however, never claim to control such miracles, nor do they cause them to occur simply on demand from others or of their own will (*see* Nadwi, pp. 75–81).

The Prophet Muhammad is considered in Islam to be the last Prophet of God. His prophetic mission was lived in the full light of history and is extensively documented. Indeed, the basic data of his life coming from his companions, the first-hand witnesses, fills volumes. We know every aspect of his life, the conditions during his times, his personal affairs as well as his social interactions, what he said and when he said it. The extent of what we know about the Prophet Muhammad can be judged by the account of Abdullah ibn Amr ibn al-As, cited by a large number of sources. It is said that Abdullah, a young Makkan, had the habit of writing down all that the Prophet said. One day his comrades rebuked him, saying that the Prophet was a human being, that he could sometimes be happy and satisfied, at other times annoyed, and that it was not desirable that one should indiscriminately note all that he uttered. When Abdullah asked the Prophet if he could take down all that he said, the Prophet replied, 'Yes'. Abdullah then asked, 'Even when thou art happy and satisfied, even when thou art annoyed?' The Prophet replied, 'Of course! By God! Nothing that comes out of this mouth is ever a lie.' Abdullah called his compilation *Sahifah Sadiqah* (the book of truth). For several generations it was taught as an independent work; later it was incorporated into a large collection of hadith compiled by ibn Hanbal and others. Similarly, a number of the Prophet's companions constantly wrote down what he said and did, the most notable being Anas who remained with the Prophet in his house night and day. Throughout his life, the Prophet had forty-five official scribes who recorded for posterity his behaviour and actions, sayings and traditions. Sira, the biography of Prophet Muhammad, is not just historic fact, it is also living history.

How the Prophet lived, what he actually did, how he accomplished his divine mission, is known as the Sunnah. The Sunnah is the actualization of the prophetic mission and, as such, is considered by Muslims to be the Qur'an in action—in his life the Prophet Muhammad showed how the Qur'an is to be lived. As the Messenger of God, he is the medium of revelation and his life is the concrete implementation of the divine will, the best example and living interpretation of the meaning of the Message in the exigencies of time. The Sunnah cannot be separated from the Message, because the very function of the Prophet is to be a model for the way people can best fulfil the divine purpose and seek God's pleasure in their daily lives. The Qur'an, for example, asks believers to pray, to fast during the month of Ramadan, to go on pilgrimage to Makkah, the hajj, at least once in a lifetime if circumstances permit. It is the Prophet who shows how to pray, how to fast and how to perform the hajj. The Sunnah is an integral part of the Message for Muslims, because it is the essential model of how to put into operation what is absolute. That is why the Prophet himself emphasized his Sunnah and taught it to his companions. He did this both orally and in written form. To make memorizing and understanding easy, he would repeat important things three times. Then he would listen to his companions to ensure that they had learned it correctly, and it was a common practice among his companions to write down the Prophet's deeds and sayings for any absentees. He also established schools in Medina to teach the Qur'an and his Sunnah. The Sunnah, then, is known in minute detail and is taken as *the* model of behaviour by every Muslim; as such the Sunnah is a living institution, which is why Muslims always speak of the Qur'an *and* the Sunnah, the one being the natural extension of the other.

Throughout Muslim history, the emphasis has been on the *fact* of the Sunnah and the sira, which is never mixed with fiction and fables. Scholars of early Islam developed a highly critical and elaborate methodology to weed out the spurious from the authentic, which involved tracing the chain of narrators back to the Prophet, examination of the character of each individual narrator, examination of the space-time questions of when and where they lived and how they met, and examination of the actual text of what the Prophet said and did and its comparison with the teachings of the Qur'an and the dictates of reason. To check a single fact or saying, scholars often travelled hundreds of miles and interviewed hundreds of individuals before reaching a conclusion. Because of the importance Muslims themselves attach to the critical examination of the facts of Prophet Muhammad's life, the fact that his Sunnah is a living example of the teachings of the Qur'an, a model of behaviour to be imitated by all Muslims, the Prophet Muhammad can never be seen as a figure of fiction: he is a fact who lived in real time. However, to conflate the Sunnah with the Qur'an goes against everything the Prophet himself taught; it also would confuse the distinct relationship which enables the Sunnah to be used for expanding the understanding of the meaning of the eternal message of God's word. It is the historical Sunnah, the living example in history that makes it possible to distinguish between the time-bound and eternal principles. Taking the Sunnah as being the same as the Qur'an, as Rushdie does, totally alters the nature and function of the Prophet as he himself taught and expressed it and as the Qur'an states it to be.

What is Rushdie's claim to fiction? He has discussed the nature of his technique in earlier novels. To change a name and enter the phantasmic style of his novels is, Rushdie alleges, sufficient insulation for being fiction, for discussing ideas in such a way that no one need take the matter too seriously. This is surely the most disingenuous of claims. If he is writing fiction, then he is ever insistent that the reader should realize the reference to solid reality on which his stories rely. He has in his earlier work made it clear that the stylistic device of naming characters points to the recurrence of ideas and experience. He is a writer who off-centres things, but that which is seen from an angle is as essential to the meaning of what he writes as to his style; it must be identifiable for his artistic intentions to work. Rushdie then claims that he is not only writing about the things he alludes to by correspondences of naming, but that his meaning and intentions are universal. It is this claim to universality that is most called into question by the very style he uses. If we take the episode of the satanic verses, there is no attempt to fictionalize the sources for this encounter between an archangel and a prophet for the simple reason that Rushdie quotes from the first eighteen verses of Qur'anic Surah An-Najam (the Star) *verbatim* by way of introduction and context.

Rushdie is not imagining an encounter; he is taking all the substance of his narrative from an historical source, closely paralleling the detail contained in the version narrated by al-Tabari. Are the verses of the Qur'an then part of Rushdie's fiction? Most important of all, is it a legitimate use of fiction to manipulate sacred text without acknowledgement? Do not facts have some rights, even in the world of art? If abundance of imagination is supposedly one of Rushdie's claims to literary reputation, then one wonders why he has so insistently to point to his actual models in real fact. He not only indicates he is speaking of the Qur'an by direct quotation but by subsequent reference to 'the true recitation, al-quran' as the text Salman Farsi is engaged in inscribing. And of course Mahound, we are told at the outset, is engaged in founding one of the world's great religions. Lest anyone still miss the point, Mahound's followers are the followers of the religion of submission, the literal translation of the word 'Islam'. There can be no doubt that Rushdie is writing about Islam and Muhammad. If his intention, or any shred of his meaning, is to sustain a claim to universality, to go from the particular to reveal something of universal significance, then we are at least entitled to require that Rushdie does justice to the particularity of the basic facts he sets forth and simultaneously off-centres.

The legal test of a slander or libel is not that a person is necessarily named directly but that any reasonable person could recognize the person intended. In all his work, Salman Rushdie takes great care in naming his characters; it is part of his word-game technique. Look at what the characters in *The Satanic Verses* have to offer: the film actor takes the stage name Gibreel Farishta, meaning the angel Gibreel, before ever encountering the experience wherein he becomes his namesake; his stardom is through appearance in theological epics, prefiguring the central events of the story. Furthermore, Gibreel Farishta's original name is Ismail Najmuddin, Najmuddin meaning star of the faith. It is of course in the Qur'anic chapter entitled the star, Al Najam, that the incident of the satanic verses is alleged to occur. So names are not random, least of all the name chosen for the prophet, Mahound. He calls his character Mahound and explains: 'our mountain-climbing, prophet-motivated solitary is to be the medieval baby-frightener, the Devil's synonym: Mahound'—that is, in mediaeval times this character was known as Mahound. *The Oxford Dictionary of Etymology* defines Mahound as 'the false prophet Mohammad; in the Middle Ages often vaguely imagined to be worshipped as a god'; 'a false god; an idol'; 'a monster, a hideous creature'; 'Used as a name for the devil', also 'as a term of execration applied to a man'. The name Mahound is most familiar in the literary genre known as the *chansons de geste* and as Norman Daniel has convincingly argued in his *Heroes and Saracens*, the characteristics these chansons gave Mahound had a deliberate, informed purpose in that genre. *Chansons de geste* were popular literature during the Crusades. The Saracens in the chansons often appear as little different from their European adversaries; the line of demarcation to distinguish why these two bodies of sturdy chaps, who otherwise could carouse and have a jolly time together, must come to blows is the question of religion. What Norman Daniel argued is that the portrayal of Islam and its Prophet, through the character Mahound, are based on knowledgeable distortions, the making of a thing into something it could not possibly be, to instill hatred and justify hostility. It is hard to accept that this significance is lost on Rushdie. He has written in *Midnight's Children* of the love of correspondences; therefore, it seems legitimate to take the full import of the correspondence as the purpose of selecting the name Mahound: a calculated, informed insult with malign intent.

But surely these events occur in a dream, and should not dreams be taken as doubly fictional? This is clearly the insulating foam advanced on Rushdie's behalf. In dreams we see reality jumbled and distorted. Yet the significance of dreams is taken to be their ability to present insight into reality by the very disjunctions they offer of what is real. The dreams of Gibreel Farishta are remarkable because they jumble only according to a strict ideological code, necessary to sustain the author's argument; the jumbling is entirely according to the canon of a well known and easily identifiable convention of writing about Islam, Orientalism. Dreams are Rushdie's stratagem for presenting his own ideas about religion, monotheism, prophethood and, specifically, about Islam and its Prophet, without having to acknowledge the limits of propriety, respect for the sensitivity of others or the complexity of the historical record. Most of all, the dream stratagem enables him to play a game with historical fact, spicing the novel with a grand sufficiency of historic detail to establish his credentials without having to be responsible to accuracy, or honesty, in handling these facts.

The City of Sand

In *The Satanic Verses*, Rushdie leaves no doubt in the minds of readers of whom and of what he is writing. He describes Mahound as a man having a high forehead, broad-shouldered, of average height, a light-footed man who takes large strides—the description that some classical scholars have given of the Prophet Muhammad. Furthermore, Rushdie cannot be satisfied with selecting a dream name which clearly identifies the Prophet, but has to emphasize the point by telling us that in reality his name correctly pronounced means 'he-for-whom-thanks-should-be-given'—in other words, Muhammad.

Mahound lives in Jahilia; Jahilia is Makkah and it is described as such. In Muslim history Jahilia is the term applied to the pre-Islamic period in Makkah. For the Muslim, therefore, it also signifies the age of ignorance and human corruption that exists outside the revelation of God's will and law. The author leaves no doubt that he is rooting his dream narrative firmly in the territory of the sira, whose main features—the prophetic mission in Makkah, the migration, the conquest of Makkah, the death of the Prophet—he describes interpolated with appropriate ideological fiction. Rushdie changes a few names to keep the pretence of fiction going. The Cave of Hira, where Muhammad received his first revelation, becomes Cone Mountain; and Abu Sufyan, the leading figure of Makkah, becomes the Grandee Karim Abu Simbel; but Hind, his wife, remains Hind. Where names are changed they maintain Rushdie's rule of correspondences. So Abu Sufyan acquires the name reminiscent of the monumental work of the Egyptian Pharoahs. The Pharoah invariably appears in the Qur'an as a figure who stands for tyranny, the antithesis and adversary of the message of monotheism.

Also retained in the dream narrative are the names of the Prophet's associates: there is Mahound's uncle Hamza, Khalid the water carrier, 'some sort of bum from Persia by the outlandish name of Salman', Bilal the slave, 'the one Mahound freed, an enormous black monster'. The historic Khalid bin Walid was not a water carrier but a general. In the overlapping resonances of the novel are we meant to see in the destructive power of water on the city built entirely of sand, Jahilia, the echo or allusion to the dream of the Imam, where water is to replace wine and blood will run like wine? The character of Salman Farsi, the Persian, certainly existed. The idols of Makkah, too, retain their original names: Lat, Uzza and Manat.

Rushdie describes the torture of Bilal in reasonably historic accuracy:

> How his master asked him . . . to enumerate the gods. 'One,' he answered. . . . They stretched him out . . . with a boulder on his chest. . . . One, he repeated, one. A second boulder was added to the first. *One one one.* Mahound paid his owner a large price to set him free. (*The Satanic Verses*, p. 102)

Here for comparison is the account of Martin Lings:

> The chief of Jumah, Umayyah, had an African slave named Bilal who was a firm believer. Umayyah would take him out at noon into an open space, and would have him pinned to the ground with a large rock on his chest, swearing that he would stay like that until he died, or until he renounced Muhammad and worshipped al-Lat and al-Uzzah. While he endured this Bilal would say 'One, One'; and it happened that the aged Waraqah came past when he was suffering this torment and repeating 'One, One'. 'It is indeed, One, One, O Bilal', said Waraqah. Then, turning to Umayya, he said: 'I swear by God that if ye kill him thus I will make his grave a shrine. (Lings, p. 79)

This example is just one of a number of passages in the novel that could be quoted in tandem with extracts from the conventional biography of Muhammad to show the direct parallels in the 'dream' sequences. The conquest of Jahilia, for example, reads like a paraphrase of Lings in Rushdie's style.

Rushdie retains the original name of Medina, Yathrib, as the name of the town to which Mahound and his followers migrate. In Yathrib most of the migrants, the *muhajirs*, worked as labourers; the sira records that in this period there were hostile incidents between the people of Yathrib and camel trains to and from Makkah; it was also in Yathrib that most of the Qur'anic verses concerning legal matters were revealed. Rushdie uses these facts in his dream-distorted fiction to present this aspect of the sira as the locus for his central and necessary logical conflation in these words:

> At the oasis of Yathrib . . . Gibreel . . . found himself [the Prophet] spouting rules, rules, rules, until the faithful could scarcely bear the prospect of any more revelation. *The Satanic Verses*, pp. 363–4)

The list given in the novel includes a prohibition against eating prawns, a subject which obviously perplexes Rushdie, since it also appears in *Shame*. There, as the obsession of the religious fanatic Maulana Dawood, it is one of the rules he selects to clean up the country. Leaving aside the vitriol, the substantive matter is that there are no Qur'anic revelations pertaining to the matters mentioned by Rushdie. He is referring to some details which are based upon the behavioural example of the Prophetic Sunnah. The point is that the Muslim community in history has extracted these details from the records of the Prophet's behaviour as the best model or example of how moral values, ethical principles and normative behaviour in keeping with the teachings and ethos of the Qur'an can be incorporated into ordinary life. The principles of the Prophet's behaviour have also been extrapolated to cover other circumstances never personally encountered by the Prophet, which include the matter of the prawn. In fairness to prawns, it ought to be pointed out that in general Muslims have no abomination for prawns. The trouble for someone as eclectic as Rushdie is that he picks up a good deal of dross along the way. Muslim tradition is a wide one that includes much diversity in interpretation. This Rushdie cannot acknowledge, even if he knows it to be the case: the above-quoted passage is presenting his essential thesis about the nature of religion, that it arises from human personality. Mahound describes the process of revelation as follows, 'You know, Salman, that I have learned how to *listen*'.

In presenting his own thesis in these terms, Rushdie is relying upon an historic body of evidence which he presents inaccurately at the most profound level and in specific detail. He asserts as direct matters of revelation things which are part of the Prophetic Sunnah, cheek-by-jowl with extrapolations—that is, interpretations and rulings that have been made by Muslim scholars in history and are anything but uniformly held to be binding by Muslims. A Malay Muslim, devout, pious and observant of the rules, would find that great national pastime, eating, inconceivable without the prawn; they are invariably served on Saudi Airlines, a carrier not noted for flouting, or being allowed to flout, any well-known Qur'anic injunction. The prawn is not forbidden.

The logical conflation arises from the most commonplace confusion in the secular mind. For secularism, religion is what people say and do about religion. So what Muslims, for better or worse, have made of their sacred text and the historical record is Islam. For the religious, this irredeemably loses the very essence of the function of sacred text and prophetic example in human history. The accurate distinction between what is divine, the literal word of God, what is divinely-guided prophetic teaching and example, as well as the total normative model of the life of the Prophet in all its richness is what enables these sources to be absolute moral, ethical and normative admonitions on the practice, ideas and beliefs of Muslims. Muslims in history must be acknowledged to be prone to error, failure and the full gamut of possibilities, including getting the wrong end of the stick. Maintaining clarity about the sources of religion is the only way in which Islam can be used as a critique, a warning and a source for reformation of human practice. These distinctions have been operated by reform movements which have occurred throughout the history of Muslim civilization, a number of varieties of which are observable among Muslims throughout the world today.

In presenting Islam as a narrow set of legalistic rules on everything, Rushdie is hardly making a novel argument. But his presentation of a rationale for this is to locate it in the very fundamentals of revelation, leaving the only possible option of 'freedom' as the rejection of religion and God, lock, stock and barrel. That may be Rushdie's own feeling and response. But to substantiate it by the most obvious of confusions—based on inaccurate presentation of basic theology and history and subtly misusing historical fact—does not makes this a testing or profound work. No one would deny the failings of Muslims. The most vituperative arguments that Muslims have gone astray in reducing their religion to narrow legalistic formulas is to be found among contemporary Muslim writers themselves. Rushdie completely ignores some of the most telling evidence provided by the sira on the character and outlook of Prophet Muhammad. He constantly cautioned his followers not to dwell on the legalities of the practice of religion precisely to avoid its becoming a kind of impositional straightjacket, and hence, a misconstruction of the spirit of Islam. Central to every Islamic reform movement is the insistent encouragement Prophet Muhammad gave to the exercise of reasoning and common sense in applying the moral and ethical norms of Islam to actual human circumstances.

In the way he handles his material and manipulates an actual historic record in his fiction, Rushdie demonstrates where he stands vis-a-vis Islam. From outside he speaks as a secular, Western observer, steeped in the Orientalist tradition, but with a significant addition of force and venom. Rushdie, by virtue of his acknowledged background, cannot claim to be unaware of the enormity of the demolition he is engaged upon, nor the significance of the conflations and confusions he makes to advance his thesis. It is perfectly reasonable from an analysis of the novel to observe that Rushdie is aiming at the jugular vein of Islam, knowing exactly how to inflict the most pain upon his target. To argue that God is dead, Rushdie knows he must deconstruct the very nature of the Qur'an—for Islam begins and ends with the Qur'an—and locate its source in the person of the Prophet, whom he can then traduce by selective dissimulation to complete his task. Each incident and every reverberation of his argument throughout the novel carries the same stamp, adds to the clear intent of his thesis.

The character of Salman Farsi is only partly based on his historic counterpart. As Rushdie is such a self-avowed delighter in correspondences, it is reasonable to see him identifying with the character and to realize that he must, indeed, be one of the author's alter egos. It is Salman Farsi who lets us know there is considerable falsification in inscribing revelation by telling Baal that he often altered the revelation recited by Mahound, who never noticed the difference. So, Salman Farsi becomes an 'author' of the Qur'an in the novel and it is he who detects the similarity between the personality and experience of the prophet and the nature of the revelation he brings. This is why the character in the novel loses his faith, and of course, this is also a thesis of the book on why faith is spurious. Rushdie makes the Persian into a scribe, a position not held by the real Salman; he makes him into an apostate, which the historic figure certainly was not. Rushdie's Salman Farsi is an amalgam of the historic figure and Abdullah ibn Abu al Sarh, who converted to Islam, became a scribe to the Prophet for a time, but later returned to the idolators as an apostate and spread tales about his falsification of the revelations. Such a claim has little historic credibility, since it is well attested that there were always a number of scribes and memorizers surrounding Prophet Muhammad, the model for all these 'fictionalized' incidents. One attempt at falsification—the novel alleges there are several undetected ones—would have stood no chance of surviving the multiple process of recording we know to have existed. Some scribes spent their entire lives with the Prophet, and in their presence a person such as Amr would have had no opportunity to falsify anything. Like Rushdie's Salman Farsi, Amr was forgiven by the Prophet after the conquest of Makkah. According to Rushdie, the Persian is pardoned because he revealed the whereabouts of the poet Baal. Here is how Muhammad Husayn Haykal described the pardon:

> As the situation settled down and the news of the Prophet's clemency and all-embracing forgiveness became fully known and appreciated by all, some companions dared to think that even the condemned could also be forgiven. Uthman bin Affan, brother-in-nursing of ibn Abu al Sarh, approached the Prophet in this regard and sought an order for the safe passage of his *protege*. Mohammad was silent for a long time sunk in thought, but he then consented to grant forgiveness. (Haykal, p. 411)

In the novel, the death of Mahound parallels the account of the death of the Prophet. While the Prophet Muhammad's last words were 'Lord! Blessed is the companionship on high', Rushdie has his character utter, 'Is this sickness then thy doing, O al-Lat?' Al-Lat replies, 'It is my revenge upon you, and I am satisfied.' It is the point at which Rushdie merges the other idea—the clash between monotheism and goddess worship—into the action. His threnody on the subject of the overthrow of goddesses, which is of course the substance of the satanic verses, recurs throughout the novel. This is an echo of his previous novel, *Shame*, where the author directly informs the reader of the existence of a 'male' and a 'female' story, and of *Midnight's Children*, with its fondness for Hindu goddesses and complex references to the female deities of this pantheon. Singularly, at the death of Mahound, he offers the final revenge of the she goddess on monotheism!

Fiction or distorted history? Or strategic dreams, encoding clear ideological arguments, presented in fiction to make distorting history legitimate with the deliberate intent of supporting the ideological position being put forward? An examination of the chapters on Mahound and Jahilia shows that Rushdie's narrative is firmly rooted in the sira. Of course, there is a great deal of fiction here, but characters and many of the events are based on historical reality. There is just enough historical fact to give the uninformed reader the feeling of solidity underlying the superstructure of the novel's argument—just enough factual rooting to suggest that this argument arises directly from the historical substance that underlies the novel and to which constant reference and allusion are made. Three things seem clear: that Rushdie is writing about the Prophet Muhammad and the events of his life; that his writing is a deliberate exercise, that he knows exactly what he is doing and has planned with care the use of historical sources and word-game references; and that the purpose of the exercise is not simply to present the sira in a distorted and fictionalized form, but to abuse, mock, malign, throw contempt and score ideological points. Why else does the author, taking great pains to tell his readers exactly who and what he is writing about, use such language? For the Muslim it is the sophistication with which the distortions and feeling of malign intent are woven into the novel that is cause for complaint. The blasphemies of which Muslims complain and to which they react are the raison d'etre of the novel—what it is seeking to convey to the reader. It is perfectly justifiable to maintain that far from examining a question—what kind of idea are you?—Rushdie, as judge, jury and executioner, is proffering the corpse of Islam as the only reasonable response to its entry into history.

This is not to say that the sira or the Sunnah are not open to critical inquiry, for they have never been closed and have attained the form in which we now know them after the exercise of critical inquiry. No Muslim could ever argue for removing these sources from reasoned inquiry, for that would be to deny the very purpose Muslims hold them to embody as the source of living history through which Islam is nurtured. But such an inquiry has to be based on history, not on fiction. And such historical criticism is open to counter-criticism. As in the argument against 'faction', where fact and creative interpretation are mingled, where history and fiction are merged, the very distinctions which make critical reasoning possible are lost. The whole argument must inevitably be rendered a matter of doubt, which, not surprisingly, is Rushdie's sole certainty, his unequivocally answered question in the novel. However, in this particular case it is not easy to hide behind the facade of fiction.

From the perspective of Islamic jurisprudence, presenting the Prophet as fiction, even in dreams, or presenting him as a devil, amounts to treason. That it is a blasphemy, Rushdie himself acknowledges through the words of Gibreel Farishta, who in his young days dreamily compares himself to Prophet Muhammad. Islamic law considers blasphemy against God to be a matter of personal conscience—it is between the indiviudal and God, and God is always merciful and forgiving. However, blasphemy against the Prophet is a social issue, for the Prophet's sira and Sunnah, are the bases of society and political order. It is from these sources that the detail that makes possible an entire communal structure is derived. Without critical analysis of the Sunnah there would be no possibility of questioning how this communal structure and its institutions can or ought to function in history.

It is doubtful whether Rushdie is aware that the process of critical questioning among Muslims has produced reform and social and political change. In his view there can be no reform in how Muslims interact with Islam because the problem is the nature of the source of Islam itself. Believing Muslims are the most gross stereotypes in all Rushdie's writing; not once can he write with sympathetic understanding of the devout Muslim struggling to make his religion relevant to the modern world. His only comment on such a movement in *The Satanic Verses* is his portrayal of the dream of the Imam, which presents one version of his consistent argument on the nature of Islam, and is analogous to the portrayal of modern Muslim society in his two previous books. Rushdie is not interested in debating with Muslims, since his thesis is to deny the validity of what makes Muslim civilization as a living, interpretive tradition possible. Rushdie, it seems, has neither the forbearance nor the available ideological premise to join in the critique of Muslim society by any other means.

It should be pointed out that in modern times there is nothing that so endears a speaker on Islam to a Muslim audience than to detail how bad the Muslims are. But then the standard that makes this argument hold is an Islam that Rushdie cannot admit, that he is determined to assert does not exist. By reducing the Prophet to a caricature, embodied in the persona of an object of fear and loathing, by abusing him and his Sunnah in the most vicious and violent manner, he has tried to destroy the sanctity of the Prophet as a paradigm of behaviour; it is as though he has personally assaulted and raped every single believing Muslim man and woman!

The Curtain of Falsehood

Rushdie's attack is not limited to ridiculing the Qur'an and maligning the personality of the Prophet Muhammad. As Islam is a monotheistic worldview based on the Ibrahimic tradition, he begins his attack with Prophet Ibrahim. He locates the incident of the satanic verses on the occasion of the Ibrahimic festival, in the Muslim calendar that would be *Id al Adha*. It should be remembered that the significance of the Ka'aba in the sacred precincts of Makkah is that it was first raised as a house of worship of the One God by Ibrahim; part of the central ritual that every Muslim pilgrim to Makkah re-enacts involves the desperate search for water by Prophet Ibrahim's wife Hagar, symbolized by running between the hills of Safah and Marwah. When Gibreel Farishta is transformed into the archangel, he arrives at the well of Zamzam, which is now part of the sacred precincts in Makkah. He experiences the arrival of revelation and witnesses the story of Ibrahim when Ibrahim brings Hagar and Ismail, their son, to a desert where he abandons them. When Hagar asks Ibrahim if this is God's will, 'he replied, it is. And left, the bastard.'

Rushdie is writing in the tradition of those who see monotheistic religions as the cause of all the oppression in the world, particularly the exploitation of women. His central incident, the satanic verses, concerns the fate of goddesses. The conflict of Baal and Mahound, the episode of the curtain and constant jibes at the monotheistic God are all manifestations of this. Rushdie echoes the anti-monotheistic stance taken by Rosalind Miles in *The Women's History of the World*, as well as the works of such other dogmatic feminists as Andrea Dworkin. Miles sees all religions and particularly monotheism as conspiracies against women:

> To women . . . the effect was broadly the same, however the message of male supremacy came packaged. All these systems—Judaism, Confucianism, Buddhism, Christianity and Islam—were presented to them as holy, the result of divine inspiration transmitted from a male power to males empowered for this purpose, thereby

enshrining maleness itself as power. . . . Historians, both male and female, have not always resisted the temptation to see the rise of monotheism as a plot against women, since the after-effects have been so uniformly disastrous for the female sex. (Miles, p. 59)

Part of the hook of Rushdie's story is then the rewriting of history within the conventions established by modern feminism. It is a predictable inclusion, echoed in his previous work. In *Midnight's Children*, he shows a fascination for the pervasive concept of goddesses in Hindu pantheism, and the loss of faith in Islam of Aadam Aziz is a precursor of vulnerability to women, since presumably faith in Islam would have taught how to keep a woman in her place. In *Shame*, his 'female' story is of the repression of women by the system, which is part of the seamless garment of repression that is Islam. In *The Satanic Verses* the theme is handled in the same manner as everything else in the novel. No one can argue that Muslims have failed to live up to the exemplary standards set for the status and rights of women by the Qur'an, but then the fault palpably lies with Muslims, men and women in history, and not the source of their religion. Secondly, Rushdie mirrors the intellectual naivete of all feminist writers on the subject in imagining that the existence of goddesses, as opposed to male gods, makes any difference to the fate, status or rights of women in historic society. Ashtoreth/Astarte, the ruling female deity of much of the ancient Near East, the abomination who is excoriated in the Bible, does not come in for criticism in the Old Testament because she is a female deity any more than do Lat, Manat and Uzza in the Qur'an. They are abominated because they detract from the unity, as well as the unknowability in human gender terms, of the transcendant, omnipotent creator. No analysis of ancient Near Eastern society can claim women, by virtue of male and female worship of Ashtoreth/Astarte, were examples of liberated femalehood, or possessors of rights that are commonly accepted by women today as essential. A further paradox that Rushdie might reflect upon is that the modern Western feminist movement was begun in the nineteenth century mostly by women inspired by non-conformist monotheism—Quakers and sectarians who uniformly questioned why, if they stood equal before their God, could they not stand equal before the legal structures of their society? He has no excuse for not being aware that the manifesto claims that have been advanced by every Western feminist campaign in modern times are actually rights given to women in the sacred word of the Qur'an, of which, unsurprisingly, not a single word is mentioned in the novel.

To a large extent the incident of the satanic verses represents the conflict between monotheistic God and the mother goddesses so beloved of feminism, and this theme is echoed throughout the narrative. Thus Rushdie makes Al-Lat a direct opponent and female equivalent of Allah. In the feminist rewriting of history, Hind is presented as a glorified figure defending mother goddesses and the honour and position of all women in history, and Ayesha as a rebel, seething with jealousy, standing against the Prophet to defend the cause of women.

> Countless women took up arms against this tyranny [of the Prophet]. Foremost among them was the Arab leader Hind al Hunnud. . . . [who] led the opposition of her tribe . . . to the forced imposition of Islam. The climax of her campaign came at the terrible battle of Badr in AD 624 where she engaged directly with Mohammad himself, but her father, uncle and brother were killed. For a time she directed a guerrilla war of vengeance against the enemy, but eventually, outnumbered and surrounded, she was compelled to submit and convert to Islam. . . . After she bowed to the will of Allah, nothing was heard of this brilliant and unusual woman. (Miles, p. 69)

Similar claims to courage, valour and independence of spirit and self-confident womanhood can be and are made on behalf of the Muslim women who took an active part in battles to defend the beleaguered Muslim community at this time, women who played an equally active part in the formation of that community. The war of this fictional Hind (both of Miles and Rushdie) is a two-pronged battle: between monotheism and female goddesses, and between the sexes. When Mahound meets Hind, she tells him that the war between them cannot end in a truce. When we come to the incident of the Imam, a naked caricature of Ayatollah Khomeini, his adversary is Empress Ayesha, the coincidence or correspondence of whose name recurs more frequently than any other in the novel. When Gibreel Farishta is ordered to take the Imam to the scene of his triumph over the tyranny of Empress Ayesha, she is revealed as the goddess Al-Lat, whom Farishta is ordered to destroy before the Untime of the Imam can commence. Alleluia Cone, the last lover of Gibreel Farishta in the novel not only echoes the name of Mount Cone, where revelation took place, but is herself the last conqueror of Chomolungma, Everest, the goddess mountain; she is sent plunging to her death from the top of the Everest Villas skyscraper by Farishta in the denouement of the novel.

Ayesha, the wife of Prophet Muhammad, is presented in a similar mixture of fact and fantasy in feminist history:

> Aishah became famous for her courageous intelligence and resistance to subordination enjoined on virtuous Islamic wives. She had no hesitation in opposing or correcting

Mohammad himself, arguing theology with him in front of his principle male followers with such devastating logic and intellectual power that Mohammad himself instructed them, 'draw half your religion from this ruddy-faced woman'. Her courage extended even to resisting the will of the Prophet when it came through the hot-line of a revelation from Allah himself. When in answer to his desire to take another wife Mohammad was favoured with a new batch of Koranic verses assuring him that Allah permitted his prophet to marry as many women as he wished, she hotly commented, 'Allah always responds immediately to your needs'. (Miles, p. 65)

The same fictionalized history occurs in *The Satanic Verses*. Both Miles and Rushdie get their material from Nawal el-Saadawi who cites ibn Saad. (Saadawi, Fatna A. Sabbah [pseudonym] and Fatima Mernissi are the principle sources of all feminist diatribes against Islam; indeed, Miles seems not to be aware of any other source.) But in ibn Saad, Ayesha is reported to say something similar as a compliment, not a rebuke! Moreover, this incident is not reported by any other authority, so it cannot be elevated to the level of established fact.

Rushdie presents the familiar feminist case that Islam subjugated women:

Our Prophet . . . didn't like his women to answer back, . . . here in Jahilia you're used to ordering your females about but up there they won't put up with it. . . . Well, our girls were beginning to go for that type of thing, . . . so at once, bang, out comes the rule book, the angel starts pouring out rules about what women mustn't do, he starts forcing them back into the docile attitudes the Prophet prefers. (*The Satanic Verses*, pp. 366-7)

Umar ibn al Khattib, who became the second Caliph of Islam is reported to have complained to the Prophet, 'we were used to having, we men of Quraysh, the upper hand over our wives, but when we came to Medina we came unto a people whose wives have an upper hand over them'. But what was the Prophet's response? 'Umar saw the suggestion of a smile cross the Prophet's face' (Lings, p. 278). And Umar is also reported to have commented, 'By God we did not use to pay attention to women in Jahiliyyah until God said about them in the Qur'an what is said, and gave them their share in matters'. The verses that are quoted as evidence of how Islam reduced all women into total submission are addressed specifically to the Prophet's wives, 'the mothers of the faithful', who have a special status in Islam. The Qur'an does not promise paradise to all submissive wives, 'walking three steps behind'. The promise of paradise is made only to the wives of the Prophet because they are 'the mothers of the faithful'— not because they were submissive to the Prophet but because they were submissive to God.

Leaving aside the wives of the Prophet, was the overthrow of the goddesses and the coming of Islam the onset of the subjugation of women as Rushdie so clearly implies? His highly selective presentation of asides neglects to mention that the Qur'an unequivocally made women full legal personalities, the objective of all early Western feminist campaigning. By virtue of Qur'anic injunction, women owned their own property and had full rights to retain all income they earned themselves for their own use; it did not become joint property of their marriage. Women also retained full rights to their dowries, which again was not communal but personal property. Women have the right to petition for divorce, a right which hadith literature shows the Prophet upheld: because a woman had been forced into marriage against her will, which is clearly prohibited, because of irreconcilable differences with her husband, or in some cases because the husband was clearly too ugly. The Qur'an made the common practice of female infanticide a crime against God and the crime of killing a woman the equal of killing a man, opposite to the custom of pre-Islamic Arabia. Not only did the Qur'an institute every measure to prevent women being chattels, their traditional legal position in many other social systems, but every injunction in the Qur'an referring to the creation of its social order is expressly directed to 'the believing men and the believing women' or 'the believing women and the believing men'. When the people of Yathrib came to invite the Prophet Muhammad to become leader of their community, he took the oath of allegiance from all those in the party, including the women. Therefore, in both sources of Islam, women have not just full legal personalities but social personalities as well, with equal responsibilities in the eyes of religion for translating the message into living practice on the socio-economic and political levels. Women also have the equal duty to pursue education, and the Prophet Muhammad is recorded to have established classes specifically to teach women. One can go further into the territory so beloved of feminists: menstruation warrants special privileges for women but does not warrant their banishment from social life. Indeed, the classical collection of hadith by al-Bukhari contains an entire book on menstruation which records how women came to the Prophet to question how they should act as fully biological women within the context of Islam. The Prophet is recorded to have shown a certain modesty over these matters, but he answered their questions. It has been the unfailing opinion of Muslim jurists, based on the primary sources of Islam, that Muslim women have a legal right to sexual satisfaction in marriage.

One could continue listing the improvements in the status and rights of women introduced by Islam, but the essence of what Rushdie's reductio ad absurdum on the vanquishing of female goddesses omits to consider is best expressed by Azizah al-Hibri:

> The major contribution of Islam towards the ultimate defeat of Patriarchy does not lie in any such list of reform. Rather, it lies in the fact that Islam replaced the 'paternal bond' of Jahiliyyah totally by the religious bond within which everyone—male or female, black or white, young or old, rich or poor—is equal. By doing that Islam struck at the heart of the patriarchal system. Tribal allegiances were weakened, with brother fighting brother for the faith. New allegiances appeared based on moral and religious principles instead of patrilineage.
>
> At the same time the prophet stressed the 'womb's bond' and made it a duty upon the Muslim to honour it. When once asked whom should a son honour and befriend most, the Prophet answered 'your mother, then your mother, then your mother, then your father'. (Al-Hibri, pp. 212–13)

Given this background, it is the most reasonable question in the world to ask why oppressive patriarchy is so evident in the Muslim world. However, the question can admit of no answer when the content of the primal sources of Islam is ignored and distorted, so that the culpability of Muslims in history is obscured. Rushdie could have had a field day, most justifiably, if only he had his facts straight. But since he falsifies both the sources and the practices of the Prophet, he has to fall back on a puerile argument about goddesses that has throughout history been devoid of any actual sociological or socio-political hope for subjugated women. Since ideologically Rushdie cannot admit of a distinction between the Qur'an and Sunnah and their interpretation and practice by Muslims in history, the locus of this and so many other problems, he has no medium to discuss real questions and turns to abuse.

On the face of it, the episode of the Curtain—the prostitutes' den where Baal, the poet satirist, seeks refuge from Mahound—might appear gratuitous to the story. Rushdie explicitly states that the prostitutes take the names of Mahound's wives and lists the names of each of the wives of Prophet Muhammad, the 'mothers of the faithful'. It is not difficult for anyone to see that this appears as a calculated disrespect. However, that is to miss the significance that underlies the whole introduction of the notion of the goddesses and the world of ideas associated with them. In the world of correspondences, the Curtain, as Rushdie himself tells us, refers to the *hijab*, the chador, or any veil that a Muslim woman uses. The prostitute is not only someone who offers her body for sexual intercourse for payment, but also someone who offers her body for a religious rite. A well established part of the worship of the goddess Ashtoreth/Astarte was the institution of temple prostitutes, ritual prostitution. When a Muslim woman puts on the hijab she is, to a degree, performing a religious rite. Rushdie's fascination with the Prophet's household, introduced early in the novel as a matter devoured by Gibreel Farishta in his phase as an omnivorous autodidact, emerges. The inference is that women who veil themselves are prostitutes, that the 'harem' of the Prophet housed in the mosque in Medina is little more than a correspondence to the temple prostitutes of pre-Islamic times. Perhaps here we are, after all, meant to remember that an exception is made of the Prophet. The Curtain is like a labyrinth from which no one 'could ever find their way, without help, either into the rooms . . . or back to the street', and it is guarded by large eunuchs who 'escorted the visitors to their goals and back again'. Are we then to see this as a metaphor for how Rushdie views Islam and its rites as labyrinthine with the followers of this rite needing the *ulama* (religious scholars), the eunuchs, to guide them?

Inside the Curtain the prostitutes adopt the names of the wives of Mahound. Once one has an inkling of the metaphor of correspondences, it becomes clear why Rushdie has to use the actual names of the wives of the Prophet Muhammad, without which this episode becomes merely a risque interlude; and that is not Salman Rushdie's kind of fiction. So he has to scour the reference works systematically to ensure he has spared no one, even allowing the actual historical timescale of real events involving real people to provide him with his most obscene jibe.

In the episode of the Curtain, Rushdie writes that Ayesha, who was fifteen, was the most popular of the whores, that the eldest and fattest of the whores was Sawdah who had married Mahound the same day as Ayesha, that Hafsah was hot-tempered, that Umm Salamah the Makhzumite and Ramlah were haughty. He names Zainab bint Jahsh, Juwairiyah, Rehana the Jew, Safia, Maimunah, Zainab bint Khuzaimah, and the most erotic, Mary the Copt.

The factual parallels cannot be missed. Ayesha was the youngest of Prophet Muhammad's wives, and Sauda was the eldest. The Prophet married Sauda, an elderly widow, to honour her and recompense her for steadfastness to Islam even in the most difficult and cruel of circumstances. Hafsa, the daughter of Umar, the second Caliph of Islam, married the Prophet at twenty-two and had the rare abilities of knowing how to read and write. Umm Salamah was a Makkan of the aristocratic tribe of Banu Makhzum; Umm Habibah, daughter of Abu Safyan and Hind was also known as 'Ramlah'; Zainab bint Jahsh was from North Arabia; Jawairiyah, who belonged to the tribe of Banul Mustaliq, was married to the Prophet after the Prophet led a mission to disperse the mobilizations of the Banul Mustaliq who were preparing to attack Medina; Sofia bint Huyiay married the Prophet after the Khaibar expedition; Maimunah bint al-Harith, who belonged to the tribe of Amir ibn Sasaa of Najd, was a widow and married the Prophet when he went to perform the lesser pilgrimage, the umra, after the Hudaibiya agreement; Zainab bint Khuzaimah, known as 'mother of the destitutes' for her generosity, died after only three months of marriage to the Prophet. 'Mary the Copt' is in fact Mariyah, a Coptic Christian slave girl who was sent by the ruler of Egypt, Muqawqis, in reply to the Prophet's letter summoning him to Islam; and Rehena was from the Jewish tribe of Bani Qurayzah.

The character of Baal, who in the novel represents the forces of art and literature throughout the ages, is our guide to the world behind the Curtain. Appropriately, within Rushdie's view of history the poet and satirist Baal is the sole victim of Mahound's triumph over Jahilia. During the time of the Prophet Muhammad, two poets were considered by common consensus to outshine the rest: Labid and Kab, the son of the chief poet of the previous generation, Zuhayr ibn Abi Salma. Baal is based on Kab, who was an arch enemy of the Prophet and wrote satirical poems against him. When Umar arrests the occupants of the Curtain, Baal responds by writing poetry to praise the beauty of each one of the wives and pins the poetry onto the prison wall. People at first simply read and enjoy the poems. Then, as Baal proceeds, they discover that Baal has set out to embarrass the prophet. Baal is sentenced to be beheaded. He shouts: 'Whores and writers, Mahound. We are the people you can't forgive.' Mahound replied, 'Writers and whores, I see no difference here.' Is Rushdie inferring that Islam does not tolerate writers, who are considered at par with prostitutes? If that is the case, then it is a most perverse inversion of history. Muslim civilization takes its inspiration from a literary nonpareil, the Qur'an, and has lived by literary endeavour, the highest mark of achievement being to have written a book. It is true that Islam has not been a civilization of novelists in the modern sense, but it is a civilization where the metier of cultural production for the entire population is poetry.

The real Kab was not killed. His brother Bujayr, himself a renowned poet, had accepted Islam before the conquest of Makkah and had urged his brother to embrace Islam. After the conquest of Makkah, Bujayr followed his previous messages with a poem:

Alone unto God, not to Uzza nor Lat.
Can be thine escape, if escape thou canst,
On a day when escape there is none, no fleeing from men,
Save for him whose heart is pure in submission to God.

Kab accepted his brother's invitation.

It is little surprise that the character who goes through the surrogate marriage with the prostitutes of the Curtain, once they have assumed the names of the wives of the Prophet, is named Baal. Baal was a generic name of the gods of the Near East. For example, the gods of the Syrian tribes all bore the name Bel or Baal, from the supreme deity of the cosmos—Baal Shamin, 'Lord of Heaven'—to the approachable personal father and weather god. All the Baals had female consorts, just as did the Baal in the Curtain; Baal Hadad of Hierapolis in north Syria had a notable consort in Arargatis, known to the Greeks and the Romans simply as the 'Syrian Goddess'. In some cases, as in Anatolia and Phrygia, Baals were involved in sacred marriage ceremonies—just as Rushdie's Baal marries the 'girls of the Curtain'. Once again the selection of a name is not eclectic but reinforces the inference of correspondences of this whole sequence of the novel.

Apart from the cult of Baal, the ancient Near East also supported a cult of non-anthropomorphic symbols of the overseers: a cult of stones and mountain tops, sky gods associated with high places, pine cones, etc. Hence, Mount Hira, where Muhammad first received revelation, is referred to as Mount Cone. We have already mentioned the echoing of Mount Cone in the name of Alleluia Cone, a modern, liberated sportswoman of the 1980s who saw the face of the divine when climbing the goddess mountain, Everest; from that encounter she learns that the infinite exists in everything. Various other pagan mysteries make an appearance in the novel, too: the Sabazian mysteries, for example, involved drawing a live serpent across the breast of the initiate in imitation of the 'God who penetrates the bosom'. Rushdie includes a scene in which Saladin Chamcha is approached at a party by a woman initiate performing a modern version of the ancient rite.

Baal knows that Mahound is coming to Jahilia when he sees 'a single teardrop the colour of blood emerging from the corner of the left eye of the statue of Al-Lat in the House of the Black Stone'. The final act of destruction is performed by Khalid:

> Then Khalid entered the temple, and when the goddess did not move the guardian said, 'Now verily do I know that the God of Mahound is the true God, and this stone but a stone.' Then Khalid broke the temple and the idol and returned to Mahound in his tent. And the Prophet asked: 'What didst thou see?' Khalid spread his arms. 'Nothing,' said he. 'Then thou hast not destroyed her,' the Prophet cried. 'Go again, and complete thy work.' So Khalid returned to the fallen temple, and there an enormous woman, all black but for her long scarlet tongue, came running at him, naked from head to foot, her black hair flowing to her ankles from her head. Nearing

him, she halted, and . . . he drew his sword and cut her down. (*The Satanic Verses*, pp. 372–3)

Rushdie's account is similar to that of Martin Lings:

> The nearest to Mecca of the three most eminent shrines of paganism was the temple of al-Uzza at Nakhlah. The Prophet now sent Khalid to destroy this centre of idolatry. At the news of his approach the warden of the temple hung his sword on the statue of the goddess and called upon her to defend himself and slay Khalid or to become a monotheist. Khalid demolished the temple and its idols, and returned to Mecca. 'Didst thou see nothing?' said the Prophet. 'Nothing', said the Khalid. 'Then thou hast not destroyed her', said the Prophet. 'Return and destroy her'. So Khalid went again to Naklah, and out of the ruins of the temple there came a black woman, entirely naked, with long and wildly flowing hair. 'My spine was seized with shivering,' said Khalid afterwards. But he shouted, 'Uzza, denial is for thee, not worship,' and drawing his sword he cut her down. (Lings, p. 424)

Lings cited the classical writer al-Waqidi, who seems to be only source for the above story. Ibn Khaldun began the forward to al-Waqidi's *The Muqaddimah* by describing the author as 'suspect and objectionable', and al-Waqidi's work as 'stories of the night'.

As Rushdie insists on following the sira closely, he is forced to kill the pagan goddesses of Makkah. He takes revenge on their behalf, however, by attacking the monotheistic God directly. First he attacks the Islamic concept of God by describing Him as a businessman. Then to complete his ridicule of monotheism and God, Rushdie himself appears as God towards the latter half of the novel, described as 'a man of about the same age as himself, of medium height, fairly heavily built, with salt-and-pepper beard cropped close to the line of the jaw. What struck him most was that the apparition was balding, seemed to suffer from dandruff and wore glasses.'

And finally, to underscore that God is dead, Rushdie the god makes a second appearance, 'I'm saying nothing. Don't ask me to clear things up one way or the other; the time of revelation is long gone.'

The fiction of Rushdie's dreams of Mahound owe a great deal to reality, often merely paraphrasing in the author's style extracts from the historical record, or selecting that which suits or can be turned to the author's ideological purposes from the sira of Prophet Muhammad. All the dreams experienced by Gibreel Farishta concern aspects of Islam. Apart from the passages dealing with Mahound, there is the dream of the Imam, who no doubt represents one face of Islam in the modern world. There is no possibility of mistaking the identity of this character when SAVAK is said to be on the loose observing the Imam. The appearance of Al-Lat, to be destroyed again in the apocalyptic triumph of the Untime of the Imam who will banish all clocks and roll back the delusion of history, has a dual inference. It is a reference both to the recurrence of the past which is the only temporal dimension possible for the Imam and to the Shah's penchant for invoking the pre-Islamic dynasties of Persia with their goddess worship and temple prostitutes. Rushdie presents his view of the Ayatollah Khomeini in lurid technicolour. He is perfectly entitled to his opinion.

The second aspect of Islam in the modern world concerns the dream of Ayesha, the orphan girl who hears the Archangel Gibreel speaking to her in the lyrics of popular songs and summons her entire village to set off on a pilgrimage, to walk to Makkah across the Arabian Sea. It is the only dream Rushdie tells with any perceptible warmth, because 'at least it suggests that the deity whom he, Gibreel, has tried unsuccessfully to kill can be a God of love.'

The dreams are integral to the fictional narrative of Gibreel Farishta and Saladin Chamcha. The dreams in Rushdie's structure explore what kind of idea Islam is, how newness enters the world. Rushdie's portrait of Islam is highly unflattering. In the only dream excursion that expresses warmth towards its subject, the faith that inspires the pilgrimage countenances, so it would seem, the cruel, intolerable stoning of a baby because it is illegitimate, and can find no time to give the common decencies to those who die along the way. The pilgrimage results in the extinction of all the marchers, even if it opens the gates of Paradise for them. The symbolism is clear and gives a highly conventional portrayal: Islam with its puritanical fanaticism barbarically consumes the innocents. It could have marched straight out of any Orientalist diatribe of the Middle Ages or, indeed, any recent Western media coverage on the Muslim world, which is obviously where Rushdie stands in relation to Islam.

What unites the dreams of the Imam and Ayesha's pilgrimage is the clear imputation that Islam is a force against the march of history, a thing of the past. The present manifestations of Islam are, therefore, prefigured in the newness of this idea and how it enters the world, which is the link between these sequences to those concerning Mahound. According to Rushdie, everything in Islam is impositional: it is itself a system of rules that leaves nothing free. There is no scope for independent reasoning by the Muslim to reform the admitted and extensive flaws in contemporary Muslim society. One quarter of the world's people—the one billion Muslims around the globe—have no route into the future with the faith that is their identity; they can only perpetually relive a restrictive past. However chilling and condemnatory this conclusion, no one could possibly deny Rushdie his right to his own view of Islam in the modern world. Nor can one object to his having his own thesis about how the present predicament is linked to the emergence of Muslim civilization. Many Muslim scholars, writers and thinkers are also trying to comprehend the nature of these linkages, though to a different purpose and obviously with a different source of inspiration. Rushdie's views on both aspects are, after all, nothing new; similar things have been said time and time again by Western observers. As much in his opinions as in his exuberant literary style, he is derivative. What sets Rushdie apart is the maliciousness of the signs and symbols with which he presents his assault. No writer in modern times has dared so much, with such a lack of respect and tolerance for the feelings of others. Anyone who has so scrupulously and partially selected from historical sources, who so insistently indicates to the reader, 'look how cleverly I'm making my point,' can lay any claim to innocent unawareness of the blasphemous nature of his material. Like Saladin Chamcha, then, he has nothing but contempt for what, at one time, were his own kind. So along with the father of Chamcha, it is not unreasonable to agree that Rushdie'e erstwhile own kind can have nothing but scorn for him.

A Black and White Universe

The dreams reverberate and have their parallels in the narrative of the central characters, Gibreel Farishta and Saladin Chamcha. Their narrative also explores another aspect of Rushdie's views about religion: the nature of good and evil. Gibreel Farishta, born of humble origins in Bombay, learned from his mother tales of the life of Prophet Muhammad, and, we are told, if inaccuracies had crept into her versions 'he did not want to know'. Farishta, recognizing his own blasphemy, begins to compare himself to the Prophet and imbibes all he can of the variety and diversity of religious ideas during his career as star of theological movie epics. Farishta has his philandering encounters with women, where he learns all the arts of dissembling, since 'the man who plays a god must be beyond reproach'. The women all forgive him, the infinite generosity of women leading to 'the deepest and sweetest corruption of all, namely the idea that he was doing nothing wrong'. In revolt against the God he has discovered to be dead, he encounters and falls possessively and jealously in love with Alleluia Cone, the novel's last echo of the goddess.

The very night after he eats 'the gammon steaks of unbelief and the pigs trotters of secularism', Farishta enters the world of his dreams. Therein, as not only his namesake, the Archangel Gibreel, but at the crucial moment as Mahound as well, he experiences the full gamut of the nature of revelation. Farishta has trouble distinguishing his dreaming from his waking, and has to acknowledge that he is suffering from paranoid schizophrenia. Under the influence of his dreams, Farishta is the latter-day agent of revelation. What is his purpose? In his dreams he had been able to fulfil the heart's desires of those who sought him out. But he fails miserably in repeating his success among the citizens of London. Eventually he realizes his purpose: 'It is for judging'. He unleashes his destructive fire on the prostitutes of the Goods Way at Kings Cross. In the burning Shaandaar Cafe, Farishta confronts his adversary/antithesis, and lives out the question, 'What happens when you win?' just as he earlier lived out the question posed to an idea when it is weak, when the ghost of Rekha Merchant offered him a compromise that he rejected. So amid the flames of the Shaandaar with Saladin Chamcha at his feet, he rescues him, 'there is a small redeeming victory for love'. And as Gibreel is taken away in the ambulance, he re-enters the pleasant dream of Ayesha's pilgrimage, that nostalgic dream of the present past, following it to its apotheosis, the death that leads the walkers to Paradise.

Farishta, the untranslated man, the man who wishes to remain continuous with his past, is forced into the experience of revelation and parallels it in his subsequent experience of madness and ultimately destruction. He ends by killing Sisodia and destroying once again the last vestige of the goddess by pushing Alleluia Cone from the top of Everest Villas. He shoots himself before the eyes of Saladin Chamcha. That is the kind of fiction Gibreel Farishta is.

Saladin Chamcha is quite another kind of fiction. Chamcha inhabits the world of the author himself, and it is hard to avoid the recognition of this character as his closest alter ego. Chamcha is the product of affluent Bombay, the dedicated admirer of the world he works so hard to join, the middle class, public school, colonial niceness of, not true-blue, toryism, but more that older unreconstituted liberalism. Chamcha sets off on an interplanetary migration to an English public school, to suffer the racism of his peers, without acquiring any desire to question the unquestioning supremacy of the world he remains determined to become part of, to conquer. Public school is followed by university, no doubt in the great liberal arts tradition. Then he determines to become an actor. Again the hand of racism bedevils his chances of success. Incorrectly pigmented, he can work only unseen as the myriad voices of frozen peas and household artefacts in advertisements, or in the children's television extravaganza, *The Aliens Show*, buried under a prosthesis. But there is no dent in Chamcha's admiration and desire to be part of the society that, however much he venerates and apes it, still excludes him.

Chamcha is the translated man, the man of selected discontinuities, a willing reinvention, his own creator. It is Chamcha who discovers that evil is not separate from good: he had, after all, followed his own idea of the good and could see no reason why he should be punished. He sets out to destroy Farishta, because he realizes that evil comes naturally, not against our natures; evil is part of our nature, because good and evil are intertwined in everything, even, asserts Rushdie, in the nature of God. But does he not also seek to destroy Farishta because he sees Gibreel, the man who wanted nothing of London and had no feel or admiration for what it represents, gaining the success denied the English hero-worshipping Chamcha? The devotee denied has nothing but contempt for what Farishta is and finds it is so easy to destroy from a consuming, concentrated hatred that contains a large measure of jealousy.

Through the particular eyes of Saladin Chamcha we enter the world of modern Britain and its ethnic minority, immigrant society. He experiences the greatest power British society possesses, the power of description. The police and immigrant officials accept his goatman deformity as normal. They take him to a detention centre where he sees the effect of this power of description upon other alleged illegal immigrants, who are translated into freakishly deformed beasts. Part of the critique of Orientalism is precisely its exercise of the power of description. Indeed, the Western tradition of anthropology with all its historic racism has arisen from the supreme arrogance that has assumed the sole right to comprehend the nature of 'other' people. Rushdie can define the nature of domination and power relationships accurately. It does not, however, lead him to question the quality and content of Orientalist writings on Islam, which he draws upon and reinforces elsewhere. Sometimes, it would seem, it is quite all right to allow the appropriation of the power of description; to know in order to subordinate is not such a bad thing, so long as Rushdie is the one doing the subordinating.

Most of the black characters in *The Satanic Verses* come out, both in their physical descriptions and behaviour, as total racist stereotypes. Dr Simba, the black activist, verges on the grotesque. Bilal, the companion of the Prophet Muhammad, is described as 'scum . . . the slave Bilal, the one Mahound freed, an enormous black monster, this one, with a voice to match his size'. Bilal, in fact, became the first great voice of Islam, and marked the beginning, as Ali Mazrui has pointed out,

> of a black vocal tradition in history—from Bilal to Paul Robeson and beyond. Black vocal power in world history began with Bilal. (Mazrui, p. 25)

Moreover, Rushdie gives neither Bilal nor Islam any credit for producing a multiracial society so early in world history.

> Bilal set the grand precedent of Islamic multiculturalism—fourteen centuries *before* President Jimmy Carter tried to persuade his own church in Georgia to go multiracial. (Mazrui, p. 25)

Rushdie, on the contrary, throws scorn at the fact that Bilal is black. The poet Baal, Rushdie's alter ego in the 'Mahound' and 'Jahiliya' chapters, tells Bilal, 'If Mahound's ideas were worth anything, do you think they'd only be popular with trash like you?' In his second reincarnation in the novel, Bilal appears as Bilal X, a black American pop singer, a convert in the tradition of Malcolm X. His vocal power is not diminished, but now he is in the service of a Shi'ite Imam and wishes to undo history. His singing talents are mobilized against history—'the greatest of the lies'. In Rushdie's depiction of Bilal and Bilal X, Mazrui sees strong anti-black and anti-semitic tendencies:

> Is Rushdie making fun of African Americans generally? Or is he satirizing Afro-American *Muslims*? Or is he ridiculing the significance of Malcolm X? But since many Afro-American Muslims regard Islam as one route back to *Roots*, is Salman Rushdie simply continuing his basic contempt for his own roots?
> Kunta Kinte—if Alex Haley is right—was a Muslim. Alex Haley went looking for his own roots. Salman Rushdie turned back on his own. To the question whether *The Satanic Verses* is as racist as *Mein Kampf*, the answer is definitely *not*. But there is an undercurrent of Negrophobia in both books. The two books are also anti-Semitic—but directed at different sections of the Semitic people. While Hitler was primarily anti-Jewish, there is an undercurrent of anti-Arabism in Rushdie. Rushdie cannot believe that Muslim Pakistanis can be pro-Palestinian without prostituting themselves to Arab governments. (Mazrui, p. 27)

The stereotypes are extended to Asians as well. In the East End deculturation of Mishal and Anahita Sufyan, Saladin Chamcha does not recognize his kind of British, does not recognize them as British at all. It is these two young women who are obviously modelled on and carry forward the incident in *Shame*, the newspaper cutting about a murdered young Asian girl. Mishal is even attacked with a carving knife by her mother when she learns of her daughter's affair with Hanif Johnson. Through Chamcha, we learn the apposite description of Thatcherite Britain: a middle-class revolution of the wrong kind of people, the hungry people, who evidently will throw out the kind of Englishness Chamcha has reinvented and bred himself to cherish.

It is with Chamcha that we learn of the inchoate struggles of the immigrant community to express and define its role. One of their mouthpieces is the radical black activist, Dr Uhuru Simba, who accuses *The Aliens Show* of racism and negative imagery, thereby succeeding in losing Chamcha his job. Simba is falsely accused of a series of hideous murders, arrested and dies by falling from his bed while in police custody. For all the pith and resonance of the description of immigrant society, the charting of the tensions, the police harrassment that sparks a riot, Chamcha is quite out of temper with and apart from this kind of Britishness. In a quite amazing way, he is disparaging, in his middle-class, colonial British niceness, of the symbolism of the radical struggles of immigrants. When he attends the protest meeting for Uhuru Simba,

> He didn't like the use of such American terms as 'the Man' in the very different British situation where there was no history of slavery; it sounded like an attempt to borrow the glamour of other more dangerous struggles, a thing he also felt about the organizers' decision to punctuate speeches with such meaning-loaded songs as *We Shall Overcome* and even, for Pete's sake, *Nkosi Sikelel'iAfrika*. As if all causes were the same. (*The Satanic Verses*, p. 415)

One wonders whether Rushdie has ever contemplated the self-evident fact that Britain may like to think of itself as different, yet every Afro-Caribbean immigrant to Britain is the descendant of slaves. And who, after all, enslaved their ancestors? Who, after all, founded American slavery, which began when it was still a British colony and which thrived in those most English country gardens of southern states? Is it not the case that the mercantile profits generated from the slave-run sugar plantations of the West Indies funded Britain's industrial revolution, a transformation that also necessitated the demolition of the Indian textile industry? The recurrent East Indian West Indians in the novel would, of course, have sprung from that other fine colonial institution, indentured labour. And when it comes to merging causes, could not Rushdie have considered that the security legislation—from which 'God Save Afrika'—was enacted by the British before they gave up administering that racially-divided nation? Surely one of the most enduring legacies of the Empire has been the draconian security legislation employed by new nations, in turn roundly condemned by the Mother of Parliaments that was responsible for its invention. Elsewhere, Rushdie has noted that Britain had its history overseas. It seems that Rushdie, nevertheless, is not ready to see the immigrants, who lived out the consequences of the wrong end of that history, repatriate it to Britain as part of their struggle against the still extant, if British, form of racism. No doubt he thinks mere liberalism cures all. Or more appropriately, we should remember his discussion of migration in *Shame*, which he asserts strips people of history. It is a dubious claim, and one much in the self/selfish interests of those who would support the notion of the power of description as a tool of subordination.

The other level of disassociation is again a function of how Chamcha/Rushdie is aloof from the immigrant society he observes. The power of description is the most potent of weapons, as he appropriately demonstrates. It has the power to invade and dominate the consciousness of the immigrant, or the devotee of Englishness. So what we see of a new generation of Britons is their willingness to inhabit the relegated idioms and images of British society and make them their own. Chamcha as the goatman becomes a cult figure whose image appears on badges, posters, sweatshirts and banners at political rallies. Mishal Sufyan tells him: 'It's an image white society has rejected for so long that we can really take it, you know, occupy it, inhabit it, reclaim it and make it our own.' With such images she can look out on Brickhall Street and announce, 'It's our turf, . . . Let 'em come and get it if they can.' Or put in the eloquence of Uhuru Simba:

> Make no mistake, we are here to change things. I concede at once that we shall ourselves be changed; African, Caribbean, Indian, Pakistani, Bangladeshi, Cypriot, Chinese, we are other than we would have been if we had not crossed the oceans, . . . It is our turn now. (*The Satanic Verses*, p. 414)

The point is the nature of the change that Chamcha/Rushdie can envisage, the kind of options he conceives as possible for these remade and remaking people. Of the woman who explains to him that Uhuru Simba means Lion of Freedom in African, he asks, 'Which language?' and clearly has only contempt that for her it matters not; it is enough that it is an African language. Wrenched from cultural roots, seeking solace or a continuity with some discrete past, however tenuous, is no option. In the Mishal Sufyans of Britain, he can only see isolated, newly uprooted persons eager for the security of an image already vacated by British society.

Nowhere in Rushdie is there any other inkling, option or idea. If the immigrants will remake Britain it will not be by the inclusion of that which is indigenous to themselves, for they have been wiped clean of history. From the perspective presented by this novel, how could they have such a thing? The growing generations of Muslim Britons have no civilization, no culture to call upon, because all that is an illusion. And as for Islam, has he not clearly consigned that to the past, as an idea that can exist only with the past and not the future. Rushdie has no conception, and no mental space to acknowledge or concede, that there are young Muslim Britons who see no contradiction between their Muslimness and being active remakers of and contributors to Britain. He knows nothing of Muslims who have gained a new insight into their faith through living and growing in Britain, where the means to improve their knowledge of the basics of Islam are better than would have been available had their parents not crossed the skies. Rushdie has no connection with and, therefore, no idea of the Muslim community that is growing in Britain, within its faith, cherishing its cultural heritage and searching and making new ways of living their Islam in this society. They are people, predominately young, but of many ages and backgrounds, who reject and abominate Rushdie's vision of Islam, because not only does it not describe them, it falsifies them, just as it falsifies Islam which is the core of their identities. Not only can and will such people participate in remaking Britain, they will be a major force in remaking the worldwide Muslim *ummah*. But Rushdie is ideologically deaf, dumb and blind, as well as totally opposed to such a notion.

Ultimately the bleakness and barrenness of what Rushdie sees is that these immigrants can only be described by dominant society, or choose to inhabit the descriptions generated from within the dominant society as new syncretists. They are the great mass unmade by the colonial encounter and they had better shape up to the fact that the only describing society is that dominant society. Rushdie, in his exposition of immigrant society, unmasks himself as a cultural supremacist of the old, familiar kind, who sees no other transplantable or donor culture or civilization. That is the kind of de-culturizer Salman Rushdie is. With his premises there is no plurality, no multicultural future, for there is only *one* culture; he speaks from its traditions and prejudices, with its signs and symbols. Even if that leaves him lonely between two worlds that will not take him in, it is still the only world there is—so much, once again, for all that doubt!

If Gibreel Farishta is the true, the untranslated, the good, who experiences revelation and the nature of the newness that enters the world, then Saladin Chamcha is his antithesis, the false, the reinvented, the selectively self-created, and also the evil. We witness Chamcha being humanized, returned to human scale and his familiar self by the concentration of his hate—a theme that echoes through the riots sequence and recurs from an idea Rushdie incorporated in *Shame*. It seems this is part of Rushdie's remedy and recipe for the migrant. But what is it that they should hate? Not, definitely, that which Chamcha selected as his idea of the good, that dominant society that so potently describes from the perspective of the only values worthy of giving description.

Deconstructing Satan

Hate, then, for the excrescences that deform that noble ideal that is the good for Chamcha, and perhaps also hate for that from which he came and abandoned. Not for the first time, in the ambiguity of his writing about immigrant society, Rushdie seems to be expressing his own angst, and the concentration of his hate can embrace each and every point on the compass. Chamcha hates the untranslated Farishta, who reveals the kind of idea Islam is. Farishta is destroyed. Chamcha survives. 'It seemed that in spite of all his wrong-doing, weakness, guilt—in spite of his humanity—he was getting another chance.' Doubt, being able to hate that which is absolute, pure, impositional, to accept the evil that arises from our nature; this is not just the survival kit but the package deal of triumphant secularism, which marches off into a new sunset of hope and an affair with Zeenat Vakil. That is the kind of fiction Salman Rushdie is.

Seven
Megalomaniacs, Mullahs and the Media

The Rushdie affair began, so far as the Western media is concerned, with the ritual burning of *The Satanic Verses* by Muslim protesters. Before this occurrence there had been no coverage of the Muslim campaign. After the book burning there was plenty of attention given to the story—but almost none to the substance of Muslim views on *The Satanic Verses*. Despite being a community long established in Britain, the Muslims were clearly a breed of people in need of interpretation every bit as much as if they had just made earthfall from Alpha Centauri. Shabbir Akhtar reflected the sentiments of every Muslim when he noted 'every evening, one came home to watch the news—and catch the name of a new expert on Islam. Christian experts, Jewish experts, Hindu experts, Marxist experts, agnostic experts, to name a few. Every kind of expert—except a Muslim expert' (*Be Careful With Muhammad!*, p. 41). This trend was merely accentuated after the intervention of Ayatollah Khomeini. It is not that there was no Muslim comment but that inclusion of such comment amounted neither to fair nor balanced reporting; a rough calculation shows a ratio of ten to one, non-Muslims to Muslims. Students of the media would find it instructive to undertake a statistical analysis of what passes for balance on a highly controversial, sensitive issue. With few exceptions, the coverage of the affair was deeply entrenched in age-old images of ignorance and classical bogies of the distorted imagination. If this was the context, then even as cursory an analysis as ours of the content of the debate, that looks only at extracts from the quality press, reveals what passed for enlightened comment, informed opinion and cogent argument to be nothing of the sort.

Ten days before *The Satanic Verses* was published, Syed Shahabuddin, a noted member of the Indian Parliament, launched a campaign to have the novel banned in India. He and a number of Muslim leaders had come to know of the novel months before its publication from the distinguished Sikh writer and editorial adviser to Penguin India, Khushwant Singh, who had advised Penguin against publishing the book. He told the campaigners, 'I read the manuscript very carefully and I was positive it would cause a lot of trouble.

There are several derogatory references to the Prophet and the Qur'an. Muhammad is made out to be a small time imposter' (*Sunday Magazine*, Calcutta, 28 October 1988). As a result of Shahabuddin's campaign, the Indian government banned the novel on the fifth of October. The Indian example was followed by Pakistan, South Africa and several Muslim countries. At the end of October, the London-based Muslim journal *Impact International* published a cover story declaring that 'Publishing Sacrilege is Not Acceptable' (28 October–10 November 1988). Within a week of the *Impact* story, well before a single demonstration against the novel, *The Independent* reported that Rushdie had hired a full-time bodyguard and was thinking of emigrating to the United States.

The Muslim protests gained momentum as *The Satanic Verses* was short-listed for the Booker Prize and then won the Whitbread Literary Award. An action committee, consisting of most of the major Muslim organizations in Britain, was formed to co-ordinate protests against the novel. As the British Muslim Action Front, they sought to have Rushdie prosecuted for blasphemy. On 11 November, British Prime Minister Margaret Thatcher declared that there was 'no ground for prosecution'; two weeks later, Attorney General Patrick Mayhew announced that the book did not constitute a criminal offence (on 27 February 1990, the Action Front asked the High Court to overturn a magistrate's refusal to issue blasphemy summonses against the author and his publishers). The British press totally ignored the Muslim protest until a copy of the book was ritually burned in Bradford on 14 January 1989. This single display finally brought out the media: Muslims were compared with Hitler's National Socialists and their actions with the Inquisition. However, the Muslim side of the story was still largely ignored. Demonstrations in Islamabad and Srinagar in Kashmir further produced accusations that Muslims were 'backward' and 'fanatics'. Then on 14 February 1989, the Ayatollah Khomeini issued his *fatwa* (juristic opinion) that Rushdie should be executed as an apostate who has blasphemed against Islam. The Western world gasped in horror, imposed sanctions, reached for ready-made historic bogies and all the other basic ingredients of the intoxicating brew that is the distorted imagination.

Here, we are not concerned with how the events played themselves out after the Ayatollah Khomeini's fatwa, but with the arguments that each side presented.

Naughty, but Nice?

As the affair began, Rushdie's salvos appeared thick and fast: an open letter to Rajiv Gandhi in *The New York Times*; a counterattack against the mullahs in the *Observer* (which also appeared in *The New York Times*, *New York Review of Books* and many other places); an explanatory interview in *The Sunday Times*; an expository interview in his friend Tariq Ali's Channel Four show, *Bandung File* (which also appeared in *The Guardian*)—all in one week. Then, into reclusion.

Rushdie's open letter to Rajiv Gandhi complained to the Indian Prime Minister:

> The book was banned after representation by two or three Muslim politicians, including Syed Shahabuddin and Khurshid Alam Khan, both members of Parliament. These persons, who I do not hesitate to call extremists, even fundamentalists, have attacked me and my novel while stating that they had no need actually to read it. (*International Herald Tribune*, 18–19 February 1989)

Naming is, of course, a Rushdie speciality, but getting the facts right seems to be a consistent problem. His labelling of Shahabuddin and Khan—both are widely recognized to have strong secular leanings—is little more than a ploy to show that only 'extremists' and 'fundamentalists' would be upset by his novels. Moreover, the two protagonists knew exactly what the novel contained: it portrayed as they had learned from someone well versed in literary criticism, 'the Prophet as a small time imposter', compared the wives of the Prophet to prostitutes, and used abusive terms to describe his companions. You do not have to be an extremist or a fundamentalist to be insulted and to object, as Rushdie knows very well; you simply have to be a believing Muslim. Rushdie continued,

> When Syed Shahabuddin and his fellow self-appointed guardians of Muslim sensibilities say that 'no civilized society' should permit the publication of a book like mine, they have got things backwards. The question raised by my book's banning is precisely whether India, by behaving in this fashion, can any more lay claim to the title of a civilized society. (*International Herald Tribune*, 18–19 February 1989)

He asked Gandhi, 'What sort of India do you wish to govern? Is it to be an open or a repressive society?' So the fate of a single book can decide whether India, the world's largest democracy, is to be included in civilized society! Is Britain 'in' or 'out' by banning *Spycatcher*? Has Ontario become 'uncivilized' by withdrawing from the school curriculum Shakespeare's *The Merchant of Venice* for its portrayal of Shylock as a 'conniving jew'? Open societies are 'open' because they protect the freedom of their members—including the freedom from abuse and religious and sectarian strife.

Rushdie said something quite astonishing:

> The section of book in question (and let us remember that the book is not actually about Islam, but migration, metamorphosis, divided selves, love, death, London and Bombay) deals with a prophet—who is not called Muhammad—living in a highly fantastical city made of sand (it dissolves when water falls upon it). . . . Moreover, the entire sequence happens in a dream, the fictional dream of a fictional character, an Indian movie star, and one who is losing his mind, at that. How much further from history can one get? (*International Herald Tribune*, 18–19 February 1989)

Is this an attempt to be too clever by half? Or does Rushdie take his Muslim readers to be total imbeciles and his Western readers to be totally ignorant of Islam and its essential themes? The book *is* about Islam. Six out of the nine chapters in the book deal *directly* with Islam complete with Islamic themes, Islamic symbolism, and real Islamic characters. The history mimics the sira—life of the Prophet Muhammad—right down to basic descriptions and small details. The fact that they are disguised as fantasy and dream hardly detracts from the fact that real history is presented with real distortion. The first theme that Rushdie says the book is about is migration, which is also a central theme of Islam. The life of the Prophet Muhammad is divided into two sections, the first part located in Makkah and the second in Medina; the dividing line is provided by his migration from one city to the other. This migration also signals the transformation of Islam from a religion of personal piety to a polity and civilization. Hence, the Muslim calendar does not begin from either the birth or death of Prophet Muhammad; it begins with the *hijra*, the migration of the Prophet and his companions from Makkah to Medina. This is also why the whole idea of migration, to flee persecution or to attain economic betterment, has a religious sanction in Islam. After deliberately abusing and falsifying Islamic history as well as basic tenets of Islam, Rushdie then, equally deliberately, falsified his own position.

Moreover, he wants one law for himself, another for others. S. Nomanul Haq took up this point, addressing Rushdie as a former friend:

> No writer, you will agree, writes in a historical vacuum. But then, a responsible artist does not, without powerful grounds, mutilate history. Nor, unless there exists a mammoth justification, does he disregard the sensibilities and sensitivities of his own milieu, especially when it forms both the subject matter and the bulk of his or her audience. Strangely, what I am saying is something that I learned from none other than yourself. You might recall your telling criticism of Sir Richard Attenborough's celebrated film *Gandhi*. You enraged Sir Richard, but in the controversy I remained your passionate supporter. You censured the film for disregarding or minimizing

certain important historical facts. And you said that in a work of an artistic nature, one cannot say everything, that there has to be a choice—but that there has to be a rationale of choice. One selects not to mislead but to make the story more meaningful. Ironically, this has precisely been your lapse in *The Satanic Verses*. (*The New York Times*, 23 February 1989)

Nomanul Haq was also unconvinced with Rushdie's defence that he had distanced himself from history.

> The veil is too thin to cover the identity of Mahound: He can be understood in no other way than as a caricature of the Muslim Prophet. (*The New York Times*, 23 February 1989)

Moreover, Nomanul Haq suggested that Rushdie had also been reckless with the character of Salman Farsi, who as a well-known Persian companion of the Prophet,

> Has been accorded a particularly elevated status by the Shiites. Given the militancy of the Shiites, when you made Salman the polluter of the revelation, you knew that you were planting your hand in the cluster of bees. (*The New York Times*, 23 February 1989)

While Syed Shahabuddin does not have the international reach of Rushdie, he was quite capable of holding his own.

> No, Mr Rushdie, contrary to your imagination, India is not being run by the 'fundamentalist lobby'. But if to seek redress of a religious grievance from the government which is the custodian of the dignity of all our people is fundamentalism in your lexicon, so be it. . . . Yes, Mr Rushdie, we are a religious people and we do not like our religious personalities . . . to be abused and vilified, directly or indirectly. Call us primitive, call us fundamentalists, call us superstitious barbarians, call us what you like, but your book only serves to define what has gone wrong with the Western civilisation—it has lost all sense of distinction between the sacred and the profane. . . . You plead innocent of the possible Muslim reaction. You depict the Prophet whose name the practising Muslim recites five times a day, whom he loves, whom he considers the model for mankind, as an imposter and you expect us to applaud you? You have had the nerve to situate the wives of the Prophet, whom we Muslims regard as the mothers of the community, in a brothel, and you expect the Muslims to praise the power of your imagination? . . . No, your act is not unintentional . . . It was deliberate and consciously planned. . . . Here in India, our laws are very clear . . . Article 295A of the Indian Penal Code says: 'Whosoever, with deliberate and malicious intention of outraging the religious feelings of any class of citizens of India,

by words either spoken or written or . . . otherwise, insults or attempts to insult the religion or the religious beliefs of that class shall be punished with imprisonment . . . or with fine . . . or with both'. I wish you were in India, Mr Rushdie, to face the music. (*Times of India*, 13 October 1988)

One should point out that Indian law is basically colonial British law, and recent additions are squarely modelled on what has been happening on the British legal scene. Shahabuddin had further advice for Rushdie and his defenders:

> Tell your British champions and advisors that India shall not permit 'literary colonialism' nor what may be called religious pornography. Not even in the name of freedom and democracy, not even under deafening and superb orchestration of your liberal band. And also tell them not to have sleepless nights over our image abroad. Our image is not so fragile as not to survive this ban or founded on the acceptance of the mores of your permissive society, but on what we can do as a nation to give a better life, a life of dignity, to our people and how we can live with each other in peace, mutual respect and harmony. (*Times of India*, 13 October 1988)

Two supporters of Rushdie concurred with Shahabuddin's conclusion that the Indian government was right in banning the book. In *The Times*, Connor Cruise O'Brien argued that 'if they had allowed the book in, Gandhi and his ministers would have been guilty of a dereliction of the most basic responsibility of any government: preventing a major breakdown of public order'. He also found Rushdie's defence that his novel is not about Islam 'disingenuous'. Wole Soyinka, the Nigerian Nobel Prize winner, while not condoning the ban, declared that he 'quite understood the action of the Indian government in banning Salman Rushdie's book, *The Satanic Verses*. . . . Given India's harrowing situation of religious unrest, I probably would have done the same if I were the Prime Minister' (*The African Guardian*, 23 February 1989).

In his defence in the *Observer*, Rushdie offered a telling line of argument for one who claimed he was not writing about Islam per se. Islam, he pointed out, differs from Christianity on several important aspects: 'the Prophet is not granted divine status, but the text is'; and 'Islam requires neither a collective act of worship nor an intercessionary caste of priests. The faithful communicate directly with God.' But in contemporary times things have changed:

> Nowadays, however, a powerful tribe of clerics has taken over Islam. These are the contemporary Thought Police. They have turned Muhammad into a perfect being, his

life into a perfect life, his revelation into the unambiguous, clear event it originally was not. Powerful taboos have been erected. One may not discuss Muhammad as if he were human, with human virtues and weaknesses. One may not discuss the growth of Islam as a historical phenomenon, as an ideology born out of its time. These are the taboos against which *The Satanic Verses* has transgressed. (*Observer*, 22 January 1989)

Yes and no; partly true and partly false. A powerful tribe of clerics (this being the Shia terminology; in the Sunni world they are known as the ulama, or the religiously learned) has indeed taken over Islam, but they have not turned Muhammad's life into a perfect life. It is the text, which alone has divine sanctions, which asks the believers to follow the example of Muhammad. His life is a paradigm of behaviour because, as a recipient of revelation, he was closest to the divine message. Moreover, Muhammad is constantly and continuously discussed as a human being, with strengths and weaknesses; but because he is the model of behaviour he has to be discussed in historically accurate terms. One cannot attribute things to Muhammad he did not say or do, any more than one can give him divine powers. Furthermore, Islam is constantly being discussed as an historic phenomenon; indeed, some of the best recent studies have analysed Islam from this perspective, Marshall Hodgson's *The Venture of Islam* being a good example. The transgressions of *The Satanic Verses* are not here but elsewhere, but Rushdie is right to suggest that 'the battle over *The Satanic Verses* is a clash of faiths, in a way. Or, more precisely, it's a clash of languages.' He is also right when he says that 'intellectual dissent is neither pornographic nor racist'. The issue is not about intellectual dissent; it is about the language in which that dissent is couched and how that language has distorted real history about real people. It is about a distorted imagination which has captured all the bogies of the Orientalist image of Islam and served them as literary *hors-d'oeuvres* to a public that cannot have enough of them.

Rushdie justified his use of Mahound by putting the derogatory term in the context of the novel. He stated, 'my novel tries in all sorts of ways to reoccupy negative images, to repossess perjorative languages.' Can perjorative language be repossessed without unleashing, and giving common currency to, the underlying factors which produced that language in the first place? Can the term 'nigger' be reoccupied without its racial connotations? Does not this reoccupation validate the substance of the negative image? Does it not also mean that the only way forward for the victims of these images is either to accept the consequences the images have for them or to be duped by their repetition into believing them and ending up actually behaving according to them, thus further reinforcing them? Significantly, one can look in vain in

Rushdie's work for an awareness of these questions or a wrestling with the legacy created by using negative imagery. Rushdie said:

> *The Satanic Verses* is not, in my view, an anti-religious novel. It is, however, an attempt to write about migration, its stresses and transformations, from the point of view of migrants from the Indian subcontinent to Britain. . . . I tried to write against stereotypes. (*Observer*, 22 January 1989)

How can one write against stereotypes while at the same time attempting to reoccupy negative images which are the stereotypes themselves? Or are we to believe that Rushdie is writing against stereotypes by using stereotypes themselves? Is this why all the characters in the novel are total stereotypes, with the religiously inclined being totally foolish and fanatic, those of leftist persuasion hell bent on revolution, all blacks being big and monstrous with not even a modicum of morals?

Rushdie concluded by invoking one of his characters: 'the forces of inhumanity are on the march. "Battle lines are being drawn up in India today", one of my characters remarks. "Secular versus religious, the light versus the dark. Better you choose which side you are on." ' What an absolute statement from someone who believes only in doubt! Secularism is light; religion is darkness—'Salman the Divine' has spoken; and there cannot be any doubt. The most notable feature of secularist doubters is that they have no doubts either about their own positions or about themselves. It is everything else that is open to doubt.

In the *Bandung File* interview, set up to give Rushdie full opportunity to present his case, he sees doubt as the spirit of the age—Espiritu del tiempo. 'Doubt, it seems to me', he told his audience, 'is the central condition of a human being in the 20th century. One of the things that has happened to us in the 20th century as a human race is to learn how certainty crumbles in your hand.' An eminently sensible statement; but Rushdie fails to see the other side of the equation. Where there is doubt, there is inner tension. The inner tension is a product of conflicting factors, opposing values, the dualism that doubt generates. The more doubt becomes the dominant force in a society, the more inner tension it generates in the members of that society. And where do people go when they are in the grip of perpetual, continuous inner tension? To religion. Doubt may be the central condition of a human being in the twentieth century, but the late twentieth century has also seen an unprecedented rise in things religious—from 'born again' Christianity to 'Islamic revivalism', from witchcraft to pagan cults, from mysticism to 'New Age' consciousness, and to that ultimate in absolutes, the religion of perpetual doubt. Where there is doubt there is always certainty: if that certainty is not sought in religious or external factors, it finds a cosy home in oneself. One becomes one's own religion; Rushdie has become a religion to himself. This is what he fails to see. The conflict over *The Satanic Verses* is indeed a conflict between two faiths: it is *Rushdie's* word against Muhammad's. No wonder Muhammad's followers are so agitated. In explaining the dream sequence, Rushdie said:

> Almost everything in those sections . . . starts from an historical or quasi-historical basis, though one can't really speak with absolute certainty about that period of Muhammad's life. The records are very partial and ambiguous. But he is, after all, the only prophet who exists even partially in history. As with all the other prophets, we have only legends and stories written hundreds of years later. The interesting thing about Muhammad is that there *is* objective information about him other than the sacred text. (*Bandung File*, 14 February 1989)

This statement revealed that Rushdie is writing specifically about Islam, but this time as historical scholar. By 'partial', Rushdie could mean Muslim history which, according to Orientalism, is biased history. By objective information he could mean non-Muslim records vital to the development of Orientalist thought. So it is a revealing admission; there is history but Rushdie maintains ambiguity. Thus, the conflict over *The Satanic Verses* is also a conflict over histories. The way in which Rushdie handles history gives greater ideological force to the myths and legends, almost exclusively ignoring the body of Muslim history. But placing this history in the context of fiction gives no one an opportunity to engage with Rushdie's own historical competence. He has created a perfect context to play fast and loose with two distinct traditions of writing history, one based on Muslim sources and traditions, the other a product of the distorted imagination.

The Mullahs' Supporters Club

The Muslim attack on Rushdie begun by Syed Shahabuddin was followed by M.H. Faruqi, editor of *Impact International*. The normally obscurantist news magazine sought to put the blame for what Rushdie had done almost squarely on the Muslim community: 'As long as the Muslim world had political and intellectual vigour and Muslim society presented itself as an open book on Islam,' wrote Faruqi, 'it was possible for the non-Muslim to compare the Orientalist version with this "open book" and decide for himself, and people went on deciding and accepting the truth of Islam. That situation has vastly changed.' That situation, in fact, changed some three to four hundred years ago. Distortions of Islam may be common, Faruqi suggested, but the journalists, columnists and leader writers who promote such misunderstandings are quite honestly 'drawing from the perceptions and resource file of their experts, Orientalist and Islamologist'. Moreover, how can they be expected to respect Islam or Muslim sensibilities when Muslims themselves show a great lack of self-respect. Thus, 'in a situation characterised by both insult and lack of self-respect, one needs a great store of patience and composure, to ignore the negatives and to concentrate on the positive.' However, Rushdie's novel has been the straw that broke the camel's back. Faruqi described Rushdie as 'a self-hating Indo-Anglian, totally alienated from his culture, who has also learnt that it is possible to make money by selling self-hate', and answered Rushdie's rhetorical question, 'how could I be anti-Muslim when my whole family is Muslim?' with the retort, 'to be a traitor, one has to belong to the community one intends to betray'. Moreover, how can Rushdie claim that 'the book is not "actually" about Islam' when 'he wants to take credit for offering "my view of revelation, and the birth of a great world religion" '? Faruqi concluded by making three demands on behalf of the Muslim community:

One—To withdraw and pulp the copies of *The Satanic Verses* and to undertake not to reprint it in the future.
Two—To offer unqualified public apology to the World Muslim community.
Three—To pay damages equal to the returns received from the copies already sold in Britain and abroad. (*Impact*, 28 October–10 November 1988)

He urged his readers to protest and seek these demands 'through all civilised and peaceful means'; and requested them to 'please leave Mr Salman Rushdie all to himself and to his charmed circle of "literary critics". We have to say this because we also sense a milling anger about the outrage committed by him.'

The late Ayatollah Khomeini did not read Faruqi's article. His judgement on what should be done about Rushdie's experiments with Islamic history was based on somewhat different criteria. His fatwa offered no reasons, but simply announced:

I inform the proud Muslim people of the world that the author of *The Satanic Verses* which is against Islam, the Prophet and the Qur'an, and all involved in its publication who are aware of its content are sentenced to death. I request brave Muslims to quickly kill them wherever they find them so that no one ever again would dare to insult the sanctities of Muslims. Anyone killed in trying to execute Rushdie would, God willing, be a *shaheed* (martyr). In addition, anyone who has access to the author of the book but does not have the strength to execute him should introduce him to the people so that he receives punishment for his action. (*The Guardian*, 6 March 1989)

Khomeini's explanation and reasoning came in an address to a select gathering of instructors and students of religious seminaries: 'The issue of *The Satanic Verses* is that it is a calculated move aimed at rooting out religion and religiousness, and above all at Islam and its clergy'. The addition of 'clergy' after Islam is important, for much of Islam (that is, about 90 per cent of the Muslim world) does not accept the clergy; indeed, the Sunnis believe that there is absolutely no place for a clergy in Islam.

The Ayatollah stated a belief that is common among most Muslims, and which is not without some historic justification:

It is interesting and indeed astonishing that so-called civilized people and intellectuals do not consider it important when a mercenary author, with the aid of his poisonous pen, hurts the feelings of over a billion people. . . . The issue for them is not that of defending an individual, the issue for them is to support an anti-Islamic current, masterminded by those institutions—belonging to Zionism, Britain and USA—which, through their ignorance and hate, have placed themselves against the Islamic world. (*The Guardian*, 6 March 1989)

Specifically about the novel, Khomeini added:

God wanted this blasphemous book, *The Satanic Verses*, to be published now, so that the world of conceit, of arrogance and of barbarism, would bare its true face in its long-held enmity to Islam; to bring us out of our simplicity. . . . Today's analysts may be occupying the seat of judgement in ten years time . . . it will not be for them to say whether the Islamic decree and the verdict of execution on Salman Rushdie was in accordance with diplomatic regulations or not; it will not be for them to conclude that—just because the expression of God's decree has led to certain consequences, and because the Common Market and the Western countries have taken positions against us—we should therefore have acted in an immature way and left alone the initiators of insults to the sacred position of the Prophet and Islam. (*The Guardian*, 6 March 1989)

Having made his position clear, Ayatollah Khomeini wondered how other

Islamic governments and states will face such a great calamity. This is no longer an issue of Arabs and non-Arabs. This is an insult to the sanctity of Muslims from the origin of Islam until now, and from today until the end of history. This is the result of foreign infiltration of Islamic culture. This will be the beginning of the end, if we remain inattentive, for colonialism has many such dangerous snakes and mercenary writers up her sleeve. (*The Guardian*, 6 March 1989)

If Salman Rushdie is a post-modernist writer, then Ayatollah Khomeini is a post-modern product. He knew how to state the sentiments of the Muslim masses; and after presiding over a bloody revolution for a decade, he became a master of panic politics. In a climate devoid of true freedom and genuine equality, the Patriarch learned from the post-modern culture that power, in whatever sophisticated guise it is presented, including the power of a writer to write what he wants to write without accountability, has to be met with power, even though it may come in the raw form of terror. Terrorism, after all, is also a form of self-expression. The logic of his argument—which he applied to all issues relating to the revolution in Iran—involves stating first what every one wants to hear; then showing that in the pursuit of the common goal (which emerges from what everyone wants to hear) the guardians of the faith, the 'clergy' and the ulamas, have always been in the forefront; then turning the 'calamity' into a challenge; and finally offering a solution that seems a natural product of the selfless interests of the guardians of the faith and, therefore, a natural solution for the masses. Because the solution is offered by those who have divine sanction and are the guardians of the faith, it is seen by the masses as a divine sanction. The 'verdict of execution on Salman Rushdie' is not 'an expression of God's decree': it is an expression of Ayatollah Khomeini's juristic opinion and political wishes. Moreover, the masses take it on faith—not least, because they have just been told that the ulama have always had their interests at heart—that the learned guardians of faith must have passed their verdict after a due process of law.

As a scholastic theologian and philosopher, Ayatollah Khomeini at least followed a kind of logic, even though the vast majority of Muslims do not agree with his conclusion. But in the twilight zone of the Ayatollah's supporters club—where the followers of the 'imam's line' take the name of the imam in the same breath as those of Moses, Jesus and Muhammad—logic and reason are conspicuous only by their total absence. Defending the Ayatollah's *fatwa* (legal ruling) in *The Times* (28 February 1989), Yaqub Zaki, who was among the first Muslims to appear in a British newspaper and whose article was extensively referred to, declared that 'when *The Independent* says that Khomeini's verdict on Salman Rushdie is acceptable only to 10 per cent (really 12 per cent) of the Muslims in the world who are Shiite, it is time for scholarship to enter the fray'. *The Independent* was actually only partially right; many Shiites themselves, not least Ayatollah Motaheri, who was to succeed Ayatollah Khomeini before his consistent criticism of the regime led to his forced resignation, also rejected Ayatollah Khomeini's *fatwa*. 'The fact is, Rushdie's book is obscene and overflows with such appalling blasphemies as no Muslim in his right mind could have uttered.' It is at this level that all Muslims agree with the Ayatollah, but his verdict on Rushdie is another matter. To prove his scholarly credentials further, Zaki produced a scholarly analogy:

> Muhammad's own role in respect of the revelatory act was that of a telephone, a mindless instrument that could in no way interfere with the transmission of the text. Unfortunately, even with the best of the telecommunication system, lines sometimes get crossed. According to two early sources (al-Tabari and ibn Saad), this is what happened on one occassion. What came through was satanic (wiswas) and not divine (wahi) revelation. (*The Times*, 28 February 1989)

So revelation is, after all, partially superior to British Telecom and American Telephone and Telegraph, whose users complain frequently of crossed lines. The countless Muslim philosophers and theologians who throughout history spent their entire lives trying to understand the nature of revelation must be turning in their graves at this learned brilliance!

On the question of apostasy, Zaki told us that 'apostasy is a capital offence in Islam, and while the death penalty may seem harsh, it is worth bearing in mind that . . . apostasy and treason are one and the same thing'. Not quite. Of the half-dozen or so who have been executed in Islamic history for treason, a few also happened to be apostates. But countless apostates have existed in Islam, a few even at the time of the Prophet, many of them great literary figures, and none of them have been executed—there is no sanction for such an action either in the Qur'an or in the sira. Moreover, Zaki's assertion that 'on the penalty for apostasy there is complete unanimity between all five schools of law in Islam (four in Sunnism, one in Shiism)' presents a monolithic unity which is not there; within Islamic law the capital punishment for apostasy is a matter of controversy and considerable debate. Moreover, *fiqh* is both an issue of power and territory as well as a matter of opinion. As the noted Muslim scholar, the late Fazlur Rahman stated categorically, 'the source of Islamic law of apostasy is not the Qur'an but the logic of Islamic imperium' (in Hovannisian, p. 15). Ayatollah Khomeini was using the logic of Iranian imperialism. What Zaki forgot to say is that a juristic opinion, like the Ayatollah's fatwa against Salman Rushdie, is *only* binding on the person who gives it and those who accept his *taqlid* (blind following). *What Zaki is thus defending is his own belief and intended action*; it has nothing to do with the position of the majority of Muslims.

The blatant and totally obnoxious political and ideological slant of Yaqub Zaki became evident towards the end of the article. 'Muslims are united as never before . . . Imam Khomeini, simply by articulating what every Muslim feels in his heart, has recouped at one stroke everything lost in the war with Iraq and emerged as the undisputed moral leader of the world's one billion Muslims.' For those Muslims whose morality is based on the *taqlid* of the imam and on killing, the statement may have certain validity; but fortunately, Imam Khomeini's 'undisputed leadership' was being challenged in his lifetime even in Iran; outside Iran only a select band of Shias endorse his authority. The logic that states that simply by one *fatwa* the losses of an eight-year war can be recouped is totally perverse, indeed demonic. The loss of two million people, including young children, razing to the ground of numerous cities, the total collapse of an economy, the politically motivated executions of thousands and thousands—all this can be recouped 'at one stroke' by simply issuing yet another command to kill? At the end of the article, *The Times* revealed that 'the author, formerly James Dickie, is a British Muslim and a visting professor at Harvard University'. It could also have added: he is an extremist who is known to the Muslim community for his perverse views and while not 'visiting' Harvard University—where he teaches architecture—he is on the payroll of the Muslim Institute which gets its financial and spiritual sustenance from Tehran.

The Muslim Institute for Research and Planning, based in London, is involved neither in 'research' nor 'planning'. It is, in fact, an extension of the Iranian Embassy and acts as a front organization for Iran, mobilizing support for Iran in the Muslim community in Britain as well as abroad, and providing post-facto intellectual, revolutionary and theoretical justification for the excesses and extremism of the Iranian regime. The Muslim Institute, like many Muslim organizations in Britain, is really a one-man affair: Kalim Siddiqui, the director, *is* the Muslim Institute. A former *Guardian* journalist, Siddiqui—who is not a Shia—believes that the late Ayatollah Khomeini was almost, if not totally, infallible, a belief which may have been strengthened by the Iranian financial support the Institute receives. Another factor which has contributed to the Institute's subservience to Iran is Siddiqui's hatred of Saudi Arabia, which dates back to the formative phase of the Institute. Siddiqui was a recipient of large donations from Saudi Arabia—some of his employees received their salaries direct from Jeddah. He was also successful in securing a very large grant for a project entitled 'The Road to Medina', which involved writing a number of studies on the life of Prophet Muhammad. When the studies did not materialize, the Saudis asked for the grant to be returned; that was not possible because Siddiqui had used some of the funds to buy the building which presently houses the Institute. After the Saudis threatened legal action, the matter was eventually settled with a portion of the grant being returned. In Iran, Siddiqui found a friend who shared his extremist and domineering tendencies as well as his hatred of Saudi Arabia. The Institute now represents an incipient minority of mainly Shia Muslims, who believe that the purity and the 'divine' nature of the revolution in Iran must be preserved at all costs.

In the first five months of the Muslim campaign against *The Satanic Verses*, Siddiqui dismissed the whole affair as a 'non-event'. The propaganda sheet of the Institute, *Crescent International*, which describes itself as the 'Newsmagazine of the Islamic movement' (considering it has only 3,000 readers, many of whom receive it free courtesy of the Iranian Embassy, the 'Islamic movement' does not amount to very much!), totally ignored the story. With the Ayatollah Khomeini's fatwa, *The Satanic Verses* affair became a matter of 'Islam versus the Western civilization'. Siddiqui, who believes that 'conflict is like sex—[it] should be enjoyed' (K. Siddiqui, *Functions*, p. iii), could not believe his luck: he was handed a conflict on a platter and as the sole spokesperson of the 'Imam's line' had a responsibility to present the case. He took over the Muslim leadership—not a difficult task, since most Muslim leaders are inarticulate and terrified of the media—and projected himself as *the* Muslim leader ('I have been advising the Muslim community . . . ' is his favourite opening line). The media played into his hand: he was saying what they wanted to hear and saying it in cogent, clearly understandable forty-second bites.

In the pages of *Crescent*, Siddiqui espoused his opinion at much greater length, first mentioning the Rushdie affair in early March. A lead story entitled 'The West and Islam on a Collision Course' began with the usual denunciation of Saudi Arabia: 'the rulers of all modern Muslim nation-states are hidden Salman Rushdies. The most obvious examples are the Saudi dynasty . . .'

> The anti-Islam smell was (first) picked up by the pro-Saudi lobby in Britain. This is the lobby that is always on the lookout for 'Islamic' causes they can champion to gain the favour of their paymasters. Their 'campaigning', as usual, amounted to letters to the British prime minster and a meeting of Muslim ambassadors in London. (*Crescent*, 1–15 March 1989)

Once that abuse was out of the way, the inevitable projection of the Ayatollah followed:

> The Imam's intervention on February 14 will go down in history as one of the greatest acts of leadership of the ummah by any political or religious leader in the history of Islam. The Imam spoke on behalf of the one thousand million Muslims of the world, and the world's Muslim community did not disappoint him. Virtually every Muslim man, woman and child agreed Rushdie should die. (*Crescent*, 1–15 March 1989)

Just as the Ayatollah Khomeini with one stroke recouped all the damage of Iran's war with Iraq, *Crescent* with one stroke, relegated the entire history of Islam to a poor second compared to the *fatwa* of Ayatollah Khomeini. Does the entire Muslim community include the Sunnis who do not accept the Ayatollah as their 'Imam'; the Saudis who, whatever the quality of their leadership, do not hide their contempt for the Ayatollah's policies; the vast majority of Muslims in Bradford, who could not distance themselves from the Ayatollah's fatwa fast enough? Evidently not. Just as for 'Islam' we should read 'Iran', for the 'entire Muslim community' we should read the 'Trotskyite-like tendency which supports the Muslim Institute'. The article finally concluded: 'that the West is spoiling for a fight with Islam is quite clear. . . . It is quite clear that the two civilizations, that of Islam and the West, are on a collision course. This is a fight only one can win.' Given the economic, technological and military might of the West, we know which side that will be.

The next issue of *Crescent* declared that there is a 'Satanic Conspiracy in the West'. The editorial told us that it is because of a conspiracy that the entire Western world is willing to 'alienate the whole world of Islam for the sake of one wretched man of brown skin living in London'. So much for Islam's uncompromising stand on racism. The lead story announced that 'the Ummah (Muslim community) stands united behind a single leader, on a single issue'.

> All the rulers of Muslim nation-states, from Morocco to Indonesia, . . . have been exposed as partners of global kufr (unbelief). None of them has had the courage, for fear of antagonizing their western masters, to condemn the book or to endorse the one and only possible verdict on its apostate author, Salman Rushdie. (*Crescent*, 16–31 March 1989)

The logic here is that of puritanical self-righteousness: there is absolutely no room for dissent—if you disagree with us, you are *kafir* (unbelievers); and despite what the Qur'an may say, what the example of the Prophet Muhammad may be, what other jurists may declare, the position declared by our 'Imam' is 'the one and only possible' one. What followed repeated the fallacy that Khomeini's fatwa is based on Qur'anic injunction: 'the Imam's unambiguous *fatwa*, based on Qur'anic sanction, electrified the Ummah and left the western leaders holding the fig-leaf of "freedom of speech" to hide their moral bankruptcy and the nakedness of western culture and civilization'. The belief that what came from the mouth of the Imam is a divine order is further reinforced by a quote from Akhundzadeh Basti, the Iranian Charge d'Affaires: 'It is a divine order; no one can change it'. When the 'divine order' is combined with a 'common well-defined goal'—that Salman Rushdie should be killed—we have a monolithic situation: one Muslim community under one leader. By this perverse logic, all the aspirations of the Muslim civilization are reduced to a single aim: kill Salman Rushdie. Yet the divinity of the fatwa seemed to have evaporated when Siddiqui was attending the Imam's funeral: 'he must be killed' turned into 'they are not sending anyone to kill him'; and 'if Salman Rushdie withdraws the book, then the British Muslims will leave him alone' (*The Independent*, 8 June 1989).

But Siddiqui was not satisfied with simply thrusting the Imam on the shoulders of all Muslim-kind, whether they wanted him or not; he wants to turn all Muslims into lemmings who, for the sake of the Imam, should turn themselves into cannon fodder so that the imperial goals of Iran can be advanced. 'The response to the Imam's fatwa confirms the existence of a global hizbullahi movement', he declared in his column in the *Crescent*. There is a 'Party of Allah' (hizbullahi movement), which, considering there is only one goal, one leader, and one true version of faith, is, of course, the one and only party. He announced that Muslims cannot be divided into 'nation-states', they must denounce their states and governments and rise up in bloody revolutions to ensure the hegemony of Iran on the international Muslim community. 'Imam Khomeini', he told his readers, 'is the best manifestation of Islamic leadership. . . . By virtue of his successful leadership of the Islamic Revolution and his position as the leader of the only Islamic state on the map today, [he] exercises a unique moral and spiritual authority over the entire world of Islam. . . . Once an Islamic State has been established, it must command the total loyalty of all Muslims everywhere.' From this totalitarian statement, Siddiqui moved into total, pathological fantasy—a strike force of lemmings has been created by the Ayatollah's successes and fatwa, ready to take over the world: 'there now exists a global hizbullahi movement ready to be led by the Islamic State of Iran and Imam Khomeini (or his successors) in pursuit of the global political goals of Islam'. And as usual, to be counted among the believers, 'the only alternative is for the ummah (Muslim community) to be led as a single global Islamic movement, and for this Islamic movement to bring about successive Islamic

Revolutions, one after the other, in all parts of the world.' Thus, the declaration to 'kill an apostate' completes its logic of 'imperium'.

In almost everything he writes, Siddiqui deliberately ignores the fact that the Sunnis have an intrinsic dislike of totalitarian theocracies: as an option, theocracy has been ruled out by all Sunni scholars. The Sunnis believe in the politics of consensus (*ijma*) and consultation (*shura*), and following the methodology of the Qur'an and the example of the Prophet, in gradual change and not in revolutionary upheaval. This is the belief, even though contemporary Muslim reality is quite the opposite. However, while the Iranian clergy could usher in a revolution because of the organized nature of their religion, to believe that this revolution can be exported to other Muslim states, despite the lessons of the last ten years, is to be intoxicated by one's own self-righteousness, power and violence—all justified by 'divine sanctions'. We can say about Ayatollah Khomeini what Kalim Siddiqui himself said about Sunni imams in Pakistan during its formative phase: 'every local imam was a leader. He led his flock down a blind alley in which the Muslim soul was sustained by faith in ultimate triumph without any evidence to promote hope based on reason'.

That Ayatollah Khomeini's fatwa is not the only possible legal opinion that can be issued against Rushdie became evident when the Al Azhar, the oldest Muslim learned institution in the world, issued another fatwa, ruling that Rushdie cannot be convicted without a trial. And as Zaki Badawi, former director of London's Islamic Cultural Centre, said: 'Yes, Khomeini reflects the entire Muslim religious view that Rushdie is on the face of it an apostate, a heretic. But neither he nor any Muslim authority has the power to sentence Rushdie to death.' Moreover, Islamic jurisprudence is a system of law and justice, involving legal procedures, a system of trial, opportunities for the accused to offer his or her defence, and an elaborate procedure for carrying out the sentence. Zaki Badawi said:

> Even if he were legitimately sentenced to death, Islamic punishment cannot be carried out by anyone other than the Islamic appointed authorities and you cannot in Islam pass any sentence, let alone the death penalty, without a proper trial. It is unacceptable in Islam to try anyone in his absence. Teachings of both the minority Shia branch of Islam and the majority Sunni . . . are identical on this. (*The Guardian*, 27 February 1989)

How the majority of Muslims felt about Ayatollah Khomeini's fatwa was made clear by the reasoned response of the Canadian Society of Muslims (CSM). In a long, closely argued declaration, CSM first categorically and clearly stated that *The Satanic Verses* is an obnoxious piece of hate literature, full of calculated abuse and blasphemies; Muslims are totally united on this assessment and want the novel banned. Then they examined the fatwa of Ayatollah Khomeini. 'It appears to constitute yet another instance in which Imam Khomeini has not proceeded in a way that would be in the best interests of Muslims, or in a way that would be in the best interest of helping non-Muslims to develop a better understanding of the Islamic religious tradition.' Reason and education are a fundamental part of Islamic religious tradition. Yet there is no evidence that Ayatollah Khomeini made any attempts to engage in an educational and reasoned dialogue with Salman Rushdie. However,

> If Imam Khomeini wishes to set an example for the West, or the rest of the Muslim world for that matter, then, sometimes, it would be nice if he would show to the West the example of patience, forbearance, compassion and forgiveness which the Prophet Muhammad displayed during the latter's dealing with those who persecuted, antagonized or attempted to kill him in their attempts to destroy Islam. The Prophet Muhammad was staunch and steadfast when circumstances warranted it. However, he also showed considerable creative flexibility and variety in his actions, without ever compromising on the basic tenets of Islam. Indeed, the insightful, and creative flexibility with which he approached the affairs of day-to-day life provided a set of standards embracing, among other praiseworthy qualities, fairness, compassion and generosity which have come to serve as guidelines for how the individual Muslim is to proceed in a whole variety of problems one may encounter in everyday life. (CSM Declaration, Toronto, 1989)

The CSM declaration wondered why Ayatollah Khomeini never seemed to display these examples of the Prophet. 'There may be many things wrong with the West but, for the most part, the people here are not evil, nor are they intrinsically antagonistic to different ways of looking at things, nor are they without sense of, and commitment to, spirituality.'

Canadian Muslims were 'deeply disturbed' that the notion of forgiveness was never considered by Ayatollah Khomeini. If Allah is constantly ready to forgive, and if one has the option of repenting to the end of one's life, then why has Ayatollah Khomeini not considered this option?

> Imam Khomeini should know that many people in the West are themselves victims of centuries of ignorance about, and have a misinformed, if not totally misplaced, hostility towards, the Islamic world. While the prejudices which arise from the years of miseducation concerning the Islamic religious tradition cannot be condoned, one still must be appreciative of why they are there and take steps to rectify, rather than exacerbate, the underlying problem. Unfortunately, Imam Khomeini . . . sometimes

does and says things which fan the fires of prejudice rather than provide an avenue for resolving them. . . . It is a cardinal principle of the Prophet Muhammad that, whenever possible, it was better to pursue conciliatory avenues of resolving difficulties, even if it meant putting the Muslim community at some disadvantage under certain circumstances. Violence was only resorted to as a defensive measure and when hostilities were thrust upon them. (CSM Declaration, Toronto, 1989)

Canadian Muslims were horrified at the idea of a bounty:

The bringing of money into the matter is highly offensive, as is, to a far lesser extent, the apparent willingness of Iranian officials to differentiate between Iranian Muslims and non-Iranian Muslims with respect to the amount being offered. (CSM Declaration, Toronto, 1989)

The Declaration concluded by stating a well known Islamic principle:

If one drop of innocent blood is spilled by anyone who feels compelled to comply with the order, then it will be as if injury has been inflicted upon the whole of humanity. This is a basic teaching of Islam, and Muslims everywhere will do well to keep it in mind. Whatever may or may not happen with respect to Mr Rushdie concerns him and no one else. Just as there are bounds of transgression which Mr Rushdie should not have crossed, there are also bounds of transgression which Muslims must not cross. (CSM Declaration, Toronto, 1989)

It was arguments such as those presented by the CSM Declaration which formed the basis of the Declaration on Joint Action to Combat Blasphemy against Islam of the Organization of the Islamic Conference (OIC). The OIC, with its forty-six member states, functions as the Muslim United Nations, and presents joint (negotiated) Muslim positions on international affairs. The OIC Declaration:

1. Resolved to protect and safeguard the Muqaddassai (Islamic sanctities) and to co-ordinate their efforts in accordance with the Shariah at national, regional and international levels effectively to combat blasphemy against Islam and slandering of Islamic personalities.
2. Announced its commitment to:
   (a) Ban the book *The Satanic Verses*.
   (b) Demand that the publishers must forthwith
       (i) Withdraw this novel from the market and pulp the same.
       (ii) Offer an unconditional apology to all Muslims.

(iii) Commit not to publish or promote it in any other form or language in the future.
3. And further:
(a) If the publishers fail to comply with the above forthwith, such publishers and their holding companies, if any, should be blacklisted and import of all their publications banned in all Muslim countries.
(b) Economic sanctions should be used against all those who extend protection to this blasphemous book against Islam.
(c) The submission in non-Muslim states be directed to contact governments of their countries (of accreditation) to take effective actions in banning this novel and seeking its withdrawal from the markets.
(d) Wide publicity be given to the measures taken by the Muslim states so that it serves as a deterrent and in future no-one dares to denigrate Islam.

The OIC Declaration, like that of the CSM, received little attention from the Western media. These moderate positions, however, in no way undermined the outrage and anger felt by all believing Muslims. Ali Mazrui's Cornell University lecture on the moral dilemma of the Rushdie affair, delivered two weeks after the Ayatollah's fatwa (1 March 1989; published by the Committee of Muslim Scholars and Learned of North America, New York) did not appear in any major Western newspaper or magazine. Mazrui detailed the personal conflict: 'I have been torn between being a believer in Islam and a believer in the open society, between being myself a writer and being a religious worshipper, between being a believer in the Shariah and an open opponent of all forms of capital punishment in the modern age.' Being a writer, novelist and broadcaster, 'I also have strong reservations about censorship.'

> This is partly because I have myself been censored over the years. I have been censored in the Republic of South Africa, in parts of the Muslim world, in my own native Kenya, in Uganda under President Idi Amin, the United Kingdom and in the United States of America. I have therefore had to argue with my very soul whether the banning of Salman Rushdie's *Satanic Verses* is any more legitimate than the censorship to which I have been subjected in different parts of the world from time to time. (Mazrui, p. 4)

Programme three of Mazrui's BBC/PBS television series, *The Africans: a Triple Heritage*, opened with a bust of Karl Marx. The voice-over told us: ' "Religion is the sigh of the oppressed culture and the soul of soulless conditions", so said Karl Marx, the last of the great Jewish prophets'. But

PBS deleted the phrase 'last of the great Jewish prophets' in order not to offend Jewish viewers in spite of the fact that 'it made it difficult for me to make the case about the Semitic impact on Africa (of Jesus, Muhammad and Marx)'. But as the series had already been shown in Britain, American journalists knew about the phrase and used it to attack Mazrui. The President of WETA was attacked at the National Press Club in Washington, D.C., for showing a television series which had *previously* had the statement 'the last of the great Jewish prophets'. 'No journalist anywhere in the USA', said Mazrui, 'took the cudgels on my behalf on the issue of my being able to say that Marx was the last of the great Jewish prophets. PBS and WETA exercised a direct form of censorship because they 'believed that a hostile alliance of rightwing gentiles and irate Jewish liberals was more than the series could cope with in the USA.' However, the Jews in Israel, where the programme was seen uncensored via Jordanian television, did not object to the phrase. Indeed, Mazrui continued,

> Everyday of the week something is being censored in the American media. Programs are denied funding for fear of offending advertisers, subscribers, mainstream patriots, mainstream religious zealots, powerful Jews, powerful gentiles. Otherwise reputable publishers turn down manuscripts, edit out ideas, or surgically remove chapters likely to offend powerful groups in the nation. Censorship in the United States is basically privatized—as befits a private enterprise system. The state lets the censorship be exercised in the market place by the forces of supply and demand. Freelance censors abound. (Mazrui, p. 17)

Mazrui contrasted his phrase which offended the American Jewish sensibilities, but not the sensibilities of the Israeli Jews, with offence and blasphemies contained in *The Satanic Verses*. Unlike his case, there is a unanimous agreement among Muslims that Rushdie had *abused* Islam and that he has been 'lionized, praised, and lavishly rewarded and financed by outright enemies and hostile critics of Islam'. Mazrui told his audience, 'the Qur'an is the most widely read book in its *original* in human history. The Bible is the most widely read book in translation. The Bible is also a multi-authored work. But the Qur'an is in a class by itself as a book which is recited by millions of believers, five times every day, in the very language in which it was first written.' Now the Americans, explained Mazrui, 'regard deliberate stepping on their flag, or purposefully urinating on the star-spangled banner, as sacrilege. Each verse of the Qur'an is like a flag to a Muslim. Has Salman Rushdie deliberately urinated on the Holy Book?'

Mazrui discussed the double-standards that Western governments regularly operate on such issues. Compare, for example, the reactions to

Ayatollah Khomeini's fatwa and the blowing up of the Greenpeace ship *Rainbow Warrior* by French secret agents. On the one hand, we have 'the European Community's collective outrage against the Ayatollah's proclamation of violence by remote control', while on the other

> No such collective outrage was evident when one of the European Community's own members sent agents to blow up the *Rainbow Warrior* in a peaceful New Zealand port. The ship belonged to the environmentalist activist group, Greenpeace, which was protesting against France's repeated nuclear tests in the South Pacific. The French authorities decided to teach both New Zealand and the Greenpeace protesters a lesson by sending agents to plant explosives on board the unarmed ship. A Greenpeace member on board was killed as a result of the French sabotage. The whole French exercise was directly intended to silence legitimate protest through an act of state terrorism. (Mazrui, p. 18)

Did the EEC show any outrage? Was there a threat of economic sanctions? 'Yes, there was a threat of economic sanctions—but against New Zealand, whose sovereignty had been violated, rather than France, which had violated it.' Moreover, there was no evidence of outrage from the Community 'when France threatened to deny New Zealand economic access to the Community as a whole if New Zealand refused to bend its own judicial procedures over the convicted agents'. Did the Community show outrage when the Israelis kidnapped nuclear scientist Mordechai Vanunu? In Israeli eyes, Vanunu was guilty of double treason: he was a traitor to Israel because he published intimate nuclear secrets in a British newspaper (September 1986), and he was also a traitor to his Jewish faith because he became a Christian at about the same time. But the Community allowed the Israelis to do what they wished with Vanunu. The logic here is, the evil we do is civilized; whatever you do is evil, barbaric and uncivilized.

Since so many commentators have compared the Muslim burning of the book with the activities of Hitler's National Socialists, Mazrui took the analogy further, offering a comparison between *The Satanic Verses* and *Mein Kampf*. 'Hitler's book was anti-Jewish while *The Satanic Verses* is anti-Muslim. Hitler had political aspirations—while Rushdie's ambitions seem to be basically literary and mercenary. But fundamentally the two books are works of alienation and basically divisive in intent and in impact. . . . In the mid-1920s, Hitler described himself as a writer. Royalties for his book and fees for newspaper articles were his principal source of income. His tax returns from 1925 to 1929 give figures which approximated closely his income from Mein Kampf . . . Hitler's original title was *Four and a Half Years of Struggle Against Lies, Stupidity and Cowardice*. I am not sure if Rushdie sees himself as engaged in many years of struggle against Muslim "Lies, Stupidity and Cowardice".' Mazrui said that had he been present and old enough he would have joined in the protests by the Jews of the United States, who 'should have done more to burn *Mein Kampf*'. Would the Jewish liberals contemplate joining him in his protest?

In Britain, the Muslim outrage found its best expression in Shabbir Akhtar, a philosopher who works for the Community Relations Council in Bradford. Writing in *The Guardian* (27 February 1989), Akhtar announced that 'having read *The Satanic Verses* twice, I am completely convinced that it is an inferior piece of literature whose popularity in the West invites one to look in the region of motives. Even on a sympathetic reading, Rushdie's book is an incoherent fantasy which will cater to an undiscerning appetite already entrenched in the Western mind.' Responding to Rushdie's claim that he was exploring revelation and the historic origins of a great religion, Akhtar declared that Rushdie need not 'flatter himself with the conceit that he has properly indulged the sceptical temper let alone discovered historical Muhammad. Rushdie is not ploughing a virgin field: sceptics there have been and always will be. What matters is the quality and integrity of their doubts.' Moreover, scepticism and doubt is neither unusual to Rushdie nor to the secularist tradition:

> A Job-like scepticism, reverent and sincere, is found in many Islamic thinkers and novelists, all the way from al-Ghazzali to Muhammad Iqbal and Najib Mahfuz. Within Rushdie's unprincipled prose, one looks in vain for the penetrating critique of a Mahfuz implying tragically that occasional divine tuition via messengership (in the Islamic style) does not suffice, human perversity being inveterate as it is. Satanic Verses falls short of the only real metaphysical achievement of an anti-religious genius, that even good and evil are (as Nietzsche would say) prejudices, albeit God's prejudices. (*The Guardian*, 27 February 1989)

In its 'Eyekay' column, the London-based Urdu daily, *Jang*, (6–7 May 1989), pointed out that despite the dominance of an incipient minority, 'it would be dangerous and insensitive to dismiss Muslim protests as the work of a zealous and unrepresentative minority of fanatics. The outrage is shared by a vast majority of Muslims, who have been informed, in no uncertain terms of the contents of the book, with the most offensive passages reproduced and distributed widely.' As the only Urdu daily in Britain, *Jang* could feel the pulse of the Pakistani, Bangladeshi and Indian communities. It noted that 'Muslim reaction has been characterised not only by anger and a deeply felt feeling of public insult, but also by an inner feeling of hurt, wounding and isolation. There is a genuine sense of resentment that no one outside the

Muslim community has yet understood or supported the Muslim cause.' Moreover, 'the unrestrained hostility of many sections of society has reinforced the Muslim minority's perception that it is not understood and that its presence in this country is merely tolerated.' *Jang* argued that freedom and liberty are not limitless absolutes:

> Both are open to abuse and both must be exercised within certain bounds. No one has the right to claim freedom of expression as an absolute defence when shouting 'Fire' in a crowded theatre and no one's exercise of liberty allows them to douse their neighbour in petrol and set them alight. Extreme examples indeed, but Muslims would argue that their suffering is no less traumatic. (*Jang*, 6–7 May 1989)

Rediscovering Rabies

From the beginning of the Rushdie affair, Muslims came under attack in newspapers, radio and television for being intolerant. But what about those who were attacking: are they tolerant and understanding?

Two common themes running through many articles in quality newspapers were expressed by John Hay in Ottawa's *Citizen* (19 February 1989): 'I cannot understand the astonishing reactions of people who have never read the book.' The argument is that one cannot pass judgement or protest against a book one has not read. But how many people have read *The Satanic Verses*? George Steiner said he could not read it. And many Muslims do not read the languages in which it has been published. How many of those who stood up against Hitler had read *Mein Kampf*? How many card-carrying Marxists have actually read *Das Capital*? What is necessary is not to have read the book, but to *know* what it contains. Muslims certainly know, for they can take the word of their brothers and sisters who have read the book and whom they trust. Even though they may not have read the book, they know what it says about themselves and the Qur'an, how it treats the Prophet Muhammad, what sacred territory it has violated.

The second common argument is that, after all, *The Satanic Verses* is a work of fiction, and why should one get all heated up about a work of fiction? Here Hay's answer is spot on: Rusdhie fully understands the differences between fact and fiction, reality and beliefs and 'to that extent, Rushdie's enemies are right. He loathes the power of Islam.'

The power of Islam, the little power it has in a world dominated by secularist thought and Western civilization, has proved too much for certain commentators. Stephen Vizinczey, in *The Sunday Telegraph* (19 March 1989), suggested that 'the almost total invisibility of the most famous book of the century is a measure of the power Islam exercises in the West'. Total invisibility? How it came to sell over one million copies in hardback if it is so invisible? Vizinczey continued, 'it also exemplifies the betrayal of Western civilization by people who believe that all cultures and values are equal and that we must never offend any of them by defending our own. But only Westerners believe that. To devout Muslims we will burn in hell. This is what the Koran says, and plenty of Western politicians and churchmen are falling over themselves to condemn a novel which suggests that this declaration doesn't come directly from God's mouth.' The real issue, Vizinczey suggested, is 'militant Islam's right to dictate to us what we can read, write, print, distribute and display'. This 'militant Islam' is a nasty piece of work and we, the West, should begin our homework immediately to decide how we are going to cope with this menace; as it is, 'we haven't even started to think about how to defend ourselves against this power which aims at world domination!'

'This power' is a totally evil enterprise. A week earlier, the same newspaper carried a piece entitled, 'Why the West is Best', by the Conservative Member of Parliament, George Walden (*The Sunday Telegraph*, 12 March 1989): 'we have been soft-pedaling on "Third World values" for too long, when even people like V.S. Naipaul regard Third World cultures as thoroughly evil; we should stand up and declare it so. It is a threat to the very survival of the West . . . the threat to our values is there, now, in front of us, perfectly cold and unambiguous; a threat directed against everything the West is supposed to believe in.' These remarks show the utility of the brown sahibs and why they are so welcome.

One should expect this kind of gunboat diplomatic jingoism from the right, but what about the middle-of-the-roaders? Peter Jenkins, who for years hogged valuable space in *The Guardian* and now regularly parades his banalities in *The Independent*, produced a number of pieces about intolerance of religion.

> Since the Bradford *auto-da-fe*, that offence has been many times compounded, not only by the death sentence from the geriatric prophet in Qom, but by the repeated demands for suppression or pulping of the book, by representations to the Home Office in favour of extending our archaic and indefensible blasphemy law to cover obscurantist Muslim fundamentalism, and by learned sophistry suggesting that we should place medieval intolerance on all fours with our own tolerant secularism. (*The Independent*, 1 March 1989)

One can see that Jenkins does not want the book suppressed, but since when has making representation to the Home Office become a crime? And that 'learned sophistry' refers literally to one-half dozen articles by Muslims that appeared in national newspapers, compared to acres and acres of pro-Rushdie, anti-Muslim venom produced by Jenkins and other 'tolerant secularists'. However, in the end, poor Peter Jenkins is totally defeated: 'there is little if anything that we as a country, nor Europe nor the West, can do about this latest surge of Islamic fanaticism save wait for it to play itself out'. But there is something that Jenkins can do: he can, for example, start using his column to put the whole issue in context, start analysing the underlying assumptions in his own and in his fellow secularists' positions. He can take a more objective look at the distorted imagination and misrepresentations which add fuel to the 'surge of Islamic fanaticism', instead of riding further on his hobby horses of religious intolerance, Naziism, and Stalinism.

Another tolerant secularist is Roy Jenkins, former Home Secretary in the Labour Government, now a leading stalwart of the Social Democratic and Liberal Party and a former President of the Commission of the European Community. Writing in the *The Independent Magazine* (4 March 1989), Jenkins observed of Muslims in Britain: 'they have obviously not merged their culture and still less their religion. . . . Nor perhaps can they realistically be expected emotionally to match modern Christian tolerance.' Is it obvious that they were supposed to? Would they have retained their cultural and religious identities had they done so? But given the fact that they are emotionally retarded anyway (for 'realistically', read ethnocentrically), how could one reasonably expect them to merge their culture or 'match modern Christian tolerance'? All this, Roy Jenkins told his readers, 'strengthens my reluctance to have Turkey, which does not incontestably meet the qualifications of being either European or democratic, in the European community.' Turkey, Mr Jenkins, is partly located in Europe, has profoundly influenced European history and is as European, at least in parts, as Greece, which, too, until quite recently, was ruled by generals. As far as their Europeanness is concerned, including the colour of the skin, Roy Jenkins would find it hard to tell them apart. The real fact is that in the eyes of Roy Jenkins, Turks being Muslims are wogs—that is why they should be kept out of the European Community.

The literary doyen Anthony Burgess announced that Muslims have declared a *jihad*; but it is obvious that he neither understands the meaning of the word nor the mechanism by which jihad is declared:

> I gain the impression that few of the protesting Muslims in Britain know directly what they are protesting against. Their Imam has told them that Mr Rushdie has published

a blasphemous book and must be punished. They respond with sheeplike docility and wolflike aggression. They forget what the Nazis did to books—or perhaps they do not: after all, some of their co-religionists approved of the Holocaust—and they shame a free country by denying free expression through the vindictive agency of bonfires. (*The Independent*, 16 February 1989)

Here misinformation combines with standard bogies. The 'Imam' appeared on the scene five months after the Muslim protest began: whatever the Imam told them, he told them after they had already known that Mr Rushdie had published a blasphemous book and had been protesting against his blasphemy. What is meant by 'some of their co-religionists approve of the Holocaust'? Burgess could be referring to—and this is the only historical incident that we can find—the meeting that the Mufti of Palestine had with Hitler. However, to suggest that the Mufti actually agreed with Hitler is historically dubious. Moreover, a meeting does not mean endorsement of ideology; after all, Chamberlain also met Hitler and no one is suggesting that he joined Hitler in his insane mission. Muslim society, like all societies, does have a fascist lunatic fringe; but that is exactly what it is, a lunatic fringe. Their actions do not constitute the norm any more than Mosley's activities can be considered the norm for British society. Anyhow, is it necessary for one to point out that it was Burgess's 'co-religionist' who instituted the Holocaust? After this absurd analysis, Burgess produced the caveat that so many writers have resorted to: 'if they do not like secular society, they must fly to the arms of the Ayatollah or some other self-righteous guardian of strict Islamic morality'. And finally, the sense of innate superiority that is the hallmark of dogmatic secularism: 'one wonders if even major religions, however sincerely held, should be allowed to prevail over those secular beliefs that no longer owe anything to theology—tolerance, charity, a sense of humour and a great deal of goodwill'. Far be it from us to suggest that these values first emerged as 'theology', as Burgess's co-religionists will no doubt tell him.

The arguments offered in various analyses in *The Independent* were summed up in an editorial (16 January 1989): 'If members of Britain's community of some two million Muslims do not want to read Salman Rushdie's novel *The Satanic Verses*, all they have to do is abstain from buying it or taking it out from the local library.' On the surface, this statement appears quite sane. However, it assumes that an ostrich-like behaviour is a wise action to follow. By 'abstaining from buying', the distorted image of Islam and Muslims presented in the book does not go away. Abstention does nothing to alleviate the products of the distorted imagination. Moreover, even in British law, one does not have to read a book to be outraged by it: the law does not ask whether you have read the book—outrage subsists and should be self-evident in what is written in the book. The counter-argument is brought home when the book is placed in some sort of personalized context. Suppose, for instance, that a novel were written about an editor of a newspaper like *The Independent*. Although the editor's name was not used exactly, his character was drawn accurately right down to the fact that he edited a newspaper called *Independence*. The fictional character was clearly identifiable as the real editor of *The Independent*. But a few extra features were added: it was suggested, for example, that the fictional editor was a leading light of the Paedophile Exchange and that he had strong sympathies with the Ku Klux Klan, often appearing, in the novel, dressed in their terrifying white robes and setting fire to innocent black people. Moreover, the fictional editor's mother was a prostitute who regularly worked London's City Road and used the offices of *Independence* for pulling in tricks. What would the real editor do? Would he, as *The Independent* leader advised Muslims, not read the novel and abstain from buying or borrowing it? Or would he take the author to court for defamation, demand that the offending passages be deleted and a compensation made? The *Spectator's* columnist, Taki (25 February 1989), made his feelings clear: 'If someone wrote that my mother was a prostitute—the old lady being a saint and having slept with one man in her life—I would make sure that his knee-caps disappear and then dare a jury to convict me.'

The editorial, like so many articles, drew parallels between the action of Muslims in Bradford and that notorious character of European history, Adolf Hitler: 'their campaign to have the book banned, on the ground that it blasphemes Islam, led to a demonstration over the weekend in Bradford in which, following the example of the Inquisition and Hitler's National Socialists, a large crowd of Muslims burnt some copies of the book'. 'Following the example' suggests that an analogy is being drawn: but is there any substance to this analogy? The Inquisition was instituted by an organized and all-powerful Church, controlling all of Europe, in which not one but countless books were burnt, and thousand-upon-thousand were tortured and burned at the stake. The Nazis were in control of a great European country and had the power and military might to impose their belief in racial superiority on others; they burned many books, most of which were not offensive to anyone, including themselves. The Muslims in Bradford are a totally powerless minority, who by all accounts are law-abiding citizens; they certainly do not believe that people should be tortured and burned at the stake or hold any beliefs that can be said to be fascist. Moreover, unlike the Nazis and the perpetrators of the Inquisition who were the culprits, in the case of the Bradford book burning, the Muslims are the *victims*; unlike the Nazis, they are not doing the ridiculing and abusing, but it is they who have been ridiculed and abused. The analogy, by any rule of logic, is totally meaningless—to have meaning, an analogy must compare like with like. What it does, however, is cast Muslims as 'Nazis' and thus make them doubly victim. However, since both the Inquisition and Hitler are European phenomena which have no counterpart in Islamic history, the Muslims themselves are not sensitive to the European emotional connotations of book burning. They were simply acting on the advice of a British lawyer who suggested that this seemed the only way for Muslims to get *The Independent* and other newspapers to take notice of their case. As *The Independent*'s editor admitted in the television programme *Hypotheticals*, protests are an everyday occurrence but book burning *is* news.

Perhaps the most ridiculous comment in *The Independent* leader, after mentioning that *The Satanic Verses* had been shortlisted for the Booker prize and won the Whitbread Literary Prize, was that the worthy and liberal-minded *literati* who sat on the panels awarding these prizes would not have thought so highly of a book which was overtly blasphemous, even of another faith.

There are a number of questionable assumptions here: that novels can be judged 'objectively' to be 'trashy' or not; that literary prizes are awarded for purely literary reasons; that politics, ego, peer-group pressure and personal prejudices have nothing to do with the exercise; and that 'worthy and liberal-minded *literati*' would recognize a blasphemy when they see it, especially of another faith. As far as *The Satanic Verses* is concerned, quite a few reviewers did not think very highly of it: Robert Irwing in *The Times Literary Supplement* found that 'in the absence of a more formal structure the novel is held together by a bemusing cat-cradle of cross-referenced names and images'; Adam Lively in the *Spectator* found the whole thing 'a mess'; Ciaran Carty of *The Sunday Tribune* found it 'verging on incomprehensibility'; John Berger, himself a Booker Prize winner, thought it was about 'irresponsibility' and described it as an 'arrogant fiction about playing God'; and not a few reviewers were just bored. So you play your politics and take your choice. And politics was up front when it came to the Booker Prize with the chairman of the jury, Michael Foot, taking a strong liking to the anti-Thatcher tone of the novel; and it was Fay Weldon, a close friend and strong supporter of the author, who secured the Whitbread Prize for 'St Salman, the Divine', as she was later jocularly to refer to him. As for the *literati* noticing a blasphemy: not a single reviewer in Europe or the United States recognized the significance of the 'Mahound' and 'Return to Jahilia' chapters. Indeed, given the antipathy and open hostility of the 'worthy and liberal-minded *literati*' towards religion in general and Islam in particular, the counter-position seems to have greater credibility: if they recognized the blasphemy in the novel, they awarded the prize, or argued in the jury for *The Satanic Verses* to be given the prize, because it was blasphemous and confirmed their worst prejudices.

The Independent leader concluded by advising Muslims that they 'must not seek to impose their values either on their fellow Britons of other faiths or on the majority who acknowledge no faith at all'. Let us suppose that the majority is always right, that minorities have no right to 'impose their values' on a majority, and look at what *The Independent* said elsewhere. In a report on the case brought against an artist who used human foetuses as earrings in a sculpture, *The Independent*'s Heather Mills (11 February 1989) reported that the jury ruled ten to two that the use of foetal earrings in a work of art was an outrage to public decency. Her report then noted, 'a ten to two majority as on the foetal earring case, could be argued to reflect the moral majority in society', and thundered, 'should they have the right to dictate to the minority?' So, you are damned if you are a majority and damned if you are a minority, but the dogmatic secularists are always right and true.

And so to the leftwallahs, where rabies and double standards were rediscovered in new and more virulent forms. Traditionally, of course, the left has been seen as the great defender of the causes of immigrants, blacks and Muslims; and Muslims themselves have always supported Labour. But the Rushdie affair has blown that fallacy wide open: the British left, as some of us suspected, is not immune to pure racism and jingoistic snobbery. In a long and rambling piece in *The Guardian*, the columnist Hugo Young concluded by telling Muslims to go back where they came from. In his various contributions as the literary guru of the same newspaper, W.L. Webb was a little more circumspect in his use of words, but on 17 February 1989 reckoned that hardly any of the demonstrators had any idea what Rushdie's book is actually about. But those in the streets do know what the book is partly—it is the part that concerns them—about: they have been taught the sira, the life of the Prophet Muhammad, since they were children, and they know that Rushdie has tried to rewrite it in his own distorted way. And that is really all they need to know. Webb seemed not to know that Muslims believe the Prophet Muhammad to have been human, not divine, but that they seek divine guidance from Allah because 'the distinction between good and evil is not always clear'. They did not need Rushdie to teach them these points. And it seems totally daft of Webb to suggest that most Arab countries 'have declared jihad, a holy war, on modernism itself'. Muslims everywhere, like most people in the Third World, are questioning modernism; they do not want to accept everything that modernism has to offer, particularly if it is at the expense of their traditions and culture; but what is good in modernism, and what enhances the quality of life, is openly accepted, which is not quite the same thing as declaring war.

A great deal of what Webb had to say and on which he based his arguments was hearsay. In one instance, he had to admit as much: 'I have been rebuked, for example, by Mahmoud Darwish, a respected Palestinian poet, for following an Arab critic who wrote in *The Times Literary Supplement* (17 February 1989) that he was banned in the Islamic World.' (He quoted Darwish as saying: 'You call blasphemy and profanity "modernism",' and ask if I consider 'a book which is cover to cover obscenities and uses such language as "bum", "scum", and "bastard" as a highly literary piece of work.'). The following day (*The Guardian*, 18 February 1989) he quoted the same 'Arab critic' and repeated the same crime: 'The satanic verses, which were the verses the Prophet rejected, concluded that they had been dictated to him not by the Archangel Gabriel but by the Devil, though the readers may not be sure about this. Fadia A. Faqir, however, reminds us of other verses the Prophet accepted: "As for poets, the erring follow them . . . they say that which they do not".'

Fadia Faqir, a Jordanian novelist, in a letter to *The Times Literary Supplement* (6–12 January 1989) responding to an article by Malise Ruthven (25 November 1988, 1 January 1989), made a number of misleading assertions. For instance, she misunderstood the Qur'an on poetry. She believed poetry to be banned, whereas when the Qur'an states, 'as for poets, the erring follow them . . . they say that which they do not', it is referring to pre-Islamic poets, not to Muslims who are poets. There have been a plethora of poets in Muslim societies throughout the ages; the most revered person in present-day Pakistan, that 'fundamentalist' Islamic state, is the poet-philosopher Mohammad Iqbal; and every newspaper in the Arab world, everyday, carries poetry as though it is the natural thing to do. The alleged conflict between literature and Islam that Faqir talks about is solely in the mind of Fadia Faqir. The Prophet himself loved poetry, and Hassan ibn Thabit was not reduced to 'writing eulogies' to survive in the face of persecution, as Faqir suggested; he wrote eulogies, among other things, because it was a common genre in his time. Moreover, to say that 'in most Islamic countries, writing has never been accepted and is considered by strict Muslims as an act of subversion' is not only to reveal a total ignorance of the basic Islamic sources and teachings and to belie history, but it also shows that Faqir's poverty (the name 'Faqir' means beggar) extends globally. She is totally oblivious to the indigenous thriving and dynamic literary scenes in Malaysia, Indonesia, Pakistan, Turkey and Egypt—all are countries which do not lack 'strict Muslims'.

In the article to which Faqir responded, Malise Ruthven, a self-proclaimed 'expert' on Islam, set out to explain the furore around *The Satanic Verses*. He noted that in 1959, Naguib Mahfouz's *Children of Our Quarter* (published in English as *The Children of Gebelawi*, 1981), led to demands that the novel be banned, and that in 1967, Taha Hussein was forced to resign his teaching post at Cairo University because of a book on Arabic criticism. Hence, there is a general, global and universal trend of book banning in Islam. And, given 'such precedents . . . the barrage of hostility that greeted Salman Rushdie's *The Satanic Verses* comes as no great surprise.' This is like saying that since *Spycatcher* was banned and Jim Allen's play *Perdition* was forced off the stage at the Royal Court Theatre even before it could open, there is a general trend of banning books and plays in Britain. How many things has Mrs Mary Whitehouse, Chairperson of the National Viewers and Listeners Association, protested against and tried to ban? Indeed, unlike the Mullahs in Egypt, her success rate is far higher—not least, her success in the *Gay News* trial! Does that mean that suppression and banning are common phenomena in Britain?

Ruthven offered the standard defence that the offending passages in the novel are presented as dream sequences and that Rushdie could not have placed his work further from historical realism. But he could have: he could, for example, have used fictional names, changed personal details and the details of their lives—that is, if he really was writing fiction and only wanted to explore certain ideas. Ruthven also argued that the story of the satanic verses is 'recorded in al Tabari and other early sources regarded by Muslims as unimpeachable'. Al-Tabari and other early sources are not regarded by Muslims as unimpeachable; they have been criticized and analysed again and again throughout history. Ruthven then announced that Muslims 'still appear to have an infantile fixation on the figure of the Prophet and the forms of their Text'. Infantile it may be, but this 'fixation' is what makes them Muslims: after all the criticisms and counter-criticisms, it is the text (i.e. the Qur'an) and the figure of the Prophet that *are* Islam. In conclusion, Ruthven suggested that we should not pay much attention to Muslim protests because 'most of the institutions calling for the banning of Rushdie are recipients of Saudi and other foreign funds'. A recipient himself of Saudi funds during his days at *Arabia: Islamic World Review*, Ruthven ought to know that Rushdie's depiction of Islam, the Qur'an and the Prophet Muhammad offends *every* believing Muslim, whether they receive foreign funds or not! The Muslim protest against *The Satanic Verses* is not surprising; what is surprising is the number of bogies one can pack into an article of a mere 3,000 words!

For a truly rabid coverage of the Rushdie affair, *New Statesman and Society* will be difficult to surpass. There is 'a stage-managed conspiracy of silence over Khomeini's unspeakable violation of rights of life and freedom of expression of Rushdie', editor Stuart Weir thundered in a lead article (24 February 1989). 'Moreover the British establishment, of which this government is part, is profoundly hostile to Rushdie, an ungratefully rich author who not only believes that writers and politicians are natural rivals, but acts on that uncomfortable belief, both in his writings and personal life. The bounder has criticized Mrs Thatcher abroad, he has signed Charter 88, above all he forgets *his place*.' Apart from the fact that governments are usually part of establishments, beyond denouncing Ayatollah Khomeini's *fatwa*, withdrawing her ambassador, presenting her case to the EC and asking its members to do the same, and isolating Iran, what else could Mrs Thatcher do? After all, Iran is not the Falklands. But Weir clearly wanted action—and the only action that is possible beyond what the government had already done is to declare war on Iran. Perhaps there is a conspiracy: it is not a conspiracy of silence, but one of sanity. Weir not only wanted Rushdie to abuse and ridicule whomever and whatever he wished at will, he also did not want the abused and ridiculed to show their hurt and displeasure. If Rushdie has thrown mud at others, is it surprising that some of it has been thrown back at him? Or to put it in Rushdie's own words, if he expresses 'contempt for his own kind, then his own kind can feel nothing but scorn for him' (*The Satanic Verses*, p. 45).

Weir asked why 'do so many accept so readily that the book is offensive, or distasteful, or both; and that its author has recklessly brought damnation down upon his head?' Perhaps so many find the book offensive and distasteful because it *is* offensive and distasteful—a possibility that totally escaped Weir. Regarding the author's having brought damnation upon his own head, either Rushdie knew what he was doing or he did not. If he did not, then the whole thing is as much a surprise to him as it was to almost all the reviewers. If he knew what he was doing, then he was taking a calculated risk—a risk that misfired—and as such brought the whole thing upon himself. By his own account and those of many of his supporters, Rushdie is some kind of expert on Islam and Islamic history. So he knew. As Hugh Trevor-Roper wrote in *The Independent Magazine* (14 June 1989), 'if an expert entomologist deliberately pokes a stick into a hornets' nest, he has only himself to blame for the result. Charitable bystanders may come to his aid. They may rescue him—at some risk to themselves—from the enraged insects. They may rush him to the chemist, or the hospital. But they need not defend his action, or hail him, as the left-wing literary establishment has hailed Mr Rushdie, as a martyr for the freedom of self-expression or literature, or scientific research.'

Weir took exception to some Labour Members of Parliament who seemed to be pro-Muslim, even though he accepted that some risked 'losing their seats, if a strong stand by Labour leaders in defence of Rushdie offended the largely Labour-voting Muslim community in Britain'. This, Mr Weir, is what is meant by democracy: politicians have to consider the feelings of the electorate. After all, if a large majority of the British public is offended by Mrs Thatcher's policies, she will lose the next election. 'There are signs that some Muslim leaders at least want more tangible results for their ability to "deliver" their vote and are seeking to emulate the influence of American Zionists over government policy. And they have observed that British Jews have been able to block the production of a historical play [Jim Allen's *Perdition*] which offends them.' In a democracy, this is what pressure groups do; and all pressure groups can learn something from the masters of the art, the Zionist lobby in the United States. Many left-wing writers joined in the protests against the play, which was said to be anti-Semitic as well as anti-Zionist. But as Jim Allen himself told the *Observer* (5 March 1989), 'I guess what it all comes down to is that there are some religions and some races that you can attack and others that you cannot'. Weir could teach us all a thing or two about double standards.

Weir attacked Max Madden, MP for Bradford West, and others who introduced an amendment to a House of Commons Bill in which 'they "noted with concern" the offence which Rushdie's novel had caused to Muslims here; drew attention "to the need to reform the law of blasphemy to permit all religious faiths to seek legal redress for blasphemy or to repeal the law of blasphemy which only allows legal action in cases concerning established Christianity"; and urged Rushdie to debate with Muslim critics on television and to allow them to insert disclaimers in all copies of the novel on sale. Protest as Madden may (and he has), that amendment reeks of appeasement.' So even agreeing to the fact, obvious for all to see, that Muslims are hurt is a form of appeasement. The basic point that Max Madden is making about the blasphemy laws is no more than a reiteration of a proposal already endorsed by the Archbishop of Canterbury long before the Rushdie affair. Max Madden, of course, should not be answerable to his constituents whose interests he represents in Parliament, but should report directly to the editor of *New Statesman and Society* and behave according to his wishes! God forbid those who actually side with Muslims, for they will be classified as criminals and hunted down. The Witchfinder General, Stuart Weir, angrily denounced Barry Seal, MEP for Yorkshire West, who 'actually spoke at the Muslim rally in Bradford at which Rushdie's novel was publicly burned', even though the poor fellow did not know that any kind of book-burning, symbolic or otherwise, was part of the day's planned activities.

Weir mentioned that it was rather ironic that 'a novel which powerfully protests against the experience of the Muslim communities in Britain should be the focus for a rage which is in part inspired by that experience'. This is a gross fallacy because the experiences that *The Satanic Verses* portrays are not of the Muslim community in Britain, which is predominantly of working-class origin. As Yasmin Alibahi (*New Statesman and Society*, 24 February 1989) reported on the very next page after Weir's rabid article, 'however "westernised" the youngsters appeared to be, they feel hurt, and humiliated by Rushdie'. This is because none of them can identify with anything in the novel. The number of Muslims in Britain who went to Rugby—where they were forced to eat kippers for breakfast—or to Oxford or Cambridge, can be counted on the fingers of one hand. *The Satanic Verses* portrays the experiences of an infinitesimally small elitest minority who were rich back home and who had a privileged existence in Britain. But it is the experience that Weir and other Rushdie supporters would like to *believe* to be the Muslim experience: that deculturation is the only option available to the Muslim community in Britain.

In closing, Weir denounced the entire British liberal tradition: 'so corrupt are Britain's liberal traditions now that our political representatives haven't the political imagination to comprehend the grievous blow that the Ayatollah has struck at our most basic freedoms'. Our political representatives are fortunately sane enough to take appropriate measures to check the Ayatollah's excesses. And if they are corrupt, then Weir has himself, as much as anyone else, to blame: he is, after all, a former editor of *New Socialist* and editor of *New Statesman and Society*, a stalwart of that tradition.

Taking on the Mullahs

A number of writers championed the pro-Rushdie cause by attacking specific Muslim targets. The noted Latin American novelist, Carlos Fuentes (*The Guardian*, 24 May 1989) took on the Ayatollahs. He deliberated on the nature of the novel, saying that it is a constant redefinition of men and women as problems, never as sealed, concluded truths. 'But this is precisely what the Ayatollahs of this world cannot suffer. For the Ayatollahs, reality is dogmatically defined once and for all in a sacred text. You can add nothing to it. It does not converse with anyone. It is its own loudspeaker. It offers perfect refuge for the insecure who then, having the protection of a dogmatic text over their heads, proceed to excommunicate those whose security lies in search for the truth.' To begin with, one is not quite sure what Fuentes meant by the 'Ayatollahs'. Was he referring to Iranian clerics only or a general state of mind of religious people of which the Ayatollahs can be said to be one, but hardly the best example? Anyhow, for most Muslims the redefinition of men and women as problems in fiction constitutes no problem. Indeed, their own literature has been doing this for centuries, long before the modern novel made an appearance. And the reality is defined by an external source, not just for the Ayatollahs but for all believers. While it is true that one cannot physically add anything to the Qur'an, it does not mean the end of knowledge, or ethics, or values. From the Muslim point-of-view, knowledge and values do not converge on the Qur'an, they diverge from it. In that sense, all new discoveries on the human condition become part of the Qur'anic message. And to say that the Qur'an does not converse with you, in the sense of pointing you to new directions, new avenues of thought, new explorations of experience, reveals a total ignorance of the divine text. There is refuge there for those who seek it; but there is also exploration there for those who wish to embark upon it. The Qur'an talks to you, listens to you, and answers you back. But to do that one first has to learn its mode of communication. In Fuentes's definition of the novel, truth can never be found in literature; it is a constant and continuous search—the search itself becomes an absolute. In the Qur'an, there are truths to be found, truths that have to be searched for, and countless other truths which man is left to discover and explore for himself. While the search is not relegated to an absolute position, it is encouraged, revered and considered as an essential prerequisite for understanding.

Fuentes told us that 'when we all understood everything, the epic was possible. But not fiction. The novel is born from the very fact that we do not understand one another any longer, because unitary, orthodox language has broken down.' We have, in fact, never understood each other, with or without the epic: *The Song of Roland* and the whole tradition of *chansons de geste* are the kinds of epics by which ignorance thrived. While the novel may increase our understanding, it does not provide us with guidance. Since, by Fuentes's own definition, fiction is a continuous, never-ending search for truth—indeed his premise being that there is no truth that can be found—the novel can hardly guide us in any direction of truth. However relative, it can never quench our thirst for certain kinds of bearings in our increasingly meaningless lives. Scripture can, and does. But believing in the sacred, or possessing a revealed text, does not mean that we understand everything, including everything about the sacred text itself. It in no way negates the necessity for exploration of human experiences in fiction. Fuentes drew his main lesson from the Rushdie affair: 'I hope everyone, after what has happened to Salman Rushdie and *The Satanic Verses*, now understands this. Fiction is not a joke. It is but an expression of the cultural, personal and spiritual diversity of mankind.' Fuentes obviously takes fiction very seriously;

but he was not willing to allow the same seriousness to religion. The question that starkly faces the West, he told us, is this: 'Can we revolt back into the sacred? Can the religious mentality thrive outside of religious dogma and hierarchy? These are questions essential to the idea of freedom. But the burdens of freedom . . . can be heavier than the chains of liberty. . . . And since God no longer exists, mankind was now responsible for its own destiny and could not shift the blame anymore.' Here then we have a neat turn of logic. First fiction is established as the only vehicle for the search for truth; it is a serious business. Then God is killed; religion becomes a joke. But for an increasing number of people throughout the world, and particularly for Muslims, religion is not a joke. It is serious business. It is but an expression of the cultural, personal and spiritual diversity of mankind in a common, universal metaphor. But by relegating religion to irrelevance (hence its personification with the Ayatollahs), and placing fiction at the level of a universal, common pursuit of truth, Fuentes is able to perform his ultimate trick: 'the modern age', he wrote, 'by liberating both the freedom for good and the freedom for evil, has placed upon us all the obligation to relativise both. . . . But the name of relativity is no longer virtue; it is value. Bad literature stays at the level of virtue; it pits good guys against bad boys. Good literature rises to the level of values in conflict with one another.' Literature, therefore, becomes a source of values: it is to literature that I turn, Salman Rushdie has said, to fill the god-shaped hole within me. Literature thus replaces religion: it is *the* serious source of values, serious pursuit of truth, serious exploration of universal human experience. This naturally makes novelists into the high-priests of modern society, even gods, way above the status of a mere Ayatollah. No wonder Fuentes declared that 'the defence of Salman Rushdie is a defence of ourselves. It is a matter of pride to say that Rushdie has given us all a better reason to understand and protect the profession of letters at the highest level of creativity, imagination, intelligence and social responsibility.' The defence of Rushdie then becomes the defence of the sacred priesthood of the novelists. While it is true, as Fuentes said, that the Ayatollahs have 'debased and caricatured their own faith', it is equally true that Fuentes, Rushdie and their *chamchas* take their fiction with all the seriousness that a religious person invests in a sacred text. For them, religion, as Oliver Leaman pointed out in *The Times* (6 March 1989), is 'at par with the colour of socks one prefers to wear or the television programmes one chooses to watch'. Notice the casual and arrogant way Fuentes stated that God is dead; there is not, despite the fact that doubt is the only absolute in his worldview, the slightest hint of doubt; yet how serious is the attempt to elevate fiction to the level of religion? While all religious worldviews acknowledge the importance and necessity of literature, Fuentes does not even have the courtesy to acknowledge that religion may at least be as important and necessary a part of the human condition as fiction. For the dogmatic secularists, the only protection for their insecurity lies in domination. No one better encapsulates than Fuentes our argument of the clash of sacred territories that underlies the Rushdie Affair.

In *The Times* (10 March 1989), Robert Kilroy-Silk, ex-Labour MP turned television presenter, countered the Muslim advertisement in the same newspaper which declared: 'No one, repeat, no one, questions Rushdie's right to express himself but to be vulgar, abusive and obscene is a misuse of this right.' Kilroy-Silk argued that 'if these criteria were accepted, very little of the heritage of English literature would escape the censor's flame. Much of it, after all, could be regarded as vulgar, abusive and obscene, including some of the classics. The fact that some people have held those opinions of certain pieces of writing has not generally been regarded as sufficient reason for banning them.' A valid argument. The advertisers clearly failed to see that simple obscenity and abuse is not good enough a reason for banning. But that abuse and obscenity was directed at someone and was aimed at presenting him and those who follow him in a particular light, thus falsifying them. It was that someone and the accompanying falsification which provided the crux of the argument. However, after making the point, Kilroy-Silk took an inductive leap: 'Yet this is the type of blanket and uncompromising censorship that the Muslims of Birmingham and elsewhere would impose on us. The Mullahs would decide what we could read.' The mullahs are too preoccupied with making sense of their own lives to worry about what Kilroy-Silk should or should not read; if he is into abuse and pornography, that is his business. But generalizing from a particular case to a grand 'blanket and uncompromising censorship' is not only shoddy thinking, it is a deliberate attempt to introduce new bogies, or bring the same old bogies back. After all, there have been numerous other books, both abusive and obscene, that the mullahs have not demanded to be banned. The issue is Rushdie's book, and this book only. However, if Muslims could be shown to be demanding a 'blanket and uncompromising censorship' on everything, then they could be shown to be totally paranoid.

The Muslim advertisement also stated that Rushdie's right to freedom of expression should be seen in a broader context. There is, for example, the situation of British hostages in Lebanon to consider: 'Is it right that the fate of the British hostages and British commercial interests should be jeopardized for a publisher's profit?' Kilroy-Silk produced his trump card: '. . . words should be applied to those who suggest that action of one person should be visited as sins on all of his compatriots. I thought only the Nazis went in for collective punishment.' Ah, the Nazis again. If the mullahs can be shown to be Nazis, then they can be dismissed not just as paranoid censors but also as fascist bigots. End of the argument. Words should also be applied to those who are reduced to such tactics to defend their sacred territory; 'liberal inquisitors' has already been suggested. But is Kilroy-Silk so naive as to believe that actions of individuals, or events at a particular place, cannot and do not have consequences for people and places far removed from them? After all, as the Chernobyl disaster happened in the Soviet Union, why should we worry about the quality of milk in Cumbria? Why should we worry about deforestation in Brazil, or could it have something to do with drought in North Africa? Rushdie's actions can jeopardize the future of the hostages in Lebanon—the mullahs in Birmingham have no power, no ability to do anything about it; they are simply pointing out that we live in an interdependent world where actions of certain individuals with power and global reach can be 'visited as sins' on others.

'The Mullahs', Kilroy-Silk averred, 'are in no position to pronounce on the "moral interests of the nation" as they affect to. In any case they should be told that their view of morality is not shared by the majority in this country, indeed would be furiously repudiated.' The mullahs, of course, have no right to impose their view of morality on anyone. But does Kilroy-Silk have a right to impose his version of morality on them? He certainly thinks so: 'their arrogance and their confidence is obvious to all. Already some of them are making bolder and more aggressive demands. The more they are given, the more they will demand.' What have they been given? How many of their demands have actually been met? They may be arrogant, but their arrogance cannot match that of Kilroy-Silk.

In *The Guardian* (10 March 1989), Michael Foot, who is impressed by the political content of *The Satanic Verses* and its depiction of 'Thatcher's Britain', and who as the chairperson of the Booker Prize jury fought hard to give the prize to Rushdie, took on Shabbir Akhtar for his piece presenting the 'fundamentalist' case in the same newspaper. Foot told us that the killings in India, during an anti-Rushdie demonstration, were not Rushdie's fault. 'The reason for this killing is to be found in the religion of the killers or those who have incited them to kill, or in the measures of the police who felt required to take protective action against the peril of even more widespread killings, inspired by the same religious appeal or provocation.' Is it possible for a former Labour leader to be so ignorant as to believe that Islam sanctions laissez-faire killings? Should we not expect an 'intellectual' of his calibre at least to check a few basic facts before putting pen to paper? Foot's justification for this malicious charge is based on Shabbir Akhtar's talk of 'militant wrath'. Did Akhtar not write that 'any faith which compromises its internal temper of militant wrath is destined for the dustbin of history, for it can no longer preserve its faithful heritage in face of the corrosive influences'? Akhtar was arguing for standing up to the liberal secularist onslaught: if Muslims do not defend themselves, he was clearly saying, they along with their religion, culture, and worldview will be totally marginalized. Docility is a one-way ticket to oblivion. But does this mean, as Foot suggested, that Akhtar 'professes a fundamentalist, absolute religious allegiance which would permit no argument with Rushdie'? Akhtar is not only a believer in Islam, he also happens to be a philosopher: and the basic trait of both is argument. Just because one is ready to express one's anger at being ridiculed does not mean that one is not ready to argue. But one argues with those who are willing to listen to arguments other then their own and who do not come to the debating table with preconceived distorted imaginations; as Alan Bloom complained in a television discussion, 'it is difficult to argue with someone who is so uncivil'!

Akhtar argued that there is a limit to tolerance beyond which tolerance should not be tolerated; and by exceeding that limit Christianity has been 'totally undermined'. Foot saw this argument as 'twisted', stating that 'the survival of Christianity has been due in part to its newfound mildness'. Well, this new-found mildness has certainly led to an ending of old rivalries—but has Christianity survived? How many Christians take their religion seriously; what moral influence does Christianity exert on international relations, public policy, science and technology? If Christianity has survived, it has survived as an underdog to dogmatic secularism. The Western world is not shaped by Christian morality and love, but by an insatiable secular greed for domination: had real Christianity stood its ground, we would not be living in the perpetual shadow of nuclear, biological and chemical weapons of mass destruction; the global economic structure would not have marginalized the vast majority of mankind to perpetual poverty and degradation; racial bigotry and hatred would not have been institutionalized; whatever one may say about Christianity in history, the Christian worldview itself would not have allowed Western civilization to drift in these directions. Akhtar's point is that to take a stand for religion is to take a stand against all this: his 'militant wrath' is rooted in social and political action.

Foot, a historian of the era of English revolution whose admiration for the Levellers is well known (the Levellers were a body of men in whom militant religious wrath was particularly strong) continued: 'For Dr Akhtar's benefit, and indeed for the general enlightenment of mankind, we might put the case the other way round: once upon a time there was little to choose between Christian and Muslim . . . in what Dr Akhtar now calls an "internal temper of militant wrath" or the preserving of ".the faithful heritage". Each side could be indiscriminate killers, and they did it in the name of religion.' For the benefit of Michael Foot and the general enlightenment of *The Guardian* readers, once upon a time there was a great deal to choose between Christians and Muslims. One only has to ask the Jews; whenever they had a choice, they chose to live in the Muslim world. Why? Because with Muslims they could live as they wished, governed by their own religious laws; they could hold important public offices, become wazirs and could produce great scholars and philosophers who were revered as much by Muslims as by Jews. In Christendom, they faced persecution and death. The Crusades were launched by Christians, not Muslims. The Holocaust happened in Europe, not in the Muslim world. Apartheid is a product of a distorted European Christianity; it has nothing to do with Islam. There was, and there still is, a great deal to choose between Christianity and Islam. But none of this detracts from the central missing link in Foot's consciousness—the 'internal temper' of 'militant wrath', as in 'Onward Christian Soldiers' or 'The General Agreement For The People'. The Levellers' expression of Christian moral mission on the social and political sphere is a moral referrent of peaceful activism as well. When it comes to Islam, that same connotation is impossible for Foot or for any of the Western commentators to conceive or concede—though it is just the same thing. If British politics has known people of militant wrath in this century, then Michael Foot is one of them or has ever aspired to be among them. One rather suspects that on the topics to which Foot's militant wrath has been directed, he would probably find Akhtar in a large measure of agreement as well as many, if not most, Muslims—but there are none so blind as those who do not want to see.

'The great persisting threat to our world,' Foot developed his argument, 'derives from this pursuit of absolute victory. Once it was Hitler's creed, and once it was Stalin's, and once it was called the Dulles doctrine, and once it came near to being adopted by a President Reagan launching fundamentalist anathemas against the evil empire.' There is only one ideology missing from Foot's list: he forgot to mention that dogmatic secularism now pursues the same goal. Having reduced Christianity to submission, and destroyed almost all the traditional cultures and worldviews of the world, it now has Islam in its sights.

The Christian fundamentalists of yore may have been, as Foot called them, 'strident or absurd or indeed wicked . . . the Khomeinis and the Akhtars, who denounced any move towards detente or rapprochement as blasphemy or treachery or godlessness', but the dogmatic secularists of today, who are equally fundamentalist about their secularism, the Foots and the Rushdies, are equally wicked and pestiferous. Underneath their benign liberal tolerance, there is the firm conviction of the truth of their position, the natural superiority of their outlook, and deep desires to see religious worldviews swept aside by the torrential force of their creed. Common human decency is not an invention of liberal secularism, as Foot would have us believe; it is there, and has been there for millenia, in the great religions of the world. It is another name for Christian love and Muslim compassion.

The R.U.S.H.D.I.E. Prize for Bogydom goes to the feminist novelist, Fay Weldon, who is not content with taking on a mullah or two, but has declared war on all of Islam. Her essay 'Sackcloth and Ashes' was presented in the *Opinion* (March 1989) slot of Britain's Channel Four television and later printed in *The Listener* (18 May 1989), *New Statesman and Society*, and the Chatto *Counterblast* series. Certain individuals seem to have a more-than-equal opportunity to exercise their freedom of expression. Combining all the elements of the distorted imagination with liberal supplies of fear and loathing, bigotry and jingoism, Weldon announced that the thought police are again about and death threats have 'developed into actual official death squads'. The fact that one official or unofficial assassin has yet to be sighted is quite irrelevant; indeed, so far as Weldon's essay is concerned, facts are irrelevant as well. She said that 'Muslims believe that words are dangerous things in themselves, able to insult and by insulting destroy the God'. For a novelist to suggest that words do not have power is daft, but to suggest that Muslims are so stupid that they think certain words will destroy God is to reveal a dumbfounding arrogance.

Weldon wants Christian churches to rethink their position on Islam, believing them far too tolerant—as their history no doubt shows! 'Put up your mosques next to our churches, scorn us as unbelievers all you like, we are too frightened by the past, too intimidated by history, to see there is a middle way between acceptance and the putting of those who believe otherwise to horrible death.' Stand up and dominate like you used to do, confront the Saracens and show them who is boss! 'I want our Church back, in the vigour of its belief that it's the one and only Church, and prepared to say so. Then I can choose not to believe its far-fetchedness.'

'Have the Christians,' she asked, 'not read the Koran? Do they not know how the believer in Muhammad regards the unbeliever?' She then produced a piece of total fabrication in inverted commas to suggest that it comes from the Qur'an or is a saying of the Prophet: 'When the unbeliever holds out his hand, take it. But when he turns his back, slay him. You have my authority.' Only a lie? Or a deliberate distortion to promote hatred? She continued:

> I recommend a thorough reading of the Koran to everyone. Allah the all-seeing, all-knowing, I am glad to see, is compassionate as well as vengeful; that is to say, he does sometimes turn a blind eye, knowing people are weak; he sometimes even rescues people from the abysmal fires of Gehenna. I just want to know what Allah has to be merciful about, what there is to forgive. It is, from the Western view, an entirely circular argument. Muhammad invents the sin in order for Allah to be seen forgiving it. To punish and chastise is the norm: compassion is when it doesn't happen. (*The Listener*, 18 May 1989)

Even from the perspective of the undoubtedly superior Western logic, there is no contradiction between being compassionate and vengeful—if Allah is indeed vengeful. Allah, if He chooses, can be compassionate in His vengeance and forgive. By any logic, if God exists He is a *de facto* God. He exists because He exists, not because we have willed Him into existence. The argument is circular only in the sense that Allah should have instituted a consultation process, with Ms Weldon as chief Goddess, before He takes revenge on anyone. But what is this? Muhammad invented sin? Is one to understand that Christianity, Judaism, Hinduism, Zoroastrianism and other religions before Islam did not have the concept of sin?

The Qur'an that Ms Weldon read 'comes in a very nice Penguin edition. Arthur Arberry did this translation.' The Penguin edition of the Qur'an, if Ms Weldon actually read it, is translated by N.J. Dawood, and it is one of the most inaccurate, misleading and distorted versions on the market (and the preferred choice of Salman Rushdie). The Arthur Arberry translation comes in a nice Oxford University Press edition (OUP hold the copyright; the American edition was published by Macmillan in 1979); it looks so different from the Penguin edition that one would have serious difficulty in confusing the two. Arberry's translation, Ms Weldon told us, 'moved him. So it should; it is a great poem.' But Weldon is not willing to allow Arberry, who spent his entire life studying the Qur'an and Muslim traditions and is considered, both by Muslims and non-Muslims, to be one of the great Orientalists of recent times, the freedom to be influenced by the Qur'an. *Her* interpretation is far superior; it has to be! So she threw scorn and sarcasm at Arberry's feelings: 'he acknowledges his gratitude to whatever power, or Power, inspired the man and the Prophet who first recited these scriptures—revelations supernaturally received, he explains'. Like all knowledgeable persons, Arberry was far more humble. This is what he actually wrote:

I have called my version an interpretation, conceding the orthodox claim that the Koran (like all other literary masterpieces) is untranslatable. . . . The task was undertaken, not lightly, and carried to its conclusion at a time of great personal distress, through which it comforted and sustained the writer in a manner for which he will always be grateful. He therefore acknowledges his gratitude to whatever power or Power inspired the man and the Prophet who first recited these scriptures. I pray that this interpretation, poor echo though it is of the glorious original, may instruct, please, and in some degree inspire those who read it. (Arberry, *Koran Interpreted*, pp. xii–xiii)

After deriding Arberry, Weldon quoted Surah Al-Kafirun (The Unbelievers) 109:1–6:

> Say, oh unbelievers
> I serve not what you serve.
> And you are not serving what I serve.
> Nor am I serving what you have served,
> Neither are you serving what I serve.
> To you your religion and to me my religion.

She added in her usual scornful manner, 'Oh yes. Except for me, the unbeliever, mine shall be the fire of Gehenna, and its mighty chastisements will never be lightened.' Had Ms Weldon actually read Arberry's interpretation of the Qur'an, she would have known that the Qur'an does not promise paradise to the believer, nor Gehenna to unbelievers. It is righteousness that the Qur'an wants; and the righteous unbelievers, unless they are Fay Weldon, need not worry too much about Gehenna. The word which is translated by Arberry as 'serve' (*ma tabadun*) alludes both to positive concepts and false objects of worship and values; among the latter are believing in one's self-sufficiency and superiority, considering one's ignorance to be superior knowledge, spreading hatred by false accusation and innuendo, seeking to suppress or dominate others and attributing superhuman and divine qualities to human beings. On all these counts, Ms Weldon has something to worry about!

Surah 109 is a supreme example of the 'live and let live' attitude of the Qur'an. But Weldon's main concern is to sow the seeds of conflict and vent her fear and hatred of Muslims:

> . . . this violent frightening poem. . . . This divine revelation from Allah to Muhammad in the seventh century, with its Bible tales retold, its rules for desert living, its rejection of monogamy, its despisal for women—yes, I know the Prophet

says treat females with kindness and respect, and I dare say it was better than what went before—only chastise them when they're rebellious, and so forth; and the women go to heaven too, but since heaven is a place full of beautiful houris and glasses of wine beneath the bough, what are the women to do? Fetch the wine, I suppose. See how awful one gets, so easily, about another culture's belief structure. (*The Listener*, 18 May 1989)

How came 'this violent and frightening poem' to lead to the creation of one of the greatest material and intellectual civilizations on the one hand, and an unparalleled tradition of mysticism on the other? There is fear and there is violence, but it is not in the message of the Qur'an. The fear is within the heart and mind of Fay Weldon: the fear of her own ignorance, her spiritual barrenness, the abject darkness that resides within her. The violence is the outcome of her intrinsic fear and hatred, her urge to dominate, her arrogant belief in her own self-righteous and superior position—violence is what she has done to the Qur'an by misrepresentation, falsification and downright ignorance. Sackcloth and ashes!

And some poem! At any one single space-time co-ordinate, it is in the hearts, minds and memories, cover to cover, of millions of people, who can recite all of it, or part of it from any one place to any other—a poem whose segments are recited, and have been recited for fourteen hundred years, five times a day by most devout Muslims—a poem that can lead ibn Haytham to lay the foundations of modern optics and Rumi to the apex of mystical ecstasy—a poem that can build or destroy empires—a poem that can shape the social structure of a society, build economic systems and construct political institutions—a poem that is a religion, a civilization, a culture, a worldview. How many poems are there like it?

Bogy after bogy. The Qur'an does have some stories that are also in the Bible. But it does not recycle them. Moreover, they are not told as stories: often they do not occur in one place, or have a beginning, middle or an end. They are used as illustration, to make a point, to draw a lesson, to correct a fallacy, to inform. Does one have to tell a novelist what a story is? But this novelist has difficulty in understanding similes and metaphors. To have significance and meaning, figures of speech have to draw on things to which ordinary people can relate; this is what the Qur'anic description of heaven and hell is all about. Only a fool would think that the only joy paradise has to offer is 'beautiful houris and glasses of wine beneath the bough'. The white, Anglo-Saxon elite of the industrialized world already have plenty of that at the expense of the rest of the world, the majority of mankind. Sackcloth and ashes!

To say the Qur'an despises women is like saying that Fay Weldon despises Salman Rushdie. In either case, it is a distortion of fact. The Qur'an never says 'men', but always 'men and women'; what applies to men applies equally to women. It is also a fact, unfortunately, that in contemporary Muslim societies, women are discriminated against. Their suppression, however, is not due to the teachings of the Qur'an but to the chauvinism and arrogance of Muslim men. It is an appalling state of affairs that cannot and should not be tolerated and that has to be fought at every juncture by all right-minded people.

First Weldon stated, with a sense of original discovery, that Muslim women are harrassed and suppressed; then she argued that among Muslims in Britain the rates of divorce, wife-beating, etc., are greater than among the more 'liberated' host community. Why did she leave out child abuse, rape, homicide, alcoholism, and drug addiction? One hopes that Muslims are not being favoured! If the champion of dogmatic secularism had checked her facts, she would have discovered that in purely percentage terms, there is simply no comparison between the low rates of divorce, children-in-care, wife-beating, etc., in the Muslim community to those in the host community.

'The mosque', Weldon announced, 'where the Muslim children go every day after school—often frightened of going, I am told by social workers, but there is no escape for them—to be taught the Koran.' But who are these social workers? Are they the same Penguin who published Arberry? If Muslim children do go to the mosque every day—a luxury many Muslim communities do not have because there are not enough mosques, enough schools, enough teachers—they may be upset about missing *Neighbours* or *Grange Hill* or playing football, but why should they be afraid? And if they are afraid, are they more afraid than any child going to school every morning? Most Muslim children go to Sunday schools, which are organized sometimes in mosques and sometimes in other community centres. They learn not just the Qur'an, Islamic history and Muslim culture, but get involved in debate and discussions, participate in sports and learn such things as karate which may come in handy when dealing with those who insist on shoving their self-righteous superiority down their throats.

As Weldon's attack on Islam continued, she said she would be frightened if she were a child being taught the Qur'an, because the Qur'an stipulates that only a believer can escape hell-fire. She attributed this pressurized fear as the reason 'why, when we in the West try to engage even the most intelligent and sophisticated Muslim in conversation about these matters, we face a blank wall of non-comprehension. Terror intervenes. The shutters of understanding come down. Minds close. Snap! The frightened child looks out of the adult's eyes.'

So there are intelligent and sophisticated Muslims after all, even though they have been frightened out of their wits by the Qur'an! Has it not occurred to Weldon that the 'blank wall of non-comprehension' may be a reaction to the lethal fusion of sheer arrogance and ignorance on her part, that it is not the Muslims' minds that are closed, but hers? They can comprehend people who do not believe, but can she comprehend people who do believe? A closed mind perceives all other minds to be closed; it can do nothing else. And that 'frightened child' who 'looks out of the adult's eyes': Muslims are really like children. Slap them and tell them to shut up and sit down. Sackcloth and ashes!

That is conditioning for you. Western culture has been conditioned to think of non-Western people as Victorian children, or if they will admit it, as animals, albeit often domesticated animals. The idea that people of non-Western cultures are nothing more than children, immature, immoral, evil, frightened savages like the boys in *Lord of the Flies*, in need of guidance from the likes of Fay Weldon is the foundation of European colonialism and imperialism, and more sadly, the basis of more contemporary notions of development and modernity. As Ashis Nandy pointed out in his essay on 'Reconstructing Childhood' (*Alternatives*, Winter 1984–5), European colonial writers often described non-Western cultures as childlike, needing moral guidance and looking after by the imperial powers. Thus John Stuart Mill, the nineteenth-century liberal who provided the intellectual justification for the colonization of India, saw the relationship between colonizers and their subjects in terms of father and son. His own childhood and how he was treated by his father became the main metaphor for the mission of civilizing the Indians. Rudyard Kipling, who had a devastatingly cruel childhood in England, projected his lost childhood as 'half savage, half child' upon India and all lesser breeds. Cecil Rhodes described the South African blacks much more darkly: 'the native is to be treated as a child and denied franchise. We must adopt the system of despotism . . . in our relations with the barbarous of South Africa.' No doubt the apartheid regime feels the same. The use of the metaphor of the child legitimizes the sense of superiority and mission to civilize that the colonial administrators felt yesterday, and dogmatic secularists feel today. What their fathers and teachers did to the colonial administrators on the playing fields of Harrow and Eton, they tried to do to the subject people they ruled. What their fathers and mothers did to the dogmatic secularists and liberal feminists, they are trying to do to Muslims and other non-Western cultures. Sackcloth and ashes!

While Muslims are childlike and immoral, evil and hateful, indeed totally black, Salman Rushdie himself is an adult, moral, good, full of love and totally white. Islam 'is not a religion of kindness but of terror'; and the Qur'an, in another one of Weldon's vicious fabrications, 'gives the believer permission to hate the unbeliever'. *The Satanic Verses* on the other hand, is a novel of love and goodness, is extraordinary poetry, which does not give permission to hate and is the stuff of revelation. The author, an 'ex-colleague of mine in an advertising agency, is too human, too modern, too witty, too intelligent, to lay down rules for the human race . . .'. Too human? Surely, a slip of the tongue? He soars high above ordinary mortals. He is, surely, god incarnate, not the childlike son but the Father himself: 'as a piece of writing, *The Satanic Verses* reads pretty much like the works of St John the Divine at the end of our own Bible . . . St Salman the Divine'. 'I'm joking', she added with a smirk. A joke? Surely not, Ms Weldon. Do you not have the conviction of your beliefs? Let us pray: Our Father who art in hiding, forgive us our sins that we are upset and angry by your ridicule and abuse . . .

Beyond the Bogies

Much of the media coverage of the Rushdie affair focused on events and catch phrases heavily loaded with emotion: book burning, death threats, mediaeval fundametalists, fanatics and the militant wrath of Shabbir Akhtar. There were, however, a number of attempts to move beyond the stereotypes of the distorted imagination. John Berger (*The Guardian*, 25 February 1989), for example, suggested that the Rushdie affair should be considered with 'global objectivity, and not used (as it is being) to confirm prejudices and high-sounding but unexamined principles'. He explained that the affair is about two books: the Qur'an which has helped, and still helps, many millions of people to make sense of their lives and their mortality; and *The Satanic Verses* which 'is a rather arrogant fiction about playing God . . . The first is a book about responsibilities, the second a story about irresponsibility.' In the West, Berger explained, art has replaced religion; but, in the final analysis, art is only a commodity. However, the distorted imagination has such a strong hold on the Western mind that Berger was forced to admit that he does not expect many to listen to his arguments because colonial prejudices are even today too ingrained.

One of Berger's high-sounding but unexamined principles is freedom of expression. Michael Ignatieff pointed out that:

> ... some liberals have taken to saying that they hold freedom sacred. This, I think, is a misuse of 'sacred'. If the word means anything it means something which is inviolate to criticism or rational scrutiny. Freedom is not a holy belief, nor even a supreme value. It is a contestable concept. How a free society marks the limits of freedom will change with time. The Muslims are correct to say this society does not believe freedom is unlimited. That is another way of saying it is not sacred. To live in a liberal society is to fight over the meaning of freedom constantly. (*Observer*, 2 April 1989)

Thus freedom, or at least the meaning of freedom, is a changing phenomenon. But sacred does not mean 'inviolate to criticism or rational inquiry'; as we have argued throughout this book, critical reasoning is an essential element in understanding and appreciating the sacred so far as Muslims are concerned. The 'leap of faith' is not a leap beyond reason. But the sacred is inviolate in the sense of being out of bounds to abuse and ridicule.

For Ignatieff, 'the debate is not between medieval fanaticism and Western enlightenment, but between incompatible conceptions of freedom, one in which freedom's limit is the sacred and one in which it is not.' Or more appropriately, one in which freedom has no limits and one in which the existence of the sacred secures multiple freedoms as the inviolable rights of people in the real world. If the sacred stops certain individuals at the boundary of abuse and ridicule, it does so to secure even greater freedom for others. Here, abuse and ridicule have the same weight as murder: just as in civilized societies an individual's freedom stops at murdering others, so in terms of expression, freedom of expression stops at the boundary of abuse and ridicule which have 'murdered' and continued to 'murder' traditional societies. A book of abuse and ridicule can turn into a lethal weapon, exposing those it has abused and ridiculed to hatred, social and personal torture, and suicide and homocide. 'A book is a complicated tool' according to Sean French, 'and it can be used for unpredictable purposes once it is let out into the world beyond the author's control' (*New Statesman and Society*, 14 April 1989). Muslims openly acknowledge that books are complicated tools, as indeed do the Jews who were right in banning *The Protocols of the Elders of Zion*, no less a work of fiction than *The Satanic Verses*. What is true of the *Protocols*, which according to some is not without literary merit, is equally true of *The Satanic Verses*.

Ignatieff's conclusions have dual connotations. While stated by a secularist, they have equal resonance for Muslims, who could readily invoke the Qur'an or examples from the life of the Prophet to support this position:

> There is nothing sacred about toleration–we're not obliged to tolerate those who threaten us because of our opinions. But it does commit us to a habit of mind and a

way of life: to listen when we do not want to listen, to endure offence when we would rather retaliate, to struggle to understand when we would rather fight and to fight, as a last resort, when intolerance will not listen to reason. (*Observer*, 2 April 1989)

In a closely argued article which is undoubtedly one of the best contributions to the debate, Jeremy Waldron explored notions of toleration. Like Berger, he placed the Rushdie affair in a global context:

Rushdie may be a British citizen, but he lives and works in a circle of authors, publishers, critics and commentators that effortlessly transcends national boundaries . . . if he contributes to the market-place of ideas, it is a world market. When he offends religious sensibilities, they are those of world religion. This is not just a British subject set upon by Iran. This is Salman Rushdie, citizen of the world, in confrontation with Islam. (*The Times Literary Supplement*, 10–16 March 1989)

The context of the problem is global and our understanding of freedom of expression must also be as wide and cosmopolitan as the perspective in which the problem, has emerged. The problem cannot be solved by one-dimensional tolerance based on mutual respect. Waldron argued that 'the religions of the world make *rival* claims about the nature and being of God and the meaning of human life. It is not possible for me to avoid criticizing the tenets of your faith without stifling my own. So mutual respect cannot possibly require us to refrain from criticism, if only because criticism of other sects is implicit already in the affirmation of my creed.' The religions of the world may make rival claims about the nature and being of God, but they do not make a rival claim about the meaning of life: all theistic worldviews agree that the meaning of life is to appreciate, love and obey the Creator. They may differ about how this is to be done, but they do not differ about the meaning of what is done.

We now move to two-dimensional toleration which concedes that criticism and discussion between rival faiths is fine, but also insists that criticism must be couched in serious and respectable terms: 'If I disagree with you about the existence of God, I may put forward my argument, but I must do so in a way that is circumspect and inoffensive, taking full account of the fact that your beliefs are not just your *views*, but convictions which go to the core or essence of your being.' Thus, two-dimensional toleration leaves ample room for debate and discussion but avoids mockery, offence, and insult. However, Waldron argued, it has a problem: 'what is serious and what is offensive, what is sober and what is mockery—these are not neutral ideas. They come as part of the package and different religions define them in different ways.' Not so. While different religions may define them differently, mockery and abuse can always be identified as such: after all, libel and defamation can be proved and are regularly proved in court. Great religions of the world, Judaism, Christianity and Islam, may have different definitions of mockery and abuse (a debatable point), but within their own traditions they have a pretty clear idea of what is an what is not mockery and abuse. Two people who hold contradictory beliefs are not offending each other; when they criticize or question each other's beliefs they are not mocking or offending each other; but when they begin to compare, or equate, each other's beliefs and sources of those beliefs with what both of them take to be common terms of abuse, mockery enters the equation. After all, if one were to equate a revered saint of any religion with a prostitute, or suggest that a religious figure was mentally deranged, most people would not have difficulty in recognizing this as mockery. Mockery and abuse may not be neutral terms, but they do have a certain objective content which most thinking people can recognize when they see it.

Nevertheless, we move towards three-dimensional tolerance. Waldron argued that:

> Persons and peoples must leave one another free to address the deep questions of religion and philosophy the best way they can, with the resources they have at their disposal. In the modern world, that may mean that the whole kaleidoscope of literary technique—fantasy, irony, poetry, word-play, and the speculative juggling of ideas—is unleashed on what many regard as the holy, the good, the immaculate and the indubitable. (*The Times Literary Supplement*, 10–16 March 1989)

However, three-dimensional tolerance actually amounts to a plea for the maintenance of the *status quo*. It neither solves the problem nor takes into account the global context in which Waldron sought to place the debate. Anything goes actually means everything stays—including the distorted imagination.

Waldron stopped at three-dimensional tolerance. But most civilized societies are actually moving towards a more holistic four-dimensional model of tolerance. Here global context is combined with the notion of social responsibility. When we view our actions as holistic, we see that they can have consequences for individuals and societies which are far removed from those actions. As assassination in one nation can lead to a stock market crash in another, and to famine in yet another. An accident in one country can produce riots in another and raise the price of a basic commodity beyond the reach of the mass of poor people in quite another. This is what the Greens and the environmentalists mean when they say we are living in an increasingly interdependent world. Indeed, different groups in society, from widely diverse areas, are coming to the conclusion that we must view the world and all that we do in it, from a holistic and socially responsible perspective. In this world, our actions have to be socially responsible or we put everyone, including ourselves, at risk. This is why even science, which is argued to be one of the most neutral and value-free enterprises, is increasingly being brought before the court of public opinion which demands that it be pursued with social responsibility, a polite secularist euphemism for moral responsibility. What is true of science and scientists is surely true of literature and writers. Both scientists and writers are free to do what they want to do, the best way they can, with the resources they have at their disposal, but they must view their activities holistically, be aware of their social responsibilities and the global context of their actions. This, it seems to us, is the only way of solving the problem.

The context in which Salman Rushdie wrote *The Satanic Verses* was higlighted by Rana Kabbani in her contribution to the *New Statesman and Society* issue devoted to 'Words for Salman Rushdie'. How Kabbani's piece, which stood in total contrast to all other contibutions, managed to slip through the enraged froth of *New Statesman and Society* is in itself an interesting academic conundrum. 'We in the Muslim East are your closest neighbours', Kabbani began,

> Coming from a world just beyond Europe's borders on that same Mediterranean with which you are so culturally familiar. Yet almost nothing is known about us, as though we hailed from a different planet altogether. If it was merely ignorance that separated us then that would be a bridgeable gap, but prejudice, preconception and even hostility have created a huge gulf between us. (*New Statesman and Society*, 31 March 1989)

The Satanic Verses, she said, perpetuates these prejudices and preconceptions; the very use of 'Mahound' for the Prophet Muhammad himself reinstates all the paranoia of the distorted imagination. 'This unpleasant polemic,' she stated bravely in the face of rabid opposition, is 'all the more surprising for its author's Muslim origins'. She asked the worthy and liberal-minded *literati*: 'Is your conscience not selective?'

> We have heard a great chorus of outrage at Khomeini's death sentence, but writers are killed in Iraq, children are tortured in front of their parents to extract confessions, some 5,000 Kurds were gassed, yet the West saw fit to side with Iraq to defeat Iran in a war it had not initiated . . . What are we to think of these double standards? Of these different responses to similar issues? (*New Statesman and Society*, 31 March 1989)

But in the end, she was far more tolerant than most contributors to the Rushdie cause. She was willing to concede, in a vain hope, that 'in the Rushdie case, it was a principle that was being defended, not a British passport.' As we have shown, that principle does not stand up to critical examination. And as we and Ms Kabbani know, a passport can overwrite all principles and make all the difference in this interdependent world.

Eight
The Limits of Forbearance

One of the most pernicious myths of modern times is that freedom of expression can only be guaranteed by a secular worldview. The corollary is that all traditional cultures enslave the individual in their social and cultural environments; it is modernization that has brought mankind liberation from social bondage and genuine freedom. To be modern is to be a free individual, to be unattached to the compulsion of anything sacred, to be indifferent to traditional and social customs, to be free to express oneself when and as one likes, to ridicule and abuse as one wishes. This freedom, however, is only an illusion. It is a freedom that ensures the silence of other points of view, for their expression is to invite ridicule or that uncomprehending raise of the eyebrow that asks, 'Can there really be people who think like that in this day and age?' It is not that there is no freedom to differ, just that those who demur from secularism have attained merely the freedom to be unheard and to become invisible. It is a freedom that has bred apologia, where those who differ must grovel for a quizzical hearing on the terms set down for them, terms that deny the validity and meaning of what they have to express. It is a freedom that enslaves others to ensure the freedom of a select few. Freedom divorced from meaning is not freedom but alienation that leads only to marginalization of those who do not subscribe to such a notion of alienated freedom.

For the Muslim scholars of the classical period, despite the fact that they spent a great deal of energy exploring the issues of free will, freedom was not a problem because of their trust in something that gave meaning to their lives. But in modern society, the issue of freedom has become an existential issue leading to acute anxiety, despair and panic. When one looks at the writings of Muslim philosophers, one cannot escape the conclusion that in their debates about free will they are playing with concepts, not struggling with existential problems. To them freedom was not a problem, for it was real by being absent as a problem. In contrast, freedom is a goal for the secularists, a value to be pursued constantly because it is intrinsically linked with their existential anxiety. In the secularist universe, the pursuit of freedom is akin to pursuit of meaning in life. As Anton Zijderveld stated in *The Abstract Society*,

> If life is experienced as concrete and meaningful, freedom will be a part of it by being absent as a problem. He is free who experiences social reality as meaningful and who knows his position and identity as traditional and taken-for-granted qualities. The moment doubt is cast upon this meaning and reality, freedom becomes a problem. When structures become alien, alienation poses itself as an existential problem. Freedom then becomes something to search for, a goal to obtain, a value to realize. (Zijderveld, p. 137)

This value is realized and is realizable only, argue the proponents of dogmatic secularism, when one is totally free to abuse and ridicule—the ultimate in freedom of expression. Conventionally in Western civilization this freedom to ridicule, this licence to abuse, has been operated by the dissident and dubious upon the dominant orthodoxy. It has been treasured as the increment of genuine liberal plurality wrested from the all-pervasive power structure. It has been the mark of tolerance within a diversifying common heritage, the balance to monopoly of power legitimated by the ideas that are ridiculed by the radically unconvinced. Such a history makes a society unprepared for plurality that is more than diversity within a common heritage. The conventional pursuit of freedom of expression in such plural circumstances makes the very exercise of abusing and ridiculing others an exercise in domination, an attempt to demonstrate the superiority of one's own intellectual stance. Those who accept such manifestations of freedom of expression, such abuse and ridicule, *ipso facto* acknowledge their inferiority and their subservience. For the secularists then, freedom of expression, is an exercise in the construction of a reality of their own choosing at the expense of the reality of non-secularist worldviews and an attempt to subdue all other notions of reality.

The distinction between the two notions of freedom, the dominant secular notion in the context of its history and that based on all traditional worldviews, including Islam, can be illustrated by looking at how the idea is treated by Daniel Defoe and ibn Tufail.

Both *Robinson Crusoe* and *Hai Ebn Yokdhan* are about individuals coming to grips with solitude and personal freedom. In Defoe's novel, published in 1715, the hero leaves home in an aimless search for adventure, is shipwrecked and finds himself on an uninhabited island. He spends twenty-eight years on the island, most of that time in solitude. Crusoe is eventually rescued by a European ship and returns to civilization, leaving behind him a small settlement to cultivate the island according to the rules *he* has laid down. In ibn Tufail's narrative, published in the middle of the twelfth century, Hai is generated spontaneously onto a desert island, where he spends thirty-five years before coming in contact with another human being. Both Hai and Crusoe learn to build a house, put up a storage place, make a cane door to keep animals out, find ways of domesticating animals. But there the similarity ends. Crusoe is gripped by a pathological fear of other men. Hai's main concern is observation and contemplation of the order he sees around him. He comes to understand that his duty is to be mindful of the needs of his body but only to the extent that this enables his soul its highest and noblest vocation—the contemplation of the Creator. On Crusoe's island, there are only two kinds of individuals: the bestial cannibals and genteel slaves; Crusoe never looks for a relationship, either with Friday or with subsequent arrivals on his island. The only way he can express his freedom is by seeking an acknowledgement of his superiority; those who deny Crusoe his superiority are consigned to the outer pale of savagery. On Hai's island, a soul more noble than his arrives and Hai learns from him.

Robinson Crusoe is regarded as a work of realism. And it is, indeed, real in the technical processes of life which Crusoe learns. But beyond that it is the product of the distorted imagination of Defoe, who had never been farther afield than Spain, as his contemporary critics were eager to point out. The external world of the island, the development of the plot, the people of the island, are not based on any observation but are the externalization of a private vision, a working-out by Defoe of 'a massive misanthropic neurosis'. The landscape and its few inhabitants are a product of the internal panic of the author. In contrast, ibn Tufail's imagination seeks the fulfilment of Hai's freedom in finding ways of teaching others what Hai has learned through the use of his reason. Because Hai had found meaning in his life, he could relate to others on the basis of equality; he could learn from them as well as teach them. Unlike Hai, Crusoe could relate to others only through an existential struggle, a struggle that gave him an identity and his life a meaning.

Robinson Crusoe personifies how the secular mind deals with the existential problems of meaning and responsibility in individual freedom, with the individual at the centre of thought and concern. Inherent in this worldview is the whole notion of conflict—the individual is constantly and continuously in conflict with his or her own ego and with a diversity of potential worlds around it. Like Crusoe, the only relationships the secular mind can have are the ones based on domination or banishment to the outer worlds of savagery. The secular mind can only tolerate the meek, humble and subservient Man Friday; or ridicule, abuse and relegate to the domain of bestial cannibals all those who refuse to acknowledge its superiority.

Conflict, domination and a sense of superiority are intrinsic to the secular worldview. The triumph of modern secularism is instrumental rationality, the dynamic, progressive truth within history whose apotheosis—the subordination, domination and inclusion of all other viewpoints within the dominant worldview—ends history. Central to the creation of this modern terminus to history has been art, the development of modes of free expression where the meaning and reality of existence have been scrutinized and radically revised. Thus the secular purveyors of art and literature consider themselves to be superior by virtue of their art and literature. As a part of this superiority, they claim to have a right to ridicule and abuse—the main weapons of domination in their armoury. This ensures that the one thing the dominated, and indeed the banished, do not have is respect; the exercise of empathetic artistic imagination that grasps their experience and knowledge is precluded. They are parodied, not represented. Like Kipling's 'half devil, half child', the best that the traditional cultures can expect from the secular onslaught is condescension.

In this secular construction, what are the freedoms of the marginalized, who have given in and accepted their inferiority and the superiority of the secular rationality, and been banished? The subservient can only express themselves when, as in the case of Man Friday, they speak in the language of Crusoe, in the terms of the secular ideology. The savages are savage and do not deserve the ear of sensible, rational individuals, even if they could be heard above the shattering clamour of abuse and ridicule.

Take, for example, the very notion of cannibalism. Defoe has no doubt savages will be cannibals and writes accordingly. Europeans have never doubted all savages are cannibals. People after people who have come into contact with the West have found they must dutifully answer questions on the organization of cannibalism among their ancestors; many must still jump through this hoop today, not just for the representatives of the press or adventure-seeking amateur travellers but for supposed scientific investigators. What is so wrong with this? As William Arens argued so cogently, the idea of cannibalism derived from the Greeks and was retailed through mediaeval literature. When Europeans first had contact with strange new peoples they immediately, without benefit of a mutual language, recounted detailed conversations where the savages explained their complex cannibalistic practices. These reports became the received wisdom of the ages. Arens's investigations, however, established that there has never been one direct eye-witness account of socially organized cannibalism in all the annals of travellers' tales or anthropological inquiry. The existence and persistence of cannibalism are predicated upon the question; the expectations of the distorted imagination constructs reality only to confirm it through every branch of endeavour from scientism to art. The abused, however, still have to answer the questions and can only learn their familiar lines: cannibalism died out in the time of their ancestors or is practised by the next people down the river or over the mountain. The overall result is that they cannot be heard; and, therefore, they do not have freedom of expression.

Fundamentalism and Frigidity

Constant abuse and ridicule of the sacred, does not, however, do away with the spiritual yearning of man. What it does do is constrain the vast majority of mankind, who see freedom in terms of constructing a reality with meaning within narrower and narrower limits. Religion, therefore, reappears not as rational interpretation of the sacred, but in the form of cults and as fundamentalism. In all its various manifestations, from born-again Christianity to Ayatollahism, fundamentalism is a direct creation of secularism. It is the last refuge from the abuse and ridicule of the secular mind, a declaration that man is much more than a manikin. Essentially, fundamentalism is a grotesque projection of the worst nightmares of secularism on the world stage, an acknowledgement of the war that the secular mind has declared on the sacred. The opposition between secularism and fundamentalism leads both sides to define the particular issues that divide them as the essential battleground; it can require both sides to internalize a distorted image of themselves as a consequence of their implacable opposition. The conflict can turn both parties into pathological expressions of their identities. Defining the battleground eradicates identification of other areas where agreement exists and accommodation or mutual support for shared ideas are possible. The pathologies of opposition in the battle for dominance prevents plurality whose essence is acknowledging limits of forbearance.

In the last resort, the issues of the absolute right of the artist to abuse and ridicule, in the name of criticism and progress, is an issue of power and territory. It emerges from the conflicts of Western history and trails the echoes of this history as neurosis on a global scale. The rise of the secular worldview has always been a power game. Little wonder that it has invoked the response it best recognizes in the power tactics of what is termed fundamentalism. In whatever guise, fundamentalism also seeks to assert authority over territory, to demarcate sacred territory wherein the faithful can be free from the domination and imposition of secularism. It is a particular expression of a form of conflict, not the total substance nor the only possible expression of the certainty for which it is battling to acquire territory. Fundamentalism is the self-assertion of the voiceless by the only means available to them to get a hearing.

Secularism once gave Western men and women an assurance about their past that legitimated the extension of political and economic control over all traditional cultures and societies. The patterns of life of all traditional societies represented stages of human social development the West had transcended in its history. The study of other people defined the progressive and superior nature of Western civilization and rationalized its mercantile expansion and assumption of colonial control over traditional societies that were living survivals of the past. Robinson Crusoe had no cause to question that he should dominate the inhabitants of his island, nor to question the institution of slavery. All that the secular outlook admitted was a distinction in the form of domination: naked force, as in chattel slavery; or benign upliftment of the inferior according to the dictates of the master. Never once does Friday, the product of benign policy, address Crusoe as anything other than Master; even after he has been inducted into the world order of his master, he is a second-class resident who must know his place, be at the disposal and bidding of the master.

Today, secularism is more ambiguous about its own past. Racism, colonialism and imperialism are deemed bad words for unfortunate historical excesses. Secularism nowadays is about relativism and development. It's assurance is all about the future, other peoples' futures, the futures of all traditional cultures and civilizations. Secularism can conceive of no modernization that is not a developmental progress to the existential condition and material formation of the West. It is for territorial control and authority over the future that secularism battles with fundamentalism. Fundamentalism must assert its past and secure its history, if it is to have any authority over the future: without history and the definition of sacred territory that made that history, there are no alternative sources of ideas that can create a future that is an alternative to becoming the second-class inhabitants of someone else's modernity. Fundamentalism as a reactive power ploy need do nothing more than assert the validity of the past. The very assertion of a discrete past is the demand for an autonomous future.

Fundamentalism is a slogan for defending the validity of the sacred words of power of a discrete past as organizing principles for the human future. Beyond that, fundamentalism is a term that obscures more than it reveals. Fundamentalism is a slogan for a reaction, it is not the name of a policy. It tells one where the policy derives its validity, not what the policy contains. The simple horror at the emergence of fundamentalism has made it impossible for commentators, especially commentators on the Muslim world, to penetrate to the substance of policy debate that exists in all Muslim countries and communities, whether they are overtly fundamentalist or not. Fundamentalism struggles for power over territory with secularism, which sees the challenge as a threat. Secularism is inherently neurotic in its arrogance, insecure in its self-assurance. It reacts to a threat with the age-old techniques it used to attain dominance: abuse and ridicule and the application of its scientific rationality to disprove the validity of the sources upon which fundamentalism relies.

This is precisely what Rushdie has attempted in *The Satanic Verses*, employing literature as the appropriate forum for his battle with Islam. It is not a conflict that can admit of understanding. As Rushdie himself has written 'in all literature, what actually happened is less important than what the author can manage to persuade the audience to believe' (*Midnight's Children*, p. 325). The distorted imagination is not ignorant by inadvertency, it is a rational instrument for deliberate purposes. The truth of secularism has superior rights and obviates any responsibility to the truth as experienced and known by other peoples. To advocate the rights of the described to self-description is to challenge the project of secularism whose legacy from history is the distorted imagination. Secularism sees any base of power that is not subservient to its definition as a threat to its own existence, an inherent threat to its own freedom. Secularism champions plurality, yet secularism can live only with plurality that accepts reformulation upon secularist principles. To do otherwise is to challenge the foundation of secularism itself. There can be other ways, only so long as they conform to the one way determined by dogmatic secularism and its rationale, scientism.

To get behind the slogans of fundamentalism is to enter the world of the marginalized and realize that theirs is an invaded, fragmented, destabilized, recreated, modified territory. The potency of fundamentalism is as a slogan for the repossession of territory so that one may proceed to make it one's own again. In a sense, the opposition between secularism and fundamentalism is a battle over discontinuities: who possesses them and how they should be responded to. The secularists view history as a series of discontinuities and ruptures of meaning through which individuals have acquired personal freedom, freedom of conscience to choose for themselves. What is repudiated is the individual as moral being accountable to something transcendant of individuality. This is not to say that the moral individual is not bound by a whole set of contractual responsibilities, but each contract is conditional, negotiable, open to criticism, revisable and inherently embraces doubt on its nature, validity, scope and meaning; all elements within the realm of individual choice are relative.

Far from being a discontinuity, this dominant secular vision of the human individual shows a marked historic continuity of allegiance to the rationale used to resolve the specific problematique of Western history. In this vision any ideology of the common collective good must be constrained by a secular political process of negotiation as the only means to achieve tolerance of diversity. The assumed nature of any collective vision is as the antithesis of diversity; therefore, the individual is always insecure within the confines of the state and must be reassured by the stress laid upon legal rights of individual personal freedom—hence, the liberal concentration upon individual human rights as political right. This is Rushdie's specific recipe for Muslim societies. At no time have new principles or the influence of ideas from outside this common Western history been consulted or included within the making of this modern paradigm.

The continuity behind vigorously asserted discontinuity is the stance taken by Rushdie. He collapses all history into the time scale of his own lifetime; the predominant interest of all his writing is working out his personal existential angst, his allegiances and conscientious position through his own rewriting of history; his interpretation of its actors mirrors the tenets of the modern Western paradigm. The artist assumes the role of the divine because the creative imagination in the universe of doubt is the sole force that brings the world into being for the free individual. The fundamental discontinuity in all Rushdie's writing is the loss of faith, the entry into the universe of doubt that sets all the other discontinuities in motion and requires that the whole of history and individual persona must be reformulated, renegotiated. It is not Rushdie's right to make this conscious choice and follow its course, nor write about it, that is at issue; rather, it is accurate identification of the position he has taken which cannot be accomplished without knowledge of other peoples. Only with such information can the effect of this exercise of individual licence upon the freedoms of others in a plural society be ascertained. The Rushdie affair is a test case on the most important question facing the contemporary world: the possibilities of making a genuinely plural future for all of humankind that properly accommodates the differences that form plurality.

There is in Rushdie no pondering of the discontinuities of traditional cultures as they operate in contemporary circumstances, striving to maintain a worldview other than secularism. The only representations of such an option in Rushdie are grostesques, vulgar caricatures, exercises in the banishment to the outer realms of savagery. As he says, every story one tells is a form of censorship precluding other stories; he also points out that in fitting together the world from scraps and fragments one must allow for the missing bits. It is of overriding importance, then, in assessing how Rushdie exercises his freedom of expression to acknowledge that the stories he censors and the bits he leaves out are the experience and knowledge of the overwhelming majority, not just of Muslims but of all people who live within traditional worldviews. One writer's freedom of expression seemingly convinces the dominant establishment to acquiesce in setting the limits of forbearance at the silence of the bulk of the world's population, for that is the position his writing confirms.

Within the world of the marginalized, censored and silenced, discontinuity is a genuine problem, and an impetus for the growth of fundamentalism; it is *the* issue of creating a plural future for the world. For the traditional worldviews, including Islam, discontinuity is not a consciously manufactured product of their own history, but the physical and mental dislocation that has been imposed and engineered from without. The result is a dual dislocation; they are ruptured from their own traditions, but they are not fully a part of the culture of modernity. The rupture in tradition has been the result of internal decline; colonization which curtailed the involvement of traditional institutions and principles in the operation of society; and the drive for modernization whose model and standards are all external to the society. The whole operation of society is deformed by the jarring between tradition, that retains authority, commitment and validity despite all the restrictions imposed upon it, and the failure of modernity to develop local roots and autonomous growth. The two poles, the traditional and modern, are like separate compartments, even though they can be part of the same individual. The ultimate meaning of reality derives from the traditional worldview, in the way that Islam as religion and belief defines the identity of the Muslim, for example; but the powerful means of making a modern society the knowledge base of science and technology and the political conventions of nation-building are governed by an imported culture heavily laden with a different set of values.

The answer that is increasingly being sought involves a different kind of modernity. It is a quest to end discontinuity by extending the moral and ethical vision of the traditional worldview to organize the needs, techniques and challenges of the contemporary world. In Western society modernity is generating meaninglessness, the condition that post-modernism embraces as axiomatic. In the Muslim world, and in many other traditional societies, discontinuity is bringing about the search for a way to recover meaning. The most common name for this response to the crisis of modernity is fundamentalism, most often applied perjoratively. In the Muslim world it means the reassertion of the fundamental Islamic vision of a unitary moral universe, where the objective for men and women as moral beings is to become good human beings by realizing their duty to themselves which includes their duty to fellow human beings and the rest of the natural world. The individual moral being is the focus of the Islamic vision, but the individual is not isolated. Community is essential, its purpose identical to that of the individual to produce conditions that foster respect for human worth and dignity and facilitate the growth of the good human being. The identity of interest of society and individual means the focus is not to secure freedom by rights for the individual in the face of society, but to ensure their participation in the exercise of those embedded rights and obligations that belong to each individual. When the focus is not the creation of the good citizen but the self-realization of the good person through their existence within society, then democracy is not an ideology but the essential procedure for participation, inclusion and consultation. The freedom to express assent and dissent are essential prerequisites of the entire system.

The freedoms, rights and obligations of a Muslim belong to the individual and must be balanced throughout the course of existence in society. The constraints that operate for the individual also apply to the state or nation, which can never be ends in themselves: the authority of the state must be justified by its allegiance to and performance of these same balanced rights, freedoms and obligations. Therefore, Islam is a religion that can never be privatized or secularized, since it sees no distinction either between the sacred and the secular or between the individual and society. To be a follower of Islam is to choose a worldview that is a whole way of life that comprehends the whole of existence. It is a view of existence that is inveterately optimistic about human potential to choose goodness and thoroughly realistic about the human capacity for evil; it is the function of human reason to distinguish, not confuse, them. But the one crucial difference that separates it from the culture of modernity is that it has no place for instrumental rationality. To be religious in the broadest sense of the term is the most rational choice of a moral human being; it is the Islamic vision. One could say this makes Islam a political creed, but it is a crude statement that misses most of the substance. It would be more accurate to say that it is essential to Islamic rationality to extend its moral vision into all spheres of human activity. When Islam operated autonomously as a stable civilization, the consequences of this moral vision were to be detected in all its fields of cultural production.

Fundamentalism is seen as a nostalgic exercise, an unquestioning assumption of the primacy of the past. This is a shallow as well as thoroughly misleading presentation of what is happening in the Muslim communities worldwide. The dislocation and discontinuity within Muslim consciousness mean that the extensiveness of Islamic law and the full range of values and principles that constructed that law from the Qur'an and Sunnah have not been in use for centuries; the same is true of Islamic philosophy, science and the whole range of intellectual endeavours that derived from the sources of Islamic civilization and were its cultural manifestations. An Islamic society is something that must be recreated today with reference to this past, precisely because it is not currently in existence. The apparent static nature of Islam as a culture is a product of the discontinuity that the appeal to the Islamic past is meant to resolve. Islam has been maintained in Muslim society as a redoubt, the minimal Islam of personal piety, personal and family law, ritual observance and rhetorical symbolism. The concentration on minimal Islam, the only areas of which could be operated while the organization of the whole of society was under the control of other principles and values, has deformed the contemporary perception of Islam as a whole. Muslims have been dislocated from knowledge of their own selves and their own heritage; they, too, are often taught about their heritage through the filter of the distorted imagination. The body of knowledge that was accumulated while Islam was an autonomous civilization has been preserved as the essential but abstract heritage, the special province of a particular group of scholars and religious adepts. This preservation is a blessing, since the resources exist to recapture the continuity of meaning locked in this abstract heritage. But preservation stresses conservation, not dynamism—a feature necessary to any living civilization and inherent in the Islamic vision. Dynamism occurs when any set of values is consulted, interpreted and operated in daily life, whether by an individual or a society. Then one's worldview ceases to be abstract; it becomes the means for cultural accommodation to change. Fundamentalism, or any other term for civilizational renewal, makes reference to the past because it must be critically examined if a transformation of contemporary society is to be made. It is the nature, extent, purpose and sophistication of this questioning that is absent from analyses of fundamentalism.

The blanket application of the term fundamentalism makes it impossible to recognize the diversity of opinion and the nature of the debate that is going on within Muslim circles. The language of this debate is unfamiliar to the outsider, since it is geared to comprehending the meaning and significance of Islamic terminology for modern society. These terms have no Western counterparts, because their content and the way they define reality are not the same as the basic categories of Western language, thought and usage. The important questions that must be debated are not the same, and similar questions present themselves in entirely dissimilar forms and at different places in the debate. To translate them into Western parlance is to subject them to the conventions of the distorted imagination and, thereby, to falsify them. To resist translation would require outsiders to learn the definitions of the terms as interpreted by Muslims, an exercise the West has, as yet, failed to undertake. When the perspective of Western analysis renders everything down to a question of for or against the Shariah, the generic term applied to Islamic law, it is impossible to make audible a debate about what is the nature, scope and appropriate means of the Shariah today. When science is taken for granted as a value-free realm of endeavour, it is hard to comprehend a debate about how values defined by a religious vision are to be used to operate critical reason in making science morally and socially responsible.

If the West tries to comprehend this movement at all, it does so in terms of its own historical experience. Fundamentalism in Western understanding is the same sort of phenomenon as early nineteenth-century romanticism, with its idealization of a nationalist, cultural ethos. From European experience this is not merely a suspect movement—it is pernicious because European romanticism was racist, obscurantist and the lineal ancestor of the phenomenon of fascism and Naziism. Romanticism stressed its own cultural roots, and idealized its folk past. Fundamentalism also emphasizes cultural roots. Indeed, the integrity of culture is fundamental to any definition of the past, present and future of non-Western societies. But in fundamentalist thought, it is also a vigorous defiance of all the categories of Western secularism. This is a profound difference and one not exclusive to Muslim society, as the Indian writer Ashis Nandy has pointed out.

> A stress on culture is a repudiation of the post-Renaissance European faith that only that dissent is true which is rational, sane, scientific, adult and expert—according to Europe's concepts of rationality, sanity, science, adulthood and expertise.
>
> Viewed thus, the links between culture, critical consciousness and social change in India become, not a unique experience, but a general response of societies which have been the victims of history and are now trying to rediscover their own visions of a desirable society, less burdened by the post-Enlightenment hope of 'one world' but by the post-colonial idea of cultural relativism.
>
> Cultural survival is an increasingly potent political slogan of our time. In the nineteenth century it seemed like an obscurantist ploy. Today, when the juggernaut of modernity threatens every non-Western culture, the slogan no longer seems a revivalist conspiracy. It has become a plea for minimum cultural plurality in an increasingly uniformized world. (Nandy, 'Cultural Frames')

Cultural plurality is a new idea in the West. Indeed, it is a distinctly unfamiliar experience for Western civilization which traces its roots to Western Christendom and its vision of a compulsory, uniform and orthodox society. One has to look to non-Western societies to find historic models of cultural plurality in operation. Western civilization has had obvious problems with and notorious lapses in accommodating cultural diversity. Cultural relativism has acquired a currency, that of the duty owed by historical guilt to marginalized peoples. But cultural relativism is constantly in conflict with the requirements of the secular worldview; it has not been internalized within secularism, for it denies the universal validity, the 'truth' upon which modern secular freedoms are founded. If cultural relativism is seen as anything more than a box within which other people confine themselves to the reservation outside the pale of modernity, then secularism automatically is on trial. Cultural plurality must challenge the dominance of secularism, because it defines limits of forbearance wherein a plurality of worldviews and their associated patterns of life coexist. Cultural plurality demands the recognition that there are a plurality of means for realizing freedom in a diversity of existential forms, not merely one way that must be appropriated by all. Cultural relativism, instead of uniting all people in the supremacy of secularism, throws Western man back upon himself to wrestle with his own demons in the solitary knowledge that other people refuse to be haunted by his ghosts.

> Many non-Western observers of the culture of the modern West—its life-style, literature, arts and its human sciences—have been struck by the way contractual, competitive individualism—and the utter loneliness which flows from it—dominates the Western mass society.
>
> From Friedrich Nietzsche to Karl Marx to Franz Kafka, much of Western social analysis, too, has stood witness to this cultural pathology. What once looked like independence from one's immediate authorities in the family, and defiance of the larger aggregates they represented, now looks more and more like a Hobbesian worldview gone rabid. (Nandy, 'Cultural Frames')

Cultural relativism casts Western man as both Faustus and Mephistopheles in Marlowe's terms. This is, as Nandy said, not to make the facile point that the West is a demon, 'but to recognise that the West and its relationship with the non-Western society has become deeply intertwined with the problem of evil in our times—according to both the West and the non-West'. The West is not demonic but it has sought, as of natural right, Mephistopheles's prize on a global scale: *Solamen miseris socios habuisse doloris*—company in its misery; it seeks companionship by the inclusion of all mankind within its kingdom of existential doubt. The limits of forbearance of a plural society, a plural world, entail the renunciation of this quest, not the end of the West, nor even the renunciation of all things Western. The limits of forbearance are the conditions for coexistence that will enable a plurality of modernity, a diversity of ways of synthesizing modernity and interpreting its content to take root. While it is widely acknowledged that the world is converging to a precarious future, the West is not only unwilling to contemplate but unable to acknowledge the possibility of a diversity of modernity that could potentially be mutually supportive of the human condition. It is only on the basis of defining such limits of forbearance that the human right to be free to choose a meaningful modernity can be expressed and enacted by non-Western peoples. Without serious consideration of how a plurality of worldviews can coexist while they set about constructing their own modernity, a whole host of freedoms that the West argues for and insists are universal natural truths will be nothing but empty rhetoric for those who hold to traditional worldviews. These supposed and insecure freedoms will have to be purchased by the falsification and meaninglessness of their own traditions.

Diversity and Domination

Peter L. Berger has called the condition of modernity 'the homeless mind'. To be homeless is the modern condition of occupying a host of different private worlds, of work, of association, of neighbourhood, of personal interest and private belief without any overarching realm of meaning that integrates these diverse facets of life. Those who seek cultural survival in a plural world are those who deny the freedom of homelessness by seeking to retain the integrative meaning of their own traditions. Most importantly, they define the nature of their home free from the prejudiced, jaundiced view of the secularist.

Ashis Nandy has examined the significance of this distinction in his writing on Gandhi. Modernists have considerable difficulty trying to accommodate the totality of Gandhi's views into the modern paradigm. 'They can neither disown the Mahatma nor digest him.' The modernist will concentrate on what is useful to modern nation-building, while confining the Mahatma's other notions, his spiritual ideals, to flights of 'insanity'. Yet Gandhi's views are a coherent totality, the significance of which is that he 'never eulogized the Indian village nor called for a return to the past. He supported the ideas of the village and traditions, and India's traditional villagers, but not extant Indian villages or traditions' (Nandy, 'Cultural Frames'). What Gandhi did, what makes him so indigestible to the modernist, was the fact that he 'rejected the modern innovations such as the nation-state system, modern science and technology, urban-industrialism and evolutionism (without rejecting the traditional ideas of the state, science and technology, civic living and social transformation)' (Nandy, 'Cultural Frames').

Gandhi accepted that he lived within an invaded territory, beset with discontinuity caused by the dislocations of externally imposed modification upon its cultural base. But Gandhi was not homeless, nor did he see his option as tearing down his home to attain a modern future. The foundation stones of his home still existed in the ideas and values upon which his tradition relied, by which it had been created. Tradition to Gandhi was a living, changing, remaking process of axioms and values that could rebuild the admittedly decrepit home into a new residence on the old domestic foundations. Nandy has argued that Gandhi saw the validity of his defence of tradition in his critique of modernity, and his critique of modernity justified his criticism of extant tradition. In consequence, Gandhi could be a more severe, constructive and effective critic of abuses within tradition than any modernist could hope to be.

Gandhi's approach has much in common, from the perspective of a different civilization, with the debate and discussion going on in the Muslim world. The fundamental principle of cultural resistance confounds the received wisdom of secularism and all its myriad branches of expertise: tradition is not static. A civilizational tradition contains the values and axioms that are a critique of extant conditions and of the modern West. To champion one's own tradition is not to defend the status quo, nor to romanticize and glorify a past, certainly not to seek the past as one's future. The option for cultural survival is to select different criteria, one's own traditional values, as the diagnostic tests by which modernity, the present and the future must be analysed and change initiated. The battle for cultural survival is the struggle to be modern and at home; the struggle for the freedom to domesticate the present and the future according to one's own tradition. The distorted image of tradition makes such an option soundless and invisible to Western observers.

The secular worldview regards traditional culture as an imposition, an instrument for control that is the antithesis of its own conception of individual freedom. Tradition is a captive condition; an option for tradition must, therefore, be an irrational, emotive flight from progress, a hideout from the awesome possibilities of personal freedom. This is Rushdie's notion of Islam as a religion of rules for everything. It is a commonplace misunderstanding of the impulse critically to reason out the normative principle applicable to all aspects of behaviour and thought; such a process can be stated as seeking the rule for everything, but it means far more than being a robot. Furthermore, the principle can remain static, a thing of continuous meaning, while at the same time there can be many forms of behavioural expression and means of putting it into practice that can change with time and circumstances. It is the principle that matters and must be maintained, not the form. This is a basic proposition, but one that is extremely elusive in Western understanding.

Visibility is attained by the proponents of cultural survival in terms of power relationships only where the domestic option becomes a direct challenge to inclusion within the modern conventions that are all Western conventions. Then, as with Gandhi, the terms of discussion centre upon the agenda set by Western convention, the challenge posed to its 'interests'. The traditionalist must answer only as questioned from the ethnocentric redoubt of modernism. Once again, the very mechanism that created the distorted imagination sets to work to apply that distorted imagination to new circumstances, recasting but never changing the character notes of the players. In the coverage of fundamentalism, history is repeating itself.

Plurality is not the acceptance of tradition as quaint exotica in private manifestations of clothing, cooking and art forms or seasonal entertainment, though even this much can be problematic. Plurality is acknowledging the existence of other axioms and values that cherish freedom, justice, equity and much more, as different modes of operation, within a different construction of life ways. Plurality is accepting that these life ways can contribute constructively to the consensus of a heterogeneous community. Plurality is seeking peaceful coexistence through difference that is denial of no party, nor imposition upon any party. Plurality is the test of the self-proclaimed freedom for all the Western worldview takes itself to be. So far this freedom has been tested only to be found wanting.

Forbearance means not insisting there is only one way, when the history of the world is replete with many ways. Forbearance is the willingness to engage in a dialogue about essential values. Such a dialogue must be founded upon a willingness to accept the validity of other life ways as derived from beliefs that have a right to be respected. Forbearance then becomes the deconstruction of intolerance and insecurity by information, through knowledgeable interaction and debate between people who mutually accept each other's right to maintain difference. If I can have freedom only as you define and construct it, I become dependent on the quality of your knowledge of my needs vis-a-vis freedom and toleration. If you and I practise distinct life ways derived from different belief systems, it is not a test of my toleration that I rely upon your comprehension of a foreign world of thought to settle the fate of my freedom to be myself and replicate my life ways—it is a test of my subservience and lack of power, a potential denial of freedom of expression of my being. Dependence and subservience make for a kind of plurality. They are not, however, akin to a plurality of freedom.

So long as freedom of expression is solely defined by and wedded to the secular worldview, it remains a function of a distorted imagination: the very construction of this freedom of expression imposes a view of normality and abnormality on other people and falsifies them. The agenda of discussion within this narrowly constructed freedom of expression confines the traditionalist in search of cultural survival to the realm of false reaction, to a false proposition. Frustration at being pushed beyond the limits of forbearance is the inevitable consequence for the falsified, whose very identity and sense of being is denied by being rendered soundless and invisible. The falsified have arguments constructed for them by an agenda of imposed interests; they do not have access to autonomous discussion of their own agenda of ideas and concern. It is hardly surprising, then, that they regard freedom of expression as lip service to an illusion.

For Western society the Rushdie affair *is* the question of for or against the person of Salman Rushdie. It *is* the question, 'have you or have you not read *The Satanic Verses*?' Neither question is pertinent to the protests that are being conducted within Western society. The organizers of the protest campaigns have consistently declined to endorse Ayatollah Khomeini's *fatwa* against Rushdie; they have not sought to further this threat to his person. Indeed they have consistently defined *the* issue as one of seeking legal, peaceful redress of a grievance through the accepted channels of Western societies, the courts. Within the conventions of Western law, any outrage that could threaten public order must be self-evident and published; it is neither required nor necessary that the outrage be personally ingested by each affronted individual. It is beyond any legal shadow of a doubt that *The Satanic Verses* has been published—it sat for many weeks at the top of the bestseller lists. The argument that freedom of expression is only seen to be done when the vertical integration of commercial publishing is complete with the circulation of an even more available paperback edition is an indication that the defence of Rushdie is not a purely principled stand; it includes the defence of the freedom to make money. This leaves us with the only substantive issue as the singular point Western society has no means to address and, therefore, ignores: is the transgressive outrage in the book self-evident? It is this substantive question that raises the issue of the limits of forbearance.

The problem is that within a plural society one must rephrase the question.

It ceases to be a simple matter of, 'is the content of the book transgressive?' The question turns upon transgressive for whom, and whether and how such transgression can be subject to scrutiny and accountability to the general interest and public order. It is arrogant effrontery to dismiss the Muslim protesters as making an uninformed, emotional response to a subtle work of literature they have neither read nor understood. It is the Western readership untutored in Islamic ideas and boggled by a convoluted novel who are unaware of the particularity of the text placed before them, but who are highly susceptible to its implications. It is the ordinary Muslim on the street who has a surer grasp of what is alleged by Rushdie; the Muslim position can be substantiated by reasoned argument that draws upon 1,400 years of intellectual endeavour. Emotion is stirred by confidence in this heritage. To allege that the Qur'an arises from the personality of Muhammad, as Rushdie does, is to say the messenger is the message and open the way to the host of inaccuracies that are asserted as the personal law built upon this premise. To allege further that the human Prophet was so unaware of his own pronouncements that the text of the Qur'an could be repeatedly falsified without his noticing and that, therefore, the textual sources are a fabulation of history is to open the Prophet to the charge of hypocrisy and his followers to the charge of allegiance to an idiotic cause. The whole is then wrapped in scurrilous language, consciously drawing upon abusive terms and images. The effect upon both the person of the Prophet and his followers is a defamation that must lead to familiar consequences: to lower them in the estimation of right-thinking people, to open them to odium and contempt and to cause them to be shunned.

Absolute freedom of expression does not exist; there is always some limit set beyond which free expression will be deemed a transgression, an infringement of the rights or freedoms of other people or the public interest in general. The concept in Western convention is freedom of expression within the law. The quality of freedom under the law is determined by context, the climate of opinion, the attitudes of a society. Any society that is not prepared to assess its own attitudes and the effect of this general climate of opinion, to be self critical, can find itself slipping into effective intolerance, no matter how noble the ideals it claims to hold dear, nor how exalted the sentiments supposedly enshrined in its legislation. The quality of freedom available within a society, the actual limits of forbearance that apply, are to be found in what constitutes a breach for which redress is attainable.

The mechanism by which a transgression is tested is trial by jury. The jury is a pressure gauge of the quality of information and opinion in a community. As the British Law Lord, Lord Devlin, has expressed it, 'A jury can do justice, whereas the judge, who has to follow the law, may not.' If the majority of right-thinking people in a society already have as common currency a distorted image of the person or group defamed, how could that person be vindicated by a jury? This is the circularity of the legal system that exists. Before defamation can become visible, the climate of disinformation must be established. In effect, to substantiate any defamation or blasphemous libel of Prophet Muhammad, the jury must be put on trial for its ability to comprehend beliefs they do not hold, do not believe to be true, and may doubt that they should tolerate. The very processes that created the conventions of literary freedom in the West, however, directly militate against this point being noticed in the clamour over *The Satanic Verses*. Justice is what a jury is capable of doing. Justice is not invariably what a jury achieves. What is at issue is not the will to see that religious freedom exists for minorities in Britain, but the ability to bring that freedom to a liveable reality.

The blasphemy law sets limits beyond which public outrage would be liable to be provoked into a breach of public order. No one seems to doubt that a book, or any publication, can outrage and that such outrage can be a provocative act. The question is what kind of publication and how does a society equip itself to judge what is reasonable outrage. The blasphemy law in Britain is limited in extent: it covers blasphemy only in the Anglican sense of the term. The legal profession tends to believe the law as it stands is unworkable and is loathe to bring such cases, fearing they will be unable to secure convictions. The last trial for blasphemy was a private prosecution brought in 1978; it was successful. The narrow scope of the existing blasphemy law is not such a blatant inequity so long as Britain is a Christian country, no matter what the diversity of Christian denominations. It becomes a glaring inequity once Britain is conceded to be a multi-faith society.

The gradual atrophy of the blasphemy law is a product of the rising tide of secularism, but this does not make the existing law inoperable—most certainly it does not mean that only Anglicans were likely to be outraged by the transgression that was the subject of the last trial for blasphemy. In the context of a multi-faith society, however, matters are different. Christian sensitivities as they have developed in history are an unreliable guide to how non-Christians view their religion, its beliefs and practices. Christian society has been secularized and the accommodation to secularism has even entered into the discourse of Christian theology; such ideas may be a nonsense in terms of non-Christian beliefs. It is patently obvious that a non-Christian is precisely not a Christian. Without general understanding and knowledge of their beliefs and worldview, the minority can have no reasonable assurance of any legal process, nor any confidence in the opportunity for legal redress. The legal confusion creates no obligation on the part of publishers to demonstrate responsibility in making choices about publication. Confusion can give them freedom but is unable to generate any definition of what constitutes licence or transgression.

The terminology of defamation is also the terminology of intolerance. The defamation can become the rationale of why the overt expression of others' believing should not be endured and can be reacted against. Just as a climate of ignorance undermines any defense against defamation, it also constructs the climate of intolerance. Intolerance, as history has shown, is never perceptible to those who practise it. Intolerance is patently obvious only to those who are its victims. History also shows that intolerance can be deconstructed. While this has seldom occurred without a struggle, in the end intolerance is vanquished not by conflict but by knowledge and the willingness to exercise self-critical reflection that makes ignorance visible. Legal formulations of principles and the ability to attain legal redress for offences are made only after the fact of change, when knowledge has already gained some currency. The real impediment to making any legal redress available to a minority is avoidance of genuine consideration of the limits of forbearance.

In matters relating to freedom of information, expression and the press, juries have a habit of supporting as little restriction as possible. Historically, this well-established tendency has had admirable effect. The willingness of juries to support the liberty of the press in the face of charges of seditious libel is how the modern understanding of freedom of expression was achieved. Sedition makes it a crime 'to stir up enmity between different classes of Her Majesty's subjects'. The Muslim would not be alone in thinking this is a prevalent practice of publishing in Britain today, that liberty of the press has been established only to permit the ease of abuse of that liberty. Muslims cannot evade the web of history that surrounds them. The great chorus of outrage that greeted peaceful Muslim agitation against *The Satanic Verses* legitimated itself by invoking this very history. The symbolic burning of the book was not seen as akin to demonstrations where effigies and national flags are burned. The symbolism of the book has been made sacred by the history of the struggle for freedom of expression. Muslim objections were silenced by the chorus of disapproval of the act of burning a book. The content of *The Satanic Verses* was irrelevant; the issue was freedom of expression as British history had defined it through its protracted, bloody and painful struggle, not as it is experienced by a powerless minority today.

Outrage is legitimated by the impact one considers the book will have on those who read it: 'in all literature, what actually happened is less important that what the author can manage to persuade the audience to believe'

(*Midnight's Children* p. 325). The repeated question, 'but have they read it?', turns out to be a smokescreen, for the real importance is the effect on those who do read the book and how it may contribute to their opinion of those people represented in the book. How many people who condemn *Mein Kampf* or *Das Kapital* as scurrilous and outrageous have actually read either? What is considered pernicious about *Mein Kampf* is the way it played upon the sensibilities and distorted the outlook of those who did read it, and the dire consequences it provoked. It contributed to and confirmed a climate of opinion where no dissenting opinions or information could circulate in society. The notion that one is unaffected by the consequences of words, or that words have no bearing on creating a climate of opinion that has real, palpable effects on the daily lives of other citizens is too naive, and too strongly against the entire evidence of Western history to be taken as anything other than self-serving nonsense.

Outrage is a potential cause of public disorder. However, the public order test neglects to question the self-censorship of the abused, vilified and ridiculed. Such a climate of self-censorship may be built up among a minority so that they would not dare challenge public order, knowing this would further impair their standing in society. Yet the only option they possess to signal the seriousness of transgression is to pose a threat to public order themselves. They are given a choice which is no choice. Not to transgress public order in such circumstances is a powerful indication of the degree of domination and subservience, not a test of toleration and freedom for all.

Legal restraints that are equitable and accepted by all are the necessary norm of communal living where freedoms must be balanced so that they can be a spur to publishers, not an imposition. The spur is the impetus the law gives to weighing the value to the public good of what they intend to publish, even if they risk prosecution; to examining the accuracy and fairness of what is published; and to being responsible within the context of society. Where no test after publication is available nor operable, then the distinction between freedom and licence has ceased to exist. The freedom from prior restraint—the prohibition of banning a book before publication—then becomes the practical means of denying freedom from imposition and transgression of the limits of forbearance to a minority. What is imposed upon them is the demand that they endure what ought not to be tolerated, a demand they can clearly see would not be made if they were members of another segment of society.

Self-censorship—prior restraint through selection according to objective and subjective criteria, curtailments of freedom of expression for a whole range of reasons advanced and accepted as being in the public interest—does exist and is in daily operation. For instance, the Jim Allen play *Perdition* was scheduled for performance at the Royal Court Theatre in London, a most prestigious home of modern drama. Thanks to a concerted and powerfully orchestrated protest, the play was abandoned prior to its first public performance; no full production of the play has since occurred. The administrator of the Royal Court stated the play had been withdrawn because inaccuracies in the text would give offence to certain segments of society. One man's interpretation was taken to be outrageously distorted by another group of people. The interpretive inaccuracy was taken as a valid reason for the exercise of prior restraint and, therefore, effective censorship.

Exactly the same principles apply to Muslim agitation prior to publication of *The Satanic Verses*. The difference in outcome has nothing to do with the arguments in either case. The difference is how the two lobbies are perceived within Britain. The Muslim lobby is not seen as representative of a loyal, hard-working, peaceful section of British society, but viewed against a global realpolitik, by judgements made on the actions of Muslims elsewhere and according to the implicit notions of the distorted imagination. It is these criteria that construct the ambit of fair comment, even when highly inaccurate and prejudicial, and mean that inflicting genuine pain and palpable vilification are tolerable within British society and must by implication be endured by Muslims. That these criteria did not apply in the case of *Perdition* is potent evidence of the existence of a double standard.

What makes the case of *Perdition* so different cannot be attributed to a conspiracy theory. Knowledge is the difference, knowledge the factor that creates the double standard. Whether the judgement made in the case of *Perdition* was right or wrong is a matter that can be responsibly debated by a public that has a range of information and opinions available. The same is true when religious debates occur within the context of Christianity. The general public has a fund of information to assess what is fair comment on the Reverend Ian Paisley and Mother Teresa of Calcutta, the present Pope and Jimmy Swaggart or Oral Roberts. Such information admits of a host of gradations between fair comment—criticism that leaves sanctity in tact—between vilification of the human failing that leaves the spiritual substance alone and that which is a transgression upon the sensitivity of others who do believe. Such information does not exist for making responsible, informed judgements on Islam, nor indeed to distinguish between the outrageous or unwarranted assertions of Muslims and the letter and spirit of Islam. Without such knowledge there can be no true forbearance on either side of the current furore. Glib stereotypes can pass for reasoned comment. Hence, the Royal Court Theatre, that previously showed such sensitivity, commissioned an instant reaction play on the Rushdie affair. *Iranian Nights* by Tariq Ali and Howard Brenton offered a cardboard cut-out continuation of Rushdie's genre to pile on the agony for a Muslim community which has hardly a chance to state its own case.

Muslims have been cast as those unable to tolerate freedom and keen to institute a thought police. Hardly anyone has thought it necessary to question what freedom of expression is intended to achieve. On all sides people have concentrated on negative positions and negative defences, but there is positive import in the concept of freedom. Democracy demands a knowledgeable citizenry; to be effective a democratic electorate must have sufficient breadth and range of information to enable it to make responsible judgements. No one from the Muslim community would dispute the point; they include themselves within this constructive purpose of freedom. The problem for Muslims is that the distorted information built upon ignorance is taken for knowledge, that inaccurate, partial information is acknowledged as fair comment. The greatest problem is that the conventions of the press, broadcasting and publishing industries operate to make the distorted imagination the sole representative opinion that has general currency.

This benign system of censorship is the hardest thing in the world to oppose, because it is operated by people who see themselves as reasonable, responsible, informed, tolerant, liberal and well intentioned. Censorship as overt restriction by authority of the right to publish is an emotive term and a dangerous precedent, the first step towards ushering in a tyranny. Overt censorship is visible and rightly opposed. The consensus of benign censorship can be as effective as any system of overt censorship, and its benign nature makes it far more insidious; it is almost impossible to tackle. The routine manipulation of the media by powerful vested interests and the consistent benign criteria of selection mean there are effective and efficient thought police at every turn in Western society; and they are all convinced they are acting impeccably. Who then has a fair opportunity to make responsible judgements?

The constructive, contribution of freedom of expression, speech and thought is to make a diversity of opinion, ideas and arguments available to the public. When the range of diversity is narrowly cast, the objective of freedom is negated by its staunchest defenders. Examine the lists of British publishers, where the overwhelming preponderance of titles dealing with Muslims, Islam and the Muslim world are works firmly within the Orientalist tradition. One can grade and sort these into trends of thought; one cannot make a comparable list of either quality or quantity of works that present Muslims, Islam or the Muslim world from the perspective and according to the cherished ideas of Muslims themselves. We have quantity of opinion but no range of opinion.

In this perverse climate it is Rushdie, the embodiment of brown sahibdom, who is hailed as the authentic voice of the subcontinent in Britain and who has access to the media. It is Rushdie, who denies being a Muslim Briton, who has the power to author the climate of opinion by which other Muslims are judged. What Rushdie represents is a specific brand of relativism. This is not the cultural relativism of plurality but the eclectic relativism of common meaninglessness. Rushdie manipulates multiple cultural genres because each genre is atomized and all are subservient to his ideology of secularism and are, therefore, dubious. The juxtaposition of ideas is made not because they adhere to his person, but because they can each be entertainingly indulged to suit his ideology.

The eclectic relativist is the international person living in the random self-made private world. Rushdie's relativism is a function of the homelessness of secular modernity. This does not invalidate the earnestness of his pondering of spiritual questions—the God-shaped hole caused by the loss of faith. It merely means one should be aware that he ponders the question from the ideological stance of regarding all potential answers as basically interchangeable, dubious human delusions, created to give mankind a reason and, therefore, untenable. It does not invalidate the seriousness of his pondering of the experience of migration. It merely means one should be aware that his ideological stance precludes the option of meaningful cultural continuity, since he has denied the only source that makes it sustainable.

Rushdie's eclectic relativism is a seductive mixture. There is a feeling of One Worldism in all his books with their seamless mingling of so many cultures. His writing is bound to have particular attraction for the growing breed of internationalists who relish indulging in Chinese acupuncture, Sufi mysticism, Ayurvedic massage and Afro-Caribbean spiritualist music to soothe the tribulations of high-pressure, modern, city living. Such internationalism appeals as a knowledgeable synthesis for a common human future, but it is not the same thing as the option for cultural survival. This brand of relativism denies the coherence of belief and thought that makes Chinese acupuncture relevant because it is part of a system of viewing the world as a whole, and viewing it differently from any other system. To take such cultural products out of their context is to falsify them and is no guarantee of gaining superior insight into the worldview from which they came. Not all relativism is plurality; eclectic relativism is subtle translation of all traditions into one tradition, by one convention. Plurality does not mean no one can sample the cultural products of another civilization; it means that at the same time they must allow others the right to maintain the interconnections of their own worldviews, to keep the bits that are not conducive to Western eclectics as well as the bits that can be enjoyed or condoned.

Muslims see misrepresentation, disinformation, prejudice, ignorance—the distorted imagination—wherever they look. It is one topic on which they can all agree—and this alone ought to give the media establishment pause for thought. The unanimity of Muslims—who agree on little else—on the subject of the media in general and *The Satanic Verses* in particular is a dangerous precedent that perilously erodes the possibilities of dialogue and mutual understanding, that builds up the potential for avoidable conflicts in the future. The West took no notice of peaceful, legitimate protest through usual channels that preceded the publication of *The Satanic Verses*. It gave shrill and blanket coverage of a distorted kind to Ayatollah Khomeini's *fatwa*. Even the *fatwa* has left the West shaken, but largely unstirred, to any willingness to engage in substantive debate with Muslims. And alternatives open to Muslims through Western conventional channels are obstructed by the pervasiveness of the distorted imagination that is confirmed by *The Satanic Verses* and manipulated as masterly panic politics by the *fatwa*.

For Muslims to persist in demands for the withdrawal of the book is an inadequate response to the needs of the time. There are numerous prerequisites to establishing commonly acknowledged grounds for adjudicating what is a reasonable outrage to an intolerable transgression. Muslims, who feel comforted by the collective outrage they have all demonstrated and vindicated by reiterating their peaceable and legal demands for redress, are marshalling the community to march headlong into renewed frustration. They, too, have an active part to play in building a plural society which requires them to become articulate on the lack of plurality and the dearth of mutual comprehension that is the status quo. Muslims must learn to articulate their vision of a dynamic Islamic civilization of the future, how they envisage their own tradition transforming itself by its own values and mores; they must make audible their own critique of extant tradition. The task for Muslims is to cease to be *re*active and become *pro*active in mobilizing their own values to contribute to remaking Western society for the betterment of all its people, as part of their inclusion in a plural society in a plural world. The task for Muslims is not to complain of the media but to seek to claim their place as of right to represent themselves in the media, to produce the range and balance of diverse opinion that is the essential currency of an informed society.

All Muslims everywhere are affected by the distorted imagination the West holds to be the truth of Islam. We are not talking of hyper-delicate sensibilities that cannot stand the rough and tumble of comment and criticism. Muslims are well aware of the practical consequences of being held in suspicion, shunned and avoided, of being considered potentially dangerous the more overtly they demonstrate themselves to be Muslims. Such is this climate of suspicion that even before the onset of the Rushdie affair, British Muslim attempts to take up the legal provision for centrally funded denominational schools for their children met with virulent opposition. Muslim women consistently find campaigns being waged to liberate them from the veil, which for most of them constitutes the wearing of a headscarf and modest attire. One wonders what would be the reaction if British women were consistently browbeaten to change their clothing? The howls at such illiberality would be ear-splitting. It seems to occur to no one that Muslim women freely choose to wear scarves and specific types of dress, which are not an imposition upon themselves or others, and would experience actual physical and psychological discomfort if pressed to wear other forms of dress. A sari is exotic and elegant, but hijab is an abomination on womankind. Western society maintains and defends its right to determine which forms of cultural expression are permissible and tolerable, and its right to practical, effective intolerance. Any exercise of the supposed freedom of religion expressed in overt behaviour demands apology or defensiveness, which inhibits the constructive exercise of religion as a coherent moral and ethical outlook upon the world.

These inhibitions imposed upon Muslims arise from ignorance, but it is ignorance militantly and assertively supported by the dominant secularist worldview. The Muslim communities in the West cannot on their own create limits of forbearance nor a dialogue upon their necessity. As a powerless and marginalized minority, they can only keep improving their skill in a constructive critique of the status quo that demonstrates how far short of its own declared aspirations of liberality and freedom Western society falls. Change has to be demonstrated as a necessity that can be embraced by the majority, because it is part of their own aspirations for a better future. Intolerance ends most conclusively with the recognition of the moral harm it is doing to the intolerant, how it is demeaning their own human dignity. Intolerance ends when the intolerant become willing to acquire the knowledge that makes the marginalized audible and visible as people sharing compatible goals. Muslims can only have peaceful cultural survival and dynamic civilizational transformation if the dominant Western hegemony also changes. Such change cannot be about dethroning of the West to set another perverse power in its place—that would be change but not progress. It is only the plurality founded on the limits of forbearance, the defining of the equal right of all people to maintain difference and pursue their vision of a better future that can offer a way out of the present intolerable and intolerant impasse.

The Satanic Verses came to be published because no one thought it important to consider Muslim opinion, despite the publishers being well informed of how strongly Muslims would react to its contents. It is the overwhelming consensus that Islam is fair game for vilification, ridicule and contempt. When such a consensus exists, there can be no requirement for justification of fair comment, because there is no balance, or equality of access to the means of freedom of expression to substantiate the unfairness contained in the book. The consensus that prevails is not freedom of expression but licence that perennially accuses the victims of its acrimony of the sin of standing against freedom. This is the looking-glass world of the distorted imagination. This upside-down world is known to the majority of Muslims; it was available to Rushdie, and eminently fits the artistic convention in which he writes. Once more he chose not to tell this story but to transgress even further with another instalment of the familiar tale.

Art is a Jealous Mistress

To the staunchest defenders of Rushdie, discussion of legal constraints in connection with *The Satanic Verses* would be an irrelevance. *The Satanic Verses*, they maintain, is fiction; furthermore, it is art. Here, different standards apply: absolute freedom is the right of the artist. This is a particular Western notion. It is quite contrary to the Islamic concept that nothing is beyond the moral and ethical scope of responsibility for one's actions and their consequences; moral and ethical judgements are part of the creation of art, as well as judgements on the art that is produced. Artistic licence is a concept of the worldview of doubt triumphant, the secularism of absolute relativism where all things are questionable because all things are merely human invention and illusory, human self-justification. Art, as demonstrated by Tom Stoppard's elegant quip in his play *Rosencrantz and Guildenstern Are Dead*, can turn legal formulations on freedom of expression on their head:

Ros: Fire!
Guil: Where?
Ros: It's all right—I'm demonstrating the misuse of free speech. To prove that it exists. Not a move. They should all burn to death in their shoes. (Act Two, p. 43)

Artistic licence has gained currency through a history where art has played a major role in liberating human thought and imagination from the old impositions of authority as error and evil. Artistic licence is seen as a liberator, because the understanding of the old authority has been reduced to its illiberal and pernicious effects as their only possibility.

There is little point in engaging in argument about the notion of artistic licence. In truth, art is not a self-evident category; the proof of any work of art is a judgement made by time. It is not the instantly popular artistic works that invariably become great art. What is taken to be great art today was often passed over or ill-favoured when first published. This makes the defence of any work of art on the grounds of artistic licence and intrinsic merit in the present a peculiar notion, though one invariably used to extend the concept of the freedom of expression. Legal arguments for artistic merit amount to saying anything and everything must be allowed to qualify as art, since no one knows what judgement the future will make of what is art. The concept of art, therefore, requires the suspension of present judgements and choices to keep the future open. It is a neat way of avoiding painful questions and responsible judgements about society today by invoking freedom for the unborn. One is just as responsible to the future by making choices and setting limits necessary for the enhancement of society today, as in refusing to make choices or set any limits in order to leave the future open.

The terms of this convention cannot be settled by appeals to art in the abstract; the future, anyway, is determined in great measure by the choices and refusals to choose that are made in the present. The terms of any convention must be referred back to the society in which they operate and the practical consequences they perpetuate, breed and harbour in the here and now. Artistic licence is a part of the quality of freedom that is lived and enjoyed by people today. Whatever claims are made for artistic licence in the long rhythms of history should not obscure subjecting it to the tests of balance, fairness and equity, and determining the contribution it makes to creating a knowledgeable society today. What kind of sane future can artistic licence compound when it insistently projects the breeding ground of conflict, denial and contempt because it is the mouthpiece of an elite, a charmed circle, who seek to falsify, silence and marginalize others?

It is arrant nonsense to argue there can be no grounds for sober evaluation of responsibility to accuracy, let alone honesty, because Rushdie has written a work of fiction. Art and fiction are powerful tools for creating a climate of opinion. A work of art may never have written a law nor caused an exact, demonstrable alteration in a particular society, but the movement of history, the trends that are about to happen as well as those that have entrenched themselves, can be demonstrated in art. It is a medium where Western society is talking to itself about itself. Art cannot be both potent and irrelevant. If it is potent, it has a duty to responsibility for its effect upon real people in society. If it is irrelevant, it has no right to stimulate the grounds of intolerance. Either way, freedom without accountability is a dangerous, illiberal and tyrannical power no person or group should be permitted to wield in a mature, sane society.

The questions of artistic licence or of art are not solvable today in terms of the Western conventions of art. What can and must be debated and resolved are the limits of forbearance. These turn out not to be matters of censorship, control and the right to prior restraint on the part of any section of a community or body of opinion. The limits of forbearance reside in the questions that have perennially been concerned with the creation of genuine freedom, proper tolerance and justice for all people. The limits of forbearance concern balance, the weight that is given to the rights of others with whom one does not agree but who nevertheless have a right to their own opinions. Most of all, forbearance is equitable opportunity for access for all to the organs of the media to represent themselves in their own terms, to express the ideals they cherish, as well as to be interpreted, criticized and condemned by others who do not share their views. The limits of forbearance also require the freedom for the dominant viewpoint to be criticized, condemned and interpreted with equal freedom by those who are now marginalized; otherwise there is no forbearance, only subservience. No dominant system can claim to uphold liberty and justice if it cannot secure these rights to a minority within its midst. Muslim protest is seeking to take the limits of forbearance so far and no further.

Western society has always shown itself to be wary of other cultures. Britain in particular is afraid that its own distinctive life ways will be swamped in the clamour for it to become a multicultural society of genuine plurality. This is just one symptom of the difficulties in recognizing the true nature of the limits of forbearance. No community can be constructive, at home and make a flourishing contribution to the general well being, when the very bedrock of its identity is constantly open to question, abuse and ridicule that leads its members to be diminished in respect, shunned and avoided. To assert that there are things which transgress the limits of forbearance, that are intolerable, is not to insist that everyone must think and believe as the Muslim does. It is to question whether other people have taken the trouble to become informed, armed with the relevant knowledge to be able to assess responsibly what Muslims think and feel. How they act upon this information will then be an indication of how much they care to extend to Muslims the limits of forbearance they insist upon for their own cherished values.

Nine
The End of Civilization?

We forever come out the same door we went in—a fitting maxim for the Rushdie affair to date. Passions have been stirred, old familiar positions rehearsed and re-entrenched, but knowledge has hardly been increased on either side of the barricades. Two mutually uncomprehending viewpoints dominate the clamour; getting no nearer to communication, they stolidly reinforce each others' stereotypes, mutually satisfying each others' self-righteous certainty in the correctness of their opinions. Arranged around the unheard fringes stand the salient issues raised by this affair, an agenda waiting for dialogue. Dialogue, in this case is no woolly idealism. It is a social and political necessity within and between communities and nations. For, while the clamour of mutual incomprehension rages, mutual intolerance acquires new recruits and mutual frustration lays the seeds of discord. What retreats further and further into the shadows is the task of making genuine plural societies in a genuinely plural world.

The Rushdie affair has consistently offered the uninviting prospect of choosing sides on the old conventional lines between Us and Them, forced to state whether one is For Us or Against Us, on both sides of intemperate battlelines. Us and Them have been severally defined and depicted in the course of outrage; yet all the pictures are familiar, another chapter to a standard work. Our course has been to suggest we investigate the nature of these battlelines before leaping to defend them. A proper understanding of the context in which offence is given, on both sides, identifies most of the rhetoric that has been generated as no more than knee-jerk conditioned responses, certainly not reasoned debate of a substantive issue. The substantive issue, which we have called defining the limits of forbearance, is one that will not go away. Viewed from a different angle, as part of an on-going story, we have tried to open up the ground for dialogue.

The battlelines that have been thrust upon us by the Rushdie affair have a long history, a history that admits of more than one or just two perennially opposed constructions. Those who have been first and loudest at the barricades do not have a monopoly on setting the context nor telling the history with which we scoff at each other today. But context is all in making the conditioned responses of both sides apparent, just as context is all in comprehending what Rushdie has written. The rise of militant dogmatic secularism, the triumphalism of the post-modern culture of panic and doubt, emerges from the history of Europe trailing its ancestry in readily reopened wounds. The knowledge of the secularist is self-knowledge, schooled by local history which is imposed upon all others, remaking all histories in its own image, according to its own issues and concerns. In this, secularism is true to its imperialist ancestor. The continuity amidst the change in Western civilization is what we have called the distorted imagination.

While the Rushdie affair has been perceived as a clash of worldviews, the true protagonists have not been identified. They are militant, dogmatic secularism which claims the realm of literature as its new religion, an absolute where unlimited freedom should be exercised by the high priests of modern culture, the artist. On the other side, there is the religious worldview wherein freedom of thought and expression arises from the existence of the sacred and the ideas of respect for sanctity, tolerance for others and responsibility in the exercise of freedom. No matter what other dimensions have been added by those seeking to dominate the course of this affair, it is this clash of worldviews that is the underlying issue, an issue that will not swiftly go away. Unless the Rushdie affair is seen in this context, then there can be no meaningful debate or appropriate responses. Without reasoned debate, panic measures will be advocated and taken on both sides, and such measures can offer no confidence that they address the real issue nor adequately deal with any facet of the problems we now face. Panic has now become a feature of the post-modern world, but to resort to panic measures rather than a measured dialogue means handing our entire future to the monolithic vision of militant dogmatic secularism.

The distorted imagination is more than a blind spot in Western perception of others. It is a distinctive construct engineered to fit traditional cultures into the conventions of the West as negative projections of the West's own fears. The distorted imagination emerged as a rationale for domination, and continues to dominate, offering only a choice of enduring subservience to non-Western peoples. The distorted imagination is not a conspiracy theory, though its effect can appear to be conspiratorial in being self-interested. Nor does possession of the distorted imagination make the West a demon bogy fit for use by the Muslim world, or any of the others, as a scapegoat for their own historic *problematique*, though it is most often used as such. The distorted imagination is the metier of crude realpolitik in a world of domination and power relationships; that is its most pernicious, pervasive and dangerous form. It is also entrenched as conventional wisdom in the attitudes and commonplace ideas of the ordinary citizen of the West, a latent suspicion and store of antipathy ever ready to resurface.

This benign version of the distorted imagination is a cultural barrier that has been turned into a barricade in the course of the Rushdie affair. The distorted imagination is a part of Western civilization, a feature of historical reality and contemporary circumstance; it is the convention that makes the Muslim world, the world of the Other, familiar to the West. To insist that the distorted imagination exists is merely to set a proper context for discussion and, hopefully, for dialogue. It is to argue that the context requires placing a powerful body of imagery in its proper home, which is within the perceptions of Western history. The distorted imagination chronicles how the West has envisioned the Other, in this case the Muslim and Islam, according to its own historical conditions, development and interests; and it is just that: a false, garbled perception of a reality that is still waiting out there to be discovered.

History is the particular record of particular people through time and space; it marches first and most easily to its own drummer. Other civilizations have their own histories which march to different drummers, a point that has totally escaped Western perception. The distorted imagination is an ethnocentric convention, which provides ethnocentrism as a universal starting point. What makes Western ethnocentrism so distorting is the confusion by which it has taken its own ethnocentric universalizing tendency for the one (and probably the only) tenable universal viewpoint. The battles that have stirred within Europe, that originated within the conventions and failings of its mediaeval history, are not taken as particular experiences, or a metaphor of general tendencies, but as *the* battles that must be endured by all peoples. World history is made one history.

Histories of non-Western civilizations then become a mere appendage to the grand history of European civilization. All other histories, all other cultures, are subsumed by the organizing principle of European society, secularism. European ethnocentrism presents a conflict-ridden view of history, honed and sharpened by the techniques employed to effect change in European consciousness. Its rallying cries are familiar: liberty, individual conscience, equality, democratic freedom, justice, fraternity, liberality, tolerance, freedom of speech. Each of these are noble qualities and enduring values. The distortion comes in understanding them only as they have been defined and delivered within the cauldron of a Western history of conflict. The problem resides in taking the way these values were denied within Western experience as the problem endured, and lingering still throughout the rest of the world—even when the rest of the world's problems of modernity have in large measure been created by Western imperialism, intervention and imposition.

The distorted imagination is taken to be an objective assessment of the reality of both the history and character of other cultures. An ethnocentric perception is elevated into the status of the truth of those cultures, but the distorted imagination has no meaning and only counterproductive utility for them. It is not the history they have lived and experienced, nor a reflection of how they experience and understand their own religions, cultures and civilizations. The distorted imagination is, nevertheless, a coherent logic in the world of power relationships. The global problem created by the distorted imagination is the way it silences mutual comprehension and communication. Whether or not the end is intentional, the effect is always the same—the predominance of the distorted imagination makes the others inaudible and invisible, unable truthfully to represent themselves. They are permanently confined to the role of contending with the distorted imagination to gain a voice. Yet the very process of argument, according to the rules and agenda of the distorted imagination, confirms its stereotypes and entrenches a false notion of itself within their community. It is this kafkaesque experience that has confronted so many Muslims during the course of the Rushdie affair. They have found their sense of hurt and pain compounded by the seeming impossibility of conveying their ideas as they understand them to a Western audience, which is deafening itself with the clamour of distorted imaginings.

In a world where domination is the rule, as well as the ruler, the distorted imagination has been appropriated within the traditional cultures through the colonization of the mind. The effect is the appearance of those who accept the logic of the distorted imagination and gratify the West, amplifying its prejudices and repudiating their own cultural patrimony. A product of a particular historical legacy, these are the brown sahibs.

The brown sahib was a conscious creation of the colonial era, as well as an opportunistic response to the realities of colonialism and neo-imperialism—that you cannot beat them unless you join them. In the years since independence, brown sahibs have continued the predominance of colonialism within the non-West and some of its most notable second generation have moved into the establishment of the West itself. The logic of the brown sahib requires destruction; its tools are constant rejection, abnegation and denigration of indigenous tradition, as a positive means of achieving the end they accept as good. The objective is the remaking of the non-West in the image of the West, according to the historical pattern of economic, political and social progress that occurred in the West and with the axioms, principles and forms of the West. It is the one-way logic of modernity that lurks even beneath the rhetoric of One-World relativism.

The trouble, so far as non-Western people are concerned, is that this involves catching a disease in order to be cured by a specific treatment. The brown sahib's fractured self is not a shared diagnosis, nor is the brown sahib's prescription acceptable to them. Many other responses to modernity exist and share a common premise: that survival in today's world depends on reaffirming cultural integrity, the wholeness of the cultural identity. This can be a road of uneasy compromise, rejection of the West or, increasingly, the reforging of traditional cultural premises. However it is expressed, it staunchly opposes any further incursions of the distorted imagination into their territory.

That is not to say that the rest of the world either today or in history has been an idyll where exemplary values were enjoyed in exemplary manner. That is the position of the nostalgics who validate tradition as it exists on the basis of a roseate vision of their own history. It is the easiest position to advocate, ministering as it does to battered pride and replacing insult with confidence-boosting assurance. But the trouble with nostalgia is that it breeds another kind of ease, that of complacency. If all questions are answered by tradition, then no real questions need be addressed. Tradition does not need to be questioned for urgent solutions to current dilemmas and disasters. Merely the application of received tradition will, in and of itself, bring the return of the Golden Age. There is a growing understanding in the Muslim world, and elsewhere in other non-Western civilizations, that nostalgia may make good slogans but produces and reifies a reductive vision of indigenous history. Both the dominance of the distorted imagination and the most visible opposing ranks of the nostalgics and their closest associates, the apologists, are an impediment to the recovery of genuine autonomous history, a realistic perspective upon what constitutes tradition and how that tradition can be employed today.

Behind the leadership of the nostalgics and apologists in the Muslim world stands a whole range of diverse positions, ideas and a genuine debate that is inaudible to the West, precisely because it takes its starting point as the validity of non-Western civilization and tradition. But the diversity and gradations of opinion that exist have little access to dialogue. The pervasive and corrosive effect of the distorted imagination lumps all positions together. The concerned Muslim is a fundamentalist, and fundamentalism is incomprehensible; it is also violent, barbaric, irrational and intolerant. It is not the kind of idea the distorted imagination invites to tea for a polite chat. Therefore, the effect of the distorted imagination is to return to the only response that comes naturally, the realpolitik of power and domination. Among Muslims, frustration fosters the support of those who understand and choose to play the Western game on their own terms, the rejectors of the West who have their own vested interest in the realpolitik of power and domination. As usual, the majority of Muslims find themselves marginalized, this time on both sides of the barricades.

We told a true story in the introduction about a Pakistani boy who knew Muslim history which was not Western history. The boy marched to a drummer that his history teacher was not even aware of. His attempt to reassert his history was an attempt to have his Muslim identity recognized. Within Muslim tradition the aspirations for liberty, freedom, equality and justice have been understood according to Islamic premises, incorporated differently in different life ways from the experience of Western society. Some of the values that define Western ideals have been absent as problems by being present as lived experiences, others have fared worse. All the noble ideals have had their domesticated construction derived from discrete Islamic sources of inspiration. Ideas about political and democratic freedom, equity and justice in politics and society, liberties of the person, conscience and the group, from family and community to the multi-ethnic, multilingual and what approximates to multinational body of the *ummah*, the worldwide Muslim community, have all been derived from the Qur'an and the Sunnah—the example of the Prophet Muhammad—where they are all respresented. They have been debated and a wide range of actions has resulted from this base, as well as a diversity of interpretation. There have always been lively arguments within the world of Islam. But none of these arguments have been about the abolition of the starting point, the foundation stone: Islam of the Qur'an and Sunnah. No tradition with a grain of sanity can be expected to contemplate suicide as a rational choice. The route to understanding and the struggle to fulfil noble ideals remains for Muslims within the conventions of their own domestic tradition. It is within these traditions that liberty, equality and tolerance have true meaning and purpose.

The Rushdie affair has demonstrated the basics upon which this whole array of positions agrees. Whatever shade or quarter people come from, wherever they wish to move, however they envision the future of Islam in the modern world, they all concur in opposing the distorted imagination and stand unanimously behind the defence of the integrity of Islam, its Prophet, the community of faith and practice instituted by Prophet Muhammad during his lifetime and that of the first four rightly-guided caliphs who were his immediate successors. This is a remarkable achievement, a measure of the surgical precision with which Rushdie's offensive outrages were aimed at the heart of Islam.

Re-understanding Islam

The Rushdie affair has some important lessons for Muslims and Muslim societies. It has brought to the fore something that thinking and concerned Muslims have known for decades: Islamic law, as it is derived from centuries-old *fiqh*, the juristic interpretive legislation, needs to be rethought. The tradition of thought upon which the Ayatollah Khomeini's *fatwa* relies, derives from *fiqh*, and not from the basic sources of Islam, the Qur'an and Sunnah. The development of the body of opinion on which the fatwa is based is a function of how jurists in history have reasoned according to their historical circumstances. Such human reasoning cannot be elevated to the same status as the eternally valid and superior sources of the Qur'an and Sunnah. But this reasoning has become a matter of power and territory: Muslim scholars see *fiqh* in terms of their own power in the community as well as a matter of survival. However, whatever Muslim jurists may say, the legal tradition upon which the *fatwa* relies is not a necessary, inflexible, unquestionable summation of Islam that must therefore be blindly followed and be incumbent upon all Muslims. The legal tradition of *fiqh* is something that has been made by Muslims in history and is the aspect of received tradition that needs most urgent reassessment and critical endeavour by Muslims today. Hence, the *fatwa* is and must be open to debate, as well as to clear and unequivocal disavowal.

Historical precedent is one thing, the fate of the law itself a much more urgent matter. With complacent pride, Muslims accept that the development of Islamic jurisprudence is one of the glories of their civilization—nothing could be more true. The jurisprudence that emerged in history was a dynamic process of critical reasoning, designed for use, developed in use, and not a codified body of imperishable, unchanging statutes. The greatest glory of the system of legislation, *fiqh*, built upon the unchanging principles of the Shariah, was that it must be attuned to the needs and context of the society and social milieu in which it operates. Many Muslims are aware that critical reasoning to develop the law is no longer a feature of Islamic legal training. Critical thought directed to the philosophy of Islamic jurisprudence and its development fell into abeyance some centuries ago. The nature and character of Muslim society has radically altered since that time. The whole corpus of Islamic law requires review and intellectual and social effort on the part of scholars and the entire Muslim community alike. There is one crowning principle of Islamic law Muslims everywhere would do well to ponder: that the preconditions of any religious obligation are themselves an obligation. This can be stated in another way: the Muslim community earns the right and the responsibility to implement the letter of the law when they have responsibly fulfilled the preconditions of the law. The limits, the *hudud* in Islamic terminology, are not bald self-subsisting impositions, they are the extreme of a system. Without the system one cannot lay claim to just imposition of the limit. To operate the limit as a substitute for the entire system is to distort and even negate the meaning of Islam as a total system of balanced and harmonious regulation of the whole of human existence.

What is certain is that the law must be exercised as a procedure of justice. Even if one could agree with the legal ruling issued from Tehran, it would have no validity except through a legal hearing, a procedure of the law courts. This raises the important question of the jurisdiction of Islamic courts, the legitimate scope of any Islamic legal ruling, *fatwa*, in the complexity of the modern world. This is another issue that has neither been debated nor considered by Muslims in the course of the Rushdie affair. It is part of the culpable negligence jointly shared by the entire Muslim community. We can find no warrant for a legal opinion, issued without benefit of a hearing, becoming the basis for a bounty hunt. Those who incite such a bounty hunt and anyone who acted upon this incitement would be beyond the pale of Islamic law, and worse, they would be bringing the law into disrepute. The status of Islamic law as the best we can achieve in the name of Islam is Muslim aspiration for the future; to denigrate its clear guidelines with their emphasis on justice, equity and fair dealing is to denigrate the law and present Islam as an obscurantist faith to the eyes of the world.

However much Muslims may wish to see the totality of Islam in operation in their societies, today they have been duped into accepting the outer limits of Islamic law before any comparable effort is made to fill in the preconditions of that system. Muslims will be held responsible, as individuals and as a community, in that final court of appeal, God's judgement in the hereafter, in so far as they are responsible for the fate of Islamic law in this world. It is the mass of Muslims who must now demand that Islamic scholars and leaders re-establish the totality of the Islamic system, with its emphasis on justice, equity, fair dealing and genuinely alive freedoms that are relevant to their daily problems in today's world. The reality of Islam exists not at the limits but in the establishment of the preconditions. Every Muslim believes in his or her heart that concentration of effort on the preconditions of the Islamic system would obviate the need to go to the limit. It is for the community itself, the mass of the Muslims to demonstrate this as a reality. However, it is not a case of the mass of the people waiting for enlightenment to be handed down by the learned. This kind of inertia has been indulged for too long. Islamic endeavour is the sacred trust of every Muslim, and concerned Muslims must now begin to act upon their own Islamically-informed initiative.

In the Rushdie affair we have not one fatwa, but two differing legal opinions that have been put forward, both grounded centrally within the tradition of Islamic legal thought, that of Imam Khomeini and that of Al-Azhar, the oldest surviving centre of Islamic learning. It is understandable, if disappointing, that only Imam Khomeini's legal ruling has attracted attention in the Western press. The truly depressing fact, however, is that while many Muslims have privately been glad of the minimal publicity given to Al-Azhar's view, it has not prompted Muslims publicly to debate the issue. The reason is not hard to find. The pressures imposed upon Muslim aspirations by the distorted imagination have bred a habit of apologetic solidarity. The consequence has been a tendency for Muslims invariably to support and defend other Muslims. The effect has been that Muslims themselves now seem to be giving credence to the view of Islam as a monolith, a uniform, inflexible system. The diversity and debate of Islamic ideas has no place in the mainstream; it has been a marginalized discourse but one that must now be brought forward. It is the Muslims themselves who bear responsibility for pressing the diversity of their opinions and ideas upon the media, and thereby making them available to the general, non-Muslim public to form their own informed and reasoned judgements.

Hyperbole and rhetorical flights of fancy have been a stock-in-trade of Muslims for many years. A fresh breath of reality needs to be breathed deep, however painful the coughing fit it is likely to produce. The Qur'anic ideal of Islam stands as the eternal challenge and potent admonition of all Muslim societies, historical and contemporary. To speak of this Qur'anic Islam as though it exists as a solid state of being in the here and now is self-delusory. All such talk achieves, for it is merely talk, is to force further and further apart the gap between aspiration and action in the urgent task of grappling with contemporary reality. This is no new argument for Muslims, but it takes new colour and context from the Rushdie affair. The Qur'anic ideal of Islam can never be reduced to what Muslims say and do in the name of Islam, any more than Christianity is merely the catalogue of the actions and sayings of Christians.

Islam is perceptible to Muslims as the eternal ideal, the totality of the eternal values to which they must aspire and the way of life they must actually produce in this far from ideal world. It is in the divergence of the ideal and reality that a divergence of opinion arises about how to change things in this world according to the ideals of Islam to produce a better world. To express a difference of opinion about how change can be effected, or the meaning of the ideal in terms of policy for change, is not to call the ideal into question but to make the ideal more central and more comprehensible to all people. It is in the open and lively exercise of critical Islamic thinking that we make Islam perceptible to ourselves and to others. It is this new language of self-expression Muslims must develop and articulate. We cannot expect to find too eager or comprehending a public in the West. But it is only by this means that we can address our own urgent agenda and continue the long war of attrition on the distorted imagination—until the old bogies simply fade away.

The End of Civilization?

The Rushdie affair has some pertinent lessons for Western society and the secularist tradition. At the very least, it has brought home the point that Muslims, however degenerate they may otherwise be, are very much alive to their traditions and sacred history. By their protests and campaigns, Muslims have clearly established the limits of ridicule and abuse they are willing to take: this far and no further, we are no longer fair game. At best, the Rushdie affair may trigger off a chain of reactions that would mean 'the end of civilization as we know it'.

'Civilization as we know it' has always meant Western civilization. Civilized behaviour and products of civilization have been measured by the yardsticks of the West. Europe, and now North America, has always contemplated itself as the focus of the world, the axis of civilization, the goal of history, the end product of human destiny. But other people can accept Europe as 'the civilization' or manifest destiny only at the expense of their historical and cultural lives. Colonial history and colonial Christianity did their utmost both to annihilate non-Western cultures and obliterate their histories. Now secularism in its post-modernist phase of desperate self-glorification has embarked on the same goal. But the Muslim protest on *The Satanic Verses* has forced the realization that the West cannot ignore the world outside, has stopped this panic doubt and panic disarray in its tracks and forced many thinking secularists to re-examine their own positions.

A common and recurring theme in contemporary Western thought and philosophy, from Nietzsche to Marx, Russell to Sartre, Ayre to Foucault, Bloom to Baudrillard, is the total and profound sense of despair at its inability to give not just a complete and satisfying account of the human being and of society, but even of being able to give an intelligible account of itself. As Leonard Binder noted, 'though it may be widely believed that there is much of value in the long philosophical heritage of the West which began in ancient Greece, we cannot offer an absolute justification for this cultural complex upon which our civilization is based; nor can we be sure that there is no better way of organizing human life.' But we can be sure that there are different ways of securing and living by those great human values which are the common heritage of all mankind: justice, freedom, equity, fair dealing and cultural authenticity. The Western way, the secularist way, is not the only way—those who think so still live in the nineteenth century.

The post-modernist environment is that of a multi-civilizational and multi-cultural world. It is not a world of 'civilization as we know it'; it is a world of civilizations—Western, Islamic, Indian, Chinese, to name the most obvious—as they will rediscover and renovate themselves and enrich and enlighten each other with synthesis and mutual respect and co-operation. In this post-modernist environment, the secularist and *homo occidentis* can adjust only by learning that not all history is the history of Western civilization and by rediscovering the modesty of their origins.

Freedom from ridicule and abuse is a prerequisite for the cultural survival of non-Western societies. However, cultural survival and critical consciousness are not the sole demand of Muslims, even though their pursuit is a common and general response of people who have been victims of history and one form or other of distorted imagination—communities, cultures, civilizations, which are now trying to rediscover their own visions of a desirable society, 'less burdened' in the words of Ashis Nandy, 'by the post-Enlightenment hope of "one world" but by the post-colonial idea of cultural relativism'. This search, this rediscovery of cultural identity, means that Muslims, or for that matter other non-Western cultures, are not going to Westernize or secularize their souls in order to find a place in a world which is not of their own making. It means that Islamic culture and other non-Western cultures have to be understood on their own terms, by their own inner dynamic, by how they see themselves, by what they think their sacred scriptures are saying—in other words, far above and beyond the distorted imagination at the level of genuine authenticity.

The basic hurdle towards the creation of a pluralistic world with genuine multicultural societies is the intrinsic seeds of domination in the vision of secularism. As long as the secularists continue to act out their Promethean vision, they force their life styles and choices on others, under pain of subjugation or cultural annihilation. Muslims have their fair share of fanatics and bigots; but fanaticism and intolerance are not a monopoly of Muslims. Secularism can be just as fundamentalist and fanatical as any worldview. The point is that the more secularism seeks to dominate, the more it places non-Western cultures against the wall, the more fanaticism and conflict it generates. As such it distorts a culture's own perceptions of itself which sees its survival only in living out a grotesque parody of itself. On the other hand, it produces distortions in that culture's perception of the West. The challenge for Muslims is not to shape a contemporary identity for themselves based on their reactions to the West; if this were so, Muslims would make the same mistakes as the West and develop a fictional image of Western society and its people. The challenge for Muslims is to rediscover a contemporary identity for themselves which is true to their own history, traditions and worldview. When Muslims look towards the Medina state of the Prophet Muhammad, they are not looking to go back to some mediaeval history; they are looking forward to capturing that sense of equality, freedom and justice of which the Medina state provided such a perfect worldly example. But that movement forward to a sacred history can only happen if Muslims can fight off the suffocating embrace of the distorted imagination and the abuse and ridicule that they continuously receive from the secularist quarter. The Rushdie affair has demonstrated that Islam is not ready to go the way of Christianity. The sooner secularism incorporates this realization into its vision, the sooner conflict will give way to mutual learning.

That learning process begins with the realization that secularism does not have an absolute right either to dominate or ridicule and abuse the sacred territory of non-Western cultures. Neither are the secular purveyors of art and literature superior to other human beings, or have absolute rights or privileges over and above the rest of humanity. In the final analysis, the absolute right of novelists to write or say what they wish, regardless of distortions or consequences, in the name of criticism and progress is an issue of power and territory. It is an attempt to accumulate further powers onto themselves and conquer new territories for secularism. It is a desire that will be resisted by any non-Western culture that wishes to survive with its sanity intact. Conflict, therefore, is writ large in this dominating vision of secularism. The way forward is to bring social responsibility into the equation and recognize that a writer is as great as the responsibility she or he shows to other cultures and human beings while illuminating some aspect of the human condition.

As far as the issue of freedom of thought in Islam is concerned, the vast and admirable creative outpouring of Muslim civilization from the seventh to fifteenth centuries testifies to the unfathomable riches of Islamic culture. The fact that philosophy could grow unabated, that mysticism could flourish and engage in a continuous argument with scholasticism, that revolutionary currents such as the Ismaelis and Kharijis existed at all, that they assaulted political and religious orthodoxy, that some thinkers were able to transcend the mentality (Islamic, Christian or otherwise) of their age, that some scholars such as al-Ghazzali first doubted and then believed and placed doubt at the prime focus of their belief ('No one believes, unless he doubts'), that poets such as Abu Nawas could openly proclaim their unbelief (and countless others thought as he did) and still be revered for their poetry—all this not only dramatically belies the usual notions about the monolithic character of Islam, it also demonstrates that thought and progress are possible without abuse and ridicule and thrived long before secularism made an appearance on the globe. As Islam teaches, and Muslims believe, argument, not abuse, is the basis for survival and progress. 'Argue and survive' could become a contemporary slogan for Muslims and secularists alike.

But before such a catch-phrase can become a rallying call, the distorted imagination must follow on the footsteps of colonialism. In *The Colonial Harem*, Malek Alloula commented on his collection of picture postcards of Algerian women, produced and sent by the French during the early part of the twentieth century. One postcard showed a woman totally covered in black, her eyes peering through and staring straight at the observer, her breasts hanging out of the two slits cut in her black chador of modesty; another, lying on a couch, was totally covered with the exception of her breasts; yet another stood by her child who was serving tea, fully clothed but her neckline had been opened to reveal her bosom; a number of couples were shown smoking water pipes, drinking tea, serving coffee, but naked at the essential areas. This is the distorted imagination in action; it is the same distorted imagination that produced *The Satanic Verses*—the colonial picture postcard of modernist fiction. 'What I read on these cards does not leave me indifferent,' Alloula recorded. 'It demonstrates to me, were that still necessary, the desolate poverty of a gaze that I myself, as an Algerian, must have been the object of at some moment in my personal history. Among us, we believe in the nefarious effects of the evil eye (the evil gaze). We conjure them with our hand spread out like a fan. I close my hand back upon a pen to write *my* exorcism: *this* text'. Like Alloula, what Muslims read in *The Satanic Verses* does not leave them indifferent: for them, it reveals the abject poverty of an historical legacy that insists on demeaning their collective history, themselves and all that they hold sacred—the ever present, the all devouring, the lurid gaze, the evil eye of the distorted imagination.

Bibliography

Abdalati, M. *The Family Structure in Islam*. Indianapolis: American Trust Publications, 1977.

Acquaviva, S.S. *The Decline of the Sacred in Industrial Society*. Oxford: Blackwell, 1979.

Ahmad, Jalal Ali (Hamid Algar, trs.). *Occidentosis: a Plague from the West*. Berkeley: Mizan Press, 1984.

Ahmad, Khurshid. 'What an Islamic Journey!', *Muslim World Book Review*. 2:3, 13–22 (1982).

——. 'What's Wrong with Western Perceptions of Islamic Resurgence?', *Muslim World Book Review*. 5:2, 3–6 (1985).

Ahsan, Manazir M. 'The Satanic Verses and the Orientalists', *Hamdard Islamicus*. 5:1, 27–36 (Spring 1982).

——. 'Orientalism and Islam', *Muslim World Book Review* 4:3, 3–5 (1984).

——. 'Orientalism: a Critique', *Muslim World Book Review*. 6:2, 3–9 (1986).

Akhtar, Shabbir. *Be Careful with Muhammad! the Salman Rushdie Affair*. London: Bellew, 1989.

Al-Attas, S.M. Naquib. *Islam, Secularism and the Philosophy of the Future*. London: Mansell, 1985.

——. *A Commentary on the Hujjat al-Siddiq of Nur al-Din al-Raniri*. Kuala Lumpur: Ministry of Culture, 1986.

Al-Farabi (Richard Walzer, tr.). *The Perfect State*. Oxford, Clarendon Press, 1985.

Al-Faruqi, I.R., and Lamya al-Faruqi. *Cultural Atlas of Islam*. London: Macmillan, 1987.

Algar, Hamid. 'The Problem of Orientalists', *The Muslim*. 7:2, 28–32 (November 1969).

Al-Ghazzali (Nabih Amin Faris, tr.). *The Book of Knowledge*. Lahore: Ashraf, 1962.

——. *The Incoherence of Philosophers*. Karachi: Pakistan Historical Society, 1964.

Al-Hariri (T. Chenery, tr.). *The Assemblies of al-Hariri*, 1867. Retold by Amina Shah. London: Octagon Press, 1980.

Al-Hibri, Azizah. *Women and Islam*. Oxford: Pergamon Press, 1982.

Alloula, Malik (Morna Godzich and Wlad Godzich, trs.; introduced by Barbara Harlow). *The Colonial Harem*. Manchester: Manchester University Press, 1986.

Al-Nadim (Bayard Dodge, ed. and tr.). *The Fahrist of al-Nadim*. New York: Colombia University Press, 1970 (2 vols).

Al-Rhazes (A.J. Arberry, tr.). *The Spiritual Physick of al-Rhazes*. London: John Murray, 1950.

Al-Sayyid, Afaf Lutfi. *Egypt and Cromer*. London: John Murray, 1968.

Al-Tabari (W.M. Watt and M.V. McDonald, trs.). *The History of al-Tabari*. Vol. VI, *Muhammad at Mecca*. New York: State University of New York Press, 1988.

Anees, M.A. (Editor), *The Kiss of Judas: Affairs of a Brown Sahib*, Kuala Lumpur: Quill, 1989.

Appingnanesi, Lisa, and Sara Maitland (eds.). *The Rushdie File*. London: Fourth Estate, 1989.

Aquinas, Thomas. *Summa Theologiae*. London: Blackfriars, 1964–76 (60 vols).

Arberry, A.J. *Revelation and Reason in Islam*. London: Allen and Unwin, 1957.

——. *Aspects of Islamic Civilisation*. London: Allen and Unwin, 1964.

——(tr.). *The Koran Interpreted*. London: Oxford University Press, 1964.

Arens, W. *The Man-Eating Myth*. Oxford: Oxford University Press, 1979.

Arnold, T.W. *The Preaching of Islam*. London: Constable, 1913.

Asad, Mohammad. *The Principles of State and Government in Islam*. Berkeley, University of California Press, 1962.

——(tr.). *The Message of the Qur'an*. Gibraltar: Dar Al-Andalus, 1964; 2nd edn, 1980.

Asad, Talal. *Anthropology and the Colonial Encounter*. London: Ithaca Press, 1973.

Ayoub, Mohmoud M. *The Qur'an and Its Interpreters*. Albany: State University of New York Press, 1984.

Azmi, M.M. *Studies in Hadith Methodology and Literature*. Indianapolis: American Trust Publications, 1977.

——. *Studies in Early Hadith Literature*. Indianapolis: American Trust Publications, 1978.

Azzam, Abdur-Rahman. *The Eternal Message of Muhammad*. New York: Devin Adair, 1964.

Azzam, Salem (ed.). *Islam and Contemporary Society*. London: Longman, 1982.

Bashier, Zakaria. *The Meccan Crucible*. London: Federation of Students' Islamic Societies (FOSIS), 1978.

Beard, C.A. 'Written History as An Act of Faith', *American Historical Review*. 39:2 (January 1934).

Beidelman, T.O. *W. Robertson Smith and the Sociological Study of Religion*. Chicago: University of Chicago Press, 1974.

Berger, Peter L. *The Sacred Canopy*. New York: Doubleday, 1969.

———. *Facing Up To Modernity*. Harmondsworth: Penguin, 1979.

———, Brigitte Berger and Hansfried Kellner. *The Homeless Mind*. Harmondsworth: Penguin, 1973.

Berndt, C.H., and R.M. Berndt. *The Barbarians*. Harmondsworth: Penguin, 1973.

Binder, Leonard. *Islamic Liberalism*. Chicago: University of Chicago Press, 1988.

Black, J.S., and G. Chrystal (eds.). *Lectures and Essays of William Robertson Smith*. London: A. & C. Black, 1912.

Blanch, Lesley. *The Wilder Shores of Love*. London: Abacus, 1954; reprinted 1987.

Bloor, David. *Knowledge and Social Imagery*. London: Routledge and Kegan Paul, 1976.

Blunt, W.C. *The Future of Islam*. London, 1882.

———. *Ideas About India*. London, 1885.

———. *Atrocities of Justice Under British Rule in Egypt*. London, 1906.

———. *Secret History of the English Occupation of Egypt*. London, 1907.

Boas, Franz. 'Changes in Bodily Form of Descendants of Immigrants', *American Anthropologist*. 14:3 (1912).

———. *The Mind of Primitive Man*. New York: Macmillan, 1938.

———. *Race, Language and Culture*. Glencoe: Free Press, 1939.

Brenan, Timothy. *Salmam Rushdie and the Third World*. London: Macmillan, 1989.

Brent, Peter. *Far Arabia*. London: Quartet, 1979.

Brodie, Fawn. *The Devil Drives*. Harmondsworth: Penguin, 1971.

Brown, S.C. (ed.). *Objectivity and Cultural Divergence*. Royal Institute of Philosophy Lecture Series: **17**. Cambridge: Cambridge University Press, 1984.

Burckhardt, J.L. *Travels in Arabia*. London, 1829.

Burton, Richard Francis. *Personal Narrative of a Pilgrimage to Al-Madinah and Meccah*. London, 1855–6 (2 vols).

——. *A Plain and Literal Translation of Arabian Nights' Entertainments*. London, 1884–6 (17 vols).
——, and F.F. Arbuthnot (trs.). *The Kama Sutra*. London, 1883.
Canetti, Elias. *The Voices of Marrakesh*. London, 1882.
Caputo, Phillip. *Horn of Africa*. London: Futura, 1982.
Carlyle, Thomas. *Heroes and Hero Worship*. London: Chapman and Hall, 1872.
Chadwick, Owen. *The Reformation*. Harmondsworth: Penguin, 1964.
——. *The Secularization of the European Mind in the Nineteenth Century*. Cambridge: Cambridge University Press, 1975.
Chaucer, Geoffrey (Donald R. Howard, ed.). *The Canterbury Tales: a Selection*. New York: Signet Classics, 1969.
Chateaubriand, Francois-Rene. *Itinerary from Paris to Jerusalem*. Paris, 1811.
Cook, Michael. *Muhammad*, in *Past Masters*. Oxford: Oxford University Press, 1983.
Cragg, Kenneth. *The Call of the Minaret*. Oxford: Oxford University Press, 1956; London: Collins, 1986.
Cromer, Lord E.B. *Modern Egypt*. London, 1908.
Crone, Patricia, and Michael Cook. *Hagarism: the Making of the Islamic World*. Cambridge: Cambridge University Press, 1977.
Cupitt, Don. *The Sea of Faith*. London: BBC Publications, 1984.
Daniel, Norman. *Islam and the West: the Making of An Image*. Edinburgh: Edinburgh University Press, 1966.
——. *Islam, Europe and Empire*. Edinburgh: Edinburgh University Press, 1967.
——. *The Cultural Barrier*. Edinburgh: Edinburgh University Press, 1975.
——. *The Arabs and Medieval Europe*. London: Longman, 1979.
——. *Heroes and Saracens, a Re-interpretation of the Chansons de Geste*. Edinburgh: Edinburgh University Press, 1984.
Dante, Alighieri (John D. Sinclair, tr.). *The Divine Comedy: Inferno*. Oxford: Oxford University Press, 1939.
Danziger, Nick. *Danziger's Travels*. London: Paladin, 1987.
Davies, Merryl Wyn. *Knowing One Another: Shaping an Islamic Anthropology*. London: Mansell, 1987.
Dawisha, Adeed (ed.). *Islam in Foreign Policy*. Cambridge: Cambridge University Press, 1983.
de Rosa, Peter. *Vicars of Christ*. London: Corgi, 1989.
Dessouki, A.E.H. (ed.). *Islamic Resurgence in the Arab World*. New York: Praeger, 1982.
d'Huart, A., and N. Tazi. *Harems*. Paris: Editions du Chene, 1980.

Diamond, Stanley. *In Search of the Primitive*. New Brunswick: Transaction Books, 1974.

Djait, Hichem. *Europe and Islam*. Berkeley: University of California Press, 1985.

Dold, Bernard E. *Carlyle, Goethe and Muhammad*. Antonini Sfameni: Edizioni Dott, 1984.

Doughty, Charles M. *Travels in Arabia Deserta*. New York: Dover, 1979; orig. edn 1888 (2 vols).

Douglas, J.D. (ed.). *Freedom and Tyranny: Social Problems in a Technological Society*. New York: Knopf, 1970.

Dozy, Reinhart. *Histoire des Musulmans d'Espagne*. Leiden, 1932.

Dumont, R. *Utopia or Else?* London: Deutsch, 1974.

Durand, Gilbert. 'On the Disfiguration of the Image of Man in the West', *Eronos*. 38:45–93 (Ipswich: Golgonooza Press, 1976).

Eberhard, W. *Conquerors and Rulers*. Leiden: Brill, 1970 (2nd edn).

Eberhardt, Isabelle (Nina de Voogd, tr.; Rana Kabbani, ed.). *The Passionate Nomad: the Diary of Isabelle Eberhardt*. London: Virago, 1987.

Eickleman, Dale F. *The Middle East, an Anthropological Approach*. Englewood Cliffs, New Jersey: Prentice Hall, 1981.

Enan, M.A. *Ibn Khaldun: His Life and Work*. Lahore: Ashraf, 1935.

Enayat, Hamid. *Modern Islamic Political Thought*. London: Macmillan, 1982.

Esposito, John L. *Voices of Resurgent Islam*. New York: Oxford University Press, 1983.

Fakhry, Majid. *A History of Islamic Philosophy*. London: Longman, 1983 (2nd edn).

Fanon, Frantz. *The Wretched of the Earth*. Harmondsworth: Penguin, 1963.

——. *White Skins, Black Mask*. London: McGibbon and Key, 1968.

Faruki, Kemal A. *Islamic Jurisprudence*. Karachi: Pakistan Publishing House, 1962.

——. *The Evolution of Islamic Constitutional Theory and Practice from 622 to 1926*. Karachi: National Publishing House, 1971.

Feyerabend, P.K. *Farewell to Reason*. London: Verso, 1987.

Flaubert, Gustave (A. Thibaudet and R. Dumesnil, eds.). *Oeuvres Completes*. Paris: Gallimard, 1952 (2 vols).

Foucault, Michel. *The Order of Things*. London: Tavistock Publications, 1970.

——. *The Archaeology of Knowledge*. London: Tavistock Publications, 1972.

Freeman, Derek. *Margaret Mead and Samoa*. Harmondsworth: Penguin, 1984.

Freire, P. *Cultural Action for Freedom*. Harmondsworth: Penguin, 1972.

Galland, Antoine (tr.) (Powys Mathers, tr. from French). *The Thousand and One Nights*. London: Routledge and Kegan Paul, 1986; from 1964 reprint.

Gardner, Brian. *The Quest for Timbuctoo*. London: Cassell, 1969.

Geertz, Clifford. *Islam Observed*. Chicago: University of Chicago Press, 1968.

——. *Interpretation of Cultures*. New York: Basic Books, 1973.

Gibb, H.A.R. *Modern Trends in Islam*. Chicago: Chicago University Press, 1947.

——. 'Islamic Biographical Literature', in Bernard Lewis and P.M. Holt. *Historians of the Middle Ages*. London, 1962.

——. *Arabic Literature: an Introduction*. Oxford: Oxford University Press, 1963 (2nd edn).

Gibbon, Edward. *Decline and Fall of the Roman Empire*. London: Bury, 1900-4.

Gilsenan, Michael. *Recognizing Islam*. London: Croom Helm, 1982.

Gimpel, Jean. *The Medieval Machine*. London: Futura, 1976.

Goody, Jack. *The Domestication of the Savage Mind*. Cambridge: Cambridge University Press, 1977.

Goonatilake, Susantha. *Crippled Minds: an Exploration into Colonial Culture*. New Delhi: Vikas, 1982.

Guillaume, Alfred. *Islam*. London, Penguin, 1954.

Haddad, Yvonne. *Contemporary Islam and the Challenge of History*. Albany: State University of New York Press, 1982.

Hakim, K.A. *The Prophet and His Message*. Lahore: Institute of Islamic Culture, 1972.

Halliday, Fred. *Iran, Dictatorship and Development*. London: Penguin, 1979.

Hamid, Abdul Wahid. *Islam the Natural Way*. London: Muslim Education & Literary Services (MELS), 1989.

Hamid, Ismail. *Arabic and Islamic Literary Tradition*. Kuala Lumpur: Utusan Publications, 1982.

Hamidullah, M. *La Vie du Prophete*. Paris: Islamic Culture Centre, 1959 (2 vols).

Hamilton, Alastair. *William Bedwell, the Arabist*. Leiden: Brill, 1985.

Harris, Marvin. *The Rise of Anthropological Theory*. London: Routledge and Kegan Paul, 1969.

Harrison, Robert (tr.). *The Song of Roland*. New York: Mentor, 1970.

Haykal, Hussain (Ismael Faruqi, tr.). *Life of Muhammad*. Indianapolis: North American Trust, 1976.

Hill, Christopher. *The World Turned Upside Down*. Harmondsworth: Penguin, 1972.

——. *The Century of Revolution*. London: Abacus, 1975.

——. *Writing and Revolution in 17th Century England*. Brighton: Harvester Press, 1985.

Hitti, Philip K. *Islam and the West*. Princeton: Van Nostrand, 1962.

Hobsbawm, E. *The Age of Revolution*. London: Abacus, 1977.

Hodgen, Margaret. *Early Anthropology of the Sixteenth and Seventeeth Centuries*. Philadelphia: University of Pennsylvania Press, 1964.

Hodgson, M.G. *The Venture of Islam*. Chicago: University of Chicago Press, 1974 (3 vols).

Hooykaas, R. *Religion and the Rise of Modern Science*. Edinburgh: Scottish Academic Press, 1972.

Hourani, Albert. *Arabic Thought in the Liberal Age*. London: Oxford University Press, 1970.

Hourani, G.F. *Averroes, On The Harmony of Religion and Philosophy*. London: Gibb Memorial Trust, 1976.

——. *Reason and Tradition in Islamic Ethics*. Cambridge: Cambridge University Press, 1985.

Hovannisian, R.G. (ed.). *Ethics in Islam*. Malibu, Undena Publications, 1985.

Huizinga, J. *The Waning of the Middle Ages*. Harmondsworth: Penguin, 1975.

Husaini, S.A.Q. *Arab Administration*. Lahore: Ashraf, 1970 (6th edn).

Hussain, Asaf, Robert Olsen and Jamil Qureshi (eds.). *Orientalism, Islam and Islamicists*. Battleboro: Amana Books, 1984.

Ibn Battuta (Sammuel Lee, tr.). *The Travels of Ibn Battuta*. London: Darf, 1984.

Ibn Ishaq (A. Guillaume, tr.). *The Life of Muhammad*. Karachi: Oxford University Press, 1978.

Ibn Khaldun (F. Rosenthal, tr.). *The Muqaddimah: an Introduction to History*. London: Routledge and Kegan Paul, 1967.

Ibn Rushd (S. Van Den Bergh, tr.). *The Incoherence of the Incoherence*. London: Pakistan Historical Society, 1954.

Ibn Taymiya (Muhtar Holland, tr.). *Public Duties in Islam*. Leicester: Islamic Foundation, 1982.

Ibn Tufail (Simon Oakley, tr., 1708). *The Improvement of Human Reason Exhibited in the Life of Hai Ebn Yokdhan*. Zurich: Georg Olms Verlag, 1983.

Iqbal, Allama Muhammad (A.J. Arberry, tr.). *Complaint and Answer*. Lahore: Ashraf, n.d.

——. *Reconstruction of Religious Thought in Islam*. Lahore: Ashraf, 1971.

—— (R.A. Nicolson, tr.). *Secrets of the Self*. Lahore: Ashraf, n.d.

Jameelah, Maryam. *Islam and Orientalism*. Lahore: Yusuf Khan, 1971.
Jarvie, I.C. *Rationality and Relativism, In Search of a Philosophy and History of Anthropology*. London: Routledge, 1984.
Johnson, Paul. *A History of Christianity*. Harmondsworth: Penguin, 1978.
Jullian, Philippe. *Les Orientalistes*. Paris: L'Office du Livre, 1977.
Kabbani, Rana. *Europe's Myths of Orient: Devise and Rule*. London: Macmillan, 1986.
——. *Letter to Christendom*. London: Virago, 1989.
Keddie, N.R. *An Islamic Response to Imperialism*. Berkeley: University of California Press, 1968.
Khosraw, Naser-e (W.M. Thackston, Jr., tr.). *Book of Travels*. New York: Bibliotheca Persica, 1986.
Kiernan, V.G. *The Lords of Human Kind*. Harmondsworth: Penguin, 1969.
Koch, Adrienne, and William Peden (eds.). *Life and Selected Writings of Thomas Jefferson*. New York: Modern Library, 1944.
Kuper, Adam. *The Invention of Primitive Society*. London: Routledge, 1988.
Kutb, S. *Social Justice in Islam*. New York: Octagon Books, 1970.
——. *In the Shade of the Qur'an*. London: Muslim Welfare House (MWH), 1979.
Lamartine, Alphonse de. *Histoire de la Turquie*. Paris, 1854.
Lane, Edward. *Manners and Customs of Modern Egypt*. London, 1836.
——. *The Thousand and One Nights*. London, 1838–41 (3 vols).
Laroui, Abdallah. *The Crisis of the Arab Intellectual*. Berkeley: University of California Press, 1976.
Lasch, Christopher. *The Culture of Narcissism*. New York: Warner Books, 1979.
Lassell, H.D., and A. Kaplan. *Power and Society: a Framework for Political Inquiry*. New Haven: Yale University Press, 1950.
Latham, J.D. 'Arabic and Islamic Studies in the UK', *New Books Quarterly*. 1:2–3, 37–8 (1981).
Lawrence, T. E. *Seven Pillars of Wisdom*. London: Jonathan Cape, 1940.
Leach, Edmund. *Social Anthropology*. London: Fontana, 1982.
Leaf, Murray J. *Man, Mind and Science*. New York: Columbia University Press, 1979.
Le Bon, Gustav. *La Civilization des Arabes*. Paris, 1884.
Levi-Strauss, Claude. *Triste Tropiques*. New York: Criterion Books, 1961.
——. *Structural Anthropology*. London: Penguin, 1968.
Lings, Martin. *Muhammad: His Life Based on the Earliest Sources*. London: Allen and Unwin, 1983.
Little, David, John Kelsey and Abdulaziz Sachedina. *Human Rights and the*

Conflicts of Culture. Columbia: University of South Carolina Press, 1988.

Maalouf, Amin. *The Crusades Through Arab Eyes*. London: Al Saqi, 1984.

Maaruf, Shaharuddin. *Malay Ideas on Development*. Singapore: Times Books, 1988.

Mackensen, Ruth S. 'Arabic Books and Libraries in the Umayyad Period', *American Journal of Semitic Languages and Literatures*. 51:83–113 (1934–5); 52:114–25 (1934–5); 52:22–33 (1935–6); 52:104–10 (1935–6); 52:245–53 (1935–6); 53:239–50 (1939–7); 54:41–61 (1937).

McLeod, Hugh. *Religion and the People of Europe 1789–1970*. Oxford: Oxford University Press, 1981.

Makdisi, George. *The Rise of Colleges: Institutions and Learning in Islam and the West*. Edinburgh: Edinburgh University Press, 1981.

Mandeville, Sir John (C.W.R.D. Moseley, tr.). *The Travels of Sir John Mandeville*. Harmondsworth: Penguin, 1983.

Manzoor, Parvez S. 'Eunuchs in the Harem of History', *Inquiry*. 2:1, 39–46 (January 1984).

——. 'Islam and Orientalism: the Duplicity of a Scholarly Tradition', *Muslim World Book Review*. 6:1, 3–12 (1985).

——. 'Cultural Autonomy in a Dominated World', *Inquiry*. 2:6, 32–7 (June 1985).

——. 'Studying Islam Academically', *Inquiry*. 3:4, 32–7 (April 1986).

——. 'Method Against Truth: Orientalism and Qur'anic Studies', *Muslim World Book Review*. 7:4, 33–48 (1987).

——. 'Islamic State: Between the Mystique of Khilafa and the Logic of Mulk', *Muslim World Book Review*. 9:1, 3–13 (1988).

Marlowe, Christopher. *Doctor Faustus*. New York: Signet, 1969.

Maundrell, Henry. *Journey from Aleppo to Jerusalem*. Oxford, at the Theatre, 1703.

Mawdudi, A.A. *Human Rights in Islam*. Leicester: Islamic Foundation, 1976.

Mazrui, Ali A. *The Satanic Verses, or a Satanic Novel? the Moral Dilemmas of the Rushdie Affair*. Greenpoint, New York: The Committee of Muslim Scholars and Leaders of North America, 1989.

Mehta, J.L. 'World Civilisation: the Probability of Dialogue', *Communication and Development Review*. 2:1, 8–13 (Spring 1978).

Michael, Donald N. *The Unprepared Society*. New York: Basic Books, 1968.

Miles, Rosalind. *The Women's History of the World*. London: Michael Joseph, 1988.

Mitchell, Basil. *Morality: Religious and Secular*. Oxford: Clarendon Press, 1980.

Montesquieu, Charles Louis de Secondat. *Persian Letters*. Harmondsworth: Penguin, 1973.

More, Thomas. *Utopia*. Harmondsworth: Penguin, 1965.

Muir, William. *Mahomet and Islam*. London, 1895.

Murad, Khurram. 'We the Civilized, they the Barbarians', *Muslim World Book Review*. **6**:3, 3–14 (1986).

Myers, Eugene A. *Arabic Thought and the Western World*. New York: Frederick Ungar, 1964.

Nadvi, Syed Habibul Haq. *Islam Aur Mustashriqin*. Delhi: Academia, 1984 (in Urdu).

Nafzawi, Shaikh (R.F. Burton, ed. & tr.). *The Perfumed Gardens*. London, 1886.

Naipaul, V.S. *Among the Believers: an Islamic Journey*. London: Penguin, 1981.

Nakosteen, Mehdi. *History of Islamic Origins of Western Education*. Boulder: University of Colorado, 1964.

Nandy, Ashis. *The Intimate Enemy: the Loss and Recovery of Self Under Colonialism*. Delhi: Oxford University Press, 1983.

——. 'Reconstructing Childhood: a Critique of the Ideology of Adulthood', *Alternatives*. **10**:3, 359–76 (Winter 1984–5).

——. *Traditions, Tyranny and Utopias: Essays in Politics of Awareness*. Delhi: Oxford University Press, 1987.

——. 'Cultural Frames for Social Transformation', *Alternatives*. **12**:1 (1987).

Netanyahu, Benjamin (ed.). *Terrorism: How the West Can Win*. London: Weidenfeld and Nicolson, 1986.

Newman, Jay. *Foundations of Religious Tolerance*. Toronto: University of Toronto Press, 1982.

Nicholson, R.A. *A Literary History of the Arabs*. Cambridge: Cambridge University Press, 1969; orig. edn, 1930.

Numani, Allama Shibli. *Sirat-un-Nabi*. Chicago: Kazi, 1981 (2 vols).

Oakley, Simon. *History of Saracens*. London, 1708–18.

Overing, Joanna. *Reason and Morality*, ASA Monograph 24. London: Tavistock, 1985.

Panikhar, K.M. *Asia and Western Domination*. London: Allen and Unwin, 1953.

Parry, J.H. *Trade and Dominion*. London: Cardinal, 1974.

Payne, John. *The Book of Thousand and One Nights*. London, 1882–4 (9 vols).

Pederson, Johannes (Geoffrey French, tr. from Danish). *The Arabic Book*. Princeton: Princeton University Press, 1984.

Penniman, T.K. *A Hundred Years of Anthropology*. London: Duckworth, 1965.

Pickthall, M.M. *The Meaning of the Glorious Qur'an*. New York: New American Library, 1953. With Arabic text, Karachi: Taj Company, 1953.

Pipes, Daniel. *In the Path of God: Islam and Political Power*. New York: Basic Books, 1984.

Piscatori, James P. (ed.). *Islam in the Political Process*. Cambridge: Cambridge University Press, 1983.

Pitts, Joseph. *A Faithful Account of the Religion and Manners of the Mahometans*. London, 1731.

Popper, K. *The Poverty of Historicism*. London: Routledge and Kegan Paul, 1957.

Qadri, Anwar Ahmad. *Islamic Jurisprudence in the Modern World*. Lahore: Ashraf, 1973 (2nd edn).

Rahman, F. *Islamic Methodology in History*. Karachi: Central Institute of Islamic Research, 1965.

——. *Major Themes of the Qur'an*. Minneapolis: Bibliotheca Islamica, 1980.

——. *Islam and Modernity*. Chicago: University of Chicago Press, 1982.

——. 'Law and Ethics in Islam'. In R.G. Hovannisian (ed.). *Ethics in Islam*. Malibu, Undena Publications, 1985.

Rahman, S.A. *Punishment of Apsotasy in Islam*. Lahore: Institute of Islamic Culture, 1972.

Ramadan, Said. *Islamic Law: its Scope and Equity*. London: Macmillan, 1970.

Redwood, John. *Reason, Ridicule and Religion*. London: Thames and Hudson, 1976.

Renan, Ernest. *Oeuvres Completes*. Paris: Calmann-Levy, 1947.

Riley, G. *Values, Objectivity and the Social Sciences*. Reading: Addison-Wesley, 1974.

Robertson Smith, W. *Kinship and Marriage in Early Arabia*. London, 1885.

——. *Lectures on the Religion of the Semites*. London, 1889.

Rodinson, Maxime. *Mohammad*. London: Penguin, 1971.

——. *Europe and the Mystique of Islam*. London: I.B. Tauris, 1988.

Rosenthal, F. *Technique and Approach of Muslim Scholarship*. Rome: Pontificum Institutum Biblicum, 1947.

——. *A History of Muslim Historiography*. Leiden: Brill, 1968 (2nd edn).

——. *Knowledge Triumphant*. Leiden: Brill, 1970.

Rushdie, Salman. *Midnight's Children*. London: Jonathan Cape, 1981.

——. *Shame*. London: Jonathan Cape, 1983.

——. *The Satanic Verses*. London: Viking, 1988.

Ruthven, Malise. *Islam in the World*. Harmondsworth: Penguin, 1984.

Sahlins, Marshall. *Culture and Practical Reason*. Chicago: University of Chicago Press, 1976.

Said, E. *Orientalism*. London: Routledge and Kegan Paul, 1978.
——. *Covering Islam*. London: Routledge and Kegan Paul, 1981.
Sardar, Ziauddin. 'Intellectual Space and Western Domination', *Muslim World Book Review*. 4:2, 3–8 (1984).
——(ed.). *The Touch of Midas: Science, Values, and the Environment in Islam and the West*. Manchester: Manchester University Press, 1984.
——. *Islamic Futures: the Shape of Ideas to Come*. London: Mansell, 1985.
——. *The Future of Muslim Civilization*. London: Mansell, 1987 (2nd edn).
——(ed.). *An Early Crescent: the Future of Knowledge and the Environment in Islam*. London: Mansell, 1989.
——. 'Surviving the Terminator: the postmodern mental condition', *Futures* 22:2, 203–10 (1990).
——. 'A Post-Modern War of Wor(l)ds: Putting Rushdie and His Defenders Through Their Paces', *Muslim World Book Review*. 10:3, 3–17 (1990).
Sazgin, Faut. *Geschichte des Arabischen Schrifttums*. Leiden: Brill, 1974–82 (8 vols pub.).
Shariati, Ali. *On the Sociology of Islam*. Berkeley: Mizan, 1976.
——. *Marxism and Other Western Fallacies*. Berkeley: Mizan, 1980.
Sharif, M.M. (ed.). *A History of Muslim Philosophy*. Munich: Otto Harrassowitz, 1963, 1966 (2 vols).
Siddiqui, Abdul Hamid. *The Life of Muhammad*. Lahore: Islamic Publications, 1969.
——(tr.). *Sahih Muslim*. Ashraf: Lahore, 1972 (3 vols).
Siddiqui, Kalim. *Conflict, Crisis and War in Pakistan*. London: Macmillan, 1972.
——. *Functions of International Conflict*. Karachi: Royal Book Company, 1975.
Siddiqui, M.M. *Islam and Theocracy*. Lahore: Institute of Islamic Culture, 1953.
Siddiqui, Mazheruddin. *The Quranic Concept of History*. Karachi: Central Institute of Islamic Research, 1965.
Sim, Katherine. *Jean Louis Burckhardt, a Biography*. London: Quartet, 1981.
Singer, M.R. *The Emerging Elite*. Cambridge, Massachusetts: MIT Press, 1964.
Smith, W.C. *Islam in Modern History*. Princeton: Princeton University Press, 1957.
Southern, R.W. *Western Views of Islam in the Middle Ages*. Cambridge, Massachusetts: Harvard, 1962.
——. *Western Society and the Church in the Middle Ages*. Harmondsworth: Penguin, 1970.
Spengler, Oswald (Charles Francis Atkinson, tr.). *The Decline of the West*.

New York: Knopf, 1939.

Sperber, Dan. *On Anthropological Knowledge*. Cambridge: Cambridge University Press, 1985.

Standord, Michael. *The Nature of Historical Knowledge*. Oxford: Basil Blackwell, 1986.

Stark, Freya. *East is West*. London: Century, 1986; original edition, 1945.

Stocking, George W. *Race, Culture and Evolution*. Chicago: University of Chicago Press, 1982.

——(ed.). *Observers Observed*, Vol. 1 of *History of Anthropology*. Madison: University of Wisconsin Press, 1983.

Stone, Caroline. 'Libraries in Arab History: a Passion for Books'. *Ur*, **3**:39–43 (1984).

Thackeray, W.M. *Notes of a Journey from Cornhill to Grand Cairo*. London, 1848.

Thesiger, Wilfred. *Arabian Sands*. London: Longman Green, 1960.

Tibawi, A.L. *English Speaking Orientalists*. Geneva: Islamic Centre, 1965.

——. *Arabic and Islamic Themes*. London: Luzac, 1976.

Torrens, Henry. *The Book of the Thousand and One Nights*. London, 1838.

Tosh, John. *The Pursuit of History*. London: Longman, 1984.

Toynbee, Arnold. *A Study of History*. Oxford and London: Oxford University Press and Thames and Hudson, 1972.

Vatikiotis, P.J. *Islam and the State*. London: Croom Helm, 1987.

Vickers, G. *Value Systems and Social Process*. London: Tavistock, 1968.

——. 'The Weakness of Western Culture'. *Futures*, **9**:6, 457–73 (December 1977).

Vittachi, V. T. *The Brown Sahib Revisited*. Delhi: Penguin, 1987.

Volney, Constantin Francois Chasse-Boeuf. *Oeuvres Completes*. Paris, 1860.

Von Leenwen, A.T. *Christianity and World History*. New York: Scribner, 1964.

Waardenburg, Jacques. *L'Islam dans le miroir de l'Occident*. The Hague: Mouton, 1963.

Watt, W.M. *Mohammad: Prophet and Statesman*. London: Oxford University Press, 1961.

Weldon, Fay. *Sacred Cows*. Chatto CounterBlasts No. 4. London: Chatto and Windus, 1989.

Wittfogel, Karl. *Oriental Despotism*. New York: Vintage Books, 1981.

Wolf, Eric R. *Europe and the People Without History*. Berkeley: University of California Press, 1982.

Zijderveld, Anton C. *The Abstract Society: a Cultural Analysis of Our Time*. London: Allen Lane, 1990.

Index

The index is arranged alphabetically word-by-word. Names with the prefix *al-* will be found under the succeeding initial letter. *Elizabeth Wiggans*

Abbasid caliphate 62
Abd Allah bin Sallam 109
Abdul Aziz al-Badri 64
Abdul Qadir Oudah 64
Abdullah b. Rawahah 106
Abdullah ibn Abu al Sarh 162
Abdullah ibn Amr ibn al-As 154
Al-Abshihi 112
Abstract Society, The (Zijderveld) 239
Abu Dawud 150
Abu l-Atahiya 107
Abu l-Tayyib Ahman b. Husayn al-Mutanabbi 107
Abu Nasr ibn al-Jahm 99
Abu Nawas 107
Abu Obaida 114
abuse
 freedom from 93, 277
 and fundamentalism 242
 of Islam 32, 276, 278
 and secularism 239, 244
 and toleration 234–5
adab literature 111
African Guardian, The 189
Age of Reason 24, *see also* Enlightenment
aggression 41
Ahmad bin Hanbal 150
Al-Ahmar 98
Ahsan, Manazir 149–50
Akhtar, Shabbir 184, 207, 223, 224, 225
Ali, Tariq 186, 259
Ali ibn Uthman al-Hujwiri 104

Alibahi, Yasmin 219
Allen, Jim 216, 218, 258–9
Alloula, Malek 279
Alvarus, Paul 35–6, 54
Amali 111
Among the Believers: an Islamic Journey (Naipaul) 82–6
Amr ibn Ubayad 102
Anas 154
apartheid 225
apostasy 93, 94, 95, 196
Aquinas, *see* Thomas Aquinas
Arabia: Islamic World Review 216
Arabian Nights (*Alf Laila wa Laila*) 50, 64
Arabic Book, The (Pederson) 98
Arabic learning and the Renaissance 37
Arabic Literature (Gibb) 106
Arabic professorships in Europe 40, 41, 42
Arberry, Arthur 63, 227, 228
Arens, William 241
Areopagitica (Milton) 23
argument 93, 279
art and artistic licence 11, 264, 265, 266
Asad, Mohammad 91–2, 102
al-Ashari, Abu Hasan 103, 104
Al-Asmai 114
al Aswad bin Sari 109
atheism 24, 28
Attenborough, Sir Richard 187–8
Augustine, Saint 15
authority 18–19

Avicenna (ibn Sina) 39, 83
Averoes (ibn Rushd) 39
al-Ayni 148
Al-Azhar 201, 275

Bacon, Roger 39, 40
Badawi, Zaki 201
Al-Baladhuri 112
Bandaraniaka, Solomon 80
Bandung File 186, 191, 192
baptism 15
Baring, Sir Evelyn (Lord Cromer) 56
al-Basri, Hasan 106
al-Basri, Rabiah 104, 106
Basti, Akhundzadeh 200
al-Bawardi 98
al-Bayhaqi 148
Becker, Carl 45
Beckford, William 51
Bedwell, William 42
belief 12
Berger, John 213, 232
Berger, Peter L. 251
Bhutto, Zulfiqar Ali 84, 85
Bible 17, 34, 35
Binder, Leonard 67-8, 277
Blanch, Lesley 52
blasphemy
  against Islam, declarations to combat 202-4
  attempted prosecution of Rushdie 185
  and civil disorder 24, 28
  in *The Satanic Verses* 150-2, 163, 164, 196, 213-4
Bloom, Alan 224
book-burning
  in European history 13-14, 17, 18, 23, 31
  of *The Satanic Verses* 11, 184, 218, 257
Booker prize 213-14
books in Muslim civilization 96-101
Books as the Tools of the Scholars (ibn Jammah) 100
Bradford 185, 207, 212
Brennan, Timothy 142
Brenton, Howard 259
Brethren of Purity 106, 113

British Muslim Action Front 185
brown sahibs 76-87, 140
  colonial elites 77, 78, 79
  post-independence rulers 79, 80
  as writers 80, 81, 82-7
Bruno, Giordano 19
al-Bukhari 94, 150, 169
Burckhardt, Jacob 59
Burgess, Anthony 210
Burton, Lady 52
Burton, Sir Richard 50, 51-2

Call of the Minaret, The (Cragg) 63
Calvin, John 19
Camus, Albert 57
Canadian Society of Muslims 201, 202, 203-4
Canetti, Elias 74
cannibalism 241-2
capital punishment 93, 94, 95
Caputo, Phillip 73-4
Carlyle, Thomas 53-4
Carty, Ciran 213
Cathars 16
censorship
  historical 15, 23, 25
  modern 204, 205, 216, 222, 258-9, 260
Chachanama 83
Chadwick, Owen 21-2, 30
chansons de geste 54, 157, 220
Chateaubriand, Francois de 54
Chatham House 71-2
Christianity, *see also* Church
  and Islam 34, 39, 40, 65, 69
  liberation theology 137
  and secularism 224
Church, *see also* Christianity
  authority 14, 15, 17, 18, 25-6
  heresies 16
  and secularism 9, 14
Citizen 208
civil rights 23
civilization 62, 86, 106, 276, 277
Civilization des Arabes, La (le Bon) 61
clergy in Islam 194, 201
Colonial Harem, The (Alloula) 279
Committee of Muslim Scholars and

Learned of North America 204
community 27, 247, *see also* ummah
Community Relations Council, Bradford 207
consensus 27
Cook, Michael 67, 68
Council of Vienna 40
Counsels in Contemporary Islam (Cragg) 63
Coup, The (Updike) 73
Cragg, Kenneth, 63, 64, 65, 66
Crescent International 198, 199
Cromwell, Oliver 23
Crone, Patricia 67
Crusades 36-7, 225
Cultural Frames (Nandy) 249, 250, 251, 252
culture 86, 249, 250, 266, 277
Cupitt, Don 31

Dagger of Islam, The (Laffin) 73
Daniel, Norman 157
Dante Alighieri 38
Danziger, Nick 85
Darwin, Charles 30
Darwish, Mahmoud 215
Dawisha, Adeed 71-2
Dawood, N.J. 91, 92, 128, 227
Dawud bin Khalaf al-Isfahani 104
Declaration on Joint Action to Combat Blasphemy against Islam 203-4
Decline of the West, The (Spengler) 61
defamation 93, 255, 257
Defoe, Daniel 239, 243
Descartes, Rene 19
development, in Hegelian thought 58
Devlin, Lord 255
Dickie, James, *see* Zaki, Yakub
Digby, Jane 52
discontinuity 9, 139, 244-6, 248, 252
distorted imagination 37, 232, 268-72, 277, 278, 279
 and British Muslims 259, 260
 and Defoe 240
 and freedom of expression 254, 264
 and fundamentalism 253
 and literature 117
 and secularism 244
Divine Comedy (Dante) 38
Djait, Hichem 46, 47, 48, 54
Doctrina Iacobi 67
Dold, Bernard 54
doubt 13, 27, 221, 251
 and Christianity 65
 and Islam 65, 88, 279
 and Rushdie 11, 12, 142, 191, 192, 245
 and secularism 10, 12, 13, 207
Doughty, Charles 53, 55
Dozy, Reinhardt 43
Dubucq, Aimee 52
Dulles, John Foster 225

East India Company 78
Eberhardt, Isabelle 52-3
education 19, 76-7, 78
Engels, Friedrich 60
English Revolution 23, 24, 25
Enlightenment 10, 15, 24, 28, 45-7
Erasmus, Desiderius 28
Essai sur les moeurs (Voltaire) 46
Eunuch (Manzoor) 59, 62
Eurocentrism 69, 76

faction (fact and fiction) 151, 152
al-Fahrist (al-Nadim) 50, 101
Fakhr ad-Din ar-Razi 108
fanaticism 72, 88
Fanon, Frantz 79
Fansuri, Hamzah 107
Faqir, Fadia A 215
Farid al Din Attar 107
al-Farra 98, 99
Faruqi, M.H. 192
fatwa of al-Azhar 201, 202, 204
fatwa of Khomeini 193-203
 al-Azhar on 201, 275
 based on *fiqh* 273, 274
 CSM Declaration 201-3
 Kabbani on 236
 Siddiqui on 199-201
 text 193-4
 Zaki on 195-7
fiction 220, 222, 265, *see also* faction
fiqh 273

Firdawsi 107
Foot, Michael 213, 223, 224–5
forbearance 246, 251, 253–5, 257, 259, 266, 267
forgiveness 202
freedom of conscience 23, 30, 268
freedom of expression 25, 253, 260, 265–6
  and Islam 88, 92, 101, 105, 238, 279
  limits to 232–3, 234, 255
  and Rushdie 8, 222, 246, 254, 257, 264
  and secularism 9, 238, 254
  and social responsibility 93, 208, 257
freedom of the press 24–5, 257
French, Sean 233
French Revolution 16
Fuentes, Carlos 219, 220, 221, 222
fundamentalism 139, 188, 242–9, 253, 271

Galileo 19
Galland, Antoine 50
Gama, Vasco da 108
Gandhi, Mahatma 251, 252, 253
Gandhi, Rajiv 185, 186, 189
Gandhi (Attenborough) 187–8
al-Ghani, Abd 112
al-Ghazzali 105, 112, 279
Gibb, H.A.R. 63, 106
Gibbon, Edward 58
Gibreel (Gabriel) 144, 147, 148
Gide, Andre 53, 57–8
goddesses, 163, 165–7, 170, 173–6
Goldziher, Ignac 44, 45
Greenpeace 206
Guardian, The, contributions from,
  Ayatollah Khomeini 194
  Carlos Fuentes 219
  Hugo Young 214
  John Berger 232
  Michael Foot 223, 225
  Salman Rushdie 186
  Shabbir Akhtar 207
  W.L. Webb 215
  Zaki Badawi 201
Guibert of Nogen 37

hadith 144, 145
Hafiz 107
Hagarism: the Making of the Islamic World (Crone and Cook) 67
Hai Ebn Yokdhan (ibn Tufail) 239–40
Hajj (Uris) 73
hakimi medicine 124
Haley, Alex 179
Halliday, Fred 69
Hamilton, Alastair 42
Haq, S. Nomanul 187, 188
al-Hariri, Abu Muhammad al-Qasim 110
Harlow, Barbara 58
Hasan al Basri 102
Hassan b. Thabit 106
Hatib bin Abi Baltaa 96
hatred of Muslims 56–7, 66–75
Hay, John 208
Haykal, Muhammad Husayn 162
health 76–7
Hegel, G.W.F. 58, 59, 62
Heroes and Hero Worship (Carlyle) 54
al-Hibri, Azizah 170
Hill, Christopher 25
Hirst, Paul 26
History of the Arabs (Hitti) 85
History of Saracens (Oakley) 41, 58
Hitler, Adolf 206, 211, 225
Hitti, Philip 63, 64, 66, 85
hizbullahi movement 200
Hodgen, Margaret 40
Hodgson, Marshall G.S. 63, 190
Holocaust 211, 225
Horn of Africa (Caputo) 73–4
House of Wisdom 100
hudud 89, 274
Hunter, William 78
Hurgronje, Snouck 45
Hussein, Taha 216

Ibn al-Arabi 106
ibn Battuta 112
ibn Fadlan 112
Ibn Hajar 113
ibn Hamdis 107, 108
ibn Hanbal 154
ibn Haqub 112

ibn Haytham 229
ibn Hazm 104
ibn Hisham 148
ibn Ishaq 112, 148
ibn Jammah 100
ibn al-Jauzi 114
ibn Jubayr 112
ibn Kathir 148
ibn Khaldun 62, 112, 113, 174
ibn Khallikan 103, 107–8, 112
ibn Khuzayma 148
Ibn Majid of Najd 108
Ibn al-Muqaffa 111
ibn al-Mutazz 114
ibn al-Nadim 101
Ibn Qutaiba of Merv 113
Ibn al-Rumi 106
ibn Rushd 105
ibn Saad 147, 168, 196
ibn Thabit, Hassan 215
ibn Tufail 110, 239–40
ibn Yaqub 112
Ibrahimi, Ahmad Taleb 57
identity 116, 240
Ignatieff, Michael 232, 233
ijaza (licence) 99
Ikhwan al Muslimun (the Muslim Brotherhood) 63–4
immigrant society 179, 180, 181, 182, 183
Immoraliste, L' (Gide) 57–8
Impact International 185, 192, 193
In the Path of God: Islam and Political Power (Pipes) 70
Incoherence of the Incoherence, The (ibn Rushd) 105
Incoherence of the Philosophers, The (al-Ghazzali) 105
Independent, The 185, 195, 200, 209–11, 212, 214
Independent Magazine, The 210, 217
Index of prohibited books 25
India 60, 186, 188, 189
India: a Wounded Civilization (Naipaul) 86
Industrial Revolution 30
International Herald Tribune 186, 187
intolerance 257, 263

Iqbal, Mohammad 61, 107, 215
Iran 83, 197
Iran Dictatorship and Development (Halliday) 69
Iranian Nights (Ali and Brenton) 259
Irwing, Robert 213
Islam 88, 90, 216, 247, 252, *see also* worldviews
  intellectual achievements 39
  prophets 153
  resurgence of 66, 70
  in Rushdie's writing 156, 187, 189, 190, 192
  and secularism 32–3
  Western image of 34, 35, 36, 37
Islam dans le miroir de l'Occident, L' (Waardenburg) 45
Islam in Foreign Policy (Dawisha) 71–2
Islam in the Modern World (W.C. Smith) 63
Islam in the Political Process (Piscatori) 71–2
Islam and the State (Vatikiotis) 72
Islam and the West (Hitti) 63, 64
Islam in the World (Ruthven) 69–70
Islamabad 185
Islamic Cultural Centre 201
Islamic law 248, 273–4
Ismaelis 279
Itinerary from Paris to Jerusalem (Chateaubriand) 54

al-Jahiz 109, 111
Jalal al-Din al-Suyuti 98
Jang 207, 208
Jefferson, Thomas 24
Jenkins, Peter 209–10
Jenkins, Roy 210
Jesus 40, 44
Jilani, Abdul Qadir 107
Jinnah, Mohammad Ali 84
John of Damascus 34
John of Segovia 40
Johnson, Paul 15–16
Journey from Aleppo to Jerusalem (Maundrell) 50
al-Jubbai 103

al-Jurjani 114

Ka'aba 127, 128, 165
Kab al Ahbar 109
Kab b. Malik 106
Kabbani, Rana 55, 56, 236, 237
Kama Sutra 52
Kashf al Mahjub (Ali ibn Uthman al-Hujwiri) 104
Kerbala 43
al-Khálil 111
Khan, Khurshid Alam 186
Kharijis 279
Khomeini, Ayatollah Ruhollah, *fatwa* 185, 193–4
  opposition to 201–4, 254, 275
  support for 73, 82, 194–200
  Western reaction 206, 262
Khosraw, Naser-e 112
Kibab al-Zuhra (Dawud bin Khalaf al-Isfahani) 104
Kilroy-Silk, Robert 222, 223
Kipling, Rudyard 81, 82, 131, 231
Kissinger, Henry 62
knowledge 97, 151
Kulturgeschichte der Kreuzzuge (Prutz) 61

Laffin, John 73
Lalla Rookh (Moore) 51
Lamartine, Alphonse de 47–9
Lane, Edward W. 53, 55
Lawrence, T.E. 53, 55–6
le Bon, Gustav 61
Leaman, Oliver 221
Lemmens, H. 43
Levellers 224, 225
libraries 99, 100, 101
Libya 70, 71
Lings, Martin 159, 174
Listener, The 226, 227
literature 105–15, 215, 221, 244
Lively, Adam 213
Luther, Martin 19, 21
Lyall, Sir Alfred 56

Maaruf, Shaharuddin 79
Macaulay, Thomas 77

MacDonald, Duncan Black 45
Madden, Max 216
Madison, James 23
madrassas 37
Mahfouz, Naguib 216
Mahomet and Islam (Muir) 44
Majalis 111
Malaya 79–80
Mandeville, Sir John 38–9
manzilah bayn al-manzilatayn 102
Manzoor, Parvez 59, 62
maqamat literature 110
al-Maqrizi 100
Mark of the Beast, The (Kipling) 131
Marlowe, Christopher 250
al-Marri, Abu l-Ala 10–8
Marx, Karl 18, 30, 60, 62, 204
Marxism 69, 70, 138
Massignon, Louis 45
Al-Masudi 113
Maundrell, Henry 50
Mawdudi, A.A. 95
Mayhew, Patrick 185
Mazrui, Ali 178, 179, 204, 206, 207
Mein Kampf (Hitler) 258
Midnight's Children (Rushdie) 115, 116–32, 157, 163, 165–6, 244
migration 187
Miles, Rosalind 165–6, 167
Mill, John Stuart 231
Mills, Heather 60, 214
Milton, John 23, 25
mockery see ridicule
Modern Egypt (Baring) 56
Modern Egypt (Lane) 55
Modern Trends in Islam (Gibb) 63
modernity 8–9, 10–11, 76, 214–15, 251, 253
modernization 123, 238, 246
Mohammad and Fanaticism (Voltaire) 46
Montague, Lady Mary 50
Montesquieu, C.L. de S. 46
Moore, Thomas 51
More, Thomas 20, 21
Motaheri, Ayatollah 195
Mufti of Palestine 211
Mughal Empire 78

muhaasabah (criticism and self-criticism) 92
Muhammad, Prophet 44, 106, 108, 154, 214
  and apostasy 93, 94
  described by early writers 35–6, 37, 42
  described by Western writers 38–9, 47–9, 51, 53–4, 73
  and Qur'an 90, 144–5
  Rushdie on 152, 156, 161, 168–9, 189–96, 255
  and satanic verses 147, 148, 149
Muhammad (Cook) 68
Muir, William 44
Mumford, Lewis 61
al-munkar 102
Muqaddassai (Islamic sanctities) 203
Muslim Brotherhood (Ikhwan al Muslimun) 63–4
Muslim civilization
  cultural identity 271, 277, 278
  development described 62
  influence on West 47
  scholarship 96–114
Muslim Institute for Research and Planning 197, 199
Muslims,
  in Britain 182, 184, 218–9, 230, 253, 259
  in a plural society 260, 262–3, 270
  solidarity 275
  in Western literature 49–50
Mustafa al-Sabai 64
Mutazilism 102–3, 104

Nadwi, Abu Hasan Ali 153, 154
Naipaul, V.S. 82–6, 209
Nandy, Ashis 81, 124, 231, 250, 277
Nasai 150
Nasser, Gamal Abdul 64
Nawas, Abu 279
Nehru, Jawaharlal 80
Nernissi, Fatima 168
New Model Army 23
New Statesman and Society 216, 219, 226, 233, 236
New York Review of Books 186

New York Times, The 185, 186, 188
Newton, Isaac 19
Nicholson, R.A. 63, 105
Nixon, Richard 61
non-Europeans 9–10, 20–1, 29
Notes on a Journey from Cornhill to Grand Cairo (Thackeray) 50
Novus Mundus (Vespucci) 20–1
Nural al-Din al-Raniri 104

Oakley, Simon 41, 58
O'Brien, Conor Cruise 189
Observer 186, 189, 190, 191, 233, 234
OIC Declaration 204
Omar Khayyam 107
Organization of the Islamic Conference 203, 204
Oriental Despotism (Wittfogel) 60–1
Orientalism
  modern 63, 66, 67, 148, 260
  in Rushdie's writing 122, 131, 140, 178
  traditional 41, 43, 44, 45, 146
Orientalism (Said) 60
orthodoxy 15, 17, 22, 23, 27, 28
Outside the Whale (Rushdie) 12

Pakistan 84, 139
Pascal, Blaise 46
Pederson, Johannes 98
Penguin India 184
Pepys, Samuel 25
Perdition (Allen) 258–9
Perfumed Garden, The 52
Personal Narrative (Burton) 50
philosophy, Islamic 39
Pipes, Daniel 70
Piscatori, James P. 71–2
plurality 8, 32, 253, 254, 261, 263
Pocock, Edward 41
post-colonial history 76–81
post-modernism 11, 195, 246, 276, 277
press 24, 25, 29, *see also* publishing
Prideaux, Humphrey 42, 54
propaganda 37, 38, 310
prophets 152, 153, 154
Protestantism 19, 22

Protocols of the Elders of Zion, The 233
Prutz, Hans 61
publishing 96–7, 98, 105, 260, *see also* press
Punishment of Apostasy in Islam (Rahman) 94–5

Qadi Iyad 148
Qudama b. Jafar 114
Qur'an
  on apostasy 93–5
  as centre of Islam 88–90, 106, 144–6, 205, 228, 232
  exemplified in the Prophet 154–5
  knowledge and reason 97, 101–2, 151, 220
  mediaeval Western opinion of 40, 47
  translations 90–92
  on women 166, 169
Quraysh 43, 90, 149, 150
Qureshi, Jamil 65, 66
al-Qurtabi 148
Qussas al Am 109
Qutb 64

racism 178, 199, 214
  and colonialism 41, 56–7, 59
  in Rushdie's writing 178–80
  and secularism 243
radicalism 123–4
Rahman, Fazlur 196
Rahman, S.A. 94–5
Rahman, Tunku Abdul 79–80
Rainbow Warrior 206
Ranke, L. von 59
al-Razi 148
Reagan, President Ronald 225
reason 26–7
Reconstruction of Religious Thought in Islam (Iqbal) 61
redemption 65–6
Redwood, John 24, 25, 28
Reformation
  in England 21, 23, 24
  in Europe 14, 18, 19, 20, 21
Reformation (Chadwick) 21–2

religion, *see also* Christianity, Church, Islam
  freedom of conscience 28
  reaction to 14, 18
  sacramental 22
  toleration 24
Renaissance 19, 37
Renan, Ernest 59
revelation 154, 196
  and Rushdie 151, 152, 177, 182, 207
revolution in England 23, 24, 25
Rhodes, Cecil 231
Ricoldo da Montecroce 38
ridicule 32, 276, 278
  and doubt 28
  freedom from 93, 277
  and fundamentalism 242
Naipaul 85
Rushdie 165
  and secularism 238, 239, 240, 241, 244
  and toleration 29, 234–5
Robinson Crusoe (Defoe) 239–40, 241, 243
Rodinson, Maxine 69–70
Rosencrantz and Guildenstern are Dead (Stoppard) 264
Royal Court Theatre 259
Royal Institute of International Affairs (Chatham House) 71–2
Royal Society 20, 27
Ruines, Les (Volney) 46, 47
Rumi, Jalal-al-Din 107, 229
Rushdie, Salman, *see also* titles of books
  Akhtar on 207
  blasphemy 120, 142
  brown sahib 140, 141
  counter-attack on Muslims 185–6
  death sentence 201
  doubt 12, 13, 245
  dreams 157, 158
  duality 120, 136
  freedom 161
  good and evil 143, 176
  Hindu patheism 129
  history 119, 132
  India 121–2
  Islam 126–8, 136, 161

on literature 221
loss of faith 118, 128, 139–40
magic 120–1
malice 176
migration 117, 133–5
Muslim attack on 185, 192–3
Naipaul on 82
offence to Muslims 150–2
Orientalism 127, 161
pagan mysteries 173
Pakistan 130–7
portrayal of Muslims 136–7
post-modernist author 11
prophethood 158
relativism 261
repression 135
revelation 160, 161
ridicule 142
secularism 142
shame 133, 135
style 117, 125
Weir on 217
Weldon on 232
women 119, 165–7, 168, 170
Rushdie affair 184–237, 245, 254, 267, 276
Ruthven, Malise 69–70, 215, 216

el-Saadawi, Nawal 168
Sabbah, Fatna A. (pseud) 168
Said, Edward 43, 45, 60, 63
Salam ibn Asim 99
Sale, George 41
Saracens 37
satanic verses 144, 146–9, 156–7, 165, 215, 216
Satanic Verses, The (Rushdie) 146–181, 213, 216, 244
 book-burning 11, 184, 257
 literary prizes 185, 213
 and *Mein Kampf* 206
 Muslim reaction 201, 203, 262, 263–4
 and Rushdie's battle with Islam 244
 and secularism 32
 Western reaction 143, 216, 218–9, 232–3
Saudi Arabia 70, 71, 197, 198, 216

Sayuf al-Dawla 107–8
science 19, 27, 59–60
Seal, Barry 218
secularism 8–33, 225–6, 268, 269, 277–8
 and blasphemy 256
 and brown sahibs 86–7
 and conflict 240–1
 and freedom of expression 238
 and fundamentalism 242–4, 249, 277–8
 and literature 268
 and modernity 76
 and plurality 250, 252
seditious libel 29, 257
self-censorship 258–9
sex 41, 51–3
Shahabuddin, Syed 184–5, 186, 188, 189
Shahzis, Sadi 107
Shame (Rushdie) 110, 115, 129–40, 179
 censorship 11
 distorted imagination 117
 migration 181, 182
 Pakistan 117, 118
 prohibition against eating prawns 160
 women 119, 163, 166
Shariah 249, 273
al-Shawkani 148
ash-Shirbani 108
Sibawaih 111
Siddiqui, Khalim 197, 198, 200, 201
sin 227
Sinclair, John D. 38
Singer, M.R. 79
Singh, Khushwant 184
Sirat ibn Hisham, 106
slavery 180
slogans 30
Smith, Adam 60
Smith, W. Cantwell 63, 64, 66
social responsibility 93, 235–6
Song of Roland, The 37
Sorokin, P.A. 61
Southern, R.W. 15, 17–18, 35–6
Soyinka, Wole 189
Spectator 212, 213
Spengler, Oswald 61, 62
Spyscatcher (Wright) 216
Srinager 185

Stalin, Josef 225
Steiner, George 208
Stoppard, Tom 264
Stranger, The (Camus) 57
Stubbe, Henry 42, 54
Study of history, A (Toynbee) 62
Sufis 103
al-Suhayli 148
Sukarno, Ahmed 80
Sunday Magazine 185
Sunday Telegraph, The 209
Sunday Tribune, The 213
Sunnah 152, 153, 154, 155
Sunnis 201
Suzuki, D.T. 61

al-Tabari 98, 147–50, 156, 196, 216
al-Tahawi 104
Taki 212
Tamin al Dari 108
al-Tanukhi, Qadi 112
al-Tawhidi, Abu Hayyan 111
terrorism 195, 206
Test Acts 24
Thackeray, W.M. 50
Thatcher, Margaret 185, 217
Thomas Aquinas, Saint 15, 37, 39
Thousand and One Nights, The (Alf Laila wa Laila) 50
Times, The 189, 195, 196, 221, 222
Times of India 189
Times Literary Supplement, The 213, 215, 234, 235
tolerance 224, 233, 234, 235, 253, 268
Toynbee, Arnold 61, 62
tradition 252
Traditions, Tyranny and Utopias (Nandy) 86
Travels in Arabia Deserta (Doughty) 55
Travels in Egypt and Syria (Volney) 47
treason 96, 164, 196
Trevor-Roper, Hugh 217
Turkey 210

Umar ibn al Khattib, Caliph 95, 168
ummah 62, 89, 182, 199, 200
United States Constitution 23, 24

Updike, John 73
Uris, Leon 73
Usama ibn Munqidh 112
usury 89
Utopia (More) 20, 21

Vanunu, Mordechai 206
Vathek (Beckford) 51
Vatikiotis, P.J. 72
Venture of Islam, The (Hodgson) 190
Vespucci, Amerigo 20–1
Vico, Giambattista 47
violence 41, 88
Vittachi, Varindra Tarzie 77, 78, 80, 82
Vizinczey, Stephen 209
Voices of Marrakech, The (Canetti) 74
Volney, C.F. C-B. 46, 47
Voltaire, F-M.A. 17, 46
voyages of discovery 20, 21

Waardenburg, Jacques 45
Wahab bin Munabbih 109
Walden, George 209
Waldenses 16
Waldron, Jeremy 234, 235
al-Waqidi 174
warraq 97–9
Wasil bin Ata 102
Watt, W. Montgomery 63
Webb, W.L. 214, 215
Weir, Stuart 217, 218, 219
Weldon, Fay 213, 226–32
Weltgeschichte (Ranke) 59
Western civilization
  conflict with Islam 199
  ethnocentrism 208–9, 269
  plurality 8, 253
  post modernism 11
  scholarship 30
  secularism 8, 9
Western Society (Southern) 15, 17–18
Western Views (Southern) 35–6
Whitbread Literary Prize 213
Whitehouse, Mary 216
Wilder Shores of Love, The (Blanch) 52
Wilkes and Liberty 29
witches 26

Wittfogel, Karl 60–1
women 119, 165–72, 229, 230, 263
Women's History of the World, The (Miles) 165–6, 167
worldviews 87, 116–7, 234, 251, 268
 discontinuity 246, 248
 religious 145, 153, 221, 222, 247, 268
 secular 238, 240–1, 242, 250, 252
Wycliffe, John 39, 40

Young, Hugo 214

Zahirite tradition 104
Zaki, Yaqub 195, 196, 197
Zamakshari 102
Zia ul-Haq, Mohammed 85
Zijderveld, Anton 239
Zindiqs 104
Zionism 69

Distorted Imagination

Designed by Little Red Cloud
Keyboarded by the authors on Wordcraft
Composed by Colset Private Limited of Singapore
in Compugraphic 11½/13pt Bembo
photographically increased by 4 per cent
Printed by Billing & Sons Limited of Worcester
on Publishers Antique Wove cream shade
Bound by Billing & Sons Limited of Worcester
in Linmaster stamped with Nuvap

Printed and bound in Great Britain